D1229590

THE ORLOFSKY EDITION

הגדה של פסח

THE PESACH HAGGADAH

Rabbi Berel Wein

הגדה של פסח

Haggadah

Through the Prism of Experience and History

THE ORLOFSKY EDITION

THE PESACH

Illustrations by
Tova Katz

Shir Hashirim / Song of Songs
translation and commentary by
Rabbi Nosson Scherman
and **Rabbi Meir Zlotowitz**

© *Copyright 2004 by* Rabbi Berel Wein and Shaar Press
First edition — First impression: March, 2004

Shir Hashirim / Song of Songs
© *Copyright 2004 by* Mesorah Publications, Ltd.

ALL RIGHTS RESERVED

No part of this book may be reproduced **in any form,** *photocopy, electronic media, or otherwise — even FOR PERSONAL, STUDY GROUP, OR CLASSROOM USE — without* **written** *permission from the copyright holder, except by a reviewer who wishes to quote brief passages in connection with a review written for inclusion in magazines or newspapers.*

THE RIGHTS OF THE COPYRIGHT HOLDER WILL BE STRICTLY ENFORCED.

Published by **SHAAR PRESS**
and Distributed by **MESORAH PUBLICATIONS, LTD.**
4401 Second Avenue / Brooklyn, N.Y 11232 / (718) 921-9000 / www.artscroll.com

Distributed in Israel by SIFRIATI / A. GITLER
6 Hayarkon Street / Bnei Brak 51127

Distributed in Europe by J. LEHMANNS
Unit E, Viking Industrial Park, Rolling Mill Road / Jarrow, Tyne and Wear NE32 3DP / England

Distributed in Australia and New Zealand by GOLDS WORLD OF JUDAICA
3-13 William Street / Balaclava, Melbourne 3183 / Victoria Australia

Distributed in South Africa by KOLLEL BOOKSHOP
Shop 8A Norwood Hypermarket/ Norwood 2196 / Johannesburg, South Africa

Printed in the United States of America by Noble Book Press Corp.
Custom bound by Sefercraft, Inc. / 4401 Second Avenue / Brooklyn N.Y. 11232

ISBN: 0-57819-319-2

In this time of והגדת לבנך, when we prepare to come to the Seder and bind generations together, we are proud to dedicate this Haggadah in honor of our parents

Baruch and Rochelle Wertenteil שיחיו

Meir and Joan Orlofsky שיחיו

Words cannot express our gratitude for all we owe them — for their example, their teaching, their help, and their wisdom, judgment and guidance. In trying times, they are an indispensable support system. Our highest ambition is to be worthy of their trust;

and in honor of our grandmothers

Mrs. Esther Kurant תחי׳

Mrs. Stella Orlofsky תחי׳

and להבל״ח

Mrs. Evelyn London ע״ה

חוה בת יצחק ע״ה, נפ׳ ערב יום כפור, תשכ״ז

Mrs. Martha Wertenteil ע״ה

מאטיל בת יהודה ע״ה, נפ׳ ז׳ תשרי, תשנ״ד

They epitomize the praises of the historic Eishes Chayil. The character and accomplishments of our families are unspoken tributes to them and their love.

We pay tribute to the memory of our grandfathers

Mr. Henry Kurant ז״ל

אלחנן בן פרץ ז״ל, נפ׳ י״א כסלו, תשנ״ט

His family was wiped out but he, in America, had the strength and spirit to build a new family, devoted to Torah and communal chessed.

Mr. Israel Wertenteil ז״ל

ישראל בן ברוך יהודה ז״ל, נפ׳ י״ח אב, תשמ״ז

He was a product of the flourishing Judaism of pre-War Galicia, and transplanted its proud tradition to America, to build generations of Torah-true Jews.

Mr. Martin Orlofsky ז״ל

משה יהודה בן צבי מאיר הכהן ז״ל, נפ׳ י״ז שבט, תשנ״ז

A famous baal chessed whose kindness and generosity were mainstays of countless people, he was especially devoted to his children and grandchildren.

Judge Jack London ז״ל

יעקב בן מאיר ז״ל, נפ׳ ערב ראש השנה, תשנ״ו

To him, time was a precious commodity, never to be wasted. Though he rose to eminence, he never lost the friendship and admiration of those who knew him.

Their legacy lives on as a model and inspiration to their offspring

Aaron and Ahuva Orlofsky

Avigail and Elana

☙ Preface

Everyone has a Haggadah book inside oneself. Just as no two people are alike, so too no two Seder services are exactly alike. So everyone has his or her own unique and special Haggadah book potential. That being the case, this is my Haggadah book. It is not so much a commentary on the Haggadah itself as it is a commentary on Jewish life, tradition, and history. It is a very personal book. It does not come so much to instruct and inform as it does to describe and hopefully to inspire.

As with many good deeds in life, one needs gentle urging and friendly prodding to get on with this task. So, I take this opportunity to thank my dear friends, Rabbi Meir Zlotowitz, Rabbi Nosson Scherman, and Shmuel Blitz for their encouragement and advice and for sticking with me during the sometimes irregular writing of this book. I also wish to thank the staff of Shaar Press for their usual superb professionalism in producing such a handsome volume. The illustrations were drawn by Tova Katz, a most talented and sensitive artist. My dear wife has sustained me all of these years and enabled me to complete this work. My family has always encouraged and indulged me and many times served as the foil for my thoughts and ideas. May they all be blessed for their efforts and kindnesses toward me.

An author once said that every book is really an autobiography of the writer. There is no doubt that in this book I intended to reveal my inner feelings about the glory of being Jewish. I hope that I have succeeded, for now, at my stage of life, though I write books and articles for the general reading public, they are meant most especially and poignantly to be read by my descendants. This is my type of living will, so to speak. And the Haggadah provides the perfect forum to speak to generations in one's family. This work is not meant to serve as a book of instructions as to how to conduct a traditional Seder service. Yet, I feel that the comments and ideas represented in this book can help make anyone's Seder service more meaningful. I certainly hope so.

I thank the Lord God of Israel Who has preserved my wife and me and our family in health and allowed me to complete this book. I am especially grateful for having the privilege, denied to so many other far-greater generations and personalities of Jews, to live in the Holy City of Jerusalem and to have written this book within its comforting and inspiring environs. For me, "Next year in Jerusalem!" has been in great measure fulfilled.

⸎ Introduction

□ The Pesach Haggadah

The night of Pesach is distinguished by the gathering of family and friends, acquaintances and strangers, the very young and the very old, at an observance that commemorates the birth of the Jewish people as a nation. The festive dinner, replete with calories and good cheer, is part of an overall ritual that Jews have observed on that night for more than thirty-three centuries, for the meal is only a secondary part of the general order of this special night. The ritual for the night, the "menu," so to speak, is outlined in the Haggadah of Pesach. Based on the opinions and words of the rabbis of the Mishnah and the Talmud, our Haggadah is a scholarly creation composed in Babylonia in approximately the sixth century. Its author/editor is fittingly anonymous since its greatness lies in its universality in Jewish life and not in any particularism or novel approach or interpretation. With only minor variations, the text of the Haggadah you have before you has been accepted by all Jewish communities throughout the world, from Yemen to San Diego and from Johannesburg to St. Petersburg. This is a remarkable feat, comparable only to the zealous guarding of the uniform text of the Torah itself among all the scattered Jewish communities of the world. Even the prayer book — the siddur — has variations of text from one Jewish community to another. But not so the Haggadah. The story that it tells, the ritual that it guides, the inspiration that it provides, are the essential elements of Jewish survival and continuity. One cannot imagine the story and destiny of the Jewish people without recourse to the Pesach Seder and its companion and instructor, the Haggadah. The central core of Jewish belief and Jewish history is contained within its pages and words.

While turning the pages of the Haggadah, one has the opportunity to meet some of the greatest figures in Jewish history —

Moses, Joshua, David, Hillel, Rabbi Akiva, and others. The story of the Jewish people is not merely one of events, monumental as those occurrences may have been. It is as much a story of people, of individual human beings who, in their service to God and humankind, have made an enormous difference in our lives as well as in the development of human civilization. The Haggadah therefore pays equal attention both to the historical occurrences and to the people involved in tracing the story of our development as a people. As such, the Haggadah becomes an invaluable tool for the transmission of Jewish self-knowledge and self-identity. This is one of the reasons why this small book has played and still plays such a vital role in the lives of Jews, even for those Jews who do not identify themselves as stringently observant or terribly committed. There is a chord deep within the soul of all Jews that the Haggadah somehow is able to reach and strike. The Pesach Seder has become the last refuge of Jewish life for many Jews. But refuge it is for it is able to revitalize Jews and endow them with a refreshing sense of eternity and self-worth. As such, the Haggadah and the attendant Pesach Seder become one of the most important components for meaningful Jewish living.

□ Preparing for the Great Day

There is no other holiday in the Jewish calendar year that engenders the preparation and anticipation that does Pesach. The house is made ruthlessly clean as Jewish housekeepers from time immemorial conquer not only forbidden *chametz* but any speck of kosher dust or dirt as well. The probably apocryphal story is told about the famous Lithuanian rebbetzin who, beginning a month before Pesach, forced the household cat to wear booties over its paws so that it would not inadvertently drag a crumb of *chametz* into the house. Her husband, the learned and scholarly rabbi, gently chided her for this, saying that the *Shulchan Aruch* (The Code of Jewish Law) did not require such stringencies. To which the rebbetzin replied: "You and your *Shulchan Aruch*! If I listened to you and your *Shulchan Aruch* our house would long ago have become *treif* (not kosher)!" I have long since stopped giving advice, let alone instructions, to my wife and daughters regarding their meticulous pre-Pesach housecleaning antics. It wouldn't be

Pesach without this preparation and anyway, since the time of our first Matriarch Sarah, the women of Israel have had a better instinct for ascertaining God's will than do we men.

The Pesach-shopping expedition is one of the great family experiences of the year. In our current society, where every imaginable food product, necessary or frivolous, is produced kosher for Pesach, shopping for the holiday has become a daunting challenge. It is also most expensive. Here in Israel, there are fewer kosher for Pesach products available than in the United States. But the number of such products keeps increasing every year and the global economy has affected Pesach products and shopping as well. The Pesach of my youth in my parents' home in Chicago was basically a matzah, meat, chicken, chicken fat, and potatoes one. A friend of the family sent us kosher-for-Pesach dairy products manufactured in St. Louis and the cheese, butter, and milk was rationed out sparingly for breakfast over the eight days of the holiday. The chief spread for the matzah snack was chicken fat (cholesterol heaven, but oh, so delicious!). Though there was commercial chicken fat available in jars in the store, my mother would begin collecting chicken fat from Chanukah time onwards and would not think of allowing any store-bought commodity to substitute for her inimitable creation. She would cook the chicken soup in a Pesach pot on a special Pesach burner and skim the fat from the top for use on Pesach. Even though I have since outgrown chicken fat, both store bought and homemade varieties, I can never think of Pesach without recalling the taste of chicken fat smeared on matzah. It also naturally reminds me of my mother. And that memory is what Pesach, the Seder, and the Haggadah is all about.

□ Tables of Generations

Pesach, and especially the Seder, are about children and generations — about telling of the past to those who will survive us and live in the future. The halachah teaches us that one is obligated to observe a Seder even if there are no children present at the table — even if one is all alone. Yet, the obvious thrust of the Seder is to fulfill the Biblical injunction, "So that you will tell into the ears of your children and grandchildren what I have wrought in Egypt."

The Seder and its attendant Haggadah is the mechanism for transmitting the story of the Jewish people to the future generations. It would not be an exaggeration to note that the entire Seder is geared toward the children. The Talmud relates to us that nuts were "thrown" at the children in a playful game at the Seder table in order to keep them awake and interested in the proceedings. A Seder is therefore a celebration of generations, of continuity, of the spiritual triumph over the passage of time itself. Even though the Exodus from Egypt occurred over thirty-three centuries ago, we can make it more immediate to us by considering the generations gathered around a Pesach Seder table. In our family, we have been blessed to have young children sit at the Seder with their aged great-grandfathers at the same Seder table. In reality, there are two hundred years of past personal memory and future life expectancy gathered at such a table. One therefore needs to imagine only seventeen more such tables of past generations gathered to celebrate the Seder in order to return to the great moment of the original Exodus from Egypt itself. Thinking in generational time makes the past much more real, vivid, and immediate to us. Jews always thought within the framework and lived their lives by the clock of generations rather than by the calendar of days.

The Haggadah has a rhythm to it, a pace of its own. To truly appreciate the beauty and holiness of the Haggadah one must surrender one's self to its order, form, and measure. When there are small children present at the Seder, the Haggadah lends itself to a more rapid recitation. Later in life, the pace of the Haggadah recitation slows and allows for greater contemplation, interpretation, and meditation. The enthusiasm of children should never be stifled at the Seder and the adults should be willing to listen to all that the youngsters have learned in school even if it is old hat to them. Read slowly or more rapidly, the Haggadah always retains its sense of relevance and majesty. It is this personality of the Haggadah itself that fascinates both children and adults and is the key to its intact transmission over many generations and centuries. Even if no words of commentary were added at the Seder table, the bare words of the Haggadah itself would suffice to infuse us with the memory of the Exodus and the story of Israel becoming a "kingdom of priests and a holy nation."

□ Daniel's Matzah

In March 1989, I wrote an article for *A Guide to Jewish Living* that pretty much sums up my view of Pesach and of the Haggadah. Since I am in charge of this book, I am taking the liberty of repeating that article for you here. The article was entitled "Daniel's Matzah" and reads as follows:

> "In the midst of my preparations for our family Seder last Pesach, my precocious four-year-old grandson, Daniel, informed me that he would be 'very quiet when eating matzah at the Seder.' When I did not respond enthusiastically to this profound statement, he pursued the matter and said, 'Don't you want to know why I will be very quiet when I eat matzah?' I, being then quite occupied with such weighty matters as choosing the appropriate wines for the Seder, grunted offhandedly, 'Tell me why, Daniel.' With a smile of wisdom that only children who are yet unaware of their limitations can muster, he said to me, 'Because I want to hear the matzah.' 'That's nice,' I said, with my typical grandfatherly diffidence. I immediately thought that 'hearing' the matzah meant the snap, crackle, and pop sounds that only dry, crisp, well-baked Pesach matzah could produce while being chewed in one's mouth. Maybe that is what Daniel meant as well. But in the time that has passed since that Pesach, I have rethought the matter.
>
> "Matzah is accustomed to hearing what we have to say to it. Most of the ritual service of the Pesach Haggadah is recited with the matzah uncovered, serving as the passive, inanimate listener to our tale of bondage and freedom, cruelty and redemption, chaos and purpose. The matzah hears our words and listens to our tale. But, I now thought, how meaningful it would be if, in the words of Daniel, we would 'hear the matzah.' I think that such a conversation would go something like this:

" 'This is Seder number 3316 (the Exodus took place in the year 2448 from Creation) for me. I began in Egypt, traveled through the Sinai Desert, and took root in the Land of Israel. I was at the Temple in Jerusalem, the palace of David, the herdsman's hut on the Golan, and the merchant's home in ancient Jaffa. I was present at the hanging gardens of Babylon, the Acropolis of Athens, and the Forum in Rome. I have been in the Atlas Mountains of Morocco, the Alps of Switzerland, the plains of Catalonia, the vineyards of Provence and Champagne, and I witnessed the splendor of ancient Byzantium. I have seen Warsaw, Vilna, Kiev, Cracow, Moscow, Berlin, Paris, Kobe, Shanghai, Cochin, and Mumbai. I have been at Seder tables spread with white linen, laden with the finest china and most ornate silver serving pieces. I have also been in hidden, dark cellars in Seville and Barcelona, expelled from London and Oxford, and unaccountably and unjustly accused of blood libels in my preparation. I was also in Auschwitz and Bergen-Belsen, under siege in modern Jerusalem and Safed, in labor camps in Siberia, and I am still in hiding in Damascus and Teheran. I have been around and I have learned a thing or two.

" 'I have observed the passing of civilizations and empires. I have witnessed profound changes in the world order and in society's beliefs. Every empire was convinced that it was invincible and immortal. Every philosophy advanced itself as being the sole panacea for the world's ills. Aristotle and Augustine, Aquinas and Locke, Marx and Nietzsche, Kierkegaard and Russell, all postulated and proposed. Monarchy and feudalism, fascism and communism, all rose to structure society and improve human life. Reason and Renaissance, humanism and socialism, imperialism and nationalism, fundamentalism and secularism, religious oppression and hedonism, all have had their day. I, as a lowly matzah, couldn't comment too loudly about these goings-on. But, I have seen them all pass. Yet the struggle for personal freedom, for meaning and commitment in life, for peace and mutual understanding, for the sanctity of home and family is yet to be won. That is why I'm so delighted to have this little chat with you. I'm always thrilled to have someone who will listen to me.

" 'For a while, people, even my people, thought that I wouldn't be around much longer. But that was not true. I am now in Scarsdale and Beverly Hills, Brooklyn and Kansas City, Bogota and Sydney, Prague and even St. Petersburg (nee Leningrad). I am back home in Jerusalem and Hebron, Tiberias and Tel Aviv. In fact, I am present wherever people care and hope, are interested and loyal regarding their heritage, treasure old values and close family, and have proscribed the violence of hatred and the lure of temporary pleasures and hedonism, and instead have chosen the path of tradition and faith. In short, for anyone who will listen to me, I am still there.'

"Please pass the matzah, Daniel. I will be very quiet while I am eating it. I also want to hear the matzah."

As the above personal reflection indicates, this commentary to the Haggadah will not necessarily be a compilation or anthology of insights, explanations, or opinions of the great rabbinic commentators to the Haggadah. Nor will it be a collection of "quickies" — basically short comments on individual sentences or words of the Haggadah. Rather, it will be a view of the Haggadah and its words as it and they fit into the great picture of Judaism and traditional Jewish life. Reproduced here are some of the words that I heard at the Seder table of my grandfather when I was very young. Others were heard by me later in life from my father and father-in-law when we shared the Seder together. I have also included some observations of my grandchildren, especially those made by them when they were still very young. There is a ring of wonder, belief, and uncanny intuition to their words, which we older, sophisticated, and more "scholarly" adults unfortunately can no longer achieve. Having delivered Pesach sermons for almost half a century, some of my homiletical gems have also been included in this commentary. In short, my dear friends and readers, I am inviting you to share the Seder table with my family, all five generations of them, may the Lord bless them all, and to overhear some of the comments and Torah conversations that have always made the Seder so special in our household. In addition, I have included thoughts, many even in a longer version, about life, Judaism, and Jewish tradition that are connected to the Haggadah, but in a broader sense I believe them to be of value all year-round. The great American thinker, Eric Hoffer, once noted that a thin book usually reveals what the author knows, while a thick book usually attempts to conceal what the author does not know. This book began as a thin book but I must admit that it has expanded during its composition. Nevertheless, I hope that you will appreciate it for what it reveals and ignore what it attempts to conceal.

☙ Preparing for *Passover

Aside from the commandment to eat matzah all of Passover and the special observances of the Seder nights, the best-known feature of the festival is the requirement not to eat, or even to own, *chametz* all during the festival. For many Jews, one of the most vivid memories of their childhood is the seemingly endless cleaning and scrubbing of their homes during the weeks and days before Passover.

Although no household can be thoroughly cleaned in only a short while, the Talmudic sages ordained that a search for *chametz* be made in every home and business on one night of the year.

The search begins upon nightfall of the fourteenth day of Nissan, the evening before Passover. The purpose of the commandment is the removal of all *chametz*, and it requires a formal inspection of all areas where *chametz* may have been brought during the course of the year — despite the fact that a thorough cleaning was made before Passover. The search should be made by candlelight, and one may not speak until it is completed — except to give instructions or make inquiries directly relating to the search.

In years when Passover begins on Saturday night, the inspection is not conducted on the evening before Passover, for this would result in a desecration of the Sabbath. Instead, it is made on Thursday night and the *chametz* is burned Friday morning.

A widespread custom calls for the distribution of ten pieces of *chametz* through the house before the search (by someone other than the person conducting the search). Of course, care should be taken that the pieces do not leave crumbs, thereby defeating the purpose of the search.

Any *chametz* intended for that evening's supper or the next morning's breakfast must be set aside carefully. After one finishes eating, leftover *chametz* should be placed with whatever *chametz* may have been found in the evening. It will be burned the morning before Passover (except when Passover begins on Saturday night, in which case the *chametz* is burned Friday morning).

בדיקת חמץ

On the night of 14 Nissan, the night before the Pesach Seder, the search for *chametz* (leaven) is made. It should be done with a candle as soon as possible after nightfall. [When the first Seder is on Saturday night, the search is conducted on Thursday night (13 Nissan).] Before the search is begun, the following blessing is recited. If several people assist in the search, only one recites the blessing for all.

The *chametz* search is initiated with the recitation of the following blessing:

בָּרוּךְ אַתָּה יהוה אֱלֹהֵינוּ מֶלֶךְ הָעוֹלָם, אֲשֶׁר קִדְּשָׁנוּ בְּמִצְוֹתָיו, וְצִוָּנוּ עַל בִּעוּר חָמֵץ.

⸙ Chametz

The main prohibition regarding Pesach is that of consuming or even possessing *chametz.* I will not enter into the technical and halachic definitions and issues that surround the word "*chametz*" as regarding Pesach. *Chametz,* however, is more than a physical fact; it is also a symbol and a characteristic trait. The Hebrew word "*chametz*" signifies delay, the loss of opportunity, a waste of time and/or effort. The symbol of redemption — Pesach — is enthusiasm, industry, alacrity, and creativity. *Chametz* represents lethargy, inertia, and sometimes even a sense of fatalism and despair. We cannot always be on a high and all of us ***do*** suffer days of inactivity and little accomplishment. Yet, Pesach does not allow for that during its yearly week of time. The preparation for Pesach, the Seder night, and its inherent rhythm and drama, all are symbols of action, motion, and accomplishment. Apparently, the message here is that freedom must be earned and continually fought for to be successfully maintained. This is true on the national level of countries and on the individual level of people's personal lives. The presence and physicality of *chametz* is forbidden in the Jewish home for the duration of Pesach. Though actual *chametz* may be eaten year-round with the exception of Pesach, the weaknesses that *chametz* symbolizes are forbidden to us throughout the year and, in fact, for all of our lives.

The night before Pesach is when the "search" for *chametz* takes place. By then, nearly all the *chametz* has been disposed of or stored away to be sold to a non-Jew on the morrow. However, the Ari (Rabbi Yitzchak Luria of 16th-century Egypt and Safed) mentions the kabbalistic custom of placing ten pieces of bread scattered throughout the house so that the "search" for *chametz* shall not be in vain. Since the idea of what *chametz* represents as discussed here is always present within us — deep in the inner recesses of our souls — it is obvious that the search for *chametz* is never in vain. Perhaps that is why the halachah provides that even if no *chametz* is found, the blessing is proper and not a wasted one; the commandment is to search, not to find. Nevertheless, the custom of placing the ten pieces of bread throughout the house is one of the pillars of the night before Pesach.

The children of the house use this opportunity to hide the bread pieces in fiendishly out-of-the-way places. When our children were young, they were very well behaved and I was always able to rather easily find the ten pieces of bread that they placed around our home. The next generation, however, our grandchildren, are much more cunning, cruel, and uncooperative (it must be the non-Wein genes that are part of them!) and the bread pieces have become much harder to find. Not only that, but one of them even attempted to extort money from me when the tenth piece could not be found! I explained

SEARCH FOR CHAMETZ

On the night of 14 Nissan, the night before the Pesach Seder, the search for *chametz* (leaven) is made. It should be done with a candle as soon as possible after nightfall. [When the first Seder is on Saturday night, the search is conducted on Thursday night (13 Nissan).] Before the search is begun, the following blessing is recited. If several people assist in the search, only one recites the blessing for all.

The *chametz* search is initiated with the recitation of the following blessing:

Blessed are You, HASHEM, our God, King of the universe, Who has sanctified us with His commandments, and commanded us concerning the removal of *chametz*.

Upon completion of the *chametz* search, the *chametz* is wrapped well and set aside to be burned the next morning and the following declaration is made. The declaration must be understood in order to take effect; one who does not understand the Aramaic text may recite it in English, Yiddish or any other language. Any *chametz* that will be used for that evening's supper or the next day's breakfast or for any other purpose prior to the final removal of *chametz* the next morning is not included in this declaration.

כָּל חֲמִירָא וַחֲמִיעָא דְּאִכָּא בִּרְשׁוּתִי, דְּלָא חֲמִתֵּהּ וּדְלָא בִעַרְתֵּהּ וּדְלָא יְדַעְנָא לֵהּ, לִבָּטֵל וְלֶהֱוֵי הֶפְקֵר כְּעַפְרָא דְאַרְעָא.

ביעור חמץ

The following declaration, which includes all *chametz* without exception, is to be made after the burning of leftover *chametz*. It should be recited in a language which one understands. When Pesach begins on *Motzaei Shabbos*, this declaration is made on Shabbos morning. Any *chametz* remaining from the Shabbos-morning meal is flushed down the drain before the declaration is made.

כָּל חֲמִירָא וַחֲמִיעָא דְּאִכָּא בִרְשׁוּתִי, דַּחֲזִתֵּהּ וּדְלָא חֲזִתֵּהּ, דַּחֲמִתֵּהּ וּדְלָא חֲמִתֵּהּ, דְּבִעַרְתֵּהּ וּדְלָא בִעַרְתֵּהּ, לִבָּטֵל וְלֶהֱוֵי הֶפְקֵר כְּעַפְרָא דְאַרְעָא.

עירוב תבשילין

It is forbidden to prepare on *Yom Tov* for the next day even if that day is the Sabbath. If, however, Sabbath preparations were started before *Yom Tov* began, they may be continued on *Yom Tov*. *Eruv tavshilin* constitutes this preparation. A matzah and any cooked food (such as fish, meat or an egg) are set aside on the day before *Yom Tov* to be used on the Sabbath and the blessing is recited followed by the declaration [made in a language understood by the one making the *eruv*]. If the first days of Pesach fall on Thursday and Friday, an *eruv tavshilin* must be made on Wednesday.

[In Israel, where only one day *Yom Tov* is in effect, the *eruv* is omitted.]

בָּרוּךְ אַתָּה יהוה אֱלֹהֵינוּ מֶלֶךְ הָעוֹלָם, אֲשֶׁר קִדְּשָׁנוּ בְּמִצְוֹתָיו, וְצִוָּנוּ עַל מִצְוַת עֵרוּב.

בְּהָדֵין עֵרוּבָא יְהֵא שָׁרֵא לָנָא לַאֲפוּיֵי וּלְבַשּׁוּלֵי וּלְאַצְלוּיֵי וּלְאַטְמוּנֵי וּלְאַדְלוּקֵי שְׁרָגָא וּלְתַקָּנָא וּלְמֶעְבַּד כָּל צָרְכָּנָא, מִיּוֹמָא טָבָא לְשַׁבַּתָּא לָנָא וּלְכָל יִשְׂרָאֵל הַדָּרִים בָּעִיר הַזֹּאת.

Upon completion of the *chametz* search, the *chametz* is wrapped well and set aside to be burned the next morning and the following declaration is made. The declaration must be understood in order to take effect; one who does not understand the Aramaic text may recite it in English, Yiddish or any other language. Any *chametz* that will be used for that evening's supper or the next day's breakfast or for any other purpose prior to the final removal of *chametz* the next morning is not included in this declaration.

Any *chametz* which is in my possession which I did not see, and remove, nor know about, shall be nullified and become ownerless, like the dust of the earth.

BURNING THE CHAMETZ

The following declaration, which includes all *chametz* without exception, is to be made after the burning of leftover *chametz*. It should be recited in a language which one understands. When Pesach begins on *Motzaei Shabbos*, this declaration is made on Shabbos morning. Any *chametz* remaining from the Shabbos-morning meal is flushed down the drain before the declaration is made.

Any *chametz* which is in my possession which I did or did not see, which I did or did not remove, shall be nullified and become ownerless, like the dust of the earth.

ERUV TAVSHILIN

It is forbidden to prepare on *Yom Tov* for the next day even if that day is the Sabbath. If, however, Sabbath preparations were started before *Yom Tov* began, they may be continued on *Yom Tov*. *Eruv tavshilin* constitutes this preparation. A matzah and any cooked food (such as fish, meat or an egg) are set aside on the day before *Yom Tov* to be used on the Sabbath and the blessing is recited followed by the declaration [made in a language understood by the one making the *eruv*]. If the first days of Pesach fall on Thursday and Friday, an *eruv tavshilin* must be made on Wednesday.
[In Israel, where only one day *Yom Tov* is in effect, the *eruv* is omitted.]

Blessed are You, HASHEM, our God, King of the universe, Who sanctified us with His commandments and commanded us concerning the commandment of *eruv*.

Through this *eruv* may we be permitted to bake, cook, fry, insulate, kindle flame, prepare for, and do anything necessary on the festival for the sake of the Sabbath — for ourselves and for all Jews who live in this city.

---

to him that all extortion had to wait until the Seder night itself when the matter of the *afikoman* (see my later discussion regarding this part of the Seder service) would have to be settled.

This symbolic search for *chametz* emphasizes to us the ideas I discussed above regard-

הדלקת נרות

The candles are lit and the following blessings are recited. When *Yom Tov* falls on Shabbos, the words in parentheses are added.

בָּרוּךְ אַתָּה יהוה אֱלֹהֵינוּ מֶלֶךְ הָעוֹלָם, אֲשֶׁר קִדְּשָׁנוּ בְּמִצְוֹתָיו, וְצִוָּנוּ לְהַדְלִיק נֵר שֶׁל [שַׁבָּת וְשֶׁל] יוֹם טוֹב.

בָּרוּךְ אַתָּה יהוה אֱלֹהֵינוּ מֶלֶךְ הָעוֹלָם, שֶׁהֶחֱיָנוּ וְקִיְּמָנוּ וְהִגִּיעָנוּ לַזְּמַן הַזֶּה.

It is customary to recite the following prayer after the kindling. The words in brackets are included as they apply.

יְהִי רָצוֹן לְפָנֶיךָ, יהוה אֱלֹהַי וֵאלֹהֵי אֲבוֹתַי, שֶׁתְּחוֹנֵן אוֹתִי [וְאֶת אִישִׁי, וְאֶת בָּנַי, וְאֶת בְּנוֹתַי, וְאֶת אָבִי, וְאֶת אִמִּי] וְאֶת כָּל קְרוֹבַי; וְתִתֶּן לָנוּ וּלְכָל יִשְׂרָאֵל חַיִּים טוֹבִים וַאֲרוּכִים; וְתִזְכְּרֵנוּ בְּזִכְרוֹן טוֹבָה וּבְרָכָה; וְתִפְקְדֵנוּ בִּפְקֻדַּת יְשׁוּעָה וְרַחֲמִים; וּתְבָרְכֵנוּ בְּרָכוֹת גְּדוֹלוֹת; וְתַשְׁלִים בָּתֵּינוּ; וְתַשְׁכֵּן שְׁכִינָתְךָ בֵּינֵינוּ. וְזַכֵּנִי לְגַדֵּל בָּנִים וּבְנֵי בָנִים חֲכָמִים וּנְבוֹנִים, אוֹהֲבֵי יהוה, יִרְאֵי אֱלֹהִים, אַנְשֵׁי אֱמֶת, זֶרַע קֹדֶשׁ, בַּיהוה דְּבֵקִים, וּמְאִירִים אֶת הָעוֹלָם בַּתּוֹרָה וּבְמַעֲשִׂים טוֹבִים, וּבְכָל מְלֶאכֶת עֲבוֹדַת הַבּוֹרֵא. אָנָּא שְׁמַע אֶת תְּחִנָּתִי בָּעֵת הַזֹּאת, בִּזְכוּת שָׂרָה וְרִבְקָה וְרָחֵל וְלֵאָה אִמּוֹתֵינוּ, וְהָאֵר נֵרֵנוּ שֶׁלֹּא יִכְבֶּה לְעוֹלָם וָעֶד, וְהָאֵר פָּנֶיךָ וְנִוָּשֵׁעָה. אָמֵן.

ing *chametz,* and makes us aware of the very serious side of Pesach and its attendant celebration of our freedom. After the search is completed, the *chametz* is "annulled" (*bitul chametz*) and stored until the morrow when it will be burned. I always have felt that the annulment of the *chametz* refers not only to the physical *chametz* but to the spiritual *chametz* within us as well. The physical *chametz* will be burned, sold, and somehow disposed of on *erev Pesach.* The spiritual *chametz* within us does not qualify for fire or sale. Instead, it is subject to annulment only by our words and thoughts and changing attitudes.

LIGHTING THE CANDLES

The candles are lit and the following blessings are recited.
When *Yom Tov* falls on Shabbos, the words in parentheses are added.

Blessed are You, HASHEM, our God, King of the universe, Who has sanctified us with His commandments, and commanded us to kindle the flame of the (Sabbath and the) festival.

Blessed are You, HASHEM, our God, King of the universe, Who has kept us alive, sustained us, and brought us to this season.

It is customary to recite the following prayer after the kindling.
The words in brackets are included as they apply.

May it be Your will, HASHEM, my God and God of my forefathers, that You show favor to me [my husband, my sons, my daughters, my father, my mother] and all my relatives; and that You grant us and all Israel a good and long life; that You remember us with a beneficent memory and blessing; that You consider us with a consideration of salvation and compassion; that You bless us with great blessings; that You make our households complete; that You cause Your Presence to dwell among us. Privilege me to raise children and grandchildren who are wise and understanding, who love HASHEM and fear God, people of truth, holy offspring, attached to HASHEM, who illuminate the world with Torah and good deeds and with every labor in the service of the Creator. Please, hear my supplication at this time, in the merit of Sarah, Rebecca, Rachel, and Leah, our mothers, and cause our light to illuminate that it not be extinguished forever, and let Your countenance shine so that we are saved. Amen.

That is why the rabbis of the Talmud taught us the importance of always saying the right words at all times. Words can heal and change situations and minds for the better. Good words can even destroy evil and render *chametz* oblivious and invisible. But wrong words can also annul previous good and cause irreparable harm and damage. *Bitul chametz* stands as a powerful lesson in the power of words.

◆§ The Seder Table

If there is ever a magnificent table set in Jewish life, it is the Seder table. Even though moderation is commended and recommended regarding table service during the rest of the year, the Pesach Seder is supposed to receive the finest treatment possible. I remember as a child that my mother had beautiful European sherbet cups, of extreme delicacy and subtle iridescent coloring, that were used only on Pesach for the Seder meal. The set of dishes that we ate from on the Seder night when I was a child were always the finest dishes that we had, far superior to our regular year-round dishes. On the Seder table of one of our daughters these sherbet cups and dishes reappear now every year. My mother would be delighted. Meanwhile, I am weeping (at least on the inside) at seeing her great-grandchildren eat from those beautiful, memory-laden dishes.

My childhood Seder table also included a beautiful tablecloth that made its appearance only once a year. It was given to my parents by a woman from Laredo, Texas who inexplicably was always present at our Seder table. I never saw a tablecloth that white (at least at the outset of the Seder) or linen that fine. Later in life when I was a rabbi in Miami Beach, a lovely lady in my congregation embroidered a beautiful Pesach tablecloth for our table. Our children loved it as much as we did. My mother's tablecloth has been passed on to her descendants together with her sherbet cups, dishes, and silver candelabra.

The custom among many Jews is to place on the Seder table fine china, silver Judaica, valuable serving pieces, and other ornaments and showpieces of beauty, even though these items will not necessarily be used during the Seder service and meal. This uncharacteristic Jewish display of opulence (even though Jewish tradition and manners frown upon any show of opulence and extravagance) is meant to ostentatiously proclaim our joy at being freed from the bondage of Egypt and our gratitude to God Who has allowed us to accumulate such fine and ornate possessions. Judaism teaches us that there is a time and a place for almost everything in life, as King Solomon taught in *Koheles*. The

Seder table is the time and place for luxury, even opulence. The other nights of the year are times for modesty and restraint, when less is really more. But not so on the Seder night, when more is really more. This is another facet to add to the answers given to why this night of the Seder is different from all other nights of the year.

☙ Cushions and Pillows and Kittel

Much of the Seder is conducted while one is "leaning" in one's chair instead of while sitting in the usual position — bolt upright. This is a throwback to the classical world of the Bible and the Mishnah in which aristocrats and people of importance ate while reclining on couches. In *Megillas Esther* we find a specific reference to such seating arrangements at royal banquets. Since the Seder commemorates our transition from slavery to freedom, from bondage to aristocratic nobility (a national reliving of the individual story of Joseph's rise from Egyptian slavery to royal nobility), we are bidden to remember this change of status symbolically, by reclining during the Seder. Halachah places certain limitations on who should recline because of constraints of modesty and respect to the host conducting the Seder. Nevertheless, the practice of "leaning" (to the left so that the danger of choking on food or drink is minimized) is universally observed by Jews during the Seder service and meal.

To facilitate the process, cushions and/or pillows are used to prop up the person who is leaning. Usually the children of the family insist on using pillows as well for their seating arrangements and this often leads to sibling disputes as to where one's seat is at the table and which pillow should be used for support. We were blessed in Miami Beach that the very same woman who embroidered our tablecloth also embroidered numerous pillowcases with a Pesach motif to be used at the Seder. This made all of our pillows uniform and spared us many an argument as to whose pillow was nicer, bigger, etc. Each of these Pesach pillowcases transformed the pillow that it covered from a mundane yet necessary sleeping aid into an item of purpose and holiness. The pillows also served the practical purpose of supporting the younger children at the Seder who invariably fell asleep at their places before the conclusion of the Seder service. But I remember that as a child, sleeping on a Pesach pillow was far sweeter than sleeping on a regular pillow the rest of the year.

In addition to the tradition of the pillows and cushions described here, there is a custom among Ashkenazic Jews that the married males of the house wear a white robe-like garment — *kittel* — which is also worn on Yom Kippur during the synagogue services. A number of reasons are offered for the custom of the white garment. A somber reason is that these white garments resemble the shrouds, which are our final clothes. Thus, even in the midst of our celebration, when we are dressed in our best finery and our table is set in the most exquisite decor and taste, we are to remind ourselves of our mortality and not succumb to excesses of drink, food, and unwarranted levity and "bad" conversation. Jewish tradition always differentiated between happiness and light-headedness.

Another reason given for the wearing of the white garment is much more upbeat. The *kittel* is seen as a recollection of the white clothing that our ancestors traditionally wore when visiting the Temple in Jerusalem. White clothing was predominant, especially on Pesach when, on the afternoon before the holiday began, the sacrifice of the paschal lamb took place in the Temple, and the entire Temple area was bathed in the dazzling white of the clothing of the hundreds of thousands of Jews gathered there. For this reason, the white *kittel* is part of the Seder service — it is, so to speak, the uniform of the night.

I know of no white *kittel* that emerges from the Seder unscathed and without stains. The wine, the *charoses,* and the meal all literally leave their work on it. My wife does her very best (and her best is unequaled in all areas of our marriage) to launder the garment after Pesach and she always succeeds in rendering it 99 percent spotless. But there is always one trace of a faint stain that refuses to disappear completely. On Rosh Hashanah and Yom Kippur when I wear the *kittel* again, this stain, unnoticed by perhaps anyone but me, is of great comfort and inspiration to me. It reminds me of Pesach, of family, of the future, immediate and long range, of generations old and young, of those who are gone and those that will yet be. I can think of no more fitting backdrop for the holiest days of the year, Rosh Hashanah and Yom Kippur, for asking Godly forbearance and forgiveness and resolving to do better in the future, than those thoughts engendered by the faint outline of a Pesach stain on my otherwise spotlessly white *kittel*.

☙ Song

The entire Seder service of the Haggadah is entitled "shirah" — song. There are traditional melodies that are sung for many parts of the Haggadah. I am completely tone deaf and cannot carry a tune. At our Seder, therefore, my grandchildren, almost all of whom sing beautifully (it is again those non-Wein genes in them!), repeat to me the mantra that I first heard in second grade from Miss McCarthy in Victor F. Lawson public school in Chicago: "Just mouth the words, the rest of us will do the singing!" Having an ego that does not bruise too easily, I cheerfully agree. But there are times during the Seder service when I indulge an irresistible urge to join in the singing. For after all, what is a Seder without song? I do not sing loudly for that would throw everyone else off key, but loud enough that my heart can hear the melody and rejoice in the feeling of exultation that the Seder always brings to me.

Naturally, the melodies sung at the Seder vary from community to community, even from family to family within the same community. There are also new melodies that are introduced in succeeding generations, especially in the recitation of the *Hallel* during the Seder service. The Seder table knows of Lithuanian and Polish melodies, of Moroccan and Turkish tunes, of age-old songs and modern innovations. Each type of musical theme, just like each different generation of Jews, has its place at the Seder table. All of the different melodies of the Jewish experience combine to create the symphony of song and praise to the God of Israel that the Seder service truly represents. The rabbis of the Talmud and Midrash stated that the beginning of the Torah is *chesed* — loving kindness — and that the end of the Torah is *chesed* — loving kindness. The beginning of the Seder service is song and the end of the Seder service is song.

◆§ Final Seder Preparations

The Seder table is to be set before the holiday actually begins. The afternoon of *erev Pesach* — the eve of the holiday — is always a busy time in the Jewish household. The kitchen staff is on duty preparing the exquisite meal that marks the Seder evening and the pious grandchildren are soaking the romaine lettuce that will be used for *maror* — bitter herbs — and inspecting each leaf to make certain that it is bug-free. My time-honored task is to prepare the *charoses* — the dip that is used in conjunction with the *maror* and that is reminiscent in texture to the lime that our forefathers used in their construction work when they were slaves in Egypt. *Charoses* is made of ingredients that in Biblical texts are symbolic of the Jewish people — apples, walnuts, dates, figs, almonds, wine, and cinnamon. Though the ingredients of *charoses* are well known to all, the exact formulation of those ingredients is what makes *charoses* really work. My recipe is so secret that I myself forget it from year to year, but somehow the *charoses* always turns out delicious and after its ritual use with the bitter herbs it becomes the spread of choice on the grandchildren's matzah during the Seder meal. There is prepackaged *charoses* "concentrate" available in stores, but I can think of no pre-Seder task as satisfying (and stomach filling, since one has to constantly taste the blend to make certain that it is up to the high standards of previous years' *charoses*) as making the Seder *charoses* from scratch from fresh ingredients.

The choice of wines for the Seder is also an important task. In my childhood there was almost no grape juice available and the wines for Pesach were either of the homemade bathtub variety (my father-in-law's brand) or the heavy, sugar-laden Concord and Malaga varieties. I remember that after the second cup, my legs were lead and my stomach well on the way to being upset. In today's world, the Seder table is graced by an enormous variety of wines. For those who cannot tolerate wine, there are many forms of grape juice available. In our family today, we drink either low-alcohol soft wines or dry red wines. Red wine is preferred over white wine if both are of equal quality. It is sad to note that in Jewish tradition, red wines often had to be omitted from the Seder service because of the nefarious blood libel of medieval Christian origin. The blood libel still is alive and well in Moslem countries today, having been imported from Europe and Christianity. Our family also prefers wines from Israel to other wines. The days of the sweet "sacramental" wines that were the original Israeli exports have long since ended. World-class kosher wines in all varieties are available from many expert Israeli wineries and many are of the highest standards of *kashrus* and quality. If one cannot actually be in Israel for Pesach, at least a product of Israel, especially its wine, should grace one's Seder table.

Rabbi Baruch Epstein, in his book, *Mekor Baruch,* relates that his uncle, Rabbi Naftali Tzvi Yehudah Berlin (known by the acronym of his name — Netziv), the great head of Volozhin Yeshivah, dressed himself in his Shabbos finery in order to welcome into his home a bottle of wine that was sent to him from the Carmel winery in Rishon L'Tzion in the Land of Israel. So many mitzvos — Torah commandments and procedures — are involved in the production of wine in the Land of Israel, commandments and procedures that are singular and exclusive to wine produced in Israel alone. This fact lends a holiness to the wine per se, over and above the fact that it will be used for other holy purposes during the ensuing Seder service.

☙ The Ka'arah

The centerpiece of the Seder table (though it is almost never placed at the physical center of the table) is the *ka'arah* — the Seder plate. The Seder plate bears the symbols of Pesach and the Seder upon it. On the *ka'arah* there is a hard-boiled egg (*beitzah*) that symbolizes the holiday offering in Temple times (*chagigah*), the bitter herbs (*maror*) that represent the slavery of Egypt, a shank bone roasted over the fire (*zeroa*) that recalls to mind the paschal lamb offering in Temple times, *charoses* (the dip for the *maror*), a vegetable such as potato or parsley (*karpas*) which is used in the first "dipping" of the Seder service, and *chazeres,* another kind of *maror,* usually translated as romaine lettuce.

☙ Artistic Plates

The Seder plate itself has been an object of Judaic artistry over the centuries. From more humble ceramic plates to silver and even

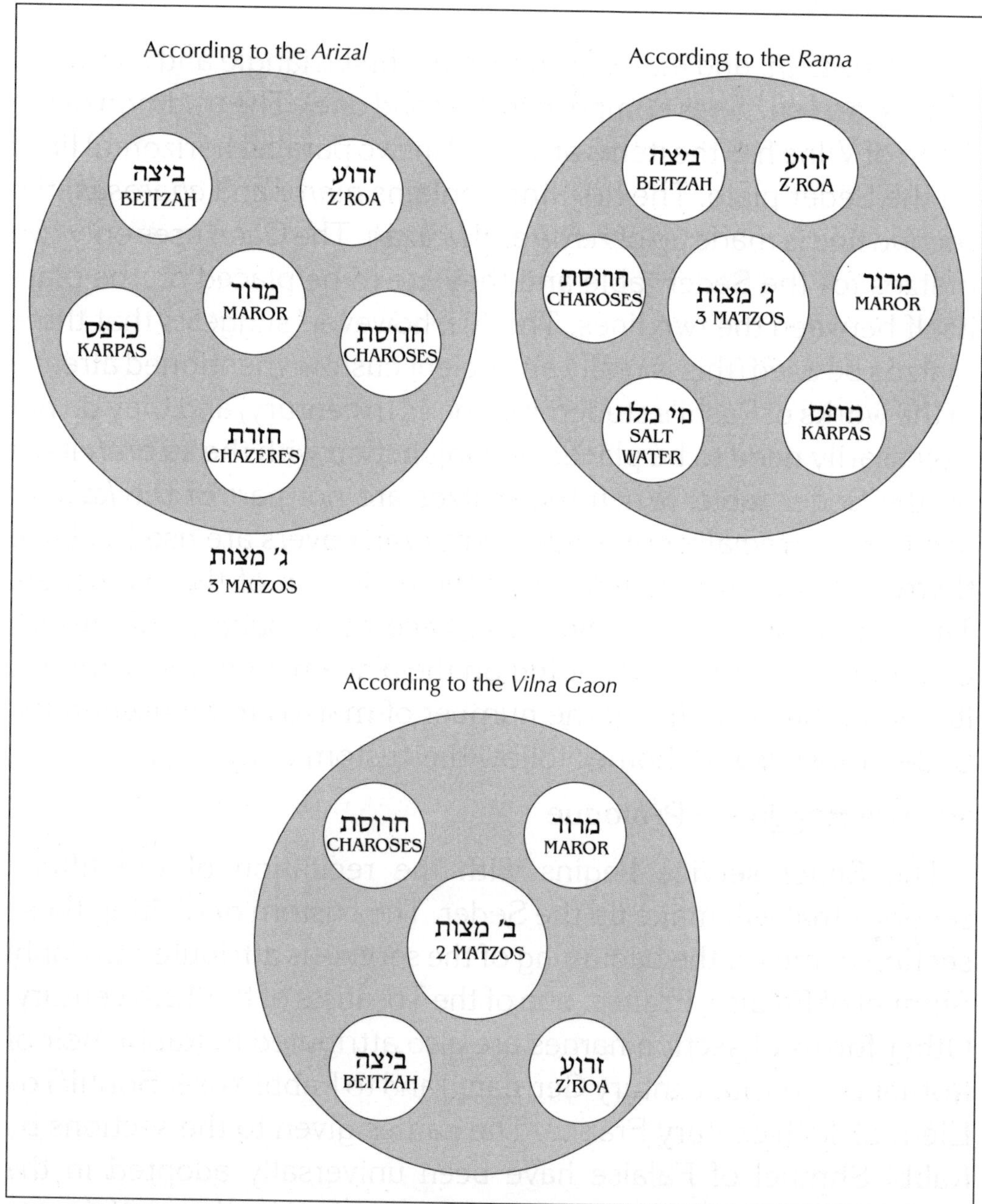

gold Seder plates, Jewish talent has attempted to beautify the Seder table. Many Seder plates combine within them space for the matzos as well, usually on shelves under the *ka'arah* itself. Designs range from old, traditional motifs to new, radically modern ones. Most Seder plates are round even though Jewish tradition does not arrange the items on the Seder plate in a circle.

The two main traditions are those of the Ari, R' Isaac Luria of 16th-century Egypt and Safed, and of the Gaon of Vilna, R' Eliyahu Kramer of 18th-century Lithuania. The tradition of the Ari calls for placing the items on the Seder plate in two inverted triangles (*zeroa, beitzah,* and *maror* compose the first triangle and *charoses, karpas*, and *chazeres* compose the second one). The tradition of the Gaon of Vilna has the items arranged in two parallel horizontal lines on the Seder plate. The first line contains *maror* and *charoses;* the second line is made up of *zeroa* and *beitzah.* The Gaon uses only two matzos for the Seder table and they are to be placed on the plate itself between the two lines. The Ari, however, suggests that three matzos be used (this is really an ancient custom mentioned already in the works of Rashi's students in the 11th century) and they do not necessarily need to be placed in conjunction with the *ka'arah* itself on the Seder table. When the matzos are not part of the *ka'arah* itself, then specially embroidered matzah covers are used to keep them covered during sections of the recitation of the Haggadah. These matzah covers have also become a subject of Jewish ceremonial artistry. In deciding on the placement of the symbolic items on the *ka'arah* and the number of matzos to be used in the Seder, most Jewish homes follow the custom of the Ari.

☙ The Haggadah Prologue

The Seder service begins with the recitation of the fifteen sections that will make up the Seder. The custom of reciting these section names at the beginning of the service is attributed to Rabbi Shmuel of Falaise, France, one of the Tosafists of the 12th century. Other forms of section names are also attributed to Rabbi Meir of Rothenburg (13th-century Germany) and to Rabbi Yosef Bonfil/Tov Elem of 11th-century France. The names given to the sections by Rabbi Shmuel of Falaise have been universally adopted in the Jewish world. These section names are recited by the participants at the Seder, usually to an accompanying melody. They are also announced by the leader of the Seder service before every respective section of the Haggadah. Over the centuries, great men have read many mystical powers into the words of this prologue to the Haggadah and invested it with a holiness and reverence that transcends the mere words themselves.

On a more mundane level, the prologue is logically necessary to the process of the Seder service. Seder means "order" and order begs for a table of contents, a direction as to where one is heading. The Torah itself is such an introduction to the universe. The Rabbis of the Talmud stated that "God looked into the Torah, so to speak, and then created the world." "Plan ahead" is a Godly motto. Life is always full of surprises and unexpected twists and turns. Our best-laid plans often are defeated by unforeseen life events. Nevertheless, purely haphazard living, without any direction or planning, is almost suicidal behavior. Akavya ben Mahalalel in *Pirkei Avos* warned us to know "where you are going." Since the Seder service is not meant to serve only as a lesson for the night of Pesach itself but rather as a blueprint for Jewish life year-round, the lesson of having a prologue to the Seder service to show "where you are going" is logical, understandable, and necessary. Life itself has many stages, just as the Haggadah has many sections. One should prepare for each stage properly — marriage, career, parenthood, midlife, senior citizenship, even for mortality itself. Life has a rhythm and a pattern — an order to living in God's world. The Seder, with its definite order, should be understood as being a one-night replica of life itself.

The word "Seder" also implies attention to detail. All of us are aware that in life, commerce, personal relationships, and fair government, the devil is in the details. Many a great concept or brilliant idea has foundered in the morass of practical detail. This prologue to the grand idea of the Seder — the relating of the experience of Jewish redemption from Egyptian bondage — deals with the nitty-gritty details of the Seder. It instructs us in how to begin and how to proceed. It provides a clear and detailed description of the night's service and governs our behavior and goals for the Seder service. In doing this, it represents the general concept of ritual observance and detailed behavior requirements, which are central to Jewish halachic tradition. We know not only that we are bound to serve God and humanity but we also know how we are to do so. Jewish history and experience has shown us that a disregard for the rules of "how" to serve God leads to a sharp decline — and eventually to alienation from God Himself. The "how" of the Seder is as important as is the "why" of the Seder.

סימני הסדר
The Order of the Seder

KADDESH	***Sanctify*** *the day with the recitation of Kiddush.*	קדש
URECHATZ	***Wash*** *the hands before eating Karpas.*	ורחץ
KARPAS	*Eat a* ***vegetable*** *dipped in salt water.*	כרפס
YACHATZ	***Break*** *the middle matzah. Put away larger half for Afikoman*	יחץ
MAGGID	***Narrate*** *the story of the Exodus from Egypt.*	מגיד
RACHTZAH	***Wash*** *the hands prior to the meal.*	רחצה
MOTZI	*Recite the blessing,* ***Who brings forth,*** *over matzah as a food.*	מוציא
MATZAH	*Recite the blessing over* ***Matzah.***	מצה
MAROR	*Recite the blessing for the eating of the* ***bitter herbs.***	מרור
KORECH	*Eat the* ***sandwich*** *of matzah and bitter herbs*	כורך
SHULCHAN ORECH	*The* ***table prepared*** *with the festive meal.*	שלחן עורך
TZAFUN	*Eat the afikoman which had been* ***hidden*** *all during the Seder.*	צפון
BARECH	*Recite Bircas Hamazon, the* ***blessings*** *after the meal.*	ברך
HALLEL	*Recite the* ***Hallel*** *Psalms of praise.*	הלל
NIRTZAH	*Pray that God* ***accept*** *our observance and speedily send the Messiah.*	נרצה

קַדֵּשׁ

Kiddush should be recited and the Seder begun as soon after synagogue services as possible — however, not before nightfall. Each participant's cup should be poured by someone else to symbolize the majesty of the evening, as though each participant had a servant.

◂§ קַדֵּשׁ / Kaddesh

Jews sanctify their meals and their food by the recitation of blessings before and after eating. The blessings have the multipurpose task of offering thanksgiving to the Creator Who provides us with the means of sustenance and also to sanctify the seemingly mundane activity of eating. On Shabbos and festivals the meal is further sanctified by the recognition of the holiness of time through the prayer of Kiddush that introduces not only the first meal of the holiday but the holiday itself. The concept of sanctifying time is a uniquely Jewish idea that was eventually adopted in a more restricted form by other cultures and faiths as well. Time is the most fragile and elusive of all Godly gifts and human values. The ceremony of Kiddush therefore combines many abstract and holy ideas within its simple ceremony and sparse words. If this is true for every Shabbos and all other festivals of the year, it is especially true as regarding the Seder night. One of the gifts that the Jews received even while yet enslaved in Egypt was the concept of a day of rest — the day called Shabbos. The entire process of freedom that the Exodus from Egypt represents is the cornerstone of all Jewish life and faith. The Kiddush text for all of the holidays and Sabbaths of the year states clearly that the mitzvos of the Torah and the celebration of all holy days are based on the concept of *zecher l'yetzias Mitzrayim* — always remembering the Exodus from Egypt. The Kiddush of the Seder is therefore the sanctification of everything Jewish in life throughout the year.

Even though the custom year round is that the head of the house recites the Kiddush and thereby discharges the duty of Kiddush for everyone at the table, the custom at the Seder table is that all the guests recite Kiddush either after or with the head of the house. In many families, even children recite Kiddush if they are capable of doing so and have an understanding of the prayer and ceremony. There is magic in hearing the Kiddush of the ages recited in the young, sweet voice of a child, especially if the child or grandchild is yours. Since the Kiddush is the first of the "four cups of wine" which are mandatory as part of the Seder service, a cup is placed in front of each of the guests and family at the table. The children will usually demand large cups since their eyes are usually bigger than their stomachs, a problem that many of us never really outgrow. Since drinking dry wine is an acquired taste, most children and many adults use grape juice as the drink for the "four cups." There are differing halachic opinions as to the propriety of using grape juice instead of wine for the "four cups," and especially for the first Kiddush cup. Although wine is definitely preferable, the vast majority of halachic decisors permit the use of grape juice. However, as I mentioned earlier, there are now quite a number of "soft" wines that have low alcoholic content and serve as an admirable replacement for grape juice among those who find drinking four cups of regular wine to be too difficult. It is interesting to note that at times of great economic and social distress in Jewish history, there is rabbinic discussion about the permissibility of the use of other liquids such as tea (and even milk!) for the "four cups." We should be grateful that our current generation in the main is not faced by any such questions or considerations.

KADDESH

Kiddush should be recited and the Seder begun as soon after synagogue services as possible — however, not before nightfall. Each participant's cup should be poured by someone else to symbolize the majesty of the evening, as though each participant had a servant.

☙§ The Four Cups

The Rabbinic injunction to drink four cups of wine during the Seder service is based on the four different verbs of redemption used by the Torah when the Exodus from Egypt was foretold to Moses (*Exodus* 6:6-7). The use of such a variety of verbs indicates that there are different stages of redemption and freedom.

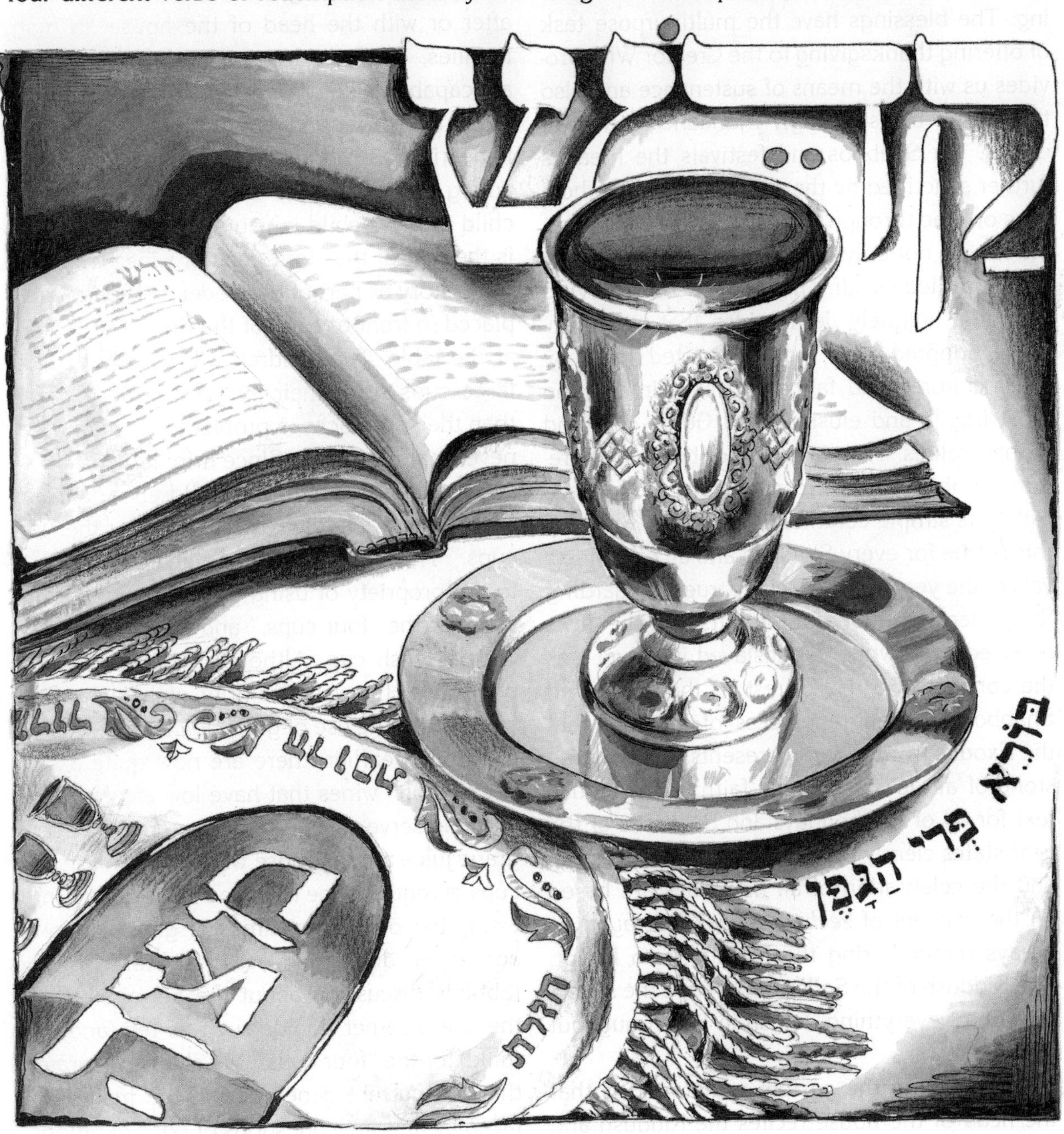

On Friday night begin here:

[וַיְהִי עֶרֶב וַיְהִי בֹקֶר]

יוֹם הַשִּׁשִּׁי. וַיְכֻלּוּ הַשָּׁמַיִם וְהָאָרֶץ וְכָל צְבָאָם. וַיְכַל אֱלֹהִים בַּיּוֹם הַשְּׁבִיעִי מְלַאכְתּוֹ אֲשֶׁר עָשָׂה, וַיִּשְׁבֹּת בַּיּוֹם הַשְּׁבִיעִי מִכָּל מְלַאכְתּוֹ אֲשֶׁר עָשָׂה. וַיְבָרֶךְ אֱלֹהִים אֶת יוֹם הַשְּׁבִיעִי וַיְקַדֵּשׁ אֹתוֹ, כִּי בוֹ שָׁבַת מִכָּל מְלַאכְתּוֹ אֲשֶׁר בָּרָא אֱלֹהִים לַעֲשׂוֹת.[1]

☐ **The First Cup:**
וְהוֹצֵאתִי, *I shall take you out.*

There is the initial redemption, of freedom from actual physical bondage, the escape from the lash of the taskmaster. But the trauma of slavery is not ended by physical emancipation alone. The entire process of the Jewish experience in the desert of Sinai was meant to raise the Jews from the mentality and personality of being a slave. Unfortunately, we see in the Torah that this effort was ultimately unsuccessful and that the generation of former slaves did not reach the Promised Land. The memories and mentality of slavery are hard to shake off. In discussing the Purim celebration, the Talmud itself ruefully states: "But we are still slaves of Achashverosh!" You can take the slave out of Egypt but it is even more difficult to take the effects of Egypt out of the former slave.

☐ **The Second Cup:**
וְהִצַּלְתִּי, *I shall rescue you.*

Therefore there comes a second verb and another cup of wine to represent redemption from traumatic memory. It comes to stop one's wallowing in self-pity and bitterness. It attempts to free us from feelings of dependency and entitlement. "Look what I went through and therefore the world owes me a living and comfort." As natural and understandable as those feelings may be, they eventually cripple the ex-slave as surely as did the physical bondage itself. The ability to move on from tragedy and sadness is a hallmark of the Jewish people. It is an unparalleled expression of freedom.

☐ **The Third Cup:**
וְגָאַלְתִּי, *I shall redeem you.*

Then there is freedom of the soul. This third cup of freedom deals with having Divine purpose to life. I think that this is part of the message that the Rabbis of the Mishnah sent us when they stated, "There is no freedom for anyone who is not engaged in the Torah." Our souls thirst for purpose and accomplishment. One of the dangers that all experts now agree upon is that in "retirement" there are great dangers, not to the body that now has more leisure time, but rather to the mind and soul of a person that has no direction or purpose. The Rabbis of the Talmud emphasized this point when they stated, "Torah scholars and personalities become wiser and more stable as they age, while those bereft of Torah knowledge and behavior become more unstable and unreliable as they age." There are only so many rounds of golf that one can play. Life has to have meaning and the soul has to have a sense of satisfaction for there to be a feeling of freedom within a person. The granting of the Torah on Sinai was a moment of freedom to the Jewish soul. It alone has given direction

On Friday night begin here:

[And there was evening and there was morning]

The sixth day. Thus the heaven and the earth were finished, and all their array. On the seventh day God completed His work which He had done, and He abstained on the seventh day from all His work which He had done. God blessed the seventh day and hallowed it, because on it He abstained from all His work which God created to make.[1]

(1) *Genesis* 1:31-2:3.

and purpose to Jewish life for all these millennia.

☐ **The Fourth Cup:**
וְלָקַחְתִּי אֶתְכֶם לִי לְעָם,
I shall take you to Me for a people.

The fourth cup of freedom represents the ability to live alone within a world of conflicting cultures and values. For all of the long history of the Jewish people, we have been a minority inundated and surrounded by foreign cultures that were antithetical to our beliefs and way of life. If the physical survival of the Jewish people over these long centuries of persecution and demonization is to be considered miraculous, as it surely is, then the spiritual survival and the loyalty of Israel to Torah over this period of time should certainly be deemed miraculous in the extreme. It is this freedom that is built upon our self-worth and true identity, on Jewish pride and vision that frees us from the oppression of majority cultures and faddish ideas. It is the freedom that allows a Jew to proclaim daily his thanks to the Creator Who has allowed him to belong to the eternal people and be a participant in the greatest drama of human existence — the story of the Jewish people.

These four steps: 1) from physical slavery, 2) from the traumatic memory and mental paralysis that physical slavery engenders even when the bondage is ended; 3) toward freedom of the soul as represented by the revelation at Sinai and the acceptance of the Torah, and 4) from the ravages of assimilation and outside foreign cultures — these are the basic concepts of Pesach and of the Seder night. The cups of wine are meant to raise us from melancholy and depression — the Bible always represented wine as the drink of comfort — and to transport us to a different sense of being and possibilities. Because wine is declared to be the most exalted of all drinks, it is the physical medium for proclaiming holiness and spirituality at the Shabbos and holiday table. It is on the night of the Seder, however, that it takes its most prominent role in serving that purpose with the Rabbinic injunction to drink four cups of wine as part of the Seder service.

The Gaon of Vilna, R' Eliyahu Kramer, states that the four cups and the use of the number four regarding other sections of the Haggadah are in line with the Talmudic rule that there are four situations in life that require the special blessings of thanks — הַגּוֹמֵל *Hagomel.*" These four situations — being saved from the sea's waves, crossing a desert, recovering from an illness, and being released from captivity — all were experienced by the Jewish people in their redemption from Egypt.

☐ **The Fifth Cup:**
וְהֵבֵאתִי, *I shall bring you to the Land.*

There is a tradition to pour a fifth cup of wine at the Seder service. This cup — universally known as the "Cup of Elijah" — represents Hashem's promise to the Jewish people regarding their settling in the Land of Israel and possessing that holy country. This additional cup of

On all nights continue here:

סַבְרִי מָרָנָן וְרַבָּנָן וְרַבּוֹתַי:

בָּרוּךְ אַתָּה יהוה אֱלֹהֵינוּ מֶלֶךְ הָעוֹלָם, בּוֹרֵא פְּרִי הַגָּפֶן:

[On Friday night include all passages in brackets.]

בָּרוּךְ אַתָּה יהוה אֱלֹהֵינוּ מֶלֶךְ הָעוֹלָם, אֲשֶׁר בָּחַר בָּנוּ מִכָּל עָם, וְרוֹמְמָנוּ מִכָּל לָשׁוֹן, וְקִדְּשָׁנוּ בְּמִצְוֹתָיו. וַתִּתֶּן לָנוּ יהוה אֱלֹהֵינוּ בְּאַהֲבָה [שַׁבָּתוֹת לִמְנוּחָה וּ]מוֹעֲדִים לְשִׂמְחָה, חַגִּים וּזְמַנִּים לְשָׂשׂוֹן, אֶת [יוֹם הַשַּׁבָּת הַזֶּה וְאֶת] יוֹם חַג הַמַּצּוֹת הַזֶּה, זְמַן חֵרוּתֵנוּ [בְּאַהֲבָה] מִקְרָא קֹדֶשׁ, זֵכֶר לִיצִיאַת מִצְרָיִם, כִּי בָנוּ בָחַרְתָּ וְאוֹתָנוּ קִדַּשְׁתָּ מִכָּל הָעַמִּים, [וְשַׁבָּת] וּמוֹעֲדֵי קָדְשֶׁךָ [בְּאַהֲבָה וּבְרָצוֹן] בְּשִׂמְחָה וּבְשָׂשׂוֹן הִנְחַלְתָּנוּ. בָּרוּךְ אַתָּה יהוה, מְקַדֵּשׁ [הַשַּׁבָּת וְ]יִשְׂרָאֵל וְהַזְּמַנִּים.

On Saturday night, add the following two paragraphs:

Hold two candles with only their flames touching when reciting the following blessing:

בָּרוּךְ אַתָּה יהוה אֱלֹהֵינוּ מֶלֶךְ הָעוֹלָם, בּוֹרֵא מְאוֹרֵי הָאֵשׁ.

בָּרוּךְ אַתָּה יהוה אֱלֹהֵינוּ מֶלֶךְ הָעוֹלָם, הַמַּבְדִּיל בֵּין קֹדֶשׁ לְחוֹל, בֵּין אוֹר לְחֹשֶׁךְ, בֵּין יִשְׂרָאֵל לָעַמִּים, בֵּין יוֹם הַשְּׁבִיעִי לְשֵׁשֶׁת יְמֵי הַמַּעֲשֶׂה. בֵּין קְדֻשַּׁת שַׁבָּת לִקְדֻשַּׁת יוֹם טוֹב הִבְדַּלְתָּ, וְאֶת יוֹם הַשְּׁבִיעִי מִשֵּׁשֶׁת יְמֵי הַמַּעֲשֶׂה קִדַּשְׁתָּ, הִבְדַּלְתָּ וְקִדַּשְׁתָּ אֶת עַמְּךָ יִשְׂרָאֵל בִּקְדֻשָּׁתֶךָ. בָּרוּךְ אַתָּה יהוה, הַמַּבְדִּיל בֵּין קֹדֶשׁ לְקֹדֶשׁ.

On all nights conclude here:

One should bear in mind that this blessing applies to all observances of the Seder.
Women who recite this blessing at candle-lighting should not repeat it now.

בָּרוּךְ אַתָּה יהוה אֱלֹהֵינוּ מֶלֶךְ הָעוֹלָם, שֶׁהֶחֱיָנוּ וְקִיְּמָנוּ וְהִגִּיעָנוּ לַזְּמַן הַזֶּה.

The wine should be drunk without delay while reclining on the left side.
It is preferable to drink the entire cup, but at the very least,
most of the cup should be drained.

On all nights continue here:

By your leave, my masters and teachers:

Blessed are You, HASHEM, our God, King of the universe, Who creates the fruit of the vine.

[On Friday night include all passages in brackets.]

Blessed are You, HASHEM, our God, King of the universe, Who has chosen us from all nations, exalted us above all tongues, and sanctified us with His commandments. And You, HASHEM, our God, have lovingly given us [Sabbaths for rest,] holidays for rejoicing, feasts and seasons for joy, [this Sabbath and] this Feast of Matzos, the season of our freedom [in love,] a holy convocation in commemoration of the Exodus from Egypt. For You have chosen and sanctified us above all peoples, [and the Sabbath] and Your holy festivals [In love and favor], in gladness and joy have You granted us as a heritage. Blessed are You, HASHEM, Who sanctifies [the Sabbath,] Israel, and the festive seasons.

On Saturday night, add the following two paragraphs:

Hold two candles with only their flames touching when reciting the following blessing:

Blessed are You, HASHEM, our God, King of the universe, Who creates the illumination of the fire.

Blessed are You, HASHEM, our God, King of the universe, Who distinguishes between sacred and secular, between light and darkness, between Israel and the nations, between the seventh day and the six days of activity. You have distinguished between the holiness of the Sabbath and the holiness of a Festival, and have sanctified the seventh day above the six days of activity. You distinguished and sanctified Your nation, Israel, with Your holiness. Blessed are You, HASHEM, Who distinguishes between holiness and holiness.

On all nights conclude here:

One should bear in mind that this blessing applies to all observances of the Seder.
Women who recite this blessing at candle-lighting should not repeat it now.

Blessed are You, HASHEM, our God, King of the universe, Who has kept us alive, sustained us and brought us to this season.

The wine should be drunk without delay while reclining on the left side.
It is preferable to drink the entire cup, but at the very least, most of the cup should be drained.

וּרְחַץ

The head of the household — according to many opinions, all participants in the Seder — washes his hands as if to eat bread [pouring water from a cup, twice on the right hand and twice on the left], but without reciting a blessing.

כרפס

All participants take a vegetable other than *maror* and dip it into salt water. A piece smaller in volume than half an egg should be used. The following blessing is recited [with the intention that it also applies to the *maror* which will be eaten during the meal] before the vegetable is eaten.

בָּרוּךְ אַתָּה יהוה אֱלֹהֵינוּ מֶלֶךְ הָעוֹלָם, בּוֹרֵא פְּרִי הָאֲדָמָה.

wine does not represent the freedoms from our past and present problems as do the first four cups of wine, but rather is the symbol of the future greatness and final redemption of the Jewish people and with them of all humanity in Messianic times. One of the unique qualities of the Jewish worldview is its ability to combine and see the past and the future simultaneously and seamlessly. Thus, if the four cups of wine represent a progression of past and present freedoms, it is natural that there should be a fifth cup that represents our future freedom. However, since this fifth cup is not mentioned in the Mishnah that describes the Seder rituals, it is not drunk at the Seder.

⇐§ וּרְחַץ / Urechatz

Washing one's hands is part of regular daily Jewish living. We wash our hands when we awake in the morning or from a nap, before we eat, upon emerging from the bathroom, before prayers, and at the end of meals. The concept of clean hands has both a literal and a moral connotation in Jewish life. The phrase, "cleanliness is next to Godliness," appears in its Jewish form in the famous statement of the great rabbinic Sage, R' Pinchas Ben Yair: "Cleanliness leads to separation [from sin and bad influences] and separation leads to purity [and eventually] to holiness." The cleanliness that R' Pinchas ben Yair speaks about is not achieved through the use of soap and water alone. It is an internal cleansing of soul and mind, ridding oneself of all of the accumulated dust and dirt that infiltrates our inner selves; it is a purging of the spiritual *chametz* and unseemliness within us. The symbolic washing of our hands is the reminder to us that cleanliness of soul and mind are necessary. Just as the physical *chametz* has to be eradicated from our possession in order for Pesach to take on proper observance and meaning, so too must we give priority to Jewish virtues and values. It is most ironic that throughout the centuries the greatest insult hurled against us by the haters of the world was, and still is, "Dirty Jew!" To call us "dirty" strikes at the very core of our being and denies our true identity. It is the supreme calumny!

There are many reasons given for the washing of hands at this early stage of the Seder ritual. It, like so many other Seder customs, is performed in order to pique the curiosity of the children who will regard this as an unusual

URECHATZ

The head of the household — according to many opinions, all participants in the Seder — washes his hands as if to eat bread [pouring water from a cup, twice on the right hand and twice on the left], but without reciting a blessing.

KARPAS

All participants take a vegetable other than *maror* and dip it into salt water. A piece smaller in volume than half an egg should be used. The following blessing is recited [with the intention that it also applies to the *maror* which will be eaten during the meal] before the vegetable is eaten.

Blessed are You, HASHEM, our God, King of the universe, Who creates the fruits of the earth.

event in the course of the expected meal, and will ask about it. It is a remembrance of Temple times when hands were washed before eating vegetables and a reminder of the complex laws of purity and impurity that were then in force and observed. Yet, I have always felt that there is another, subtler, reasoning in play here as well. In the order of the Haggadah, this stage is called *urechatz, and wash,* and not simply *rechatz, wash.* The ו *U* — the connecting *vav,* and — binds the washing of the hands to the *Kaddesh* section. There cannot be *Kaddesh* — holiness along with the rest of the commandments and ritual of the Seder — without there being clean hands. The two terms — holiness and cleanliness — are interlinked and mutually dependent on each other. If one wishes to strive for holiness — *Kaddesh* — then *Urechatz* — one must immediately cleanse one's hands. A Seder conducted with dirty hands is an absurd contradiction.

☙ כַּרְפַּס / Karpas

The vegetable used for *karpas* should preferably be green and usually eaten raw, such as celery or cabbage. However, it has become customary in many families to use potatoes (as our family does) or parsley. Nevertheless, any vegetable will do for *karpas,* provided its blessing is *borei pri ha'adamah* — Who has created the produce of the earth. This blessing also applies to the eating of the *maror* — the bitter herb — later in the Seder service. By having this later eating of the *maror* in mind now when reciting the blessing over the *karpas* vegetable, one is exempt from repeating that particular blessing later, at the actual time of eating the *maror.*

However, the truth is that when we recite the blessing regarding produce taken from the earth, it also serves to remind us of the bitterness of our human lot after the expulsion of Adam and Eve from the Garden of Eden. The *Midrash* relates that Adam, upon being driven out of the Garden of Eden, complained to God that he would now be forced to eat grass, as the animals do: "Shall I be forced to eat at the same trough as my donkey?" The Lord "blessed" Adam and his descendants that, through the sweat of their brow, humans would be able to produce bread and other finished food products from the raw materials grown by the earth, something that animals cannot do. The blessing on the *karpas* reminds us of God's gift to man of that ability to produce tasty foods from a wide variety of products that the earth gives forth.

יחץ

The head of the household breaks the middle matzah in two.
He puts the smaller part back between the two whole matzos,
and wraps up the larger part for later use as the *afikoman*.
Some briefly place the *afikoman* portion on their shoulders,
in accordance with the Biblical verse recounting that Israel left Egypt
carrying their matzos on their shoulders, and say
בִּבְהִלוּ יָצָאנוּ מִמִּצְרָיִם, *"In haste we went out of Egypt."*

The Exodus from Egypt and the subsequent Divine revelation on Sinai restored Israel temporarily to the status of Adam before his expulsion from the Garden of Eden. We were redeemed from the "sweat of our brow." Thus, the gift of manna from heaven that nurtured Israel in the desert of Sinai required no human intervention to produce it. The later sins of Israel in the desert once again drove us out from the status of being in the Garden of Eden. On this Seder night we remember that we are yet capable of achieving reentry into the Garden of Eden and therefore this blessing of *borei pri ha'adamah,* like many other Seder matters, differs on this night from all other nights of the year.

Karpas is an appetizer. Like all good appetizers, it promises that there is more to come. It is the forerunner of all of the unique Seder commandments that will be fulfilled this night with our mouths. The ceremonial presence of *karpas* at the beginning of the Seder arouses the curiosity of the children at the table. The vegetable is dipped into salt water or wine vinegar or apple-cider vinegar before being eaten. This is also done to raise the curiosity of the children at the table. The salt water represents the ocean of tears shed by the Jewish people over the centuries, from the time of Egyptian slavery to the present-day Arab suicide bombings. While Jewish memory is always tinged with sorrow, the Jewish future is always bright and happy. The Seder skillfully combines these two emotions into one seamless whole.

Dipping vegetables into a sharp or salty solution (salt water, wine vinegar, or apple-cider vinegar) is mentioned in the Talmud in connection with neutralizing any harmful, unseen parasites that the vegetable may contain. It must also be admitted that the dip adds flavor to otherwise bland, if not almost tasteless food. But it is not the dip itself that is so important. It is the act of dipping that draws attention and piques curiosity. Again, it is the symbolism of the fresh Jewish future as represented by the vegetable of *karpas* having to be dipped in the sorrow of the past, that reminds us of the inseparable connection between our future and our past.

The word *karpas* is mentioned only once in the Bible. It appears in the Scroll of Esther but its meaning there is either a woven curtain or a multicolored silk couch cushion. There is no reference there whatsoever as to its being the name of a food. Since Hebrew words almost always are based on three-letter roots, there is a difference of opinion among Jewish scholars and grammarians of the ages as to whether a word with a four-letter root, such as *karpas* — *kaf, reish, pei,* and *samech* — is non-Hebrew in origin (R' Eliyahu Bachur and others) or whether it is a Hebrew contraction of what were originally two Hebrew words (R' Abraham Ibn Ezra, R' David Kimchi, and others). There are also those that say that *karpas* is in reality a word taken

YACHATZ

The head of the household breaks the middle matzah in two.
He puts the smaller part back between the two whole matzos,
and wraps up the larger part for later use as the *afikoman.*
Some briefly place the *afikoman* portion on their shoulders,
in accordance with the Biblical verse recounting that Israel left Egypt
carrying their matzos on their shoulders, and say
בִּבְהִלוּ יָצָאנוּ מִמִּצְרָיִם, *"In haste we went out of Egypt."*

from Sanskrit. However, the Talmud (*Megillah* 12a) apparently considers it to be a combination of two Hebrew words — *kar*, meaning a pillow or cushion, and *pas*, meaning iridescent silk or a many-colored item. How the word *karpas*, whatever its origin in language, came to mean parsley or celery is a mystery to me. Nevertheless, it should be noted that the Talmud (*Kesubos* 61a) mentions a vegetable, probably celery, as being called *karpasa*. Perhaps the green color of the celery and/or parsley matched the color of the iridescent silk cushions of the Persian court and thus the transference of the name occurred. In any event, *karpas* is famous today as a Seder vegetable and not as a couch cushion.

◆§ יַחַץ / Yachatz

The middle of the three matzos is broken into two. For those who use only two matzos, the bottom matzah is broken into two. Anyone who uses hand-baked matzos for the Seder knows from experience that it is impossible to break a hand-baked matzah into two equal portions. Thus, one is always left with a larger piece and a smaller one. The smaller one is returned to its original place between the other two whole matzos while the larger piece is now wrapped in a cloth or placed in a bag to become, later in the Seder service, the *afikoman* — the "dessert" of the Seder meal. (I will discuss the entire matter of the *afikoman* later in this Haggadah.) There is a custom that in order to keep the children intrigued with the goings-on at the Seder, they are allowed to "steal" this larger piece of matzah and hold it for reasonable ransom pending its return when the time to eat the *afikoman* finally arrives, at the conclusion of the meal. This beloved but seemingly strange, morally questionable, and challenging custom is also related to another Seder custom. In memory of our forefathers leaving Egypt with the unfinished matzos being carried on their shoulders, the adults in some communities march around the house for a moment with their *afikoman* bags on their shoulders. This custom also affords them the ability to try and find a safe hiding place in which to secure the *afikoman* from the clutches of the avaricious younger generation. There is nothing that causes me more joy than being pursued by squealing little grandchildren who are vitally interested in where I will place the *afikoman* bag. I have never been able to successfully hide the *afikoman* bag from them. To tell the truth, I don't really want to. I will discuss the propriety of this custom that apparently condones "teaching" children to "steal" when I discuss the *afikoman* ceremony itself later in this Haggadah commentary.

The two pieces of broken matzah also symbolize a reality that threads its way through all of Jewish history. The word *yachatz* appears in the Torah in connection with our father Yaakov's meeting with Esav upon Yaakov's return from the house of Laban and his self-imposed exile in Aram. There the Torah tells us that Yaakov broke his camp and family into two sections, saying that if Esav attacked and destroyed one group, the other group would still be able to flee

מַגִּיד

The broken matzah is lifted for all to see as the head of the household begins with the following brief explanation of the proceedings.

and survive. Throughout most of Jewish history, even when there was a Jewish sovereignty in the Land of Israel and the Temple stood in its place in Jerusalem, there was a Jewish Diaspora. When the Jewish community in the Land of Israel was destroyed by the Byzantine Christians in the fifth century, the Jewish community in Babylonia survived and prospered. When Babylonia began to decline, the Jewish communities of North Africa, Spain, and France arose to lead the Jewish world. When these countries in turn destroyed or persecuted their Jewish communities, the Jewish communities of Central and Eastern Europe arose to fill their roles of destiny in the story of Israel. The Holocaust and Communism destroyed European Jewry, but the Jews of America and the Land of Israel survived and continued. *Yachatz* therefore represents the eternal promise of God: "You, the children of Yaakov, will never be annihilated." Whatever the fate of the broken piece of matzah, there will always be a remnant that survives as the *afikoman* of our guaranteed future and eternity.

The broken matzah is the symbol of poverty and slavery. Poor people are forced to eat scraps of bread, not necessarily whole loaves. The broken matzah symbolizes the "*lechem oni*" — the bread of poverty and affliction that was the society of Egypt for our forefathers. The large piece of matzah that is put away and hidden until later symbolizes the great future that yet awaits Israel and mankind. The *afikoman* piece is our future. That future is greater and larger than even our glorious past. And it is certainly symbolic, therefore, that the *afikoman* — our future — is accompanied by the squeals of laughter of the members of our youngest generation who are busy pursuing that *afikoman* — our future greatness.

מַגִּיד / Maggid

The main part of the Seder is *Maggid* — the recitation of the Haggadah and the table discussions surrounding it. (Unfortunately some people feel that *Maggid* is less important than the meal itself. This misplaced priority has given rise to the pithy Yiddish aphorism to describe insincere behavior, especially insincere religious behavior: "He does not mean the Haggadah; he means the *kneidlach*/matzah balls.") The word "*maggid*" means to speak, to tell. In Yiddish and Hebrew colloquialism, the word became a noun describing a preacher, sometimes of note and fame, and other times of itinerant, journeyman quality. *Maggid* here means not only to speak, but also to tell a particular story — the story of the Exodus of the Jews from Egyptian bondage.

The basic structure of the Haggadah is outlined in *Mishnah Pesachim,* which is in turn built upon the tradition of the Men of the Great Assembly, which again, in turn, reflects the traditions of the prophets and scholars of Judaism in First Temple times. The Haggadah is composed of numerous sections that logically follow one another. I have already discussed the sections of *Urechatz, Karpas,* and *Yachatz,* all of which are meant to raise questions and curiosity among the children and guests at the Seder table. This leads to the actual asking of the questions themselves, the traditional *Mah Nishtanah,* the Four Questions of the Seder. Then come the answers to these questions and the thanks to the Lord for all of our children and

MAGGID

The broken matzah is lifted for all to see as the head of the household begins with the following brief explanation of the proceedings.

generations, whatever their current state of scholarship or piety. Then we recite the Talmudic proof that the commemoration of the Exodus from Egypt must take place on this particular night and in this particular format. This is followed by the *Hallel* of Egypt, the praise of God Who delivered us from Egypt. The recitations until the drinking of the second cup of the four cups of wine are all part of this section of *maggid.* The second cup concludes this section.

Then we observe the other special mitzvos and customs of the night — matzah, *maror,* the sandwich of Hillel, the eating of eggs and salt water, the meal, and the *afikoman.* After the conclusion of the meal and the blessings after the meal, *Hallel* is concluded and other songs of praise of God are recited including the "Great *Hallel,*" the *Hallel* of Egypt. The Seder concludes with poems, songs, and other traditional sayings that have been added over the centuries to the original format of the Haggadah.

One of the characteristics of *Maggid* is מַתְחִילִים בִּגְנוּת וּמְסַיְּמִים בְּשֶׁבַח, we begin the recitation of *Maggid* by recalling the unsavory past of our ancestors, but we conclude by declaring the eventual glory of Israel and God. People rarely advertise the fact that their immediate ancestors were dishonorable people. Yet, we begin *Maggid* by declaring our origins — idolaters — and only then do we proceed to discuss our more positive history starting from the story of our father Abraham. All of this is in line with the basic Jewish idea that we cannot get to where we are supposed to be going if we do not know where we are coming from. And we must always be honest with ourselves regarding our past. False claims, invented glories, and fantastic stories about the past only complicate our assessment of the present and cloud our vision of the future. Inventing history and falsifying biographies lead to eventual disillusion about our current less-than-perfect situation and our human leadership. Abraham is greater in our eyes precisely because his father Terach was a pagan. Ignoring Terach would make Abraham a lesser figure as the founder of Judaism. Knowing the weaknesses of our past only strengthens the wonder of Jewish survival throughout the ages and confirms the fact that "now the Lord has brought us closer to Him and His service." For if it were not for God's choosing the Jewish people for a special role in human history and His omnipresent if unseen direction of that pivotal role, why would Israel be so unique among all of the peoples of the earth? Only by beginning *v'genus* — with brutal honesty about our past — can we rise to the level of concluding *b'shevach* — in praise of the Almighty and His people who have remained faithful to Him throughout the entire story of human civilization.

Maggid has many subdivisions to it, as outlined above. I will attempt to give each of these sections its due as we continue our review of the Haggadah together. As with all Torah topics, the range of discussion and the depth of analysis that the Haggadah engenders are limitless. That is why every year at the Seder there are fresh insights and new understandings regarding the Haggadah to be shared at the great holiday table. It is especially important to hear what the children have to say. Some of the deepest insights into Pesach that I have ever heard came from the mouths of 8- and 9-year-olds. Innocence and simplicity often breed great wisdom.

הָא לַחְמָא עַנְיָא דִי אֲכָלוּ אַבְהָתָנָא בְּאַרְעָא דְמִצְרָיִם. כָּל דִכְפִין יֵיתֵי וְיֵיכוֹל, כָּל דִצְרִיךְ יֵיתֵי וְיִפְסַח. הָשַׁתָּא הָכָא, לְשָׁנָה הַבָּאָה בְּאַרְעָא דְיִשְׂרָאֵל. הָשַׁתָּא עַבְדֵי, לְשָׁנָה הַבָּאָה בְּנֵי חוֹרִין.

הָא לַחְמָא עַנְיָא — *This is the bread of affliction.*

This declaration in Aramaic is not really part of the original text of the Haggadah. The Haggadah and the order of the Seder were already established in the time of the Talmud (fourth — fifth century) and are themselves based upon the words and teachings of the Mishnah in *Meseches Pesachim.* (As I will mention later in this work, the poems and songs at the conclusion of the Seder service are of much later origin, dating to medieval rather than Talmudic times.) This Aramaic paragraph of הָא לַחְמָא עַנְיָא was apparently first recited in Geonic times (sixth–seventh century) in Babylonia (Aramaic was the spoken language of the Jews in Babylonia of that time) in order to focus the attention of the children on the matzah and to arouse their curiosity so that they would then ask with true wonder why there is matzah tonight instead of the usual bread. It is therefore a custom, followed at our family Seder, to lift the matzahs and exhibit them to the Seder participants when reciting הָא לַחְמָא עַנְיָא. In general, it is obvious that many, if not most, of the Seder customs are intended to pique the curiosity and interest of the children at the Seder table. The purpose of the Seder is the transmission of the story of the Exodus from Egypt to the next generations, and thus the interest and attention of those children is vital.

לַחְמָא עַנְיָא — *bread of poverty or affliction* — is the Aramaic name given to matzah. But the original Hebrew term לֶחֶם עֹנִי *"lechem oni,"* that appears in the Torah itself was subject to various interpretations. The Talmud states that it is *lechem she'onim alav devarim harbei* — food upon which much will be said, i.e. the entire first part of the Seder service is recited with the matzah present on the table. I think that this explains why matzah, which was the bread of affliction — the poor, almost tasteless, sometimes difficult to digest bread of slavery and misery — is also the bread of triumph, hope, and freedom. For the matzah represents God's covenant with Israel, the uniqueness of the Jewish people, and their story. The covenant with our father Abraham included slavery in Egypt and redemption from that slavery (*Genesis* 15:13-16). The whys of the covenant are often difficult for humans to fathom and sometimes to even deal with. But the realities of the fulfillment of the covenant over the long history of the Jews are obvious to all.

The terms of God's covenant with us and His guidance of our affairs remain unchanging, whether in times of deep trouble and abject slavery or in times of Jewish triumph and power. So, too, does the symbol of the matzah remain unchanging, the food for all times, good or bad, for it is the food of God's will, so to speak. The bread of affliction is a permanent fixture in human existence. Many answers — *devarim harbei* — have been given as to why this is so. But all answers that exist outside the realm of faith and belief always appear to be superficial and eventually unsatisfying. The basic answer of the Haggadah is "no answer," except that the faith and tradition of Israel has been sustained till this day and it alone will continue to do so in the future as well. This theme will be repeated many times during the service of the Seder.

This is the bread of affliction that our fathers ate in the land of Egypt. Whoever is hungry — let him come and eat; whoever is in need — let him come and partake of the pesach. Now, we are here; next year may we be in the Land of Israel! Now, we are slaves; next year may we be free men!

The second part of the paragraph deals with the basic concept of Jewish communal life: hospitality, and care for one another. Slaves are not in a position to really help each other. One of

The Seder plate is removed and the second of the four cups of wine is poured. The youngest present asks the reasons for the unusual proceedings of the evening.

מַה נִּשְׁתַּנָּה הַלַּיְלָה הַזֶּה מִכָּל הַלֵּילוֹת?

the hallmarks of freedom is the ability to share material and social benefits with others. Traditionally, the Seder meal always brought guests, even strangers, into one's home. During my years as a rabbi in Miami Beach when our children were still quite young, my wife and I always had guests for Shabbos, the holidays, and especially Pesach. I remember that once there were no guests invited for Shabbos. However, while in the synagogue on Friday night, a stranger approached me and asked to eat with us that evening. I sent my 8-year-old son scurrying home to tell my wife to set an extra place at our table. She later told me that our son burst into the house with a huge smile on his face and announced: "Mama, good news! Daddy found a guest for the Shabbos meal!"

The tradition of Israel is that the process of the redemption of Israel and the world is fueled by good deeds of lovingkindness. Therefore, once we have invited guests to our Seder table and shown them compassion and extended help to others who need it, we can confidently assert that whatever our status and troubles today may be, there is legitimacy to our vision of a Jewish society living next year in the Land of Israel as a truly free people. As part of this idea of goodness to others that must come before the Seder service itself begins, the holiday of Pesach is preceded by the annual *Maos Chittim* food and funds drive on behalf of the indigent and needy. The custom of *Maos Chittim* is the first ruling mentioned in the laws of Pesach as they appear in the *Shulchan Aruch.*

At the beginning of the Seder and at its conclusion, as well, is the expression of the undying Jewish hope to return to the Land of Israel and build a Jewish life there. It is this constant expression of the Jewish longing for the Land of Israel and Jerusalem that remained embedding in the psyche of even secular Jews and inspired the creation of the State of Israel in 1948 and that continues to nurture its growth and self-realization. Although Jews can find personal freedom individually outside of the Land of Israel as well, only in the Land of Israel can there be a visionary Jewish society governed by the Torah and Jewish tradition.

מַה נִּשְׁתַּנָּה — *Why is this night different from all other nights?*

To a great extent, this section of the Haggadah is emblematic of the Seder. This is not only because of the children's role in asking the "Four Questions," though that is undoubtedly the most emotionally appealing reason for its importance. Even if there are no children present at the Seder table, the Four Questions must be asked. More so, even if there are no guests at the table and the person conducting the Seder is alone — even then the Four Questions must be asked out loud, albeit the one who asks is addressing himself. All of Jewish scholarship is based upon asking and answering. The Talmud is comprised of "*shakla v'tarya,*" discussions between scholars, questions and answers, opinions and counteropinions. The great rabbinic works of the ages are encompassed in "*shaylos u'teshuvos*" — questions and responses to problems arising from halachah, circumstances, and life itself. In fact, when the great halachic works of the Rambam (*Mishneh Torah,* 12th century) and R' Joseph Caro (*Shulchan Aruch,* 16th century) were published and disseminated, they were criticized by some because of their departure from the traditional question-and-answer format that had always dominated Jewish scholarship. Tradi-

The Seder plate is removed and the second of the four cups of wine is poured. The youngest present asks the reasons for the unusual proceedings of the evening.

Why is this night different from all other nights?

tionally, the great men of Israel maintained that children and students who are empowered and encouraged to ask questions will eventually rise to the level of being capable of answering questions for others.

There is nothing as stifling to a student's intellectual and spiritual growth as the refusal by a teacher or parent to allow questions to be aired and discussed. The Talmud tells us of a teacher who was considered to be great because he allowed his student to repeat a question to him four hundred times (!) and he answered

שֶׁבְּכָל הַלֵּילוֹת אָנוּ אוֹכְלִין חָמֵץ וּמַצָּה,
הַלַּיְלָה הַזֶּה - כֻּלּוֹ מַצָּה.
שֶׁבְּכָל הַלֵּילוֹת אָנוּ אוֹכְלִין שְׁאָר יְרָקוֹת,
הַלַּיְלָה הַזֶּה - מָרוֹר.

---

every time until the student was satisfied. Even difficult questions of faith and doubt are allowed to be asked and even encouraged. Otherwise, those questions fester deep in the soul and mind of the student and child, and may eventually lead to rebellion and alienation from Torah and tradition. The Seder can have meaning only if the question, "Why the Seder?" is asked and answered. This basic question is therefore not only reserved for small children. Everyone must ask it. It is the driving imperative for the entire Pesach Seder.

Jewish children, from a very early age, and from time immemorial, have been coached to recite the מַה נִּשְׁתַּנָּה / *Mah Nishtanah* at the Seder table. There are traditional melodies that are used for asking the Four Questions. They are asked in Hebrew, and usually translated into the languages of the parents and grandparents. The children have been cajoled, bribed, and coerced into doing so by doting parents and grandparents over all of the generations of Israel. I feel that the emphasis placed on the child asking the Four Questions stems not only from trying to explain to the child why this night of Pesach is different from all other nights of the year. It is also an attempt to implant in the mind and heart of the child the idea of why he or she is different. It is an attempt to educate the child in the necessary concept of Jewish uniqueness and its sense of personal and national mission. By training the child to ask, "Why is this night different from all other nights?" we urge the child to ask, albeit silently but I think no less importantly, "Why am I different?" No one can be expected to remain a loyal and steadfast Jew if this latter question is not properly addressed and answered. Therefore, the questions should be recited not only in their original Hebrew text, but also in the language in which the child is fluent. And this is true of the answers as well, which must be geared to the level and language of the child. The Haggadah recitation should not be a rote reading of the Hebrew text. Rather, it is a key educational tool used to transmit the heritage of the Torah and of the sages of Israel to the coming generation. Thus, Haggadah recitation requires patience, wisdom, common sense, and a great deal of love and tenderness. I am hard pressed to think of any better milieu for parents' education of children in Judaism than the Seder table.

Why "four questions"? There are really five questions involved in this section: "Why is this night different . . .?" and then the four specific questions. Nevertheless, this section is always referred to as the Four Questions. There have been many answers put forth to this question about the questions. The accepted answer is that the first question, the מַה נִּשְׁתַּנָּה, is really part of each and every one of the individual four questions and is only a preface to each of the questions. Thus the questions are "Why is this night different from all other nights in that on all other nights we eat ...." There are those that read the prefatory question, "Why is this night different?" not as a question but as a statement of wonder — "How different is this night from all other nights!" The problem with this approach is that the Four Questions then

1. For on all other nights we may eat *chametz* and matzah, but on this night — only matzah.

2. For on all other nights we eat many vegetables, but on this night — we eat *maror*.

---

also become declaratory statements and are no longer questions. I have felt that though the Haggadah concentrates on the number four — four questions, four cups of wine, four sons, four redemptions — there lurks behind each of these a fifth item — a fifth question, a fifth son, a fifth redemption, a fifth cup of wine. Though we call everything in the Haggadah by the number "four," we really allow for a fifth category throughout its pages and ideas. The obvious and certainly purposeful use of five questions to make up the "four questions" indicates this concept of the relative elasticity of the numbers of the Haggadah. Earlier in this commentary, in the section dealing with the cups of wine, I discussed the idea and custom of pouring a fifth cup of wine at the Seder. I will have more to say about this invisible "fifth" factor as each section relating to the number "four" is reviewed here in this commentary.

□ Chametz or Matzah

On every night of the year except for the nights of Pesach, we may eat either *chametz* or *matzah.* On the Seder night, we are obligated to eat matzah. I have discussed the concept of *chametz* earlier in this book. Tonight — the Seder night — is an "only matzah" occasion. The question implies, correctly so, that not only are we forbidden to eat *chametz* on this night, but we are obligated to eat matzah. Judaism is always a two-tiered faith in that it balances acts of commission with positive actions that are obligatory. It is insufficient to merely abstain from eating *chametz.* One must eat matzah tonight. And that is really the thrust of this question and the other three questions as well. On all other nights we may eat what we wish — *chametz,* matzah, bitter herbs, sweet vegetables, dipped foods, or dry ones — and in the way we wish — reclining, sitting, in leisurely comfort or on the run. So why is this night different? Why the obligations regarding eating tonight? One can perhaps understand the historical significance of not eating *chametz* as being a remembrance of the exodus from Egypt, but being obligated to eat matzah, to eat bitter herbs, to recline, to dip — that is already a curtailment of the very freedom that Pesach allegedly grants us. As one of my recalcitrant grandchildren stated to me, "Why do I have ask the Four Questions?" Abstaining from doing something feels much less coercive than having to do something that is obligatory. There is a psychological tendency to resist doing something that is required. That is why the Talmud teaches us that the reward for performing an obligatory act is greater than the reward for volunteering to do something that one is not obligated to do. What rankles is the infringement on our freedom that obligations entail. But the lesson of Pesach is that freedom automatically carries with it obligations, duties, and responsibilities. I explained all of this to my little grandson and told him that this is why he had to recite the Four Questions. I told him that it is the beginning of his education as to how to be a truly free person — responsible and proud. (In order to help him understand this important and basic idea, I also offered him a sizable bribe of a toy that he wanted. He immediately understood the philosophy of the true definition of freedom, and enthusiastically asked the Four Questions.)

□ Why Bitter Herbs?

Eating bitter herbs on the Seder night is also seemingly a strange matter. After all, the Seder

שֶׁבְּכָל הַלֵּילוֹת אֵין אָנוּ מַטְבִּילִין אֲפִילוּ פַּעַם אֶחָת,
הַלַּיְלָה הַזֶּה - שְׁתֵּי פְעָמִים.
שֶׁבְּכָל הַלֵּילוֹת אָנוּ אוֹכְלִין בֵּין יוֹשְׁבִין וּבֵין מְסֻבִּין,
הַלַּיְלָה הַזֶּה - כֻּלָּנוּ מְסֻבִּין.

The Seder plate is returned. The matzos are kept uncovered as the Haggadah is recited in unison. The Haggadah should be translated if necessary, and the story of the Exodus should be amplified upon.

---

celebrates victory and triumph, not the bitterness of continuing slavery and tragedy. Yet, victory can never be truly appreciated unless one has previously tasted defeat in one's life as well. Unfortunately, Jewish history has more shadow than light to it. It is really the taste of the bitter herbs — an obligatory taste, again — that allows us to savor all of the other tastes of the Seder table. On other nights we have a choice of tastes, of memories, both bitter and sweet. Even on the Seder night we eat different vegetables as well. Nevertheless, on the Seder night our memory focuses on the great story of the Exodus from Egypt. As such, tonight we are to eat the bitter herbs as our obligatory service to remember the bitterness of centuries of Egyptian bondage and servitude. Eating any other vegetables, even on this Seder night, is a matter of choice and personal preference. Eating the bitter herbs is not. So again, this question, like the others of the Four Questions, is really, "Why do I have to eat those bitter herbs?" I will have more to say about the obligation to eat the bitter herbs later in this commentary on the Haggadah.

☐ **Dipping**

In the ancient world, vinegar or other types of pungent liquids were used for dipping vegetables and were considered the salad dressing of that time. Even though the custom to do so was widespread, this was a matter of personal choice. On the Seder night, however, we are bidden to dip vegetables twice — the *karpas* in salt water and the bitter herbs in *charoses.* The symbolism of dipping twice can be understood in the recollection of the depths of agony of the enslaved Jews in Egypt. It is one thing to lose national and personal independence and to be subject to the rule and whim of the mighty and tyrannical. That is one dipping. But it is even more painful to realize that the sole purpose of all of the hard labor extracted from the enslaved was really of no lasting benefit to anyone. This terrible waste of human beings is psychologically even more damaging than the physical privation they endured. This is represented by the second dipping. The entire Soviet Gulag slave-labor system, which included over eighteen million hapless victims in its decades of operation, profited the Soviet economy not one ruble. Slavery and forced labor is inefficient and usually ends as a losing economic venture. So the question here is really a subtler one, a philosophical one, an attempt to understand the mind of human cruelty. Why should we have to dip twice? Why should irrational hatred of others blind humans to such an extent as to cause them to become slave masters, torturers, and hardened criminals, all against their own best social and economic interests? The answer to mankind's woes will come only if this question of why we have to always "dip twice" is addressed and somehow answered satisfactorily.

3. For on all other nights we do not dip even once, but on this night — twice.

4. For on all other nights we eat either sitting or reclining, but on this night — we all recline.

The Seder plate is returned. The matzos are kept uncovered as the Haggadah is recited in unison. The Haggadah should be translated if necessary, and the story of the Exodus should be amplified upon.

☐ Reclining

The final question of the Four Questions deals with the manner of how we sit while involved in the Seder. Tonight we all recline while eating and attending the Seder. While on other nights one may eat sitting erect or leaning, tonight we are all leaning. In our current 21st-century Western society, no one eats leaning any longer. Therefore, this question, perhaps more than any of the other three questions, now truly piques our interest and that of the child asking it. My grandchildren asked me many times why we continue to lean at the Seder table when doing so today is not necessarily known as a symbol of freedom. In their inimitable irreverence they asked, "Why do we have to sit the way they did at the time of the Mishnah?" The question, though phrased rather inelegantly, is nevertheless a valid one. I answered them that this leaning is a method of staying connected to our ancestors, to our history. Everyone on the night of Pesach is bidden to see oneself as though he or she left Egypt in that remarkable Exodus over thirty-five centuries ago. To help us get into such a mental mood, we should first go back twenty centuries and imagine ourselves at the Seder of R' Akiva in long-ago Bnei Brak. At that Seder everyone was leaning. To connect ourselves to that Seder and thereby enable us to continue our imaginary journey even farther back in time to the original Pesach Seder, concrete physical actions and behavior are necessary. If we are leaning, then we can truly imagine ourselves attending R' Akiva's Seder, while if we are sitting erect (something which my grandchildren rarely, if ever, do), it is much harder to connect to R' Akiva. My grandchildren agreed that it would be "cool" to be part of R' Akiva's Seder. By leaning, we are somehow attending R' Akiva's Seder.

In many homes, more than one child asks the Four Questions. The participation of as many children as possible in the actual Seder is to be encouraged. Children's memories of the Seder last their entire lives. One must always remember that the Seder is *the* vehicle for binding the generations together. It is unthinkable, therefore, that we should allow this opportunity to grasp eternity in our families to slip by because of time constraints or other factors that are always present at any Seder. I have found that the Seder can be a tension-filled event if not handled correctly. Serenity, satisfaction, optimism, and infinite patience should govern adult behavior during this evening. All of these insights and advice should be elementary to us. However, decades of rabbinic experience in Jewish family life, along with the countless problems that people have asked me to help them solve, have taught me that nothing should be taken for granted — even the recitation of the Four Questions on the Seder night.

עֲבָדִים הָיִינוּ לְפַרְעֹה בְּמִצְרָיִם, וַיּוֹצִיאֵנוּ יהוה אֱלֹהֵינוּ מִשָּׁם בְּיָד חֲזָקָה וּבִזְרוֹעַ נְטוּיָה. וְאִלּוּ לֹא הוֹצִיא הַקָּדוֹשׁ בָּרוּךְ הוּא אֶת אֲבוֹתֵינוּ מִמִּצְרַיִם, הֲרֵי אָנוּ וּבָנֵינוּ וּבְנֵי בָנֵינוּ מְשֻׁעְבָּדִים הָיִינוּ לְפַרְעֹה בְּמִצְרָיִם. וַאֲפִילוּ כֻּלָּנוּ חֲכָמִים, כֻּלָּנוּ נְבוֹנִים, כֻּלָּנוּ זְקֵנִים, כֻּלָּנוּ יוֹדְעִים אֶת הַתּוֹרָה,

---

עֲבָדִים הָיִינוּ — *We were slaves*

Complicated and technical questions rarely receive a relatively simple answer. Yet, the answer to the Four Questions — in fact, the answer to all of the whys and hows of Judaism and its traditions and life-style behavior — is rather simple and straightforward. We were slaves to Pharaoh in Egypt. We were a small family that grew into a nation on alien soil and in a foreign culture. The Egyptians, forgetting what contributions Joseph and his family and their descendants had made and were continuing to make to the advancement and enrichment of Egypt, saw the Jewish people as a threat and not as an asset. As such, the Egyptians enslaved the Jewish people. At first, like all dictatorships, Egypt thought it would benefit from the "free" slave labor. However, as all tyrants and oppressors have learned or, more accurately, failed to learn over the ages, slave labor is eventually costly and inefficient and it breeds a society and economy that will surely collapse. When Pithom and Ramases did not quite turn out the way Pharaoh had hoped, the slave labor of the Jews lost its economic purposes and simply descended into the sadism and unreasoning hatred of the "other" by the Egyptians.

In the 20th century, a vivid example of this type of tyranny and cruelty occurred in the establishment of the infamous Soviet Gulag that affected eighteen million people directly and tens of millions indirectly. The Gulag never paid for itself economically and destroyed any pretense of morality or idealism that Soviet communism originally claimed for itself.

The Torah tells us how we became slaves in Egypt — the story of Joseph and his brothers, Joseph's rise to power, the great famine, Jacob's descent to Egypt, and the passing of that entire generation. The Torah does not really discuss the "why" of the Egyptian slavery. Why were 210 years of Egyptian sojourn — 86 of which were years of terrible forced labor and cruel persecution — necessary to create the people of Israel? Though many explanations of this difficulty have been offered over the ages by the great commentators to the Torah, the Torah itself offers no explanation for God's will in this matter. It is sufficient in the eyes of God, so to speak, for the Torah to tell us that God apprised Abraham of the fact of Egyptian bondage generations before it was to occur. No reason need be given. God's will is inscrutable; the finite cannot grasp or understand the infinite, and apparently without the experience of Egyptian slavery and the Divine redemption from it, the eternal people could not have been forged and created. Part of the lesson of the Haggadah is the appreciation that God need not conform to our rules of logic nor is God bound to make Himself understandable to us. The entire Haggadah, as we will continue to see, is a lesson in humility and human frailty. Upon a focused and deep analysis, we realize that the Haggadah's answer to the Four Questions cannot really be the *complete* answer; it is the beginning of our humility lesson for the night.

We were slaves to Pharaoh in Egypt, but HASHEM our God took us out from there with a mighty hand and an outstretched arm. Had not the Holy One, Blessed is He, taken our fathers out from Egypt, then we, our children and our children's children would have remained subservient to Pharaoh in Egypt. Even if all of us were wise, all of us understanding, all of us old, all of us knowledgeable in the

---

□ Vestiges Of Slavery

Being a slave leaves a lasting legacy on an individual and a people. Moses redeemed Israel from Egyptian bondage but, as the saying goes (I think this is a saying), "You can take Israel out of Egypt but you can't always take Egypt out of Israel." The entire forty-year sojourn of Israel in the Sinai desert, as well as the period of the Judges that lasted for centuries even when the Israelite nation was created and ensconced in its homeland, testifies to the accuracy of the above saying. The slave mentality within the Jews lasted far longer than did the actual years of slavery. In the desert, any time there were difficulties and frustrations the call was always, "Let us turn around and go back to Egypt!" In fact, the slave mentality even came to glorify Egypt and wax rhapsodically about its watermelons and leeks and squash (*Numbers* 11:5). A slave mentality always embellishes and makes mythical the past, which was known and certain, albeit unpleasant, over current situations and the responsibilities of freedom and statehood, which are fraught with uncertainty and potential dangers. In answering "עֲבָדִים הָיִינוּ," *we were slaves*, we state not only a fact of history but also an explanation (explanations should never be confused with acceptable excuses) as to why so much has gone wrong in the Jewish past and even in the present. It would not be until the times of Samuel, Saul, and David that the mentality of servitude and paganism that Egyptian bondage foisted upon Israel would be mitigated, though not completely eliminated even then. The Lord, through Moses, redeemed us from Egyptian slavery. The task of redemption from the mental state of mind of that slavery He left up to us.

□ Gratitude

A byproduct of the slave mentality is the ingrained evil habit of malevolent ingratitude. A slave is never grateful since whatever is given to the slave by the master cannot compensate for the lack of freedom that he feels. Rare is the servant who does not come to resent his master, no matter how kind that master is to the servant. In the case of Israel, this attitude of ingratitude affected its relationship with God. The Jewish people transferred their understandable feelings of ingratitude from the Egyptian Pharaoh to the God of Israel. Even while being saved from Pharaoh and his army at the Reed Sea, we are told that there were Jews who complained: "In Egypt our feet were muddied in the lime pits and here we also are walking in mud!" Their cynicism and ingratitude did not allow them to discern the obvious difference between mud and mud. The same streak of ingratitude applied to their attitude toward the manna from heaven that fell in the desert, the miraculous well of water that sustained them there, and even to the gift of the Torah that God had granted them. Being grateful and expressing such gratitude for favors and blessings bestowed upon a person by God and other humans is the mark of a truly free individual.

As a further example of the importance of gratitude in Jewish life and thought, one need only consider the fact that the Torah prohibits the revulsion of an individual Egyptian by Jews, "for you were a sojourner in his land." Eventually, Egyptian converts to Judaism are allowed to become part of the Jewish nation. Even though we were severely mistreated by the Egyptian nation as a whole and enslaved and tortured by its rulers, the individual Egyptian is still owed a debt of acknowledgement, if not gratitude, for allowing us to have sojourned in his land. In God's system of justice and morality, every good deed, even unintentional and minimal ones, does not go unnoticed, just as every evil deed eventually never goes unpunished. Ingratitude to other humans and/or to God is a cardinal sin in Jewish life.

□ Still in Egypt?

We acknowledge in the Haggadah that God alone took us forth from Egyptian bondage and that He did so "with a strong hand and an outstretched arm." We also state that if God would not have done so, we would still be enslaved to the Pharaoh of Egypt for all of our generations. At first glance, this seems to be a strange statement, even an inaccurate one. No empire in history has lasted forever; all have eventually collapsed and disappeared. If we would not have left Egypt in 1312 B.C.E. (2448 from Creation), we certainly would have left it in one way or another by now. It is obvious, therefore, that the Haggadah is not only speaking of physical bondage as well. It is speaking of spiritual bondage. If God had not redeemed us powerfully — "with a strong hand and an outstretched arm" — in a spectacular and miraculous fashion, our attention would be focused on the natural collapse of the Egyptian empire and not on the God of Israel Who redeemed us and, unaided by any "natural" forces, crushed the Egyptian might.

Spiritually, emotionally, even mentally and logically, we would still be under Pharaoh's influence and be beholden to the "natural" forces that make empires wither and pass away. God's hand, so to speak, is always present in human events and history. However, it usually reveals itself in "natural" causations and explanations that form the bases for Ph.D. theses and academic studies and books. We are witness in our time to the miraculous collapse of the Soviet Union, the evil empire that terrorized the free world for decades on end. Yet, even this is treated by almost all as being "natural," understandable, and, in perfect hindsight, even predictable. If that attitude were to be the case regarding the Exodus from Egypt as well, Jews would never have felt themselves special, chosen, a different and unique people. Thus, full freedom from Pharaoh could not have been attained and the later acceptance of the Torah at Sinai would have occurred, if at all, under a vastly different mental state of the Jewish people. When one feels beholden to Pharaoh, it is difficult to say to Moses and to God, "We will do and we will listen." The Jewish people would not have been willing to "go after Me into a trackless desert, into a land never sowed or planted." Thus, the outstretched and powerful hand, the miracles and the destruction of the Egyptian taskmasters, were all necessary ingredients in the story of the Exodus from Egypt. Nothing less than God's miracles — "the strong hand and the outstretched arm" — would have made us truly free from Pharaoh's rule and lasting influence.

◆§ וַאֲפִילוּ כֻּלָּנוּ חֲכָמִים —
Even if all of us were wise.

The obligation of reciting the story of the Exodus is independent of our previous knowledge and understanding of the story. All knowledge needs constant reinforcement in order to remain truly useful. It is easy for humans to relegate historical events and lessons derived from them to the back of their minds, especially events that are thousands of years old by now. But the Exodus from Egypt is the basis of Judaism and the Jewish story. Many of the mitzvos of the Torah are זֵכֶר לִיצִיאַת מִצְרָיִם —

עבדים
היינו
לפרעה

מִצְוָה עָלֵינוּ לְסַפֵּר בִּיצִיאַת מִצְרָיִם. וְכָל הַמַּרְבֶּה לְסַפֵּר בִּיצִיאַת מִצְרַיִם, הֲרֵי זֶה מְשֻׁבָּח.

מַעֲשֶׂה בְּרַבִּי אֱלִיעֶזֶר וְרַבִּי יְהוֹשֻׁעַ וְרַבִּי אֶלְעָזָר בֶּן עֲזַרְיָה וְרַבִּי עֲקִיבָא וְרַבִּי טַרְפוֹן שֶׁהָיוּ מְסֻבִּין בִּבְנֵי בְרַק,

---

a memorial to our redemption from Egyptian bondage. Therefore, the constant repetition and memory of the Exodus is basic for an understanding of Torah and Jewish life. The Seder and the Haggadah provide the yearly review lesson that keeps the story of the Exodus fresh and vital in our hearts and minds. Even the wisest and most knowledgeable scholars are plagued with memory loss and changing priorities and values in their lives. No one, therefore, is exempt from the obligation of remembering the Exodus from Egypt "all the days of your life."

My years as a teacher, both in yeshivah and synagogue, have taught me that one of the most difficult parts of teaching is motivating the student to review the knowledge that he feels he has already obtained and knows. I once interviewed a promising eighth-grade student who was considering attending my yeshivah for high school. In the course of our discussion (it soon became apparent to me that he thought he was actually interviewing me!), he asked me what tractate of the Talmud the ninth grade would be studying next year. When I informed him of the name of the tractate that the yeshivah planned to study the following year, he frowned and said to me, "I don't believe I will attend your yeshivah. You see, I did that tractate already in sixth grade." Only the true Talmud student understands that every review of a Torah subject is in reality a new and fresh learning experience. Yet, the temptation of always wishing to learn new things, even without truly digesting and understanding what has already been learned, is a great one, especially for people of a creative bent of mind. Hence the wording here in the Haggadah, that even the wisest, most creative and knowledgeable Torah scholars are nevertheless ordered to review the lesson of the Exodus from Egypt on this Seder night. And the wonder of it is that every Seder night is a new and fresh experience with added insight and knowledge enhancing our previous understanding of the event. The mere fact that a year, along with all of its experiences and events, has passed is sufficient to allow us to read the same old words of the Haggadah with a new approach and a deeper understanding and appreciation of the eternal and timeless quality of the story of our redemption from Egyptian bondage.

The Haggadah here praises the one who expands on the simple narrative of the Haggadah and tells the story of the Exodus in detail and with insights and explanations. From this statement arose the custom of discussing the Haggadah and its contents at great length at the Seder table. Many of our children and grandchildren come to the Seder table laden with the notes taught to them in school. Usually they vie with one another in showing and sharing their knowledge with others and this can be a very positive learning experience, as long as it is not allowed to get out of hand. It should be noted that the Haggadah states that the one who "tells, relates the story to others" is to be complimented. Again, as a teacher, I know that in explaining something to others, I gain new insights and understanding into the subject mat-

Torah — it would be an obligation upon us to tell the story about the Exodus from Egypt. The more one expands upon the discussion of the Exodus, the more he is praiseworthy.

It happened with Rabbi Eliezer, Rabbi Yehoshua, Rabbi Elazar ben Azaryah, Rabbi Akiva, and Rabbi Tarfon, who were gathered (at the Seder) in Bnei Brak. They spoke of

---

ter being taught. Therefore, the one who relates the Pesach story in detail and care to others will not only feel complimented for doing so, but will be "מְשֻׁבָּח" — he will feel enhanced and improved thereby. Having to explain great and often complex ideas to others always benefits the teacher as much as it does the student. R' Meir said, "From my students I have learned the most." By that he meant that having to teach students, being forced to answer their questions and doubts, creates a greater source of knowledge and insight for the teacher. The Pesach Seder and Haggadah are outstanding examples of this truism of educational policy.

מַעֲשֶׂה בְּרַבִּי אֱלִיעֶזֶר — *It happened with Rabbi Eliezer.*

Theory and practice often differ. Good ideas, even great thoughts, are frequently unworkable in the real world. Therefore, the Jewish genius occasionally provides for plans, thoughts, and decisions that are theoretically correct — *l'halachah* — but are not to be required in everyday practice and life — *aval lo l'ma'aseh*. Therefore, in order to reinforce the previous assertion in the Haggadah, that even the wisest scholars are bidden to actually recite the story of the Exodus on the night of Pesach, the Haggadah tells us *l'ma'aseh* — a story about the greatest scholars of Israel in the second century C.E. who spent the entire Seder night of Pesach retelling the story of the exodus from Egypt. There is a concept in Jewish life called *ma'aseh rav* — the behavior and actions of great teachers and mentors. Judaism does not allow for "do as I say and not as I do." We follow what great people, our holy leaders and recognized scholars, actually did, and not only what they said and taught. It was in their practical, actual behavior that their Torah views were tested and made firm. It is one thing to conduct a symposium about the necessity of telling the story of the Exodus. However, it is the actual retelling of that story that is the commandment and the requirement of the hour. The *ma'aseh* of R' Eliezer, R' Yehoshua, R' Elazar ben Azaryah, R' Akiva, and R' Tarfon — their real-life behavior — teaches us the necessity of retelling the Exodus story on Pesach night in a way that no intellectual explanation could.

(There is an anecdote popular in Israeli academia poking fun at theoreticians who lack practical common sense, about a professor who passed on and arrived at the gates of Heaven reserved for those academics that inhabit the World to Come. There he saw two signs over two entrances to Paradise. One sign read: "This is the gate to *Gan Eden* — to Paradise itself." Over the second entrance there was a sign that read: "This is the gate to the symposium about *Gan Eden*.")

These great rabbis lived at the time of the Bar Kochba rebellion and the subsequent terrible persecutions of the Jews, and especially of their Torah scholars, by Hadrian. Because of this, many have read into the phrase, "they spoke of the Exodus of Egypt כָּל אוֹתוֹ הַלַּיְלָה, *all of that night*," as being a reference to the "night" of the Roman persecutions of that century. And the

וְהָיוּ מְסַפְּרִים בִּיצִיאַת מִצְרַיִם כָּל אוֹתוֹ הַלַּיְלָה. עַד שֶׁבָּאוּ תַלְמִידֵיהֶם וְאָמְרוּ לָהֶם, רַבּוֹתֵינוּ הִגִּיעַ זְמַן קְרִיאַת שְׁמַע שֶׁל שַׁחֲרִית.

אָמַר רַבִּי אֶלְעָזָר בֶּן עֲזַרְיָה, הֲרֵי אֲנִי כְּבֶן שִׁבְעִים שָׁנָה,

---

hidden and yet not so subtle message here is that even in the midst of the night of persecution the great men of Israel never despaired. They never lost their faith in the better tomorrow and in the

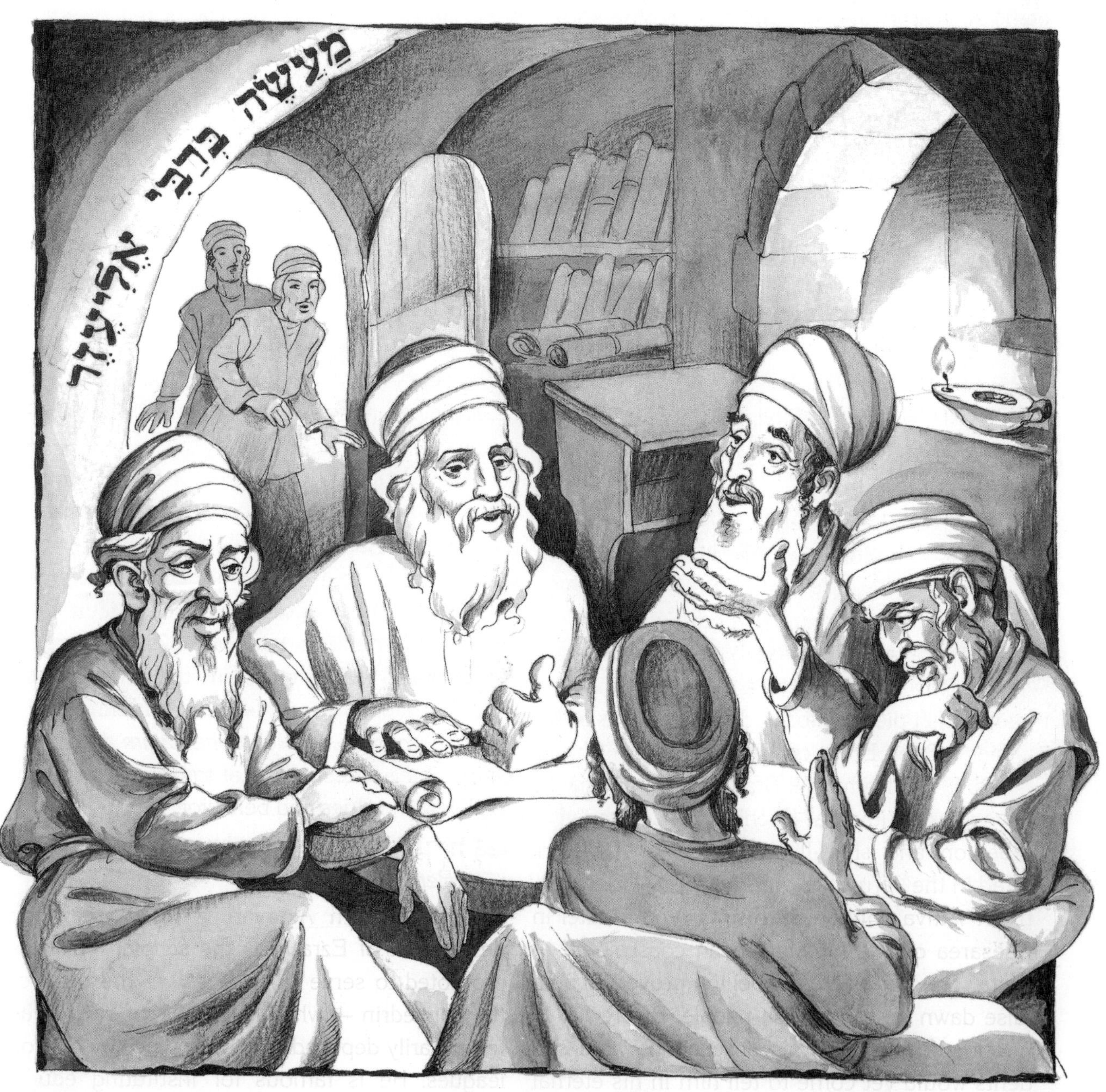

the Exodus from Egypt all of that night until their students came and said to them: "Our teachers, the time has come for the reading of the morning *Shema*."

Rabbi Elazar ben Azaryah said: I am like a seventy-year-old

---

ultimate vindication and redemption of the Jewish people. They constantly retold the story of the first Exodus in the unshakable belief that the last Exodus would also arrive and redeem Israel from its enemies and troubles. Eventually, no matter how many generations later and no matter how long the night is, their students — and, in fact, we, almost two millennia later, are still their students — will come and report to them that the dawn is breaking over Israel and let us, therefore, recite the *Shema* in gratitude and service to the God of Israel Who has sustained us miraculously through this long night of exile and tragedy. And it must certainly be said that it was the rabbis who triumphed over the Romans. There have been hundreds of thousands of Jews named Akiva in the centuries since his death. There were and still are very few persons who are proud to call themselves or their children Hadrian.

In the times of R' Akiva, Bnei Brak, which was the location of his yeshivah, was a rather small farming community. Today's Bnei Brak, with a population of nearly 150,000 Jews and famous the world over as a city of Torah study and Jewish piety, is located near the site of the ancient Bnei Brak of Biblical and Mishnaic times. It was from Bnei Brak that R' Akiva journeyed east to join Bar Kochba, whose desperate rebellion and short-lived kingdom were centered in the Jerusalem/Hebron area of the country. R' Akiva would meet his martyrdom later in Caesarea on the Mediterranean coast south of Haifa. The Bar Kochba rebellion proved to be a false dawn for the Jewish people. But R' Akiva never lost faith that his descendants and students would yet come to tell him in his eternal resting place that the true dawn of Jewish deliverance had in fact arrived.

Althouh the five rabbis sitting together at that Pesach Seder in Bnei Brak were united on the essentials of faith and law, they were five distinctly different individuals. They occasionally differed with each other over matters of halachah, rabbinic behavior, politics, and policy for the Jewish people vis-a-vis the Romans and the potential messianic aspirations of Bar Kochba. They were also different personalities, some strong and mostly unbending, and others more gentle and conciliatory. But these differences were in reality the exhibition of their strengths and all of their opinions and policies were *l'shem Shamayim* — for the sake of Heaven and Israel's welfare. Since it was this overriding concern — *l'shem Shamayim* — that united them, it is not surprising that they joined together in friendship, respect, and harmony to celebrate the Pesach Seder as one group. Judaism was never built on the basis of personal conformity or the stifling of individuality and personality. It was and is built on the combination of many individuals' talents and with the unity of purpose to serve God and Israel in a manner befitting the concept of *l'shem Shamayim* and in the spirit of the preservation of tradition, halachah, and Jewish values and behavior.

אָמַר רַבִּי אֶלְעָזָר בֶּן עֲזַרְיָה — *Rabbi Elazar Ben Azaryah said:*

R' Elazar ben Azaryah, a tenth-generation descendant of Ezra, was the scholar who was promoted to serve as the *Nasi* — the head of the Sanhedrin — when R' Gamliel of Yavne was temporarily deposed from that office by his colleagues. He is famous for instituting educa-

וְלֹא זָכִיתִי שֶׁתֵּאָמֵר יְצִיאַת מִצְרַיִם בַּלֵּילוֹת, עַד שֶׁדְּרָשָׁהּ בֶּן זוֹמָא, שֶׁנֶּאֱמַר, לְמַעַן תִּזְכֹּר אֶת יוֹם צֵאתְךָ מֵאֶרֶץ מִצְרַיִם כֹּל יְמֵי חַיֶּיךָ.[1] יְמֵי חַיֶּיךָ הַיָּמִים, כֹּל יְמֵי חַיֶּיךָ הַלֵּילוֹת. וַחֲכָמִים אוֹמְרִים, יְמֵי חַיֶּיךָ הָעוֹלָם הַזֶּה, כֹּל יְמֵי חַיֶּיךָ לְהָבִיא לִימוֹת הַמָּשִׁיחַ.

בָּרוּךְ הַמָּקוֹם, בָּרוּךְ הוּא. בָּרוּךְ שֶׁנָּתַן תּוֹרָה לְעַמּוֹ

---

tional changes and increasing the numbers of students among the scholars during the time of his reign.

R' Elazar was a very young man when he assumed that august post. There is Talmudic opinion that he was either 18 or 21 years old at that time. Nevertheless, he looked much older than his years — "I am like a 70-year-old man!" Some say that he prayed to look aged so that his words and authority would be accepted by his older colleagues. Others state that the intensity of his Torah study was so great that it made him look aged. Still others state that he meant to say that even though he was a very young person, he had acquired vast Torah knowledge as though he were a 70-year-old scholar. A more cynical view is that anyone who assumes a leadership role ages automatically overnight. When R' Gamliel was restored as the leader, R' Elazar continued to serve as a co-leader, assuming the leadership position one week out of four.

Here, R' Elazar states that he was of the opinion that the third section of the *Shema* prayer — the one that contains references to both the mitzvah of *tzitzis* and to the Exodus from Egypt — should be recited at night (during the *Ma'ariv* service) as well, even though the commandment regarding *tzitzis* is effective only during the day. It was because of the reference to the Exodus that R' Elazar maintained that the paragraph should be recited at night as well. However, the rabbis of the Mishnah disagreed with him and he was unable to win the point with them until his colleague, (Shimon) Ben Zoma, supported his position by proving its correctness from the verse in the Torah itself — "In order that you shall remember the day of your Exodus from Egypt *all* the days of your life" — the word כָּל, *all,* indicates even during the nights. Ben Zoma's support allowed R' Elazar not to have to stand alone as an individual opinion against the opinion of the rabbis, one against many. Now it was the opinion of more than one against the opinion of those who also were more than one. Until Ben Zoma came along, R' Elazar said in effect, "I was unable to overcome the opinion of my colleagues but now with his help, I have become vindicated in my long-held opinion that this paragraph should be recited at night due to its specific mention of the Exodus from Egypt." Shimon ben Zoma was famous in the Mishnah for being the last of the *darshanim* — the men who were able to deduce insights from the texts and words of the written Torah. Therefore, his interpretation — his *derash* — of this verse, namely, that remembering the Exodus refers to the nights as well, carried great weight among the scholars and therefore allowed R' Elazar's opinion to become the law and custom of Israel.

Regarding the verse, "*all* the days of your life," the opinion of the rabbis of the Mishnah

man, but I could not succeed in having the Exodus from Egypt mentioned every night, until Ben Zoma expounded it, as it says: "In order that you may remember the day you left Egypt all the days of your life."[1] The phrase "the days of your life" would have indicated only the days; the addition of the word "all" includes the nights as well. But the [other] Sages declare that "the days of your life" would mean only the present world; the addition of "all" includes the days of Mashiach.

Blessed is the Omnipresent; Blessed is He. Blessed is the One Who has given the Torah to His people Israel; Blessed is

(1) *Deuteronomy* 16:3.

---

differed from that of Ben Zoma and R' Elazar. They hold that the word כָּל, *all,* in that verse refers not to nighttime but rather to messianic times, for even then, the story of the Exodus from Egypt will be remembered and recited. In fact, the Exodus from Egypt will then serve as the basis for comparison of the miracles and wonders that will appear in the final processes of the messianic era. This is a further reinforcement of the idea mentioned previously, that the Exodus from Egypt is the cornerstone upon which the entire structure of Jewish life and history rests and that therefore the era of messianic redemption will be a further reminder of our original redemption from Egyptian bondage. Chassidic masters add that "all the days of your life" should be devoted to the good works and positive deeds that will then help bring us to that longed-for era of messianic redemption — "לְהָבִיא לִימוֹת הַמָּשִׁיחַ"

בָּרוּךְ הַמָּקוֹם — *Blessed is the Omnipresent;*

Blessed is God — that is our message to our Creator. We bless God in all of our prayers and this expression of blessing is repeated numerous times — at least one hundred times a day. But we should never make the mistake of believing that God is affected by our blessings or that He is somehow enhanced by them. Therefore we immediately say, "בָּרוּךְ הוּא" — *blessed is He;* the Creator is blessed by the very fact of His existence itself, without anything that we can add to that concept of blessedness. We bless God for granting Israel the Torah — the most precious of all Godly gifts. But even that gift to Israel does not affect God's innate blessedness. Independent of God's covenant with Israel and of the gift of His Torah to Israel, God reigns alone and perfect in the universe of His creation. Thus the response of Jews to the recitation of God's Name is to say בָּרוּךְ הוּא — Blessed is He, and there is nothing that we can add to that quality. Part of the blessedness of God is that He tolerates all kinds of people (this will lead us to the section of the Four Sons) and is the symbol of patience and forgiveness in dealing with His human creatures. Because of this alone, humans must always proclaim the innate blessedness of God.

At our family Seder, we always sing בָּרוּךְ הַמָּקוֹם with a special tune. The only problem is that my sons-in-law and grandchildren and I

יִשְׂרָאֵל, בָּרוּךְ הוּא. כְּנֶגֶד אַרְבָּעָה בָנִים דִּבְּרָה תוֹרָה – אֶחָד חָכָם, וְאֶחָד רָשָׁע, וְאֶחָד תָּם, וְאֶחָד שֶׁאֵינוֹ יוֹדֵעַ לִשְׁאוֹל.

never are able to agree what that special tune should be. I am a very good musical person in my head, but my voice and ear have always betrayed me. As noted above, my second-grade teacher advised me just to mouth the words and not bother to try and sing the melody. So I know that they are singing the wrong tune to בָּרוּךְ הַמָּקוֹם but I am unable to teach them our family's traditional and correct tune. So, בָּרוּךְ הַמָּקוֹם is always a bittersweet moment for me at the Seder table. However, if God can endure all of the different types of humans that comprise His world, I can also smilingly suffer through the incorrect tune for בָּרוּךְ הַמָּקוֹם.

אַרְבָּעָה בָּנִים — *The Four Sons*

The Torah includes within it all types of Jews. It predicates itself on the awareness that not all Jews are the same and that not all of them have the same opportunities and life experiences as far as Jewish knowledge and life are concerned. Thus the רָשָׁע, the evil son, is also part of our Seder table because as a Jew he is also now redeemable, even though originally in Egypt he would probably not have survived. The difference between now and then as regards the status of a רָשָׁע, will be discussed shortly. It is noteworthy to examine the language used here in the Haggadah in connection with the Four Sons. Each of the Four Sons — the wise, the evil, the simple and the unlettered — finds himself preceded by the word אֶחָד, *one:* אֶחָד חָכָם, *one is the wise one,* וְאֶחָד רָשָׁע, *one is the wicked one,* and so on. They are not counted as being numbers one, two, three, and four. Rather, each one is an אֶחָד, a singular, unique individual. Many times, it is the fact that one was never treated as an individual in one's home or school that allows a Jew to slip down into the *rasha* category. Remembering that each child, each student, each individual human being is an אֶחָד is a fundamental rule for success in raising a family, running a school, and maintaining harmonious social relationships.

The *rasha* would have died in Egyptian bondage because of a number of reasons, all advanced by our commentators on the Haggadah. The *rasha* excludes himself from the shared fate of the Jewish community, believing that he is entitled to "follow the control and wantings of my own heart." He views the service of God and the responsibilities of Jewish halachic behavior and values of the Torah as being oppressive, burdensome, and not worth the effort. He mocks the lifestyle of observant Jews and associates himself with those that deny Israel's uniqueness. At the beginning of our history — in Egypt — such attitudes removed one from the Jewish community completely. According to the *Midrash*, as many as 80 percent of the Jews in Egypt did not live to leave Egypt, having died during the three days of the plague of darkness. A *rasha* is without hope or faith, optimism or perseverance. Such a person could never have survived the slavery of Egypt. The later *rasha,* however, the person who is present at our Seder table can be shocked into becoming a better person and a more loyal Jew. The Haggadah says of the *rasha,* שָׁם לֹא הָיָה נִגְאָל, *there* in Egypt, he would not have been redeemed, but now here, by being at the Seder table, there is a good possibility of his being elevated.

Today's "secular" Jew is not really the *rasha* of the Haggadah. The difference between then in Egypt and now in our current world is summed up succinctly by R' Abraham Yehoshua Karelitz in his great work, *Chazon Ish, Yoreh De'ah, Hilchos Shechitah:*

He. Concerning four sons does the Torah speak — one is wise, one is wicked, one is simple, and one is unable to ask.

It is my opinion that the laws [of the Talmud regarding disregarding the life of the Jewish nonbelievers] applied only to those times when the Lord's guidance of the world was obvious to all, with open miracles present and a Heavenly echo [*bas kol*] present and operative. But in a time when God's presence is hidden from us and the faith has been torn away from classes of Jews, then giving these Jews a lower status will not in any way contain the breach [of faith within our people] but will rather widen that breach for they will think our behavior to be

חָכָם מָה הוּא אוֹמֵר? מָה הָעֵדֹת וְהַחֻקִּים וְהַמִּשְׁפָּטִים אֲשֶׁר צִוָּה יהוה אֱלֹהֵינוּ אֶתְכֶם?[1] וְאַף אַתָּה אֱמָר לוֹ כְּהִלְכוֹת הַפֶּסַח, אֵין מַפְטִירִין אַחַר הַפֶּסַח אֲפִיקוֹמָן.

רָשָׁע מָה הוּא אוֹמֵר? מָה הָעֲבֹדָה הַזֹּאת לָכֶם?[2] לָכֶם וְלֹא לוֹ, וּלְפִי שֶׁהוֹצִיא אֶת עַצְמוֹ מִן הַכְּלָל, כָּפַר בְּעִקָּר – וְאַף אַתָּה הַקְהֵה אֶת שִׁנָּיו וֶאֱמָר לוֹ, בַּעֲבוּר זֶה עָשָׂה יהוה לִי בְּצֵאתִי מִמִּצְרָיִם.[3] לִי וְלֹא לוֹ, אִלּוּ הָיָה שָׁם לֹא הָיָה נִגְאָל.

> immoral and violent, God forbid. And since the purpose of this law [of lowering the status of nonbelievers] is to improve the society and the enforcement of such behavior and attitudes will in no way accomplish that, the law has no effect in our days. It is rather our duty to bring these Jews closer to us [and to Torah] with bonds of love and to enlighten them to the best of our abilities.

The *rasha* in Egypt was witness to miracles, plagues, and the leadership of Moses. Our *rasha* at today's Seder table is a product of tsarist persecution, the false gods of communism and pure nationalism, the Holocaust, a lack of any meaningful Jewish education, a century of Arab terrorism against Jews in the Land of Israel, the prevalent Western culture of materialism and assimilation, and a climate of hedonism. He is much more the son who knows nothing than he is the son of evil.

I have always enjoyed looking at Haggados from different periods of Jewish life and history. One of the more fascinating things that I have discovered in perusing these Haggados is the illustrations that are used to represent the evil son. He is always portrayed as wearing the most stylish and provocative clothes of that period, be it Roman armor and toga, Renaissance Italy, Dutch feathery, Cossack Eastern Europe, foppish Victorian England, or Roaring Twenties America. These depictions of the evil son may be inaccurate and even unfair, but they reflect the belief that being too radically up to date and "cool" is not really the Jewish way. The wise son always seems to be dressed more conservatively than his evil brother. Apparently, appearances do count in this world of ours, even in our illustrated Haggados. It is true that a person may be wise and pious and yet dress wildly differently from the norm, and a person may dress in rabbinic garb and have "his *tzitzis* showing on the outside visible to all while his heart may be far away from his Father in Heaven," in the words of R' Menachem HaMeiri (*Sotah* 20b). Yet, how a person looks and dresses often says a great deal about his character, beliefs, and behavior. One can also note how the garb of the wise son has changed over the centuries of illustrated Haggados.

The *rasha* in Egypt would not have gone free, but the fact that the great majority of the Jewish people in Egypt — as mentioned above, four-fifths of them died in Egypt — could be classified as wicked did not prevent the Exodus from happening. Chassidic thought (*Shem MiShmuel*) teaches us that the Jews were taken out of Egypt in order to later accept the Torah and observe mitzvos and not because of their pre-

The wise son — what does he say? "What are the testimonies, decrees and ordinances which HASHEM, our God, has commanded you?"[1] You, too, tell him about the laws of the *pesach* offering: that one may not eat dessert after the final taste of the *pesach* offering.

The wicked son — what does he say? "Of what purpose is this service to you?"[2] — [implying] "to you," but not to him. By excluding himself from the community of believers, he denies the basic principle of Judaism. Therefore, blunt his teeth and tell him: "It is because of this that HASHEM did so for me when I went out of Egypt."[3] "For me," but not for him — had he been there, he would not have been redeemed.

(1) *Deuteronomy* 6:20. (2) *Exodus* 12:26. (3) *Exodus* 13:8.

---

vious good moral behavior. And that is the answer that is given to the *rasha* at the Seder, that the Lord took me out of Egypt so that in the future I would serve Him and accept His Torah. It was God's will to do so, not Israel's merit in achieving it. The Jews were redeemed not because of their past behavior, but because of the potential of their future behavior. Therefore, the Lord rejected the complaint of the angels that the Jews should not be saved at the Sea of Reeds for they were then no better than the Egyptians. God stated that since the Jews will be judged on their future behavior and not on what they were within Egypt, they are worthy of His miracles. Nevertheless, those Jews who refused to agree to a future of Godly service, who lobbied constantly for a return to Egyptian slavery, a condition that allowed them to continue to wallow in Egyptian paganism and immorality, died in Egypt and in the desert of Sinai. The first step in extricating oneself from the danger of being categorized as a *rasha* is to look forward to better days and more positive accomplishments and not to dwell upon past errors and weaknesses.

In light of what I have written above regarding the *rasha* and tomorrow, I relate at my Seder the following insight which I value greatly. In the verse in *Deuteromony* (6:20) that concerns itself with the question asked by the wise son, the Torah states that he will ask you the question מָחָר, *tomorrow.* Rashi there comments that there is a tomorrow that comes after time, that is not necessarily immediate. In *Exodus* (13:14) there appears the question of the simple, nave son. There, too, the word מָחָר appears in the verse. But there Rashi interprets the verse differently and states that there is a מָחָר that is immediate and there is a מָחָר that comes after time. The verse in *Exodus* that deals with the question of the *rasha* does not contain any mention of מָחָר at all. Thus in utter simplicity the three sons who speak at the Seder are therewith clearly defined: The wise son plays a long game — a distant tomorrow. His behavior is not to be judged by immediacy or current political or social correctness, nor is the reward for his good deeds always readily and immediately present. He retains the perspective of ages and history and the prophetic promises of Jewish

תָּם מָה הוּא אוֹמֵר? מַה זֹּאת? וְאָמַרְתָּ אֵלָיו, בְּחֹזֶק יָד הוֹצִיאָנוּ יהוה מִמִּצְרַיִם מִבֵּית עֲבָדִים.[1]

וְשֶׁאֵינוֹ יוֹדֵעַ לִשְׁאוֹל, אַתְּ פְּתַח לוֹ. שֶׁנֶּאֱמַר, וְהִגַּדְתָּ לְבִנְךָ בַּיּוֹם הַהוּא לֵאמֹר, בַּעֲבוּר זֶה עָשָׂה יהוה לִי בְּצֵאתִי מִמִּצְרָיִם.[2]

יָכוֹל מֵרֹאשׁ חֹדֶשׁ, תַּלְמוּד לוֹמַר בַּיּוֹם הַהוּא. אִי בַּיּוֹם הַהוּא, יָכוֹל מִבְּעוֹד יוֹם, תַּלְמוּד לוֹמַר בַּעֲבוּר זֶה. בַּעֲבוּר זֶה לֹא אָמַרְתִּי אֶלָּא בְּשָׁעָה שֶׁיֵּשׁ מַצָּה וּמָרוֹר מֻנָּחִים לְפָנֶיךָ.

---

destiny. The *rasha* lives only for the here and now. No מָחָר figures in his life and none therefore appears in the verse that asks his question. Consumed by his present passions, he is oblivious to what awaits him tomorrow as a consequence of his present actions. The תָּם, the simple, naive son, believes that one can have both the present and the future, without having to choose or at least grant priority of one over the other. Hence, one's relationship to מָחָר, *tomorrow*, becomes the deciding factor in categorizing the sons of the Haggadah who are seated at our Seder table.

◆ שֶׁאֵינוֹ יוֹדֵעַ לִשְׁאוֹל, *The Son Who Is Unable to Ask*

The method for dealing with the son who is even unable to ask is straightforward: אַתְּ פְּתַח לוֹ, you must open his mouth, engage him in conversation, give him the knowledge to ask wisely and think knowingly. The word "you" is used in feminine gender — אַתְּ instead of אַתָּה – to indicate that this must be done softly and gently and not coercively and autocratically. Unlike the *rasha* who requires shock and trauma to get him to readjust his ways, the ignorant son requires warmth and gentleness to urge him to begin the task of learning about his faith and his people. The Talmud has taught us that the words of the wise men are heard when they are spoken softly and gently. If the ignorant son is not taught and brought close, then the likelihood that he will eventually, and even unintentionally, join the *rasha's* camp is far greater than are the chances of his becoming allied with the wise son. Thus a conscious, continuing effort must be made by those who are knowledgeable and Jewishly committed to help the son who is ignorant and mute in all Jewish matters. This may often appear to be a herculean task but that affords no excuse for not attempting to improve the situation.

◆ יָכוֹל מֵרֹאשׁ חֹדֶשׁ — *One might think [that the obligation to discuss the Exodus commences] with the first [day] of the month.*

The obligation to recite the story of the Exodus from Egypt is limited to the night of the Seder itself. "Only when there is matzah and *maror* lying on the table before you" is this obligation to be discharged. In the times of the Temple in Jerusalem the formula recited was,

The simple son — what does he say? "What is this?" Tell him: "With a strong hand did HASHEM take us out of Egypt, from the house of bondage."[1]

And as for the son who is unable to ask, you must initiate the subject for him, as it says: You shall tell your son on that day, saying: "It is because of this that HASHEM did so for me when I went out of Egypt."[2]

One might think [that the obligation to discuss the Exodus commences] with the first [day] of the month of Nisan, but the Torah says: "You shall tell your son on that day." But the expression "on that day" could be understood to mean only during the daytime; therefore the Torah adds: "It is because of this that HASHEM did so for me when I went out of Egypt." The pronoun "this" implies something tangible, thus, "You shall tell your son" applies only at the time when matzah and *maror* lie before you — at the Seder.

(1) *Exodus* 13:14. (2) *Exodus* 13:8.

"Only when there is the meat of the *pesach* sacrifice and matzah and *maror* lying on the table before you."

There is logic to support the idea of reciting the Exodus story on *Rosh Chodesh Nisan*. After all, it was on *Rosh Chodesh Nisan* that the Lord related to Moses the tidings of the Exodus and the laws of the *pesach* sacrifice and holiday. One can also understand that the recitation should take place on the afternoon of the fourteenth of Nisan since that was the time when the *pesach* sacrifice was offered in the Temple. Yet the Torah is insistent that the story be told only on the Seder night when the *mitzvos* of Pesach — matzah, *maror*, etc. — are before your very eyes. The important lesson here is that abstract, even historical events and/or ideas never become real to a person unless there is an actual physical reminder of the event and/or idea present. Because we eat matzah and *maror* on the Seder night, we are able to remember the Exodus from Egypt. Without the tangible performance of the mitzvos of Pesach, the event of the Exodus would have disappeared from Jewish memory. The genius of the obligation to physically perform mitzvos is that only in that way are they able to translate amorphous, abstract ideas and memories into tangible, understandable human behavior and action. This is the method of transforming the abstract and unseen into reality that then may be communicated to later generations. Eating matzah and *maror* accomplishes more for Jewish survival and continuity than all of the symposiums, lectures, and media publicity about the necessity for such survival and continuity. In Judaism the *na'aseh* — we will do — always precedes the *nishma* — we will listen and debate and try to understand.

מִתְּחִלָּה, עוֹבְדֵי עֲבוֹדָה זָרָה הָיוּ אֲבוֹתֵינוּ, וְעַכְשָׁו קֵרְבָנוּ הַמָּקוֹם לַעֲבוֹדָתוֹ. שֶׁנֶּאֱמַר, וַיֹּאמֶר יְהוֹשֻׁעַ אֶל כָּל הָעָם, כֹּה אָמַר יהוה אֱלֹהֵי יִשְׂרָאֵל, בְּעֵבֶר הַנָּהָר יָשְׁבוּ אֲבוֹתֵיכֶם מֵעוֹלָם, תֶּרַח אֲבִי אַבְרָהָם וַאֲבִי נָחוֹר, וַיַּעַבְדוּ אֱלֹהִים אֲחֵרִים. וָאֶקַּח אֶת אֲבִיכֶם אֶת אַבְרָהָם מֵעֵבֶר הַנָּהָר, וָאוֹלֵךְ אוֹתוֹ בְּכָל אֶרֶץ כְּנָעַן, וָאַרְבֶּה אֶת זַרְעוֹ, וָאֶתֶּן לוֹ אֶת יִצְחָק. וָאֶתֵּן לְיִצְחָק אֶת יַעֲקֹב וְאֶת עֵשָׂו, וָאֶתֵּן לְעֵשָׂו אֶת הַר שֵׂעִיר לָרֶשֶׁת אוֹתוֹ, וְיַעֲקֹב וּבָנָיו יָרְדוּ מִצְרָיִם.[1]

☙ **מִתְּחִלָּה** — *Initially.*

This section of the Haggadah fulfills the Talmudic injunction of מַתְחִילִים בִּגְנוּת, to begin the recitation of the Haggadah with a description of our original spiritual lowliness and then to trace our development into a holy nation and to end with praise for the God and people of Israel. At my stage of life, climbing the hills of Jerusalem — anywhere you walk in Jerusalem always seems to be uphill — is not as easy as it once was, neither physically nor psychologically. So, I have begun the habit of stopping every so often and turning around and looking back at how much of the hill I have already climbed. I find this to be most comforting and encouraging to me, certainly psychologically and even physically. By realizing how steep was the hill that I started climbing and how far I have already climbed, I am heartened by my accomplishment and I have the will to proceed further.

This is pretty much illustrative of the idea that we begin the narrative by recalling our lowly origins. Not only do we readily say that we were once a nation of slaves, with all the baggage that slavery imposes on its victims, but we also recognize that our spiritual pedigree is tainted. We stem from idolaters and pagans. We were also part of the ancient world that glorified superstition and ignorance, violence and indecent behavior. While boasting that we are the seed of Abraham, we are also recognizing and admitting that Terah is our grandfather. But that was then — מִתְּחִלָּה — originally at the dawn of our national creation. Now — וְעַכְשָׁיו — however, the Lord has helped us climb the hill of service and civilization. And to appreciate, therefore, how far we have actually come, we must stop and look back and downwards at the spot and status that were our beginning. Terah was the father of Abraham and of Nahor, he lived מֵעֵבֶר הַנָּהָר — on the other side of the river, figuratively and actually — far away from God and the Holy Land and any ideas of monotheism and moral values. And here it is that God took a direct role in our ascension from being the grandchildren of Terah to becoming the children of Abraham.

The Lord brought us close to Him and His service. Human beings alone would not be able to reach out to God and serve Him if it were not for God's own aid in the matter. Therefore, we pray unto God that He bring us closer to Him and allow us to serve Him. Abraham recognized on his own that there must be a God in the

Originally our ancestors were idol worshipers, but now the Omnipresent has brought us near to His service, as it says: Joshua said to all the people, "So says HASHEM, God of Israel: Your fathers always lived beyond the Euphrates River, Terach the father of Abraham and Nahor, and they served other gods. Then I took your father Abraham from beyond the river and I had him travel through all the land of Canaan. I multiplied his offspring and gave him Isaac. To Issac I gave Jacob and Esau, to Esau I gave Mount Seir to inherit, but Jacob and his children went down to Egypt."[1]

(1) *Joshua* 24:2-4.

---

world. But God is the One Who brought him close, Who spoke to him and instructed him. The Talmud reinforces this idea when it states: "He who comes to purify is aided by Heaven." Or when it further states: "Every day the evil inclination of our hearts threatens to overwhelm us and if it were not for Divine help we would be unable to defend ourselves against it." The Lord is not passive in these matters. The original choice of doing good or evil is left exclusively to humans. However, once that choice is made, then, again in the words of the Talmud: "Heaven facilitates the ability to walk down the road in life that one has chosen." Abraham wished mightily to serve his Creator and the Lord therefore granted him many opportunities to do so. Evil people are unfortunately also provided with the wherewithal to commit evil. Here in the Haggadah, when recounting our antecedents and Abraham's break with the idolatry of his father, Terah, we thank God for reaching out to Abraham and to his descendants, the people of Israel, and for bringing us close to Him and His service.

But there is always a price to be paid for coming closer to our Creator. One has to continually purify oneself as he comes closer to God. There is a winnowing process in society and self-development on the road to a connection with Godliness. It was Isaac and not Ishmael who continued Abraham's work and way of life in the world. The price there for Issac was being bound on the altar and coming within a hairsbreadth of being killed, all in the service of God. Jacob suffered greatly in his lifetime. It was he who went into Egyptian exile, albeit initially willingly. It is from there — the bondage of Egyptian slavery — that Israel was toughened in the fires of pain and tragedy to become the people that would forever represent the search for God in the story of human civilization. Jacob's brother, Esau, happily refused the pain of Egypt and marched off in a different direction to Seir and later to Rome. It was a shortcut to power and pleasure for Esau. But Jacob chose the long road to reach God and eternity. And by Divine decree, that road had to run through Egypt and enslavement. It is God's willingness to continually bring us closer to Him and His service that is the guarantee of our survival and eventual triumph over the forces of evil that have always attempted to undermine and even destroy Jewish existence.

בָּרוּךְ שׁוֹמֵר הַבְטָחָתוֹ לְיִשְׂרָאֵל, בָּרוּךְ הוּא. שֶׁהַקָּדוֹשׁ בָּרוּךְ הוּא חִשַּׁב אֶת הַקֵּץ, לַעֲשׂוֹת כְּמָה שֶּׁאָמַר לְאַבְרָהָם אָבִינוּ בִּבְרִית בֵּין הַבְּתָרִים, שֶׁנֶּאֱמַר, וַיֹּאמֶר לְאַבְרָם, יָדֹעַ תֵּדַע כִּי גֵר יִהְיֶה זַרְעֲךָ בְּאֶרֶץ לֹא לָהֶם, וַעֲבָדוּם וְעִנּוּ אֹתָם, אַרְבַּע מֵאוֹת שָׁנָה. וְגַם אֶת הַגּוֹי אֲשֶׁר יַעֲבֹדוּ דָּן אָנֹכִי, וְאַחֲרֵי כֵן יֵצְאוּ בִּרְכֻשׁ גָּדוֹל.[1]

The matzos are covered and the cups lifted as the following paragraph is proclaimed joyously. Upon its conclusion, the cups are put down and the matzos are uncovered.

וְהִיא שֶׁעָמְדָה לַאֲבוֹתֵינוּ וְלָנוּ, שֶׁלֹּא אֶחָד בִּלְבָד עָמַד עָלֵינוּ לְכַלּוֹתֵנוּ. אֶלָּא שֶׁבְּכָל דּוֹר וָדוֹר עוֹמְדִים

בָּרוּךְ שׁוֹמֵר הַבְטָחָתוֹ —
Blessed is He Who keeps His promise

God's promises to Israel can be relied upon. Unlike agreements, promises, treaties, and commitments made between human beings that often prove to be worthless and unfulfilled, the Divine word is sacred and reliable. God's promise to Abraham that the Jews would leave Egypt בִּרְכוּשׁ גָּדוֹל, *with great wealth*, was fulfilled. The Jews left Egypt with gold, silver, precious stones, and fine clothing. To the just-freed slaves this material wealth was undoubtedly רְכוּשׁ גָּדוֹל. But in God's promise to Abraham, the רְכוּשׁ גָּדוֹל was not merely material goods. It was the gift of the greatest wealth of all, the Torah that would be given to Israel at Mount Sinai. The appreciation of the worth and true value of Torah, like all spiritual things, is a matter of passing time and enhanced maturity. At the moment of the Exodus from Egypt, many, if not most, Jews would have chosen "real" wealth — gold, silver, precious stones, fine clothing — over spiritual greatness. They had no concept as of yet of the greatness and eternity of Torah. Therefore, God's promise to Abraham had to be fulfilled in a manner that even the simplest Jew could recognize and appreciate. Of course, the gold and silver did not really last too long, some of it being squandered in the Golden Calf and some of it finding its way into the holy *Mishkan*, Tabernacle. Money and wealth is always fungible, always being transferred from one person to another. Torah, however, remains an eternal gift that can never be taken from the one who has acquired it. It is truly רְכוּשׁ גָּדוֹל — *great wealth*.

Another insight regarding this "great wealth" is worth mentioning. The Midrash comments here that God granted all of this רְכוּשׁ גָּדוֹל — actual material wealth — to the Jews so that Abraham would not have a chance to complain that the slavery part of the prophecy regarding Egypt was fulfilled while the "great wealth" part was unfulfilled, since the simple Jew escaping from Egypt would not yet be able to appreciate that the Torah was really the "great wealth" promised. From this it seems that both God and Abraham somehow felt themselves to be subject to public opinion, to what the simple Jew would say about the promised "great wealth." Why should God care, so to speak, what shallow understandings the Jewish public would have regarding His promises and plans? God is cer-

Blessed is He Who keeps His promise to Israel; Blessed is He! For the Holy One, Blessed is He, calculated the End in order to do as He said to our father Abraham at the *Bris bein Habesarim*, as it says: He said to Abram, "Know with certainty that your offspring will be aliens in a land not theirs, they will serve them, and they will oppress them four hundred years; but also upon the nation which they shall serve will I execute judgment, and afterwards they shall go out with great possessions."[1]

The matzos are covered and the cups lifted as the following paragraph is proclaimed joyously. Upon its conclusion, the cups are put down and the matzos are uncovered.

And it is this that has stood firm by our fathers and us. For not only one has risen against us to annihilate us, but in

(1) *Genesis* 15:13–14.

tainly above all human criticism. His greatness is not enhanced or diminished by anything that humans think or do or say. Yet we see throughout the Bible that God is somehow sensitive, as it were, to this argument of what public opinion will say regarding the matter. Moses uses this argument effectively a number of times in order to protect Israel from God's wrath when the Jews sinned badly in the desert of Sinai. Moses says: "Why should You allow the Egyptians to say that God took them (the Jews) out of Egypt in order to destroy them in the desert?" And God was responsive to that argument. Abraham, in his appeal to God to spare Sodom, boldly asks, "Will the Judge of the entire world Himself not do justice?" Of course, Abraham knows that God is just. But his question is prompted by what the rest of the world will say about the destruction of Sodom. This is a reminder that we Jews do not live in a vacuum. The attitude, "Who cares what the others will say?" is not really a productive one. Jews are meant to be influential vis-a-vis one another and in the world in general. For if God, so to speak, is sensitive to public opinion, so should we be as well.

וְהִיא שֶׁעָמְדָה —
It is this that has stood firm.

The custom of raising one's cup of wine while reciting this paragraph of the Haggadah is based on the verse in *Psalms* (117:13): "I will lift up a cup of salvation and call out the Name of the Lord." This paragraph is a statement of Jewish survival and salvation and thus we raise our cups of wine in consonance with its recital. God's promise to Abraham that his children would be redeemed from Egyptian slavery centuries later — עָמְדָה — stood the test of time and was fulfilled. It was not only the promise of redemption from Egypt that was part of God's covenant with Abraham, but it was the implicit promise that Israel would always somehow be redeemed from its oppressors in all ages and times and never be allowed to be annihilated. From Pharaoh to Hitler, from Titus to Arafat, our enemies have attempted to solve the "Jewish problem" by the genocidal destruction of the Jewish people. In spite of all of these attempts and in spite of the horrendous losses suffered by the Jews at the hands of their enemies, the Jewish nation has outlasted and sur-

עָלֵינוּ לְכַלּוֹתֵנוּ, וְהַקָּדוֹשׁ בָּרוּךְ הוּא מַצִּילֵנוּ מִיָּדָם.

צֵא וּלְמַד מַה בִּקֵּשׁ לָבָן הָאֲרַמִּי לַעֲשׂוֹת לְיַעֲקֹב אָבִינוּ, שֶׁפַּרְעֹה לֹא גָזַר אֶלָּא עַל הַזְּכָרִים, וְלָבָן בִּקֵּשׁ לַעֲקוֹר אֶת הַכֹּל. שֶׁנֶּאֱמַר:

---

vived all of its foes. It is more than ironic that Natan Sharansky has been a minister in the government of Israel while Mikhail Gorbachev is reduced to appearing in Pizza Hut commercials. Pharaoh, Haman, Titus, Godfrey of Bouillon, Czars Alexander and Nicholas, the Nazis, and Stalin, all are on the ash heap of history. Not so the Jewish people, who remain vital and the center of the world's attention. One would think that the non-Jewish world would "get it" by now and use the Jews as a resource and an asset and not as a target. But for whatever reason, God has not yet willed that to be the case.

☙ A Continuous Struggle

The paragraph also includes the sad reality that this struggle for Jewish survival is a continuous one. In every generation "they rise against us to annihilate us. But the Holy One, Blessed is He, rescues us from their hand." The Tosafist, R' Eliezer of 13th-century Germany, in his commentary to the Haggadah (*Rokeach*), tells us of an incident in Minchenburg in the year 1185 in which a non-Jewish woman accidentally fell into a well in the Jewish neighborhood of town and drowned. A mob gathered and accused the Jews of purposely throwing her into the well in order to kill her. The governor of the town came to the aid of the Jews and his soldiers dispersed the mob that was bent on a massacre of the Jews. R' Eliezer recorded this event as his personal testimony to the exquisite accuracy of the words of this paragraph of the Haggadah. However, in many cases in the Middle Ages and later, the Jews did not fare as well. The Holocaust stands as an indictment of Christianity and an enormous test of Jewish faith and resilience. Our generation thought for a while that after the Holocaust and Stalin, we would be given a pass as far as blatant anti-Semitism is concerned. That belief has been proven to be hopelessly naive. The 21st-century Moslem world and still much of the Christian world as well is badly infected by the virus of anti-Semitism. The Rabbis of the Talmud, in commenting upon the name *Sinai* as the name of the mountain where the Torah was given to Israel, associated *Sinai* with the Hebrew word *sinah* — unreasonable hatred. And so it is. Ruefully, we, along with our ancestors, can therefore repeat with fervor the words of the Haggadah: "In every generation they [our enemies] rise against us to annihilate us and it is the Lord God Who saves us from their hand."

A number of years ago, an "intellectual" friend of mine remarked to me that this paragraph of the Haggadah was a prime example of the hysterical Jewish paranoia that plagues the Jewish world. I responded that his comment made me recall an anecdote I heard regarding Richard Nixon, who allegedly once told his aides that "you too would be paranoid if the whole world were against you!" Unfortunately and dangerously, real events and not imagined fears continue to prove that Jewish paranoia is justified. This paragraph of the Haggadah is a statement of fact and not an expression of unjustified concern. In our hope for a better tomorrow we should not blind ourselves to the realities of today. That is really the message of this paragraph in the Haggadah.

every generation they rise against us to annihilate us. But the Holy One, Blessed is He, rescues us from their hand.

Go out and ascertain what Laban the Aramean attempted to do to our father Jacob! For Pharaoh decreed only against the males, and Laban attempted to uproot everything, as it says:

☙ **צֵא וּלְמַד** — *Go out and ascertain.*

The word צֵא — go out — is the key to understanding this part of the Haggadah. Jewish tradition looks at history with different eyes than do secular historians. If one wishes to understand anything about the Jewish story and people, then

אֲרַמִּי אֹבֵד אָבִי, וַיֵּרֶד מִצְרַיְמָה וַיָּגָר שָׁם בִּמְתֵי מְעָט, וַיְהִי שָׁם לְגוֹי, גָּדוֹל עָצוּם וָרָב.[1]

וַיֵּרֶד מִצְרַיְמָה – אָנוּס עַל פִּי הַדִּבּוּר.

וַיָּגָר שָׁם – מְלַמֵּד שֶׁלֹּא יָרַד יַעֲקֹב אָבִינוּ לְהִשְׁתַּקֵּעַ

---

one must leave all preconceived notions, theories, and descriptions of historical events at home. One needs to go outside one's previous self in order to appreciate and have some understanding of the story of the Jews. When God makes His covenant with Abraham regarding the great nation that he will found, He tells Abraham, "צֵא" — go outside of yourself and your previous way of thinking and acting. Abraham is told to free himself from the conformity of thought and viewpoint that oftentimes blinds even the most knowledgeable of academicians. Jewish history will not conform to the pattern of general history, even though it is a part of that general history. Only by accomplishing צֵא — going out — will one come to the level of וּלְמַד — learning and understanding the story of the Jews and their attachment to Torah and the God of Israel. There is an inner soul to Jewish life and our story. It is difficult to understand Judaism and Jews without knowing and appreciating that inner soul. Paradoxically, that inner soul can be found only if one goes outside of one's self and one's ordinary and mundane views and perspectives. There was a movement in 19th-century Germany that promoted "scientific" knowledge of Jewish history and of Judaism itself. It was full of Jewish knowledge but devoid of any inner Jewish soul. The great R' Ezriel Hildesheimer whose yeshivah was on the same street as the Institute for Scientific Judaism once told a wavering student: "If you want to know what color clothes Rashi wore, then go down the street. But if you want to know Rashi, then you must stay here." Scientific Judaism has remained an academic relic in the Jewish world while the yeshivos continue to grow and prosper.

Laban is the prototype of all of the hateful enemies of Israel. He exploits Jacob, treats him unfairly, cheats him abusively, and at the end poses as the righteous and aggrieved party. Laban is the one who wishes to destroy all of Jacob — his family, his material possessions, and his faith. Laban will claim that Jacob's "sons are my sons and that his daughters are my daughters." There is no reasoning with Laban, no argument that will mitigate his jealousy and hatred. It is only God's intervention that stays the hand of Laban. Laban sulks in his inability to destroy Jacob but Laban will produce many more Labans down through the ages. The Haggadah sees Jacob's eventual descent into Egypt as a result of Laban's actions. The family tensions engendered by Laban's behavior towards Jacob and towards his own daughters and grandchildren lead to the strains and tensions in Jacob's own family, as exemplified in its finality by the story of Joseph and his brothers. And it is that tale of family disharmony that eventually brings Jacob and the Jews down to Egypt, initially as welcomed guests and then some time later as abject and persecuted slaves. Laban's venom was injected into Jacob's family and it would take the furnace of the experience of Egyptian slavery to burn off that dross from Israel. The small band of Jacob's family would grow into a large and mighty people through the experience of that Egyptian slavery. But it would not be without cost and pain.

An Aramean attempted to destroy my father, and he descended to Egypt and sojourned there, with few people; and there he became a nation — great, mighty and numerous.[1]

And he descended to Egypt — compelled by Divine decree.

He sojourned there — this teaches that our father Jacob did

(1) *Deuteronomy* 26:5.

◆§ וַיֵּרֶד מִצְרַיְמָה — *And he descended to Egypt.*

Jacob went to Egypt — in forced chains of familial love. He was happy and anxious to be reunited with his beloved son, Joseph. But nevertheless, the trip down to Egypt was forced upon him by the Lord, in fulfillment of the covenant with Abraham that his descendants would be slaves in a strange land for centuries before being redeemed by God. There is exile and then there is exile. Sometimes and in some places in Jewish history, exile was not only tolerable but it was even comfortable. Tenth-century Spain, 14th-century Poland, 19th-century Germany, 20th-century America are examples of such an exile of comfort and privilege. When I was a rabbi in Miami Beach, a great rabbi from Toronto, a survivor of the Holocaust, weak in body but powerful in faith and Torah knowledge, would come there to spend the winter months. I arranged a daily study session with the scholar. We sat under a grapefruit tree in our shirtsleeves, basking in the Florida sun and studying God's Torah. It was what I imagined Paradise would be like. However, apparently noticing my smug comfort in our surroundings, the great rabbi once said to me, "Miami Beach is not bad at all as far as exiles go. But it is still exile!" Egypt, when Jacob arrived there, was also not bad at all as far as exiles went. But Jacob knew in his heart that it was still exile, and therefore, mixed with his joy over being reunited with Joseph was his feeling of trepidation over the long centuries of exile that his descendants would have to endure in Egypt. And Jacob was well aware that his arrival in Egypt was not a random affair of chance but rather it was "עַל פִּי הַדִּבּוּר" — by Divine fiat.

עַל פִּי הַדִּבּוּר — compelled by the decree. Whose saying and from whose mouth? The obvious answer is that God is the subject of the sentence here. Some say that it refers to the word of God at the time of God's covenant with Abraham. Others say that it was the word of God to Jacob when Jacob is already on the road down to Egypt and the Lord tells him not to fear the consequences of his descent into Egypt. However, there is also an interpretation that the mouth and the saying were those of Joseph who practically commands his father to come down to Egypt to be reunited with him. In any event, it is obvious that Jacob feels impelled to go down to Egypt, even if his basic instinct is to remain in the Land of Israel.

◆§ וַיָּגָר שָׁם — *He sojourned there.*

Jacob intended to return home to the Land of Israel as soon as he could, but the opportunity to do so never arose. Only in death was he transported home by his children to be buried in the Cave of Machpelah. Presumably, he had no right to leave Egypt unless God commanded him to do so. It is also possible that he had to take into account that the famine in Canaan might resume, the difficulty of separating himself from Joseph and Joseph's children, the premonition that without his presence the tension between Joseph and his brothers might flare up once more. All these

בְּמִצְרַֽיִם, אֶלָּא לָגוּר שָׁם. שֶׁנֶּאֱמַר, וַיֹּאמְרוּ אֶל פַּרְעֹה, לָגוּר בָּאָֽרֶץ בָּֽאנוּ, כִּי אֵין מִרְעֶה לַצֹּאן אֲשֶׁר לַעֲבָדֶֽיךָ, כִּי כָבֵד הָרָעָב בְּאֶֽרֶץ כְּנָֽעַן, וְעַתָּה יֵשְׁבוּ נָא עֲבָדֶֽיךָ בְּאֶֽרֶץ גֹּֽשֶׁן.[1]

בִּמְתֵי מְעָט – כְּמָה שֶׁנֶּאֱמַר, בְּשִׁבְעִים נֶֽפֶשׁ יָרְדוּ אֲבֹתֶֽיךָ מִצְרָֽיְמָה, וְעַתָּה שָׂמְךָ יהוה אֱלֹהֶֽיךָ כְּכוֹכְבֵי הַשָּׁמַֽיִם לָרֹב.[2]

וַיְהִי שָׁם לְגוֹי – מְלַמֵּד שֶׁהָיוּ יִשְׂרָאֵל מְצֻיָּנִים שָׁם.

---

conspired to keep Jacob in Egypt. Of course, these were the manifestations of the Divine Will that decreed that Jacob and his descendants would have to remain in Egypt.

In spite of the comforts of life that Joseph lavished upon his father, Jacob always felt himself to be a גֵּר — a stranger in a strange land — while living in Egypt. The idea of a comfortable exile has always been a problem for the Jewish people in terms of its leading to assimilation and lost Jewish identity. The great Rabbi Meir Simcha HaCohen of early 20th-century Dvinsk, Latvia, wrote prophetically: "Woe unto those who think that Berlin is Jerusalem!" No matter what, no matter how long the sojourn in Egypt would be, Jacob came there only as a temporary visitor. His presence would bring many blessings to Egypt — prosperity, culture, peace. But Egypt was not Jacob's home and never would be. Jacob is the prototype of the Jew living in the Diaspora. His lesson of וַיָּגָר שָׁם — that he is merely a sojourner in the land of Egypt — should not be ignored. All of Jewish history proves its uncanny accuracy.

בִּמְתֵי מְעָט — *With few people.*

The Jewish nation, the descendants of Jacob, began as a small family. Seventy is the number that the Torah provides us for the size of that family when it first came to Egypt. What is clear, and this is certainly the main point of the Haggadah here, is that the Jewish nation began its Egyptian sojourn as a small, numerically insignificant family, easily subject to assimilation and disappearance, and left Egypt centuries later as a nation of millions. The next sections of the Haggadah attempt to give us an insight as to how such a phenomenon occurred.

וַיְהִי שָׁם לְגוֹי —
There he became a nation –

How did the Jewish people become a "nation" while living in the midst of an oppressive and culturally overwhelming Egyptian society? How was Israel able to retain its self-identity? The Haggadah tells us that the Jews made a conscious effort to be outstanding — different — in that society. Their method of dress, their names, their speech and language, and their values separated them from the dominant society of the time. I don't know what kinds of clothing Jews wore in Egypt. It could very well be that the clothing itself was similar to the clothing that the Egyptians wore. The difference lay in how that clothing was worn. Modesty in dress, both for men and women, has

not descend to Egypt to settle, but only to sojourn temporarily, as it says: They (the sons of Jacob) said to Pharaoh: "We have come to sojourn in this land because there is no pasture for the flocks of your servants, because the famine is severe in the Land of Canaan. And now, please let your servants dwell in the land of Goshen."[1]

With few people — as it is says: With seventy persons, your forefathers descended to Egypt, and now HASHEM, your God, has made you as numerous as the stars of heaven.[2]

There he became a nation — this teaches that the Israelites were distinctive there.

(1) *Genesis* 47:4. (2) *Deuteronomy* 10:22.

---

always been the hallmark of Jewish life. Thus in the Middle Ages, Jews wore the same type of clothing as their neighbors, but they wore them in a modest and clean fashion. This has been true for all of Jewish history, whether it be the costumes of 17th-century Amsterdam, 18th-century Poland, 19th-century Germany or 20th-century America. It was not so much that the actual clothing was different as it was the manner in which that clothing was worn and how a sense of modesty and privacy in dress was preserved. And of course, over the ages the rule of *bigdei Shabbos* — special clothing and finery to be worn on the Sabbath and holy days — also served as a symbol of Jewish "difference" and a support of Jewish self-identity.

Throughout the history of the Diaspora, Jews have developed a language of their own. In many countries they continued to speak Hebrew and/or Aramaic (also considered a holy and "Jewish" tongue) for centuries after their exile from Jerusalem and the Land of Israel. Ashkenazic Jewry created Yiddish as its vernacular and Ladino was popular among many Sephardic communities. Even the Jews who spoke Arabic as their lingua franca wrote that language with Hebrew characters. Only in the 19th century did German Orthodoxy speak and write German almost exclusively, as 20th-century English and North American Orthodoxy used English. The emergence in the American yeshivah world of "yinglish" — a jargon of English and Talmudic and Yiddish words, terms, and sentence forms — semi-humorous as it may often sound, may be seen as an attempt to build self-identity in the face of a dominant and oftentimes morally hostile societal environment.

Another facet of being "outstanding" is the disproportionate influence of Jews in society, relative to their small numbers. From commerce to academics, from Nobel Prize laureates, from medicine to politics, Jews are present and successful in numbers greatly disproportionate to their population. This was the case in Egypt as well, for even though the Jews were slaves and persecuted, their presence and influence was felt throughout Egyptian society. I feel that this was a great contributing factor as to the large amount of non-Jews — *eirev rav* — that chose to accompany Israel into the desert and eventually associate themselves with the

גָּדוֹל עָצוּם – כְּמָה שֶׁנֶּאֱמַר, וּבְנֵי יִשְׂרָאֵל פָּרוּ וַיִּשְׁרְצוּ וַיִּרְבּוּ וַיַּעַצְמוּ בִּמְאֹד מְאֹד, וַתִּמָּלֵא הָאָרֶץ אֹתָם.[1]

וָרָב – כְּמָה שֶׁנֶּאֱמַר, רְבָבָה כְּצֶמַח הַשָּׂדֶה נְתַתִּיךְ, וַתִּרְבִּי וַתִּגְדְּלִי וַתָּבֹאִי בַּעֲדִי עֲדָיִים, שָׁדַיִם נָכֹנוּ וּשְׂעָרֵךְ צִמֵּחַ, וְאַתְּ עֵרֹם וְעֶרְיָה; וָאֶעֱבֹר עָלַיִךְ וָאֶרְאֵךְ מִתְבּוֹסֶסֶת בְּדָמָיִךְ, וָאֹמַר לָךְ, בְּדָמַיִךְ חֲיִי, וָאֹמַר לָךְ, בְּדָמַיִךְ חֲיִי.[2]

Jewish people, for good or for better. The primitive and undeveloped ideas of Egyptian monotheism, which have been a source of study and scholarship for historians of the ancient world and which coincide with the centuries of Jewish exile in Egypt, undoubtedly bear the marks of Jewish influence. All of this Jewish creativity and contributions to the advancement of civilization over the millennia are a fulfillment of the Divine promise to Abraham, that "through you [and your descendants] will all the families of humankind be blessed."

גָּדוֹל עָצוּם — *Great, mighty.*

The explosion of the Jewish population in Egypt was extraordinary. The rabbis of the *Midrash* taught that the birth of sextuplets was common. They derived this from the use in the verse in the Torah of the six Hebrew words — פָּרוּ וַיִּשְׁרְצוּ וַיִּרְבּוּ וַיַּעַצְמוּ בִּמְאֹד מְאֹד — to describe this phenomenal increase in the numbers of the Jews in Egypt. "And the land [of Egypt] was filled with them [the Jews]." The Egyptians recoiled in fear and disgust at the number of Jews in their land. The Jews "became thorns in their eyes." But having committed themselves to a policy of enslavement of the Jews and an adamant refusal to consider their emancipation, the Egyptians had no good solutions to the "Jewish problem." From their perspective, it then became expedient to institute a policy of extermination. Newborn sons were to be fed to the crocodiles in the Nile. By this policy, the Jews would eventually disappear. Pharaoh bathed in the blood of Jewish children and Jewish babies were used as substitutes for bricks and mortar in the walls of the building projects that were being built by Jewish forced labor. But miraculously, the Jewish population remained large and growing. Thus did the eternal "Jewish problem" begin in Egypt. This, like the preceding paragraph, is a dose of hard reality that the Haggadah transmits to us in all of our generations.

וָרָב — *Numerous.*

The Hebrew word רְבָבָה is usually translated as *ten thousand.* However, the commentators to *Tanach* point out that the word — from רָב, *many* — refers to great numbers; sometimes it means one thousand, or two thousand, or ten thousand, depending upon its usage in the particular verse. The Jewish people were numerous in numbers but they were considered to be עֵרֹם, *naked.* This word is used in Hebrew to describe not merely physical nudity but also more subtly a spiritual and emotional vacuum within a person. The Jewish people were ready for redemption physically, they were mature physically and longed to be freed from bondage — but emotionally and spiritually they were still in bondage, stripped of the dignity and purpose of life that only a feeling of divinity and eternity can instill. They were without the connection to God that only observance of mitzvos can create within a Jew. Thus they were now granted the

Great, mighty — as it says: And the Children of Israel were fruitful, increased greatly, multiplied, and became very, very mighty; and the land was filled with them.[1]

Numerous — as it says: I made you as numerous as the plants of the field; you grew and developed, and became charming, beautiful of figure; your hair grown long; but you were naked and bare. And I passed over you and saw you downtrodden in your blood and I said to you: "Through your blood shall you live"; and I said to you: "Through your blood shall you live."[2]

(1) *Exodus* 1:7. (2) *Ezekiel* 16:7,6.

---

mitzvah of the *korban pesach* — the paschal lamb, that was sacrificed and eaten as part of the first Seder service of Israel. Only circumcised males were permitted to participate in this service, and thus the mitzvah of *milah* — circumcision — was effectively renewed and revived. The innate symbolism of the blood of the circumcision and the blood of the paschal lamb uniting to create the impetus for continued Jewish life through the observance of mitzvos is represented by the twice-repeated words of the prophet Ezekiel — בְּדָמַיִךְ חֲיִי בְּדָמַיִךְ חֲיִי — "through your blood [of circumcision] shall you live, through your blood [of the paschal lamb] shall you live." In recognition of the pain involved at any time in drawing blood, even at the occasion of performing a mitzvah, some families remove a drop of wine from their cups when this verse is recited.

The blunt truth is that the Jewish people have been forced to wallow in its own blood for its entire history. It is true, therefore, that through our willingness to shed our blood on behalf of our faith and nation, we have survived and continue to live on. An old teacher of mine in the yeshivah remarked to us — then less-than-eager students of Jewish history — that the entire Jewish story can be summed up in the words "blood and books." Like all overly clever statements, that is not exactly the whole story of the Jews, but it certainly is a major part of the story. The Seder reminds us not only of the glory of Judaism and the worth of being a Jew, but also of the cost and sacrifice demanded over the ages to maintain Judaism and the Jewish people. It is only through the bitterness of our blood, spilled in cruelty by others and in sacrifice by ourselves, that we have survived and even prospered against all odds and foes.

The word עָרוּם — naked — is first used in the Torah in connection with Adam and Eve and the sin that led to their expulsion from *Gan Eden*. There the Torah tells us that after eating from the Tree of Knowledge they realized that they were עֵירֻמִּם, *naked*. Rashi, based on *Midrash*, comments that they were now naked of mitzvos, of spiritual content and godly purpose. "They had one mitzvah — the commandment not to eat from the Tree of Knowledge — and now they were stripped of it."

Rabbi Meir Don Plotzki (early 20th century Poland) in his monumental work, *Kli Chemdah*, notes that Adam and Eve were not completely stripped of mitzvos since the first commandment of God to them — פְּרוּ וּרְבוּ, "be fruitful and multiply" — was still in place. So why were

וַיָּרֵעוּ אֹתָנוּ הַמִּצְרִים, וַיְעַנּוּנוּ, וַיִּתְּנוּ עָלֵינוּ עֲבֹדָה קָשָׁה.[1]

וַיָּרֵעוּ אֹתָנוּ הַמִּצְרִים – כְּמָה שֶׁנֶּאֱמַר, הָבָה נִתְחַכְּמָה לוֹ, פֶּן יִרְבֶּה, וְהָיָה כִּי תִקְרֶאנָה מִלְחָמָה, וְנוֹסַף גַּם הוּא עַל שֹׂנְאֵינוּ, וְנִלְחַם בָּנוּ, וְעָלָה מִן הָאָרֶץ.[2]

וַיְעַנּוּנוּ – כְּמָה שֶׁנֶּאֱמַר, וַיָּשִׂימוּ עָלָיו שָׂרֵי מִסִּים, לְמַעַן עַנֹּתוֹ בְּסִבְלֹתָם, וַיִּבֶן עָרֵי מִסְכְּנוֹת לְפַרְעֹה, אֶת פִּתֹם וְאֶת רַעַמְסֵס.[3]

---

they called עֵירֻמִּם, naked from mitzvos, when in fact they still possessed the first mitzvah given to them? He therefore makes the telling insight that after Adam and Eve ate from the Tree of Knowledge and the *yetzer hara* — evil instinct — became a permanent feature of the human makeup, procreation lost its holiness and became a physical act of passion and desire. The mitzvah attribute of the act of procreation was stripped from human life, or at least greatly sublimated to pure physical desire, and thus Adam and Eve were עֵירֻמִּם, spiritually naked.

◆§ וַיָּרֵעוּ אֹתָנוּ הַמִּצְרִים — *The Egyptians did evil to us.*

The Jewish people were sorely oppressed by the Egyptians, and unnecessarily so. There is bondage and then there is bondage. Ramban, in discussing why the Egyptians were punished for enslaving the Jews — after all, it was God's will as revealed centuries earlier to Abraham — states that the punishment was for their excessive cruelty toward the Jews. It was not the slavery itself that was so unjustified, but the barbarous methods used to enforce it that brought Divine retribution. Hitler's concentration camps and Stalin's Gulag are modern examples of how a mindset of illogical hatred and sadistic cruelty overwhelm the original production-oriented ideas of slave-labor regimes.

There is an alternative reading to this verse that states that the Egyptians transformed good Jews into bad and violent people. Slaves become cruel toward their fellow slaves just as prisoners in labor camps and jails usually are cruel to one another. In the Holocaust, Jewish ghettoes had their own Jewish police forces that under Nazi direction were cruel to their own people; there were Jewish kapos in all the concentration camps. This was a product of the unimaginable and surrealistic nature of the terrible environment in which these people suddenly found themselves. Thus, the Germans were responsible for the cruelties that some Jews inflicted on one another in those terrible times and conditions. Part of the indictment of the Egyptian taskmasters and the society that produced them is that they also weakened the moral character of their Jewish victims. They made ordinarily good Jews into bad people and this, therefore, is also part of the guilt and crime of the Egyptian society of that day.

The true Egyptian motivation for enslaving the Jews, whatever it may have been (there are many different interpretations offered in rabbinic literature), was masked behind the guise of national security. The Jews were accused of being disloyal, not trustworthy, an unassimilated foreign entity in the country that would prove dangerous to Egyptian hegemony in the

The Egyptians did evil to us and afflicted us; and imposed hard labor upon us.[1]

The Egyptians did evil to us — as it says: Let us deal with them wisely lest they multiply and, if we happen to be at war, they may join our enemies and fight against us and then leave the country.[2]

And they afflicted us — as it says: They set taskmasters over them in order to oppress them with their burdens; and they built Pithom and Raamses as treasure cities for Pharaoh.[3]

(1) *Deuteronomy* 26:6. (2) *Exodus* 1:10. (3) *Exodus* 1:11.

---

region in the future. Thus, already in Egypt at the dawn of our history, we already stood accused of disloyalty to our host country. This charge has been repeated throughout all of the ages and in all of the Diasporas of Jewish history. It matters not that this accusation was false and even ludicrous on its face. The Torah tells us that Pharaoh pretended not to know of Joseph. What is shocking is that this sort of attitude and its resultant behavior has continued to accompany us throughout our long history.

Similarly, Germany, in the 1930's, ignored the fact that tens of thousands of Jews had fought in the German army in World War I and that more than twelve thousand of them had lost their lives fighting for German victory. "Jews are our misfortune," was the Nazi slogan and it resonated in the ears and minds of millions of Germans. This malicious canard was also broadcast in Stalin's Soviet Union after World War II and in almost all Moslem lands after the 1948 creation of the State of Israel. Pharaoh's statement about potential Jewish disloyalty — that the Jews will eventually drive the Egyptians out of their own country — is the forerunner of malevolent conspiracy theories about Jews and Jewish power that infect much of the world even in the 21st century. Pharaoh's patently false statement about the "Jewish danger" created the fear and loathing of Jews that eventually became the hallmark of Egyptian society. That attitude of fear and loathing grew into a mindset of persecution, violence, and murder.

⁂ וַיְעַנּוּנוּ — *And they afflicted us.*

The Jews were physically tortured in their slave labor. There were special taskmasters — sadists all — appointed to make the lives of the slaves as unbearable as possible. I have often wondered what makes a person a torturer, an executioner. There never seems to be a shortage of people willing to do such horrid work. That is a frightening fact about human nature. Though the Torah is not pacifist in its theoretical and intellectual instructions, in practice it is nonviolent. Jewish courts rarely if ever executed criminals and torture was not part of the Jewish police or judicial system. The Talmud even interpreted the verse "Love your neighbor as yourself" as meaning: Choose as painless a death as possible for criminals who were guilty of a capital crime. The Torah certainly never allowed physical or verbal abuse of laborers or slaves. The Torah's rules regarding slavery placed such obligations upon slave owners that the institution of slavery was never viable in Jewish circles, though there were individual Jews in

וַיִּתְּנוּ עָלֵינוּ עֲבֹדָה קָשָׁה – כְּמָה שֶׁנֶּאֱמַר, וַיַּעֲבִדוּ מִצְרַיִם אֶת בְּנֵי יִשְׂרָאֵל בְּפָרֶךְ.[1]

וַנִּצְעַק אֶל יהוה אֱלֹהֵי אֲבֹתֵינוּ, וַיִּשְׁמַע יהוה אֶת קֹלֵנוּ, וַיַּרְא אֶת עָנְיֵנוּ, וְאֶת עֲמָלֵנוּ, וְאֶת לַחֲצֵנוּ.[2]

וַנִּצְעַק אֶל יהוה אֱלֹהֵי אֲבֹתֵינוּ – כְּמָה שֶׁנֶּאֱמַר, וַיְהִי בַיָּמִים הָרַבִּים הָהֵם וַיָּמָת מֶלֶךְ מִצְרַיִם, וַיֵּאָנְחוּ בְנֵי יִשְׂרָאֵל מִן הָעֲבֹדָה, וַיִּזְעָקוּ, וַתַּעַל שַׁוְעָתָם אֶל הָאֱלֹהִים מִן הָעֲבֹדָה.[3]

Biblical and Mishnaic times and even later who did own slaves. While allowing for slaves, the Torah's thrust is so anti-slavery oriented as to make it undesirable in Jewish society, both economically and socially. The Talmud states: "He who acquires a slave to serve him in reality has acquired a master over himself."

Pithom and Raamses were "storage" cities constructed in the Delta. Though the location of these cities is not known with exactitude, archeologists have uncovered the ruins of such "storage" cities at a number of sites in the Nile Delta. In Jewish folklore these two cities came to represent any and all projects of immense scope, effort and cost. Such projects were always called "building Pithom and Raamses." The names Pithom and Raamses are of Egyptian origin — Raamses was a name used by the Pharaohs themselves — though, as is the wont of the *Midrash*, many different ideas and interpretations were derived from these two Egyptian words. This is in line with the rule of Torah exegesis that every word written in the Torah, even those of foreign non-Hebraic origin, gains holiness and is to be treated as a source of interpretations and hidden meanings the same as any word of pure Hebrew origin.

וַיִּתְּנוּ עָלֵינוּ —
They imposed hard labor upon us.

The Egyptians worked the Jewish people בְּפָרֶךְ, hard labor. Not only was the work backbreaking, it was purposely nonproductive. Masons were assigned to be hod carriers, and unskilled laborers were driven to maddening frustration by being assigned sophisticated and delicate tasks. The Soviet Union's Gulag was tremendously inefficient and wasteful and never came close to achieving economic viability also because of the inability to assign its forced laborers to their proper tasks. In the case of the Soviets, this was due to the bungling bureaucracy that ran the Gulag. In Egypt it was maliciously and purposely enforced in order to destroy the morale of the Jewish slaves, denying them any feeling of accomplishment in their hard work. Backbreaking labor, frustrating labor, cruel taskmasters, and the systematic murder of Jewish children all combined to make the last decades of Jewish slavery in Egypt a living hell.

Another popular interpretation of the word בְּפָרֶךְ renders the word into two separate Hebrew words: בְּפֶה רַךְ, with a soft, enticing mouth. The Jews were suckered into eventual slavery by the

They imposed hard labor upon us — as it says: The Egytians subjugated the Children of Israel with hard labor.[1]

We cried out to HASHEM, the God of our fathers; and HASHEM heard our cry and saw our affliction, our burden, and our oppression.[2]

We cried out to HASHEM, the God of our fathers — as it says: It happened in the course of those many days that the king of Egypt died; and the Children of Israel groaned from the servitude and cried; their cry because of the servitude rose up to God.[3]

(1) *Exodus* 1:13. (2) *Deuteronomy* 26:7. (3) *Exodus* 2:23.

blandishments of the call to Egyptian patriotism. The work was meant to be a project of volunteer labor in which all Egyptians would participate. Even Pharaoh himself appeared at the work site on the first day of the project, spade in hand. Jews have always been superpatriotic to the country in which they resided. Even though badly persecuted by the czar, the Jews of Russia supported him over Napoleon, even though the French emperor promised them equality and liberty. World War I found Jews in all of the armies of the major combatants. This legendary Jewish loyalty to the country wherein they reside began in Egypt. The Jews were over-represented in the volunteer workers who came forth to build Pharaoh's projects. Soon, the Egyptian volunteers left the project and stopped coming to work, but the Jews continued to show up. Pharaoh soon converted the patriotic Jewish volunteers into abject slaves and the Jews were thus caught in the trap of the פֶּה רַךְ — the soft, seductive mouth of seeming loyalty and patriotism — that has destroyed many a Jew and Jewish community over the ages.

וַנִּצְעַק — *We cried out.*

The shouts of the Jewish people ascended now to heaven. Their cry of anguish grew even louder with the death of Pharaoh. According to some commentaries, Pharaoh's death was really incapacitation, due to a malignant skin disease, the "cure" for which was bathing in the blood of newly born Jewish infants! The Jews expected that things would get better for them now that their hated enemy was no longer in power. Instead, the new Pharaoh not only continued the cruel policies of his predecessor, but even intensified them. The frustration and disappointment at this turn of events brought the Jews into a greater state of anguish and depression than before. When one expects a situation to improve and it does not, one is much more downhearted than if one had never had any hopes for such an improvement. Dashed hopes always lead to emotional turmoil and depression. Having nowhere else to turn, the Jews cried out in anguish to heaven and the Lord heard their cries. He "remembered" the covenant with Abraham, Isaac, and Jacob, the promise to redeem their descendants from slavery and restore them to the Land of Israel, to make them a special people, a kingdom of priests and a holy folk. Thus this cry to heaven became the catalyst for the redemptive process to begin.

וַיִּשְׁמַע יהוה אֶת קֹלֵנוּ – כְּמָה שֶׁנֶּאֱמַר, וַיִּשְׁמַע אֱלֹהִים אֶת נַאֲקָתָם, וַיִּזְכֹּר אֱלֹהִים אֶת בְּרִיתוֹ אֶת אַבְרָהָם, אֶת יִצְחָק, וְאֶת יַעֲקֹב.[1]

וַיַּרְא אֶת עָנְיֵנוּ – זוֹ פְּרִישׁוּת דֶּרֶךְ אֶרֶץ, כְּמָה שֶׁנֶּאֱמַר, וַיַּרְא אֱלֹהִים אֶת בְּנֵי יִשְׂרָאֵל, וַיֵּדַע אֱלֹהִים.[2]

וְאֶת עֲמָלֵנוּ – אֵלּוּ הַבָּנִים, כְּמָה שֶׁנֶּאֱמַר, כָּל הַבֵּן הַיִּלּוֹד הַיְאֹרָה תַּשְׁלִיכֻהוּ, וְכָל הַבַּת תְּחַיּוּן.[3]

וְאֶת לַחֲצֵנוּ – זוֹ הַדְּחַק, כְּמָה שֶׁנֶּאֱמַר, וְגַם רָאִיתִי אֶת הַלַּחַץ אֲשֶׁר מִצְרַיִם לֹחֲצִים אֹתָם.[4]

There are those, especially among the Chassidic masters of the late 19th century, that infer from this that all Jewish redemption throughout the ages has to be initiated by the Jews themselves, through intense prayer and action taken with the belief that the help of God will be forthcoming. Then He intervenes and moves the redemptive process forward.

§ **וַיַּרְא אֶת עָנְיֵנוּ** — *And saw our affliction.*

The word עָנְיֵנוּ usually means "our affliction." However, the Haggadah here chooses to interpret it as the absence of normal marital relations. The word עָנְיֵנוּ here therefore is seen as being related to the word עוֹנָה, a term used in the Bible to describe such relations. The Egyptians separated the male slaves from their wives and had them sleep in barracks or in the fields where they labored in order to prevent them from returning home to their families. This type of deprivation has since become common in all forced slave-labor camps, with dreadful results to all concerned. The phrase here וַיֵּדַע אֱלֹהִים, *and God "knew,"* is also related to the subject of marital relations, since the Hebrew word וַיֵּדַע — and he "knew" — is often used in the Bible as a euphemism for marital relations.

The Torah's disciplined treatment of Egyptian interference with Jewish family life is worthy of a book in its own right. In the context of the Haggadah reading it is sufficient to say that forced celibacy was seen as a form of enslavement, a distinct negative in human life and that the women of Israel were praised for taking the initiative and coming out into the fields and inducing their spouses to live with them, thus guaranteeing the continuity of the Jewish nation. It is recorded that many Jewish men — even Amram, the father of Moses — abandoned family life out of the despair of the cruel conditions of enslavement and infanticide practiced by the Egyptians. This understandable attitude was certainly suicidal. The women of Israel, in opposing such an attitude and in winning the hearts of their husbands in spite of the apparent bleakness of the Jewish situation — and the young Miriam, who convinced her parents to reunite — became the true heroines of the story of the Exodus. It would be their very bronze mirrors that they had used to entice their husbands to family life in Egyptian slavery that would be used to make the כִּיּוֹר, the *Laver,* from which

Hashem heard our cry — as it says: God heard their groaning, and God recalled His covenant with Abraham, with Isaac, and with Jacob.[1]

And saw our affliction — that is the disruption of family life, as it says: God saw the Children of Israel and God knew.[2]

Our burden — refers to the children, as it says: Every son that is born you shall cast into the river, but every daughter you shall let live.[3]

Our oppression — refers to the pressure expressed in the words: I have also seen how the Egyptians are oppressing them.[4]

(1) *Exodus* 2:24. (2) *Exodus* 2:25 (3) *Exodus* 1:22. (4) *Exodus* 3:9

---

the Kohanim washed their hands and feet before performing the sacrificial service in the *Mishkan* of the Sinai Desert and of later generations in the Land of Israel. Their behavior is a prime example of how family life should be exalted and made holy by noble purpose and human sensitivity and disciplined passion.

וְאֶת עֲמָלֵנוּ — *Our burden*

The word עָמָל that is used here refers to continuous labor, tension, concern, and cost, and the Sages comment that it refers to the Jewish children in Egypt. All parents will agree that raising children is all of the above and more. There is an interpretation of the verse אָדָם לְעָמָל יוּלָּד — humans are born to toil — that the main עָמָל is the duty to guarantee the spiritual, emotional, and physical well-being of the next generation. In any event, the emotional investment of parents in children is enormous. At every stage of children's lives, there lurks in the mind of the parent a feeling of anxiety and apprehension regarding their future. In completely inhuman situations such as the Holocaust or the Gulag, the despair of parents over the fate of their children is unbearable and indescribable. Thus Pharaoh's decree to drown the male children of the Jews and preserve the females for the pleasure of the Egyptians was the harshest blow of all to Jewish morale and belief. We read in the Torah of the lengths to which Moses's mother, Jochebed, went in order to try and save her infant son. All survivors of such traumatic ordeals, of which the Holocaust is a prime example, generally face this challenge of rising over extraordinary עָמָל in order to be able to rebuild the Jewish people and its families in a turbulent and dangerous world.

וְאֶת לַחֲצֵנוּ — *Our oppression.*

לַחַץ is pressure. The Egyptians, like all slave masters, established work norms nearly impossible of fulfillment. The Jews were pushed and crushed into despair and complete loss of hope. I keep harping back to the Soviet Gulag as a modern adaptation of the Egyptian slavery. There the work norms were so cruelly unrealistic that they led only to widespread cheating on the figures of work accomplished and at the same time to the deaths of hundreds of thousands who were killed trying somehow to accomplish the humanly impossible. In Egypt,

וַיּוֹצִאֵנוּ יהוה מִמִּצְרַיִם בְּיָד חֲזָקָה, וּבִזְרֹעַ נְטוּיָה, וּבְמֹרָא גָּדֹל, וּבְאֹתוֹת וּבְמֹפְתִים.[1]

וַיּוֹצִאֵנוּ יהוה מִמִּצְרַיִם – לֹא עַל יְדֵי מַלְאָךְ, וְלֹא עַל יְדֵי שָׂרָף, וְלֹא עַל יְדֵי שָׁלִיחַ, אֶלָּא הַקָּדוֹשׁ בָּרוּךְ הוּא בִּכְבוֹדוֹ וּבְעַצְמוֹ. שֶׁנֶּאֱמַר, וְעָבַרְתִּי בְאֶרֶץ מִצְרַיִם בַּלַּיְלָה הַזֶּה, וְהִכֵּיתִי כָל בְּכוֹר בְּאֶרֶץ מִצְרַיִם מֵאָדָם וְעַד בְּהֵמָה, וּבְכָל אֱלֹהֵי מִצְרַיִם אֶעֱשֶׂה שְׁפָטִים, אֲנִי יהוה.[2]

---

the pressure to fulfill such work norms overwhelmed the Jewish slaves and their own Jewish foremen. The psychological pressure — לַחַץ — was omnipresent in Egyptian slavery. It probably took as great a toll among the slaves as did the backbreaking physical toil itself. People under constant לַחַץ are affected negatively in a physical, emotional, and spiritual way.

Not only did the living feel the לַחַץ of the Egyptian slavery but so did the dead. The *Midrash* records for us the pain that the Patriarchs and Matriarchs of Israel experienced even in their graves at the enslavement of their descendants. The Hebrew word גַּם, meaning *also* or *as well,* always indicates that more is included in the subject matter than is actually expressed by the words. The גַּם here therefore includes the dead as well as the living, in consonance with the concept that the souls of our founders are aware of the situation of their descendants. Perhaps this is an insight into the words of the Talmud that the righteous people have no rest either in this world or in the spiritual world after death. Living on spiritually means knowing much and being subjected to the pressures that accompany such knowledge. The World to Come is apparently a very active place.

The *Midrash* also includes the angels of Heaven in the burden of shared לַחַץ. They, too, felt the pressure to somehow intervene on behalf of Israel, so that Heaven became an active site, so to speak, to lobby for Jewish redemption. It is also mentioned here by commentators that even God, so to speak, found Himself under לַחַץ. However we choose to understand this, it is apparent that God had to intervene now to save Israel. Later I will discuss the concept that God "calculated the end" of the Egyptian exile in an unusual manner in order to save Israel. Had the Egyptian לַחַץ continued, it would have destroyed the Jewish people physically and spiritually. Thus God, so to speak, also found Himself under pressure — a heavenly לַחַץ — to redeem Israel quickly and completely. This is consistent with the oftrepeated idea that God, so to speak, is in exile with Israel in all of its troubles and situations. Therefore, the pressure on the Jews is reflected in pressure on the Lord as well.

וַיּוֹצִאֵנוּ יְהוָה מִמִּצְרַיִם —
HASHEM took us out of Egypt.

The emphasis here is that God Himself took us out of Egypt — not through angels and seraphim and other supernatural interveners and not through human messengers and agents either. Moses is seen as the emissary of God to speak to Pharaoh but not as God's agent to take Israel out of Egypt. It was He alone Who accomplished that. The Jewish people believed in God and in His servant, Moses, but Moses was never

HASHEM took us out of Egypt with a mighty hand and with an outstretched arm, with great fear, with signs, and with wonders.[1]

HASHEM took us out of Egypt — not through an angel, not through a seraph, not through a messenger, but the Holy One, Blessed is He, in His glory, Himself, as it says: I will pass through the land of Egypt on that night; I will slay all the firstborn in the land of Egypt from man to beast; and upon all the gods of Egypt will I execute judgments; I, HASHEM.[2]

(1) *Deuteronomy* 26:8. (2) *Exodus* 12:2.

---

to be seen as anything more than God's servant. Only God was able to identify who was firstborn and who was not, which dwelling housed Jews and which housed Egyptians, who was to live and who was to die.

The deeper meaning of all this is that Israel and God operate on a direct line, so to speak, and their relationship is not dependant upon intermediaries. Paganism is based upon the concept of intermediaries who deal with ruling powers on behalf of humans, be they natural or supernatural. Rambam in his *Mishneh Torah* points out that the beginnings of paganism lay in the belief that worshiping God's agents — such as the sun, moon, stars, etc. — was the way of reaching God. It soon deteriorated into outright paganism and worship of these entities, to be deified directly in their own right. Much of the original Jewish objection to Christianity was caused by the blatant use of an intermediary between God and man that necessitated the eventual elevation of that intermediary into an equal God or a part of God, all of which was and is blasphemous to Jewish thought and faith. Because of the importance of this concept of the elimination of intermediaries between God and man and the danger of humans somehow elevating another human to the status of a god, at the very birth of the Jewish nation in its release from Egyptian bondage, God asserts Himself, so to speak, and declares: "I am Hashem" — no angels, seraphim, agents or intermediaries fashioned you as a free people.

Rabbi Meir Simcha of Dvinsk (late 19th–20th century) points out that an underlying cause of Moses' not being allowed to enter the Land of Israel and lead the Jewish people there was the danger that the new generation now grown in the desert — who had seen Moses only as the person who drew water from a rock and manna from Heaven, defeated the great Emorite kings and giants, wore a mask over his face to shield them from the "spiritual radioactivity" of the radiance of Divinity, lived partly a celibate life and was the greatest and most humble person at the same time that ever walked the earth — would now view Moses as a god, an intermediary between God and them instead of being a servant of God and Israel. The older generation, some of whom knew Moses as a young man in Egypt before his rise to leadership, was in no danger of converting him into a god. "I went to school with him!" is a cry that cuts the great down to size in every generation. But the new generation, raised in awe of the great man, may have been in danger of misconstruing his human greatness, and thus the Lord ended his life and career in the desert of Sinai.

וְעָבַרְתִּי בְאֶרֶץ מִצְרַיִם בַּלַּיְלָה הַזֶּה - אֲנִי וְלֹא מַלְאָךְ. וְהִכֵּיתִי כָל בְּכוֹר בְּאֶרֶץ מִצְרַיִם - אֲנִי וְלֹא שָׂרָף. וּבְכָל אֱלֹהֵי מִצְרַיִם אֶעֱשֶׂה שְׁפָטִים - אֲנִי וְלֹא הַשָּׁלִיחַ. אֲנִי יהוה - אֲנִי הוּא, וְלֹא אַחֵר.

This is also perhaps an insight into the Haggadah's quotation of God's statement: "and upon all the gods of Egypt will I execute judgments." The paganism of Egypt was worship of the Nile, the snakes, the dead, the sun and moon and stars — all as intermediaries to gain favor with the natural powers of life and death that surround all human existence. The presence of the Lord Himself at the moment of the Exodus from Egypt gives the lie to this pagan concept of intermediaries that need be worshiped, honored, and feared. There is no clearer indictment of pagan beliefs and practices than the statement "I am Hashem," which is the key motto of the entire Exodus story. The Lord declares: "I am Hashem — there is no other!" Once man understands and accepts the principle that "there is no other," then the road to a pure and true monotheistic faith is created and opened. As long as there is a possibility that there does exist an "other" in any possssible form, way, or shape, there is also the possibility that a slide toward paganism, superstition, and disbelief in God and His Unity can gain acceptance and adherents.

The deliverance of the Jews from Egypt through the destruction of the Egyptian firstborn was not done through the instrument of angels or messengers but by God Himself. The concept of angels is well known in Jewish tradition. They are creatures that have no free will, are apparently immortal, and are at times assigned specific tasks here on earth. We meet angels in the Biblical narratives regarding our father Abraham, Hagar, Jacob, the prophet Elijah, the mother of Samson, the destruction of Sennacherib's army, the prophesies of Zachariah and Daniel, and in other instances as well. There is apparently a qualitative difference between acts accomplished by angels at God's bidding and those same acts when accomplished by God Himself. It was God alone Who redeemed us from Egyptian slavery without the use of intermediaries, Heavenly or otherwise.

Neither were messengers or agents used in the destruction of the firstborn Egyptians. In human life, the Lord sends us messengers — other human beings — who through their behavior or speech influence us and many times change the course of all human history, unbeknown even to themselves. Such an incident is related to us in the Torah in the story of Joseph and his brothers. Joseph, at the behest of his father, goes searching for them to bring them regards from Jacob and to inquire after their welfare. He cannot find them since they are tending the sheep in a different location than originally planned. Joseph is about to return home, mission unfulfilled, and thus avoid the catastrophic ambush that awaits him if he does indeed find his brothers. All of human history, certainly Jewish history, would perhaps be changed if Joseph had returned to Jacob without encountering his brothers. And then, while wandering in the fields, Joseph meets an enigmatic stranger who directs him to his brothers and sends Joseph to his fate, and eventually brings Israel into Egyptian bondage. Who was this stranger who is so pivotal to the story? Rashi states that he was the angel Gavriel. Ramban, while not disputing Rashi's statement,

"I will pass through the land of Egypt on that night" — I and no angel; "I will slay all the firstborn in the land of Egypt" — I and no seraph; "And upon all the gods of Egypt will I execute judgments" — I and no messenger; "I, HASHEM" — it is I and no other.

offers another possibility. He states that God many times sends us messengers — other human beings — through whose actions and statements, innocuous as they may seem at the time, alter our destinies and lives. This man who Joseph met was one of those human agents whom God employs to guide His world and shape human history.

I know a wonderful person who has slowly but steadily restored his ties to Judaism and to observance of a Torah lifestyle. I once asked him what particular incident, if any, was the catalyst for his beginning this road from one life to another. He related to me that once he was driving to a rock concert with his non-Jewish girlfriend. They were slightly late for the concert and were therefore horrified to find themselves locked in a long line of cars being stopped at an intersection by a formidable-looking police officer. A large stream of people were continually walking across the intersection and even though the traffic light changed a number of times, the policeman allowed the pedestrians to continue crossing the intersection.

My friend left his car and stormed up to the policeman demanding to know why the automobile traffic could not proceed. The policeman told him: "Buddy, tonight is Yom Kippur and all of these people are walking to the synagogue for services. When they finish crossing in a minute or two, I will let the cars proceed." My friend then thought: *The policeman knows that tonight is Yom Kippur and I who am Jewish did not even know that tonight is Yom Kippur!* And that incident got him to think about himself and his Jewishness and begin to discover his faith and soul. God sent him a messenger: the policeman directing traffic at that intersection. The truth is that God sends messengers in our daily lives to all of us, to jog our souls and minds. Whether or not we recognize those messengers and react wisely when they enter into our lives is really a test of our spiritual perception and our Jewish maturity.

One of the great debates that still rages in Jewish life and thought is the place and use of intermediaries, human beings, both dead and alive, to intercede on our behalf with God. This book is not the venue to explore such a debate. Suffice it to say that Judaism does not require middlemen or intermediaries in order for one to approach God, as do other faiths. Rabbi Yisrael Meir of Radin (the Chafetz Chaim) when once asked by a Jew for a blessing responded, "One pauper asks another pauper for a donation. Why don't you ask the rich one himself — God Almighty — for your needs?" Nevertheless, the blessings and influence of such "paupers" as the Chafetz Chayim are recognized as being significant in Jewish life and tradition. The point here in the Haggadah is that when dealing with the Exodus from Egypt, neither God nor Israel made use of any intermediaries.

⁂ וּבְכָל אֱלֹהֵי מִצְרַיִם —
And upon all the gods of Egypt.

There are commentators who, with Midrashic backing, took these words literally, that God destroyed the pagan gods of Egypt that night. The idols collapsed, rotted, broke, and were physically destroyed. God did this to demonstrate the impotence of the pagan idols and to show how bizarre and illogical it was to worship

בְּיָד חֲזָקָה – זוֹ הַדֶּבֶר, כְּמָה שֶׁנֶּאֱמַר, הִנֵּה יַד יהוה הוֹיָה בְּמִקְנְךָ אֲשֶׁר בַּשָּׂדֶה, בַּסּוּסִים בַּחֲמֹרִים בַּגְּמַלִּים בַּבָּקָר וּבַצֹּאן, דֶּבֶר כָּבֵד מְאֹד.[1]

וּבִזְרֹעַ נְטוּיָה – זוֹ הַחֶרֶב, כְּמָה שֶׁנֶּאֱמַר, וְחַרְבּוֹ שְׁלוּפָה בְּיָדוֹ, נְטוּיָה עַל יְרוּשָׁלָיִם.[2]

וּבְמֹרָא גָּדֹל – זוֹ גִּלּוּי שְׁכִינָה, כְּמָה שֶׁנֶּאֱמַר, אוֹ הֲנִסָּה אֱלֹהִים לָבוֹא לָקַחַת לוֹ גוֹי מִקֶּרֶב גּוֹי, בְּמַסֹּת, בְּאֹתֹת, וּבְמוֹפְתִים, וּבְמִלְחָמָה, וּבְיָד חֲזָקָה, וּבִזְרוֹעַ נְטוּיָה, וּבְמוֹרָאִים גְּדֹלִים, כְּכֹל אֲשֶׁר עָשָׂה לָכֶם יהוה אֱלֹהֵיכֶם בְּמִצְרַיִם לְעֵינֶיךָ.[3]

---

them in any form or manner. The destruction of the Egyptian idols was not so much a punishment for Egypt as much as it was intended to be a lesson for the departing Jews. Idolatry and pagan worship threatened Jewish life both from without and within for a millennium after the Exodus from Egypt. In order to strengthen the Jewish resolve to oppose paganism at all costs, God demonstrated publicly and unequivocally the bankruptcy of paganism, by physically destroying the very idols that were worshiped as being all-powerful. The sight of the destruction of the Egyptian idols helped to implant the rejection of paganism in the souls and minds of the Jewish people. Even though the attraction to idolatry remained among Jews for centuries after the Exodus, the memory of the gods lying in ruins helped many Jews resist that attraction.

Other commentators hold that the term אֱלֹהֵי מִצְרַיִם means not the *gods* of Egypt, but rather the powerful leaders and noblemen of Egypt. The word אֱלֹהֵי in this context thus refers to human beings and not to pagan idols. We find numerous times in the Bible that the word אֱלֹהִים or אֱלֹהֵי means *power* or *authority*. Thus in the Exodus story God destroyed those human beings who were in power and who had enforced the poverty and slavery of the Jews. Only Pharaoh himself was temporarily spared and through him and his unrepentant stubbornness the great miracle of the splitting of the sea was made possible. God's justice, as represented by the word שְׁפָטִים in this verse, is always exquisitely exacting, fair, and correct.

בְּיָד חֲזָקָה — *With a strong hand.*

The Haggadah interprets the *strong hand of God* as the striking down of the Egyptians' cattle. Since God is incorporeal and has no physical "hand," the anthropomorphic descriptions of God and His attributes that are found in the Bible are never meant to be understood literally. Accordingly, the Haggadah, based on the *Midrash*, searches for a verse that will define what is meant by the term God's "hand." The *Midrash* finds the answer in *Exodus* 9:3, which the Haggaddah now quotes. This verse deals with the destruction of the Egyptian cattle, the fifth plague inflicted upon Egyptian society.

With a strong hand — refers to the pestilence, as it says: Behold, the hand of HASHEM shall strike your livestock which are in the field, the horses, the donkeys, the camels, the herds, and the flocks — a very severe pestilence.[1]

With an outstretched arm — refers to the sword, as it says: His drawn sword in His hand, outstretched over Jerusalem.[2]

And with great fear — refers to the revelation of the *Shechinah*, as it says: Has God ever attempted to take unto Himself a nation from the midst of another nation by trials, miraculous signs and wonders, by war and with a mighty hand and outstretched arm and by awesome revelations, as all that HASHEM your God did for you in Egypt, before your eyes?[3]

(1) *Exodus* 9:3. (2) *I Chronicles* 21:16. (3) *Deuteronomy* 4:34.

The next sentence in the Haggadah — וּבִזְרֹעַ נְטוּיָה, *with an outstretched arm* — must also be understood as a metaphor, and derives from *I Chronicles* 21:16 that the metaphor of the outstretched arm alludes to a "drawn sword." Even though the verse regarding the drawn sword does not refer to the Exodus from Egypt, it shows that the term "outstretched arm" refers to a drawn sword. The "drawn sword" here refers to God's slaying of the Egyptian firstborn sons. The *Midrash* tells us that in fact there was a civil war with drawn swords within the Egyptian society itself, with the firstborn sons, who were condemned to die because of Pharaoh's intransigence, demanding that the king release the Jewish slaves immediately, before the plague would descend upon them. Thus the drawn sword is also a reference to this inner battle among the Egyptians themselves.

וּבְמוֹרָא גָּדוֹל — *And with great fear.*

The word מוֹרָא is usually translated as *fear* or *awe*. Here, however, most commentators translate it as *sight* or *vision*. God's revelation in Egypt to the Jewish people was of such a nature that even the lowliest of Jews glimpsed His magnificence, so to speak, in a manner that even great prophets such as Ezekiel could not do. God's revelation to Israel in Egypt and at Sinai is the basis for our faith and beliefs and practices. That is the thrust of the verse that states that there is no comparable example of a nation being taken from the midst of another nation to the accompaniment of miracles, plagues, signs, and direct Godly revelation. This statement of the Torah therefore establishes Israel as unique among all other nations and societies. The necessity to foster this awareness of Jewish uniqueness is part of the reason why we are bidden to tell the Pesach story over and over again all the days of our lives. Without an appreciation of Jewish uniqueness, the chances for meaningful Jewish survival are severely compromised. The uniqueness of Israel is based upon God's revelation to us. The Torah calls it "a great vision." It is this vision that has accom-

וּבְאֹתוֹת – זֶה הַמַּטֶּה, כְּמָה שֶׁנֶּאֱמַר, וְאֶת הַמַּטֶּה הַזֶּה תִּקַּח בְּיָדֶךָ, אֲשֶׁר תַּעֲשֶׂה בּוֹ אֶת הָאֹתֹת.[3]

וּבְמֹפְתִים – זֶה הַדָּם, כְּמָה שֶׁנֶּאֱמַר, וְנָתַתִּי מוֹפְתִים בַּשָּׁמַיִם וּבָאָרֶץ:

---

panied us throughout the thousands of years of our history.

וּבְאֹתוֹת – זֶה הַמַּטֶּה — *With signs — refers to [the miracles performed with] the staff.*

The staff of Moses was the "sign," the symbol of his acting at God's behest. According to tradition the staff had the acronym of the ten plagues — דְּצַ"ךְ עֲדַ"שׁ בְּאַחַ"ב — engraved on it. Also according to tradition, the staff passed through ten hands before it finally fulfilled its mission in Egypt. The ten owners of the staff were Adam, Enoch, Noah, Shem, Abraham, Isaac, Jacob, Joseph, Jethro, and finally Moses.

The staff is the symbol of God's concern for the human race and for His promotion of a sense of justice and civilization among His creatures through the righteous ones of every generation, and eventually through the Jewish people and its uniqueness. Human beings, especially those in leadership roles, often feel lonesome and abandoned. The symbol of the staff reminds us that we are never truly alone and without someone to turn to. Moses originally refuses the mission assigned to him, but God employs Moses' staff to convince him to accept the task. The staff becomes the symbol of the past and the future, of God's grace and guidance in human affairs. A similar staff would become the symbol of Aaron's priesthood and be placed next to the Ark of the Covenant itself in the Holy of Holies in the Temple. The staff became the symbol of Jewish continuity. It is therefore no mere linguistic coincidence that the tribes of Israel were called מַטּוֹת, staffs.

וּבְמֹפְתִים – זֶה הַדָּם— *With wonders — alludes to the blood.*

The Torah itself teaches us that "blood is the life force" of all creatures. Blood is also the symbol of death and destruction. The transformation of life-giving water to life-spilling blood — the first of the plagues visited on the Egyptians — was the symbol of God's coming judgment of the slave masters. It was also the first sign and miracle that Moses employed in convincing the Jewish people that God had sent him to redeem them from Egyptian bondage. Blood makes a noise in the world. God tells Cain that "the voice of the bloods of your brother shout to Me." The circulatory system of humans and the awesome mysteries of how blood functions in our physical bodies testify to the Creator's genius, so to speak.

The Haggadah quotes *Joel* 3:3 to show that the word מֹפְתִים, *wonders,* is closely associated with the word דָּם, *blood.* Blood is a מוֹפֵת, a wonder and a miracle, both for good and for better. *Ritva* (Rabbi Yom Tov ibn Ashbili, 14th-century Spain), based on *Mechilta* of R' Shimon ben Yochai (second-century Land of Israel), states that the plague of blood in Egypt turned the blood as hot as fire and the steam emanating from this boiling blood covered Egypt like a pillar of smoke. Thus this verse in *Joel,* which links miracles with blood, is not only a prophecy about future miracles and bloody punishments, but it is in fact a description of the past as well — of the plague of blood that befell Egypt in the story of the Exodus.

With signs — refers to [the miracles performed with] the staff as it says: Take this staff in your hand, that you may perform the miraculous signs with it.[1]

With wonders — refers to the blood, as it says: I will show wonders in the heavens and on the earth:

(1) *Exodus* 4:17.

The custom of removing drops of wine from our cups when reciting the words, דָּם, וָאֵשׁ וְתִמְרוֹת עָשָׁן, is to illustrate our discomfiture that other humans had to suffer — justifiably so, but

וְאֶת הַמַּטֶּה הַזֶּה
תִּקַּח בְּיָדֶךָ
אֲשֶׁר תַּעֲשֶׂה בּוֹ
אֶת הָאֹתֹת

As each of the words דָּם, *blood,* אֵשׁ, *fire,* and עָשָׁן, *smoke,* is said, a bit of wine is removed from the cup, with the finger or by pouring.

דָּם וָאֵשׁ וְתִמְרוֹת עָשָׁן.[1]

דָּבָר אַחֵר – בְּיָד חֲזָקָה, שְׁתַּיִם. וּבִזְרֹעַ נְטוּיָה, שְׁתַּיִם. וּבְמֹרָא גָּדֹל, שְׁתַּיִם. וּבְאֹתוֹת, שְׁתַּיִם. וּבְמֹפְתִים, שְׁתַּיִם.

אֵלּוּ עֶשֶׂר מַכּוֹת שֶׁהֵבִיא הַקָּדוֹשׁ בָּרוּךְ הוּא עַל הַמִּצְרִים בְּמִצְרַיִם, וְאֵלּוּ הֵן:

---

suffer nevertheless — for our freedom to be achieved. Thus when we recite the list of the ten plagues in the next portion of the Haggadah we again resort to removing drops of wine from our cups. Wars and punishments are perforce ruthless and unsparing, but, the Torah does not allow for uncalled-for violence, and is sensitive to the damage that retribution can cause in the hearts and psyches of victims turned victors. Therefore, even this small symbolic act of spill-ing drops of wine from our full cups of wine is sufficient to remind us of the balance of emotions and values present when humans are seen to be punished painfully for their transgressions and evil.

God's system of justice allows for no errors. But from the story of our father Abraham praying that God spare the evil people of Sodom, we see that God appreciates, if not demands, our compassion for the suffering of humans, even if they justly deserve that suffering. Emotionally speaking, it is difficult to raise oneself to such a level of selflessness and compassion, but in the intellectual construct of Judaism such an effort at goodness and mercy is nonetheless required.

דָּבָר אַחֵר — *Another explanation.*

The use of the plural forms for אתות and מֹפְתִים, instead of the singular form את and מוֹפֵת, indicates that these words refer to two plagues each. The use of the double words זְרֹעַ נְטוּיָה, *outstretched arm,* יָד חֲזָקָה, *strong hand,* and מֹרָא גָּדֹל, *great fear,* all indicate that each of these phrases refers to two plagues. Thus these verses imply that ten plagues befell the Egyptians. The Haggadah now enumerates the ten plagues in the order that they appear in the Biblical narrative. The effects of the plagues on Egyptian society were cumulative in nature. One plague built upon the woe and havoc created by the previous one. The plagues destroyed the water supply, the food chain, the agriculture, and eventually the entire economy of Egypt. It was this realization of the impending doom of Egypt as the plagues continued that caused Pharaoh's advisers to tell him: "Do you not realize that Egypt will be destroyed?!" The great and mighty Egypt was reduced to poverty and darkness by the plagues. Yet, through all of this Pharaoh remains hardhearted, stubborn and adamant in his refusal to free the Jewish slaves. The question therefore arises as to why Pharaoh is so stubborn, to his own detriment and to that of his nation.

The Torah explains that Pharaoh's stubbornness was necessary to demonstrate God's participation in the Exodus of the Jews from Egypt. God hardened the heart of Pharaoh in order to accomplish this end. The commentators to the Torah wrestle with the moral prob-

As each of the words דָּם, *blood,* אֵשׁ, *fire,* and עָשָׁן, *smoke,* is said, a bit of wine is removed from the cup, with the finger or by pouring.

Blood, fire, and columns of smoke.[1]

Another explanation of the preceding verse: [Each phrase represents two plagues,] hence: mighty hand — two; outstretched arm — two; great fear — two; signs — two; wonders — two.

These are the ten plagues which the Holy One, Blessed is He, brought upon the Egyptians in Egypt, namely:

(1) *Joel* 3:3.

---

lem of God apparently removing freedom of choice from Pharaoh and nevertheless punishing him for his stubbornness in refusing to free the Jewish slaves. Many comments have been made on this matter. The one that I find most insightful is advanced by *Rambam* (Rabbi Moses ben Maimon, 12th-century Spain, Morocco, and Egypt). God gave Pharaoh the courage of his convictions. The choice between good and evil, freedom and slavery, was always exclusively in the hands and heart of Pharaoh. However, the pressure of the plagues was so strong that Pharaoh would have succumbed to Moses' demands, not out of his own free choice but rather out of the coercion of the difficulties that the plagues caused. By strengthening and hardening the heart of Pharaoh, God allowed Pharaoh to stick by his choice and enforce his own will, and not bow to the pressures engendered by the plagues. The truth of this view is clearly seen in the fact that immediately after the Exodus and the slaying of the firstborn Egyptians, Pharaoh nevertheless raises an army and pursues the escaping Jews into the desert to return them to slavery. Pharaoh's freedom of will and action was preserved by God at all costs during the struggle that resulted in the Exodus of the Jews from Egyptian bondage.

☙ The Ten Plagues

The listing of the ten plagues in the Haggadah is meant to illustrate to us the exactness of God's judgment and the nature of the Exodus from Egypt. The Jews did not leave Egypt in one fell swoop and instant. The redemption came about gradually and as a combination of many factors. The Lord could have redeemed us in an instant, but apparently that is not His way. Each of the plagues was a different factor that led to the final redemption.

I think that this is the basis for the next part of the Haggadah that describes the redemption from Egypt in terms of hundreds of plagues. Each of the ten plagues contained many factors and consequences within it. For instance, the plague of blood that destroyed the Egyptian water supply also brought with it the plagues of not being able to bathe, to do laundry, to cook, etc. Each of these discomforts was a plague unto itself, another factor that eventually led to the redemption of the Jews from Egyptian slavery. Though at times redemption may appear to be sudden and unexpected, it is in reality a gradual and progressive phenomenon. Each of the ten plagues is therefore to be viewed as a separate rung up the ladder of freedom and independence.

As each of the plagues is mentioned, a bit of wine is removed from the cup.
The same is done as each word of Rabbi Yehudah's mnemonic is pronounced.

דָּם. צְפַרְדֵּעַ. כִּנִּים. עָרוֹב. דֶּבֶר. שְׁחִין. בָּרָד. אַרְבֶּה. חֹשֶׁךְ. מַכַּת בְּכוֹרוֹת.

◆§ דָּם — *Blood*

The first plague that struck the Egyptians was דָּם — turning the water supply into blood. As mentioned earlier, it was also one of the signs that Moses used to convince Israel of God's mission to him to redeem Israel from Egyptian bondage. The symbolism here is that both water and blood are necessary for life to exist. Dehydration and loss of blood can both be fatal. One cannot live only on water and one cannot live only by having blood circulating through the body. It is rather the balance of life-giving ingredients within our bodies that sustain life itself.

One of the most negative factors regarding slavery is the lack of balance that it creates in society. A society of slaves who have no rights and of masters who control all rights is eventually doomed to collapse. All of human history, from ancient Greece and Rome to the antebellum American South to the Gulag of the Soviet Union, proves this point. All blood and no water creates only death and destruction.

The plague of דָּם thus speaks symbolically to the inequity and iniquity of human slavery. In *Meshech Chochmah*, Rabbi Meir Simchah of Dvinsk repeatedly emphasizes that the Torah attempted to uproot the concept of human slavery from ancient Israel. "You are my slaves" is God's statement to Israel "and not slaves to other slaves." Humans are servants of the Creator exclusively and are not meant to be held in thrall by other humans. There has to be a balance between blood and water, employer and employee, manager and worker. Thus the plague of דָּם, attacking as it does the institution of slavery, fittingly served as both the sign to Israel of its impending redemption and as the first plague and rung on the ladder of Egyptian punishment and the release of the Jewish slaves from bondage.

◆§ צְפַרְדֵּעַ — *Frogs*

The Talmud teaches us that the decision of Hananyah, Mishael, and Azaryah to allow themselves to be thrown into the furnace of Nebuchadnezzar rather than bow down to his pagan idols was based on the example of the frogs in Egypt. The frogs jumped into the burning ovens of the Egyptians to fulfill God's mission for them regarding this plague against the Egyptians. If the frogs sanctified God's Name in this matter, certainly Jews who experienced Godly revelation were bidden to do so, as well. The rabbis used this metaphor to emphasize that we are bidden to make sacrifices in order to live a Godly existence. Thus the lesson of the frogs lies not only in the punishment of the Egyptians but in the lesson they taught to the Jews as well. The frog was worshiped in Egyptian society as one of the gods of the Nile, together with the crocodile. Turning the Egyptians' own god into the instrument of punishment of the Egyptians was meant to show the impotence of paganism and its utter nonsensical falsehood.

◆§ כִּנִּים — *Lice*

The plague of כִּנִּים — a type of lice that infested the human body — brought all Egyptian life to a halt. Even the royal court of Pharaoh was affected, for the plague infested all of the courtiers. The lesson here is how fragile man really is. Despite all of the wealth and power amassed by these courtiers, they were unable to function because of microscopic lice-

As each of the plagues is mentioned, a bit of wine is removed from the cup. The same is done as each word of Rabbi Yehudah's mnemonic is pronounced.

1. Blood 2. Frogs 3. Lice 4. Wild Beasts 5. Pestilence 6. Boils 7. Hail 8. Locusts 9. Darkness 10. Plague of the Firstborn.

---

like creatures that invaded their skins. Again, how fragile and puny man truly is!

The entire concept of enslaving other human beings is based on hubris and arrogance. As the Talmud so succinctly puts it: "Why is your blood redder than your fellow's? Perhaps his is

redder than yours!" Out of all of the plagues that affected Egyptian life, כִּנִּים was perhaps the most humbling of all.

Rambam (Maimonides), based on the *Mishnah* in *Avos,* posits that one must go to all extremes to overcome haughtiness, false pride, arrogance, and hubris. It, together with anger, forms a most dangerous defect in one's character, behavior, and world outlook. The microscopic, almost unseen, little lice effectively cut the Egyptian power structure down to size. We should be reminded always of our vulnerability and fragility. Our body tells us that all of the time. It is one of the reasons that Jews recite a blessing after attending to their bodily functions. The slightest problem with our bodies, even just a painful hangnail, renders us useless and impotent. So, where is there room for arrogance and domineering behavior? It is our foolishness that blinds us to our faults of arrogance and unjustified prideful behavior. The lowly כִּנִּים should serve to remind us of the true nature of things.

◆§ עָרוֹב — *Wild Beasts*

The plague of עָרוֹב — a staggering mixture of wild animals of prey — brought home to Egyptian society God's control of the world. Wild animals are instinctive creatures, very hard to train and domesticate. As any of the aficionados of *National Geographic* knows, these animals, mainly those of the big-cat family, are beautiful, but deadly killers all the same. One can only imagine the chaos and consternation that an attack of such animals on Egyptian communities must have wrought. The animals arrived "on time" as Moses had foretold and left "on time," again on Moses' instructions. That was no longer instinctive behavior; that was trained behavior. Who trained them and how was this accomplished? How was it possible that there be such a varied mixture of these wild animals, creatures who ordinarily move and hunt only with their own species and do not ever mix together? And how was it that the natural enemies among the *arov* did not prey on one another?

It must have slowly begun to dawn on the average Egyptians that something supernatural was afoot here. But because of their attachment to paganism, they undoubtedly attributed the plague to a god of the animals, which they must now try to pacify. It would take more plagues, more warnings from Moses, more thought and prescience on the part of the Egyptians to make them realize that the pagan gods they worshiped were powerless to help them or to hurt them. That is why the Torah tells us that God judged and punished the gods of Egypt by these plagues, since slowly but steadily the Egyptians' faith in these pagan gods was weakened. Perhaps the historically recorded rise of a turn to monotheism, albeit still imperfect and not without continuing pagan overtones, in Egyptian society and even among the Pharaohs at that time was a result of the effect that the plagues had upon the beliefs and faith of Egyptian society.

◆§ דֶּבֶר — *Pestilence*

The plague that killed most of the Egyptian cattle devastated the economy of the country. In our modern world, mechanized and machine driven as it is, domesticated animals serve only as a source of food (meat, milk, etc.) or as unlikely pets or sports objects (horses). Not so in ancient Egypt, where all transport, agricultural work, and military operations depended upon horses, oxen, cows, and other domesticated animals. Without a plentiful supply of domesticated animals, the Egyptian economy and way of life would grind to a halt. We hear in the Song of Moses at the Sea of Reeds the exultation over the drowning of the Egyptian warhorses. Egypt was famous for its animals. The Talmud teaches us that even in later centuries no animals were allowed to depart Egypt unless they were first made sterile in order to preserve the Egyptian monopoly on pure-bred animals.

Thus, the plague that decimated the Egyptian animal supply surely must have wreaked havoc in that society. When conducting war, one of the major tasks of the attacker is to destroy the economic infrastructure of the enemy. The destruction of the economy perforce brings about a crisis of morale and a failure of will in that enemy's society. In God's war against the Egyptian empire, the destruction of much of Egypt's animal supply caused Egyptians to feel that they were losing or already had lost the struggle to retain their Jewish slaves. However, as with all of the plagues except the final one, Pharaoh was still not convinced that his cause was lost. From the remaining animals that survived the plague he rebuilt the Egyptian animal supply. The later plague of hailstorms would again destroy most of the Egyptian supply of animals. But Pharaoh's stubbornness would prove equal to that trial as well.

◆§ שְׁחִין — *Boils*

The plague of boils and lesions on the human skin resembled the previous plague of lice, except that it was far more painful and intense in terms of human discomfort. The plagues seem to follow a certain pattern. There were three groups of three: The first set consisted of plagues that affected all life — blood, wild beasts, hailstones. The second set consisted of economic plagues — frogs, pestilence, locusts — which struck at the economy. Finally, there were three plagues that affect the human body itself — lice, boils, darkness — which affected people's ability to see or move. The plagues culminate with the tenth and last one, the death of the firstborn Egyptian males. The increasing intensity of the plagues was intended to show the Egyptians that further opposition to Moses' demand that the Jews be freed was useless.

Boils certainly must have been much more painful than lice. Boils also disfigured the sufferer, adding psychological and emotional angst to the physical pain already involved. Often the scars left by boils and lesions continue to haunt the sufferer long after the pain is gone and the boil itself has been lanced and healed.

Some commentators link the scars from boils on the bodies of the Egyptians to the scars from the whiplash that remained on the backs of the former Jewish slaves of those very Egyptians. The "measure for measure" rule of reward and punishment in God's world never wavers. Exploitation of others eventually leaves a lasting, if sometimes unrecognizable, scar on the psyche of the exploiter as well.

◆§ אַרְבֶּה — *Locusts*

The locust plague that descended upon Egypt continued the pattern of the systematic annihilation of the Egyptian agricultural economy. In Biblical description, especially in the words of the prophet Joel, the locust plague is presented as an invasion of a great despoiling army that leaves nothing untouched or undamaged in its wake. Many decades ago, my family and I were driving on a highway in Kansas when suddenly a horde of locusts flew, jumped, and proceeded across the highway. It was a small horde and the ordeal was over in a few minutes. Naturally all traffic stopped. Some cars were unable to proceed afterwards, for too many locusts had invaded their engines. The road was slippery from them and I must admit that it was quite a scary sight. I remember thinking to myself then what an awesome and terror-filled experience it must have been in Egypt when the onslaught of the locust plague occurred.

The devastation wreaked on the remnants of the Egyptian agricultural economy must have been horrendous in scope and nature. Locusts take no prisoners and they strip everything bare. They invade homes and shops, workplaces and public structures. But since locust plagues occur from time to time in all agricultural societies, it was the intensity and degree of damage wrought by the plague that impressed the Egyptians as being out of the ordinary. The

רַבִּי יְהוּדָה הָיָה נוֹתֵן בָּהֶם סִמָּנִים:

דְּצַ״ךְ עֲדַ״שׁ בְּאַחַ״ב.

The cups are refilled. The wine that was removed is not used.

רַבִּי יוֹסֵי הַגְּלִילִי אוֹמֵר: מִנַּיִן אַתָּה אוֹמֵר שֶׁלָּקוּ הַמִּצְרִים בְּמִצְרַיִם עֶשֶׂר מַכּוֹת וְעַל הַיָּם לָקוּ חֲמִשִּׁים מַכּוֹת?

---

plague of locusts at the time of the prophet Joel that struck the Land of Israel was apparently even greater than this plague in Egypt. However, Joel's plague consisted of many (at least five) different types of locusts and grasshoppers, while in Egypt the plague was restricted to only one species of locust.

חֹשֶׁךְ — *Darkness*

The plague of darkness was employed by God, so to speak, to winnow the ranks of the Jewish people. The majority of Jews did not live to leave Egypt with Moses. According to the *Midrash* they perished in the period of Egyptian darkness, so that the Egyptians would be unaware that a plague of death was affecting the Jews as well. I have always thought that there is a great symbolic lesson taught to Israel by the fact that the Jewish deaths occurred only in consonance with the plague of darkness.

In the Torah we read that for the Jewish people "there was light in all of their dwelling places" while the Egyptians were paralyzed by darkness. Yet even then, when in the light of the difference between the situation of the Jews and of the Egyptians, when things were starkly black and white, light and dark, there were many Jews who still preferred remaining in Egypt and being pagan to following Moses and accepting Torah and its values and lifestyle. It is one thing (nevertheless still a wrong decision) to reject Torah when the differences between traditional Jewish life and values and general society's mores are not blatantly different. But when the differences are clear and sharp — light and darkness — to choose darkness over light and to be blind to Torah and its blessings, the rejection of Torah becomes something not understandable and eventually unforgivable.

מַכַּת בְּכוֹרוֹת — *Plague of the Firstborn*

To put this final and decisive plague in some sort of current perspective I think that one could say that it was a preemptive strike to decapitate the leadership of Egypt and prevent the Egyptians from attempting to regain their Jewish slaves during the long sojourn of Israel in the neighboring Sinai desert. I think that it is highly significant that Egypt, after the Exodus and the Sea of Reeds, does not figure again in Jewish history for many centuries. It was the destruction of the firstborn Egyptians and the national memory of that catastrophe that made Egypt very wary of tangling with the Jews again. It would take a long time before the memory of the plague of the firstborn sons would fade in Egyptian society. The plague affected all families. "There was no house that there was not death present." The impact of the plague was therefore person-al, universal, and of great and dramatic impact.

It was only the total defeat of Germany and Japan in World War II that cured those countries, at least temporarily, and I hope permanently, of their aggressive intents and natures. The plague of the destruction of firstborn sons in Egypt was equivalent to the total destruction of Egyptian society and its slaveholder mental-

Rabbi Yehudah abbreviated them by their Hebrew initials:

D'TZACH, ADASH, B'ACHAV.

The cups are refilled. The wine that was removed is not used.

Rabbi Yose the Galilean says: How does one derive that the Egyptians were struck with ten plagues in Egypt, but with

---

ity. It provided a lasting lesson of centuries-long duration to Egypt and to Israel. Having accomplished this, it must truly be seen as the most pivotal and central of the ten plagues visited by God upon Egypt.

רַבִּי יְהוּדָה — *Rabbi Yehudah*

R' Yehudah was wont to deal with such acronyms and abbreviations (for example, see *Mishnah, Menachos*, Chapter 11, *mishnah* 4). This acronym of the plagues has the numerical value of 501, thus including all of the opinions of the different rabbis regarding how many plagues — and plagues within plagues — the Egyptians actually suffered during the process of the Exodus. (See below,) The order of the plagues as mentioned in *Psalms* (Chapters 78 and 105) is different than the order that appears in the Torah itself. Therefore, through the means of this easily remembered acronym, R' Yehudah asserts that the correct order of the plagues is as it appears in the Torah, while the different orders that appear in *Psalms* are in poetic but not chronological order.

According to the *Midrash*, the acronym appeared on the staff of Moses, which had been the staff of Adam, the original man. The acronym remained a mystery until millennia had passed and when the ten plagues in Egypt unfolded in that order, its meaning then became clear. The lesson of this *Midrash* is really a very simple one. Many of the apparent mysteries of life and history take decades, centuries, and even millennia to be understood and deciphered. The inscription on Adam's staff was always there but never really understood. It took on clear meaning only with Moses' use of that staff to deliver Israel from Egyptian bondage.

As mentioned earlier, a drop of wine is removed from our cups while reciting each of the names of the ten plagues and each of the three phrases of R' Yehudah's acronym. This is to signify that we take no special joy at the destruction of our human enemies, deserving as those enemies are of such destruction. Rabbi Meir Simchah of Dvinsk points out in his *Meshech Chochmah* that the Lord purposely made the first day of Pesach a holiday even though our deliverance from Egypt was not complete until the seventh day of Pesach when the Egyptians were drowned at the Sea of Reeds, so that we would not see Pesach as solely a commemoration of the destruction of our enemies (as represented by the seventh day of Pesach) but rather as an expression of gratitude for our deliverance from bondage (as represented by the first day of Pesach). The removing of drops of wine from our cups represents the wisdom of Solomon in *Proverbs*: "When your enemy is brought low, rejoice not!"

רַבִּי יוֹסֵי הַגְּלִילִי אוֹמֵר — *Rabbi Yose the Galilean says:*

The Torah here mentions that the people had faith in Moses as being the servant of God. The greatness of Moses lay in his humility and self-effacement. Even while performing supernatural miracles, seemingly at will and without end, he conveyed to the people that it was not he but rather God Who was ordering nature to produce these miracles. Moses, like Abraham before him, allowed ordinary mortals to see that

בְּמִצְרַיִם מָה הוּא אוֹמֵר, וַיֹּאמְרוּ הַחַרְטֻמִּם אֶל פַּרְעֹה, אֶצְבַּע אֱלֹהִים הִוא.[1] וְעַל הַיָּם מָה הוּא אוֹמֵר, וַיַּרְא יִשְׂרָאֵל אֶת הַיָּד הַגְּדֹלָה אֲשֶׁר עָשָׂה יהוה בְּמִצְרַיִם, וַיִּירְאוּ הָעָם אֶת יהוה, וַיַּאֲמִינוּ בַּיהוה וּבְמֹשֶׁה עַבְדּוֹ.[2] כַּמָּה לָקוּ בְאֶצְבַּע? עֶשֶׂר מַכּוֹת. אֱמוֹר מֵעַתָּה, בְּמִצְרַיִם לָקוּ עֶשֶׂר מַכּוֹת, וְעַל הַיָּם לָקוּ חֲמִשִּׁים מַכּוֹת.

רַבִּי אֱלִיעֶזֶר אוֹמֵר. מִנַּיִן שֶׁכָּל מַכָּה וּמַכָּה שֶׁהֵבִיא הַקָּדוֹשׁ בָּרוּךְ הוּא עַל הַמִּצְרִים בְּמִצְרַיִם הָיְתָה שֶׁל אַרְבַּע מַכּוֹת? שֶׁנֶּאֱמַר, יְשַׁלַּח בָּם חֲרוֹן אַפּוֹ – עֶבְרָה, וָזַעַם, וְצָרָה, מִשְׁלַחַת מַלְאֲכֵי רָעִים.[3] עֶבְרָה, אַחַת. וָזַעַם, שְׁתַּיִם. וְצָרָה, שָׁלֹשׁ. מִשְׁלַחַת מַלְאֲכֵי רָעִים, אַרְבַּע. אֱמוֹר מֵעַתָּה, בְּמִצְרַיִם לָקוּ אַרְבָּעִים מַכּוֹת, וְעַל הַיָּם לָקוּ מָאתַיִם מַכּוֹת.

רַבִּי עֲקִיבָא אוֹמֵר. מִנַּיִן שֶׁכָּל מַכָּה וּמַכָּה שֶׁהֵבִיא הַקָּדוֹשׁ בָּרוּךְ הוּא עַל הַמִּצְרִים בְּמִצְרַיִם הָיְתָה שֶׁל חָמֵשׁ מַכּוֹת? שֶׁנֶּאֱמַר, יְשַׁלַּח בָּם חֲרוֹן אַפּוֹ, עֶבְרָה, וָזַעַם, וְצָרָה, מִשְׁלַחַת מַלְאֲכֵי רָעִים. חֲרוֹן אַפּוֹ, אַחַת. עֶבְרָה, שְׁתַּיִם. וָזַעַם, שָׁלֹשׁ. וְצָרָה, אַרְבַּע. מִשְׁלַחַת מַלְאֲכֵי רָעִים, חָמֵשׁ. אֱמוֹר מֵעַתָּה, בְּמִצְרַיִם לָקוּ חֲמִשִּׁים מַכּוֹת, וְעַל הַיָּם לָקוּ חֲמִשִּׁים וּמָאתַיִם מַכּוֹת.

---

through the servant one could also glimpse the Master. The highest appellation and greatest title that Moses achieved was being called by both God and humans "the servant of God." It is only through abject humility that true greatness can be seen and recognized.

Rabbi Yose the Galilean derives his numbers of plagues from the verses of the Torah. His colleagues, R' Eliezer and R' Akiva, derive their numbers of plagues from a verse in *Psalms*, Chapter 78. The Gaon of Vilna points out that the attempt of the rabbis to magnify the number of plagues that struck the Egyptians is in line with the tradition that one should attempt to tell more and more regarding the Exodus. The Hebrew letters of the word לְסַפֵּר, *to tell* or *recite*, can be vocalized as לִסְפֹּר, *to count*. Thus the one who can

fifty plagues at the sea? — Concerning the plagues in Egypt the Torah states: The magicians said to Pharaoh, "It is the finger of God."[1] However, of those at the sea, the Torah relates: Israel saw the great "hand" which HASHEM laid upon the Egyptians, the people feared HASHEM, and they believed in HASHEM and in His servant Moses.[2] How many plagues did they receive with the finger? Ten! Then conclude that if they suffered ten plagues in Egypt [were they were struck with a finger], they were stricken with fifty plagues at the sea [where they were struck with a whole hand].

Rabbi Eliezer said: How does one derive that every plague that the Holy One, Blessed is He, inflicted upon the Egyptians in Egypt was equal to four plagues? — as it says: He sent upon them His fierce anger: wrath, fury, and trouble, a band of emissaries of evil.[3] [Since each plague in Egypt consisted of] 1) wrath, 2) fury, 3) trouble, and 4) a band of emissaries of evil, therefore conclude that in Egypt they were struck by forty plagues and at the sea by two hundred!

Rabbi Akiva said: How does one derive that each plague that the Holy One, Blessed is He, inflicted upon the Egyptians in Egypt was equal to five plagues? — as it says: He sent upon them His fierce anger, wrath, fury, trouble, and a band of emissaries of evil. [Since each plague in Egypt consisted of] 1) fierce anger, 2) wrath, 3) fury, 4) trouble, and 5) a band of emissaries of evil, therefore conclude that in Egypt they were struck by fifty plagues and at the sea by two hundred and fifty!

(1) *Exodus* 8:15. (2) *Exodus* 14:31. (3) *Psalms* 78:49.

---

count more plagues suffered by the Egyptians is praiseworthy.

The Gaon also states that since God promised Israel that "all of the plagues and sicknesses of Egypt will not be visited upon you (Israel)," it is understandable that the more plagues suffered by the Egyptians, the greater the immunity of the Jews. Finally, *Sfas Emes* points out that the total number of all of the plagues presented here in the Haggadah (the

כַּמָּה מַעֲלוֹת טוֹבוֹת לַמָּקוֹם עָלֵינוּ.

אִלּוּ הוֹצִיאָנוּ מִמִּצְרַיִם,
וְלֹא עָשָׂה בָהֶם שְׁפָטִים, דַּיֵּנוּ.
אִלּוּ עָשָׂה בָהֶם שְׁפָטִים,
וְלֹא עָשָׂה בֵאלֹהֵיהֶם, דַּיֵּנוּ.

---

ten plagues, listed in the Torah, the three phrases of the acronym of the plagues as advanced by R' Yehudah, sixty plagues according to R' Yose the Galilean, two hundred-forty plagues according to R' Eliezer and three hundred plagues according to R' Akiva) equals six hundred-thirteen, the number of mitzvos in the Torah. The observance of the six hundred-thirteen mitzvos is the spiritual defense against both the physical and spiritual plagues of Egypt.

☙ דַּיֵּנוּ — *It would have sufficed us.*

After enumerating all of the plagues that befell the Egyptians, the Haggadah reverts to telling us of the wonders that befell us during the Exodus from Egypt and later in the desert of Sinai. Implicit in this recitation of the fifteen stanzas of *Dayeinu* is the lesson that in one great miracle there are always present many "minor" miracles as well. It is comparable to two people who are recovering from an illness and/or surgery. One is recovering in comfort with good care and encouraging surroundings. The other is in a bleak and lonely room; practically left to fend for himself. Both patients will eventually recover and be restored to health, but there is no comparison as to how this recovery will occur. So, too, when the Lord redeemed us from Egypt, He did so in a manner of comfort and consideration for Israel, interspersing the "minor" miracles of comfort and convenience within the major miracles of the Exodus and the granting of the Torah on Sinai and the entry of Israel into the Land of Israel and the building of the Temple.

In life, all of us know that many times it is the small things that count. A great event can be ruined or diminished by a small flaw in planning or execution. I have often seen how the wonder of a transcontinental flight in a jumbo jet is erased by a minor discomfort or a surly flight attendant. God, therefore, knowing our human frailties all too well, arranged for a "perfect" Exodus and sojourn in the desert for the Jews. Even this perfection did not prevent the people from complaining, but there is no doubt that it was God's intent, so to speak, to please us completely.

There are many comments to be made on each of the fifteen stanzas of *Dayeinu*. Allow me to share some of them with you. Each stanza implies that the good that eventually came to us by God's grace could have come differently and without such direct intervention by God. The Jews could have been saved at the Sea of Reeds had the waters merely blocked the advance of the Egyptians. The Jews had sufficient sheep and cattle of their own with them in the Sinai desert to allow them to eat meat on their own. Food and water could have been purchased from neighboring tribes without having to resort to manna and Miriam's miraculous rolling well. The seabed at the Sea of Reeds could have been wet or muddy and we still would have been saved. Since we had a *Mishkan* — a Tabernacle with all of its holy vessels and artifacts — the

The Omnipresent has bestowed so many favors upon us!

Had He brought us out of Egypt,
but not executed judgments against the Egyptians, it would have sufficed us.

Had He executed judgments against them,
but not acted against their gods,
it would have sufficed us.

---

construction of the Temple in Jerusalem was an extra bonus to us. As thousands of years of exile and dispersion have taught us, if we have and keep the Torah, then the Land of Israel is not necessarily vital to our survival as a people. All of these ideas help explain the basic thrust of the *Dayeinu* section of the Haggadah.

The one stanza that draws the most attention from the commentators to the Haggadah is the one that states that if God only brought us to Mount Sinai without giving us the Torah, that too would have been enough for us. Of what benefit can appearing before Mount Sinai be without the granting of the Torah? The answer that I like best is based on the idea mentioned in the Talmud and quoted by Rashi in his commentary to the Torah. When the Jewish people came to Mount Sinai, even before God's revelation to them, they came as a united entity, "as though they were one person with one heart." This, therefore, was the moment that the people as a whole fulfilled the lofty ideal of "וְאָהַבְתָּ לְרֵעֲךָ כָּמוֹךָ — feeling for one's fellow as for one's own self." This is the whole Torah according to Hillel and the basic rule of Torah according to R' Akiva. Thus the Torah, so to speak, was already "given" to Israel simply by the Jewish people's arrival at Mount Sinai in a united "one-person one-heart" group. The actual giving of the Torah at Sinai was, again in the words of the noble Hillel, now included in his concluding concept, of "as for the rest of the Torah, go and learn."

Dayeinu ends with thanks to the Lord for having given us the Temple that brings atonement. When the Temple will again be built, it will serve to cleanse us of all our sins. We are taught in *Pesikta* that Jews never slept in Jerusalem as sinners, for the morning *tamid* sacrifice provided forgiveness for all sins of the night and the evening *tamid* sacrifice brought forgiveness for all sins of the day. Thus the building of the Temple will automatically again bring us to a status where our sins will be forgiven by a merciful Creator.

Because of our recognition of God's grace to us not only regarding the causation of the miracles of the Exodus but also in the manner and detail by which they occurred, we extend thanks and gratitude to the Lord for all of the above. The language of the vote of thanks, עַל אַחַת כַּמָּה וְכַמָּה טוֹבָה כְפוּלָה וּמְכֻפֶּלֶת, *how much more so, a redoubled goodness*, appears at first glance to be a bit hyperbolic and exaggerated. However, the Rabbis taught us that this section of the haggadah refers not only to the past miracles of the Exodus but also to the future miracles of the final redemption of Israel and mankind. The miracles that will accompany that event will be far greater than those of the Exodus from Egypt. Therefore, the exaggerated use of language in describing that redemption will in fact be no exaggeration at all.

The word "*Dayeinu*" also includes a darker side. In our thanks to God for the miracles per-

אִלּוּ עָשָׂה בֵאלֹהֵיהֶם,
וְלֹא הָרַג אֶת בְּכוֹרֵיהֶם, דַּיֵּנוּ.
אִלּוּ הָרַג אֶת בְּכוֹרֵיהֶם,
וְלֹא נָתַן לָנוּ אֶת מָמוֹנָם, דַּיֵּנוּ.
אִלּוּ נָתַן לָנוּ אֶת מָמוֹנָם,
וְלֹא קָרַע לָנוּ אֶת הַיָּם, דַּיֵּנוּ.
אִלּוּ קָרַע לָנוּ אֶת הַיָּם,
וְלֹא הֶעֱבִירָנוּ בְתוֹכוֹ בֶּחָרָבָה, דַּיֵּנוּ.

---

formed on our behalf, *Dayeinu* as a prayer and an idea is certainly in order. However, regarding *our own* accomplishments we should definitely not say *Dayeinu*. The Rabbis point out to us that

Had He acted against their gods,
  but not slain their firstborn,
    it would have sufficed us.
Had He slain their firstborn,
  but not given us their wealth,
    it would have sufficed us.
Had He given us their wealth,
  but not split the sea for us,
    it would have sufficed us.
Had He split the sea for us,
  but not led us through it on dry land,
    it would have sufficed us.

אִלּוּ הֶעֱבִירָנוּ בְתוֹכוֹ בֶּחָרָבָה,
וְלֹא שִׁקַּע צָרֵינוּ בְּתוֹכוֹ, דַּיֵּנוּ.
אִלּוּ שִׁקַּע צָרֵינוּ בְּתוֹכוֹ,
וְלֹא סִפֵּק צָרְכֵּנוּ בַּמִּדְבָּר אַרְבָּעִים שָׁנָה, דַּיֵּנוּ.
אִלּוּ סִפֵּק צָרְכֵּנוּ בַּמִּדְבָּר אַרְבָּעִים שָׁנָה,
וְלֹא הֶאֱכִילָנוּ אֶת הַמָּן, דַּיֵּנוּ.
אִלּוּ הֶאֱכִילָנוּ אֶת הַמָּן,
וְלֹא נָתַן לָנוּ אֶת הַשַּׁבָּת, דַּיֵּנוּ.
אִלּוּ נָתַן לָנוּ אֶת הַשַּׁבָּת,
וְלֹא קֵרְבָנוּ לִפְנֵי הַר סִינַי, דַּיֵּנוּ.
אִלּוּ קֵרְבָנוּ לִפְנֵי הַר סִינַי,
וְלֹא נָתַן לָנוּ אֶת הַתּוֹרָה, דַּיֵּנוּ.
אִלּוּ נָתַן לָנוּ אֶת הַתּוֹרָה,
וְלֹא הִכְנִיסָנוּ לְאֶרֶץ יִשְׂרָאֵל, דַּיֵּנוּ.
אִלּוּ הִכְנִיסָנוּ לְאֶרֶץ יִשְׂרָאֵל,
וְלֹא בָנָה לָנוּ אֶת בֵּית הַבְּחִירָה, דַּיֵּנוּ.

---

this attitude of *Dayeinu* was the main difference between Noah and Abraham. Noah rises to pass the great test of the flood and the ark that he constructed. But after that great and traumatic event, Noah says, *Dayeinu*, so to speak. He plants a vineyard, with disastrous consequences soon to follow. וַיָּחֶל נֹחַ, Noah becomes mundane, ordinary, not interested in any more challenges or spiritual adventures. Abraham, on the other hand, is tested over and over, ten times in all and rises to every new challenge. He is always looking to do more, influence more, to continue to spread the Name of God and the idea of monotheism throughout the world. We are called the children of Abraham and not the children of Noah. Even after surviving the worst of traumas, such as the Holocaust in the past century, we are not allowed to say *Dayeinu,* to say we have done enough and now we will retire from the fray.

On *Shabbos Chol Hamoed Pesach*, the *Haftarah* (reading from the Prophets) concerns the great vision of Ezekiel in the valley of the dry bones. The skeletons of the dead grow flesh and sinews and are revived to life. This is symbolic of the rebirth of the Jewish people and the eternity of Israel. The *Haftarah* ends on an optimistic and inspirational note of rebirth and redemption — in short, the message of Pesach itself. However, the Talmud in Tractate *Sanhe-*

Had He led us through it on dry land,
but not drowned our oppressors in it,
it would have sufficed us.
Had He drowned our oppressors in it,
but not provided for our needs in the desert
for forty years, it would have sufficed us.
Had He provided for our needs in the desert
for forty years,
but not fed us the manna,
it would have sufficed us.
Had He fed us the manna,
but not given us the Shabbos,
it would have sufficed us.
Had He given us the Shabbos,
but not brought us before Mount Sinai,
it would have sufficed us.
Had He brought us before Mount Sinai,
but not given us the Torah,
it would have sufficed us.
Had He given us the Torah,
but not brought us into the Land of Israel,
it would have sufficed us.
Had He brought us into the Land of Israel,
but not built the Temple for us,
it would have sufficed us.

---

drin is not satisfied with this ending. It asks the all-important question: "What happened to these revived people after they were restored to life again?" The Talmud advances differing opinions. One opinion is that Ezekiel's vision was only that — a vision but not reality. Another opinion is that these dead people arose from the dead but immediately fell dead again — a one-time, temporary miracle. *Dayeinu.*

But the Talmud concludes that R' Yehudah ben Beseira then stood on his feet and proclaimed in the study hall of Torah: "God forbid that this was only a vision or that they died again immediately. No, they lived a life, married, fathered and mothered children, built families, and I am a descendant of one of them. As proof of the matter, look, I hold my grandfather's *tefilin* in my hands!"

עַל אַחַת כַּמָּה, וְכַמָּה טוֹבָה כְפוּלָה וּמְכֻפֶּלֶת לַמָּקוֹם עָלֵינוּ. שֶׁהוֹצִיאָנוּ מִמִּצְרַיִם, וְעָשָׂה בָהֶם שְׁפָטִים, וְעָשָׂה בֵאלֹהֵיהֶם, וְהָרַג אֶת בְּכוֹרֵיהֶם, וְנָתַן לָנוּ אֶת מָמוֹנָם, וְקָרַע לָנוּ אֶת הַיָּם, וְהֶעֱבִירָנוּ בְתוֹכוֹ בֶּחָרָבָה, וְשִׁקַּע צָרֵינוּ בְּתוֹכוֹ, וְסִפֵּק צָרְכֵּנוּ בַּמִּדְבָּר אַרְבָּעִים שָׁנָה, וְהֶאֱכִילָנוּ אֶת הַמָּן, וְנָתַן לָנוּ אֶת הַשַּׁבָּת, וְקֵרְבָנוּ לִפְנֵי הַר סִינַי, וְנָתַן לָנוּ אֶת הַתּוֹרָה, וְהִכְנִיסָנוּ לְאֶרֶץ יִשְׂרָאֵל, וּבָנָה לָנוּ אֶת בֵּית הַבְּחִירָה, לְכַפֵּר עַל כָּל עֲוֹנוֹתֵינוּ.

רַבָּן גַּמְלִיאֵל הָיָה אוֹמֵר. כָּל שֶׁלֹּא אָמַר שְׁלֹשָׁה דְּבָרִים אֵלּוּ בַּפֶּסַח, לֹא יָצָא יְדֵי חוֹבָתוֹ, וְאֵלּוּ הֵן,

---

[As an aside, I have always felt that this statement of R' Yehudah ben Beseira is the origin of the common practice that grandparents purchase *tefillin* for their grandson's bar-mitzvah, or that a grandfather's *tefillin* are refurbished for the use of the grandson.]

But to return to the topic at hand, here is the example of the choice that one has after a traumatic experience and unexpected salvation. There are those who say: "Enough! I survived. *Dayeinu*." They, in a sense, die again immediately. Others rise and say: "I was saved and revived and I will therefore build families, Torah, the Jewish people, humankind. I was not saved to die again; to say, *Dayeinu* to the holy work always left to be performed in this world. And as proof of this, look at the heritage left in my hands — my grandfather's *tefillin*." In our time, the Jewish people, Torah, the State of Israel, all have been built and rebuilt by individuals who survived the Holocaust, Stalin, the Arabs, and the other enemies of Israel and traumas over the past century. They were all people driven by a vision and a cause, unwilling to say *Dayeinu* — it is good enough that we survived. *Dayeinu* is an appropriate expression of humans to God for his continuing grace and bounty. But it is not the motto of Abraham and his descendants, the Jewish nation.

◆§ רַבָּן גַּמְלִיאֵל — *Rabban Gamliel*

Rabban Gamliel II of Yavneh, a descendant of Hillel, was one of the central figures of the period after the destruction of the Second Temple. He was a very strong leader and was determined to uphold the honor of the office of *nasi,* which he occupied during that time. He remained one of the great sages and leaders of his time and great weight was given to his opinions in both Mishnah and Talmud.

Rabban Gamliel outlines here three mitzvos that are the essence of the Seder and the Haggadah: the *pesach* offering, the eating of the matzah, and the obligation to eat the bitter herbs of *maror*. After the destruction of the Second Temple, the offering no longer figured in the Seder service, but the idea behind it remained alive and vital as before. The Lord, so to speak, skipped over the houses of the Jews when the

Thus, how much more so should we be grateful to the Omnipresent for all the numerous favors He showered upon us: He brought us out of Egypt; executed judgments against the Egyptians; acted against their gods; slew their firstborn; gave us their wealth; split the sea for us; led us through it on dry land; drowned our oppressors in it; provided for our needs in the desert for forty years; fed us the manna; gave us the Shabbos; brought us close to Mount Sinai; gave us the Torah; brought us to the Land of Israel; and built us the Temple, to atone for all our sins.

Rabban Gamliel used to say: Whoever has not explained the following three things on Pesach has not fulfilled his duty, namely:

---

plague of death swept Egypt. God protected Israel from being destroyed, even though strict justice saw little to choose between the Egyptian idolaters and their Jewish slaves. The Egyptians "knew not Joseph," because many of the Jews no longer resembled their father, Joseph. This theme of Jewish culpability in sin and idolatry is repeated often in the story of the Exodus.

It is obvious that, based upon their then merits, Israel was still unworthy of redemption, but God redeemed us on the basis of our potential. The Lord always seems to take potential into account. The salvation of Lot from Sodom is based on the fact that his descendants — Ruth and Naamah — will be great people and play an important role in Jewish life and survival. Ruth was the great-grandmother of King David, and Naamah was the queen of Rechavam, the son of King Solomon. In judging others and certainly as regarding our children and our students, potential should play a great part in our assessments. The Lord spared the Jews in Egypt from the plague of death because of what they would yet be — "a kingdom of priests and a holy people." I think this concept is implicit in the word "פָּסַח," *to skip over*. The Lord, so to speak, skipped over not only the houses of the Jews but also the generations of the Jews; skipped over the present to realize the future; saved the Jewish homes not because of their spiritual status now in Egypt but rather because of their future exalted spiritual level and achievements at Sinai and thereafter.

In my years of heading a yeshivah and being a congregational rabbi, I have seen how anyone who aspires to leadership or guidance of others must be acutely aware of the role of potential when dealing with people. I have seen students loll through the first three years of high school, attaining average or even poor grades, to the frustration of their teachers and parents, and yet somehow then mobilize their talents and energies and grow into excellent students and become leaders in their chosen fields of endeavor in life. Our father Jacob realized the potential that lay in his son Joseph, so that when the others mocked Joseph's dreams, Jacob guarded and nurtured them.

Rabban Gamliel II himself was taught this lesson. The Talmud tells us that when he headed the yeshivah in Yavneh he refused to accept students whom he felt were insincere or not worthy. He judged them on their present status before they entered the yeshivah. When he was removed from office temporarily, his successor R' Elazar ben Azariah (quoted earlier in the Haggadah) opened the doors of the yeshivah for all to attend. Even if they were temporarily unworthy, they possessed great potential that their attendance at the yeshivah would enable them to realize. When Rabban Gamliel II was restored to office by his colleagues, he no longer instituted his previous policy of admittance to the yeshivah, based solely on current status and achievement. Rabban Gamliel II thus became a living example of his own interpretation of "פֶּסַח" — potential — as being not only the basis of the Seder but also the basis of Jewish life generally.

I have previously discussed matzah and its different representations in this review of the Haggadah. What I wish to add here is the idea that matzah — "no time to allow the dough to leaven" — represents the fact that Pharaoh finally drove us out of Egypt. He did not offer to improve the living conditions of the Jews or lighten their burdens so that they would remain in Egypt. Had he done so, undoubtedly many Jews would have opted to stay rather than leave for an uncertain future in the trackless desert of Sinai. But Pharaoh wanted Egypt now to be *Judenrein*. So the Jews embark on their millennia-long journey of destiny.

I know of a family that lived in Germany in the early 1930's when the Nazis came to power. Part of the family lived in an area of Germany that was immediately Nazified and anti-Semitic acts of violence took place on a regular and continuing basis. Despairing of remaining in Germany, this group immigrated to the Land of Israel, where they lived and eventually prospered. The second part of the family lived in a German town that opposed the Nazis and the Jews there felt that they would be able to ride out the storm, and hence did not leave Germany. Needless to say, they were eventually destroyed down to the last infant. The matzah is the symbol of God's grace toward us in having Pharaoh drive us out completely from his land and not allow the Jews to fool themselves — something which we are very good at — into thinking that they still had some future left in Egypt.

I read a fascinating article in a book called *Six Thousand Years of Bread* by H. E. Jacob, in which he posits that baking leavened bread was an Egyptian invention and that such bread was so revered that it eventually became the currency of the realm, and furthermore evolved into a deity. As such, the Jewish matzah was meant to uproot this concept of paganism from the Jewish society. This is in line with the principle enunciated by Rambam in his *Moreh Nevuchim* (*Guide to the Perplexed*) that all mitzvos of the Torah aim to uproot idolatry and paganism from Jewish society. It is no wonder, therefore, following that line of thought, that all of the flour offerings in the Jewish Temple were of unleavened bread (except in only two instances), since the Egyptian offerings to their gods were always of leavened bread.

The matzah symbolized therefore the end of any attachment of Jews to Egyptian society. For forty years after leaving Egypt the Jews did not eat bread but rather Heavenly manna. This is as well, perhaps, another nuance in the great statement of Moses to Israel that "man does not live by bread alone." Bread and Egypt seem to have been synonymous to the minds of the people of that ancient world. Matzah served to break that chain of thought in Jewish society.

Pesach — the *pesach* offering;

Matzah — the unleavened bread;

Maror — the bitter herbs.

Maror is certainly the symbol of Jewish affliction in Egypt. Our remembrance of Egyptian bondage conditioned us to deal with all of the myriad troubles that would yet be our lot in our long history. People tend to forget their past troubles when they are able to escape from them, but the ability to deal with *maror* is one of the strengths of Jewish history and life.

פֶּסַח שֶׁהָיוּ אֲבוֹתֵינוּ אוֹכְלִים בִּזְמַן שֶׁבֵּית הַמִּקְדָּשׁ הָיָה קַיָּם, עַל שׁוּם מָה? עַל שׁוּם שֶׁפָּסַח הַקָּדוֹשׁ בָּרוּךְ הוּא עַל בָּתֵּי אֲבוֹתֵינוּ בְּמִצְרַיִם. שֶׁנֶּאֱמַר, וַאֲמַרְתֶּם, זֶבַח פֶּסַח הוּא לַיהוה, אֲשֶׁר פָּסַח עַל בָּתֵּי בְנֵי יִשְׂרָאֵל בְּמִצְרַיִם בְּנָגְפּוֹ אֶת מִצְרַיִם, וְאֶת בָּתֵּינוּ הִצִּיל, וַיִּקֹּד הָעָם וַיִּשְׁתַּחֲווּ.[1]

The middle matzah is lifted and displayed while the following paragraph is recited.

מַצָּה זוּ שֶׁאָנוּ אוֹכְלִים, עַל שׁוּם מָה? עַל שׁוּם שֶׁלֹּא הִסְפִּיק בְּצֵקָם שֶׁל אֲבוֹתֵינוּ לְהַחֲמִיץ, עַד שֶׁנִּגְלָה עֲלֵיהֶם מֶלֶךְ מַלְכֵי הַמְּלָכִים הַקָּדוֹשׁ בָּרוּךְ הוּא וּגְאָלָם. שֶׁנֶּאֱמַר, וַיֹּאפוּ אֶת הַבָּצֵק אֲשֶׁר הוֹצִיאוּ מִמִּצְרַיִם עֻגֹת מַצּוֹת כִּי לֹא חָמֵץ, כִּי גֹרְשׁוּ מִמִּצְרַיִם, וְלֹא יָכְלוּ לְהִתְמַהְמֵהַּ, וְגַם צֵדָה לֹא עָשׂוּ לָהֶם.[2]

The *maror* is lifted and displayed while the following paragraph is recited.

מָרוֹר זֶה שֶׁאָנוּ אוֹכְלִים, עַל שׁוּם מָה? עַל שׁוּם שֶׁמֵּרְרוּ הַמִּצְרִים אֶת חַיֵּי אֲבוֹתֵינוּ בְּמִצְרַיִם. שֶׁנֶּאֱמַר, וַיְמָרְרוּ אֶת חַיֵּיהֶם, בַּעֲבֹדָה קָשָׁה, בְּחֹמֶר וּבִלְבֵנִים, וּבְכָל עֲבֹדָה בַּשָּׂדֶה, אֵת כָּל עֲבֹדָתָם אֲשֶׁר עָבְדוּ בָהֶם בְּפָרֶךְ.[3]

בְּכָל דּוֹר וָדוֹר חַיָּב אָדָם לִרְאוֹת אֶת עַצְמוֹ כְּאִלּוּ הוּא יָצָא מִמִּצְרָיִם. שֶׁנֶּאֱמַר, וְהִגַּדְתָּ לְבִנְךָ בַּיּוֹם הַהוּא לֵאמֹר,

---

Maror is inescapable in personal and national life. The fact that we even make a blessing over *maror* before eating it confirms our ability to accept adversity and deal with it without losing our faith, belief, and religious practice. It is a practical illustration of the Talmudic dictum that "just as one blesses God over good events, so too is one bidden to bless Him over sad events as well."

Remembering the *maror* of Egypt should also serve to dampen any possible enthusiasm to return there or to willingly acquiesce to domination by any foreign powers or cultures. Perhaps that is the basic positive contribution of *maror* to Jewish society — the sense of memory and the experience of being dominated by others, physically and culturally. Forgetting or not knowing our past dooms us to making serious mistakes in life. Ignoring the lesson of *maror* is done at great personal and national peril.

Pesach — Why did our fathers eat a *pesach* offering during the period when the Temple stood? Because the Holy One, Blessed is He, passed over the houses of our fathers in Egypt, as it says: You shall say: "It is a *pesach* offering for HASHEM, Who passed over the houses of the Children of Israel in Egypt when He struck the Egyptians and spared our houses"; and the people bowed down and prostrated themselves.[1]

The middle matzah is lifted and displayed while the following paragraph is recited.

Matzah — Why do we eat this unleavened bread? Because the dough of our fathers did not have time to become leavened before the King of kings, the Holy One, Blessed is He, revealed Himself to them and redeemed them, as it says: They baked the dough which they had brought out of Egypt into unleavened bread, for it had not fermented, because they were driven out of Egypt and could not delay, nor had they prepared any provisions for the way.[2]

The *maror* is lifted and displayed while the following paragraph is recited.

Maror — Why do we eat this bitter herb? Because the Egyptians embittered the lives of our fathers in Egypt, as it says: They embittered their lives with hard labor, with mortar and bricks, and with all manner of labor in the field: Whatever service they made them perform was with hard labor.[3]

In every generation it is one's duty to regard himself as though he personally had gone out of Egypt, as it says: You shall tell

(1) *Exodus* 12:27. (2) *Exodus* 12:39. (3) *Exodus* 1:14.

בְּכָל דּוֹר וָדוֹר — *In every generation*

The story of Egyptian bondage, attempted genocide, Jewish assimilation, and miraculous salvation is not one of past history alone. Everything that was in those days is in our time, as well. This is really the basic lesson of the Seder itself. We are talking about now — about pharaohs and dictators, haters and slave masters, millions of Jews being alienated from their tradition and roots. Everyone, therefore, relives the Pesach Exodus experience in every age and in every circumstance. All our oppressors are the same Pharaoh of old and all of our countries and places of persecution are the same Egypt

בַּעֲבוּר זֶה עָשָׂה יהוה לִי, בְּצֵאתִי מִמִּצְרָיִם.[1] לֹא אֶת אֲבוֹתֵינוּ בִּלְבָד גָּאַל הַקָּדוֹשׁ בָּרוּךְ הוּא, אֶלָּא אַף אוֹתָנוּ גָּאַל עִמָּהֶם. שֶׁנֶּאֱמַר, וְאוֹתָנוּ הוֹצִיא מִשָּׁם, לְמַעַן הָבִיא אֹתָנוּ לָתֶת לָנוּ אֶת הָאָרֶץ אֲשֶׁר נִשְׁבַּע לַאֲבוֹתֵינוּ.[2]

The matzos are covered and the cup is lifted and held until it is to be drunk. According to some customs, however, the cup is put down after the following paragraph, in which case the matzos should once more be uncovered.

לְפִיכָךְ אֲנַחְנוּ חַיָּבִים לְהוֹדוֹת, לְהַלֵּל, לְשַׁבֵּחַ, לְפָאֵר, לְרוֹמֵם, לְהַדֵּר, לְבָרֵךְ, לְעַלֵּה, וּלְקַלֵּס, לְמִי שֶׁעָשָׂה לַאֲבוֹתֵינוּ וְלָנוּ אֶת כָּל הַנִּסִּים הָאֵלּוּ, הוֹצִיאָנוּ מֵעַבְדוּת לְחֵרוּת, מִיָּגוֹן לְשִׂמְחָה, וּמֵאֵבֶל לְיוֹם טוֹב, וּמֵאֲפֵלָה לְאוֹר

---

of old. Jews nevertheless were free people within their souls and personalities even when physically in bondage in later exiles.

The Lord took us forth from Egypt to bring us to the Land of Israel, the land that He by oath promised to our forefathers. We also have to feel that the goal of Jews is the return to the Land of Israel, a goal that in our time is realizable in a fashion that has not been available to Jews for many many, centuries. Rabbi Nachman of Breslav is reputed to have said: "Every step that I take in life is meant to bring me closer to Jerusalem." We are all survivors, all having passed through the furnace of fire in one way or another over the difficult and terrible events of the past centuries. Thus we can all truly feel that we have left Egypt — "we were taken forth from there" — and that we too somehow are on the way to fulfill the Lord's promise to us — "in order to bring us and to give us the land that the Lord took an oath to our forefathers [to so do]."

לְפִיכָךְ אֲנַחְנוּ חַיָּבִים —
Therefore it is our duty

The cup of wine is raised while reciting this paragraph, as it is during the entire *Hallel* prayer, for this is a song of joy and thanksgiving and in Jewish tradition, all such moments of song, joy, and thanksgiving are accompanied by a cup of wine. There are nine expressions of praise of God in this paragraph, plus the usual word for praise of God, הַלְלוּיָהּ, thus constituting ten expressions of praise and thanksgiving to God. These ten expressions of praise parallel the ten types of praise that David used in the *Book of Psalms*, where they usually serve as the introductory word to individual psalms. The greatest form of praise of God is the word הַלְלוּיָהּ, for it embodies praise of God combined with His Name in one word.

The symbolism of the number ten in Jewish thought is obvious and especially so at the Pesach Seder where the ten plagues have been minutely discussed and explained. It may be that since a quorum for prayer in Jewish law is ten, the proverbial *minyan,* the quorum for necessary expressions of our praise of God is also ten. Just as in prayer quorums, a *minyan* of ten is equal to a *minyan* of thousands, so too in our praise of God, which is essentially unlimited and therefore unattainable by mere mortals, ten expressions

your son on that day: "It was because of this that HASHEM did for 'me' when I went out of Egypt."[1] It was not only our fathers whom the Holy One, Blessed is He, redeemed from slavery; we, too, were redeemed with them, as it says: He brought "us" out from there so that He might take us to the land which He had promised to our fathers.[2]

The matzos are covered and the cup is lifted and held until it is to be drunk. According to some customs, however, the cup is put down after the following paragraph, in which case the matzos should once more be uncovered.

Therefore it is our duty to thank, praise, pay tribute, glorify, exalt, honor, bless, extol, and acclaim the One Who performed all these miracles for our fathers and for us. He brought us forth from slavery to freedom, from grief to joy, from mourning to festivity, from darkness to great

(1) *Exodus* 13:8. (2) *Deuteronomy* 6:23.

---

of praise will suffice for the otherwise unlimited number of types of praise and thanksgiving that God truly deserves. Ten is therefore the bar that we need to cross and that number is within our ability to achieve. More expressions of praise will not really add anything to God and will only be futile words for us as well.

We were delivered from slavery to freedom, grief to joy, from mourning to holidays, from foggy darkness to see a great light, and from slavery to redemption. Each of these phrases represents a different form of salvation and comfort. Slavery to freedom is the physical release from bondage. But even a freed slave can be enslaved once more. In Jewish history, Pharaoh has had many successors in oppressing the Jews. The rabbis of the Talmud said that after the miracle of Purim, we were still the servants of Ahasverus, the Persian king. Ahasverus is a symbol of all of those who rule over Jews in foreign lands.

Grief to joy are the two sides of the same emotion of the spirit within us. Both grief and joy are eventually mitigated by time, though both leave a lasting impression on our subconscious psyche.

Mourning to festivity represents the halachic view that the advent of festivals cancels ritual forms of mourning. Great people are able to reprogram their feelings of sadness and loss in order to celebrate the festivals in true emotional happiness. But realistically, these are rare people. Most of us, while observing the *halachah* that forbids ritual mourning on the holidays, nevertheless carry a heavy feeling of sadness within us when we recall those who are no longer with us, even on the holidays. It was not accidental, therefore, that the custom of reciting *Yizkor* and reciting memorial prayers for the dead on the holidays was accepted and instituted in the Jewish world. It helps alleviate the ache in our hearts regarding those who are now missing from our holiday table. Thus, this deliverance from mourning to holidays is also only a partial one, with the advent of the holidays ironically often deepening the feeling of loss.

Darkness to great light requires adjustment of eyesight. Our pupils are not prepared for such

גָּדוֹל, וּמִשִּׁעְבּוּד לִגְאֻלָּה, וְנֹאמַר לְפָנָיו שִׁירָה חֲדָשָׁה, הַלְלוּיָהּ.

הַלְלוּיָהּ הַלְלוּ עַבְדֵי יהוה, הַלְלוּ אֶת שֵׁם יהוה. יְהִי שֵׁם יהוה מְבֹרָךְ, מֵעַתָּה וְעַד עוֹלָם. מִמִּזְרַח שֶׁמֶשׁ עַד מְבוֹאוֹ, מְהֻלָּל שֵׁם יהוה. רָם עַל כָּל גּוֹיִם יהוה, עַל הַשָּׁמַיִם כְּבוֹדוֹ. מִי כַּיהוה אֱלֹהֵינוּ, הַמַּגְבִּיהִי לָשָׁבֶת.

---

sudden change. The Jews who left Egypt found it difficult to adjust to their new free status. It required forty years to raise a new generation whose eyes would be able to adjust and function properly in the environment of the light of personal autonomy and physical freedom. So, although this deliverance was from darkness to light, it also contained a problematical element within it. It is the final statement of deliverance from slavery to redemption, and it remains both the immediate and permanent feature of the Exodus from Egypt.

The redemption described here is not only the physical one. As mentioned above, after all the Talmud wryly remarks that we are still the servants of Ahasverus, meaning that much of the Jewish world still lives under the domination of foreign governments and cultures. Rather we are speaking of a spiritual redemption, a freedom of heart and mind and soul that has characterized Israel ever since its leaving of Egypt. It is regarding this redemption of spirit and morale, of the achievement of inner worth and self-pride, that our true praise to God is extended. For that freedom of our inner self can never be taken from us and is not subject to the vagaries of time, place, and circumstance.

The commentators to the Haggadah saw in the use of these five carefully chosen and unique phrases of redemption — slavery to freedom, grief to joy, mourning to festivity, darkness to great light, and slavery to redemption — the symbolic references to the five exiles of the Jewish people: Egypt, Babylonia, Persia, Greece, and Rome (the present and by far the longest exile). Thus the final phrase of redemption, from servitude to redemption, refers to the final redemption of Israel, to messianic times, to the better world that all humanity hopes for. Pesach is not only a time to remember past greatness and miracles. It is just as much a commemoration of our hopes for our great future and our enlightened destiny. This is a theme repeated often in the Seder service. We are not only a people of our past. We are even more a people of our future and destiny.

שִׁירָה חֲדָשָׁה — *A new song*

The "new song" is really of ancient origin, since we are about to sing the chapters of *Hallel* from the *Book of Psalms / Tehillim*. Its origin is even older, since the Rabbis teach that the first two chapters, which we are about to recite, were originally sung by the Children of Israel at the Sea of Reeds, and King David incorporated them into *Tehillim* hundreds of years later. The old song of *Hallel* becomes a *new* song when it is recited by a new generation of Jews with youthful gusto and enthusiasm.

There is nothing so depressing and squelching the enthusiasm of the young by saying that what they find new and inspiring is really old hat and used up. I remember that as a 12-year-old, I made my debut as a public speaker at a large banquet in Chicago on behalf of the local

light, and from servitude to redemption. Let us, therefore, recite a new song before Him! Halleluyah!

Halleluyah! Praise, you servants of HASHEM, praise the Name of HASHEM. Blessed is the Name of HASHEM from now and forever. From the rising of the sun to its setting, HASHEM's Name is praised. High above all nations is HASHEM, above the heavens is His glory. Who is like HASHEM, our God,

---

Torah schools organization. I told a story in that speech, a story that I had only first heard the very day of the banquet itself and that I really liked. After the speech, an older person in the audience came over to me and said to me that the story that I told was an old one that he had heard before. I replied that to me it was a new story. I still remember the damper that the remarks of that man cast over me.

An old story, an old song, is a new story and a new song to the next generation, since the Seder is so oriented to the young generation coming to take its place in the chain of Jewish continuity. To them the *Hallel* of King David, millennia old though it is, is to the youngsters at our Seder table a new song, and it should be. The Torah itself exhorts us to consider its teachings and commandments as new and fresh. And if it is invigorating and vibrant to the young, then it has a renewed quality to the older generation as well, and we sing it with a renewed sense of joy and thanksgiving and appreciation.

שִׁירָה חֲדָשָׁה, *new song*, is in the feminine form. This alludes to the Jewish woman as the conduit of tradition, for Jewish continuity is molded in the Jewish home. King Solomon exhorts, "Do not forsake the teaching of your mother." Furthermore, the Rabbis teach that the Jews were redeemed from Egypt in the merit of the righteous Jewish women, so that the Exodus and its eternal message reverberates to this day, for throughout the generations, noble and courageous women have strengthened and preserved the Jewish spirit.

On the other hand, in the blessing following these two chapters from *Tehillim*, we pray for the coming of Mashiach when we will sing a different "new song." The song of Mashiach, however, is expressed in the masculine form, שִׁיר חָדָשׁ. We do not yet know the text of that song, but the thrust of all Jewish tradition is that the events of the final redemption of Israel will dwarf even the events and miracles that accompanied the Exodus from Egypt. Thus the old song will not do any longer, but the new masculine, strong, definitive song of Jewish world redemption will be sounded from millions of throats.

◆§ הַלֵּל / Hallel

Until the 15th century, many great scholars insisted that the usual blessing for the recitation of the *Hallel* should indeed be recited. The prevailing custom today is not to recite that blessing, because the Haggadah's blessing regarding the redemption of the Jews from Egypt — and thereby our personal redemption — suffices for the recitation of the *Hallel* as well. Another reason advanced is that since the recitation of the *Hallel* is interrupted by the eating of the matzah and the meal, we will not read *Hallel* as a complete unit, and therefore no specific *Hallel* blessing is required.

The *Hallel* itself states many important principles of Judaism. Its very words and methods of expressing praise of God define the Jewish attitude toward the Creator. It is a prayer of thanks-

הַמַּשְׁפִּילִי לִרְאוֹת, בַּשָּׁמַיִם וּבָאָרֶץ. מְקִימִי מֵעָפָר דָּל, מֵאַשְׁפֹּת יָרִים אֶבְיוֹן. לְהוֹשִׁיבִי עִם נְדִיבִים, עִם נְדִיבֵי עַמּוֹ. מוֹשִׁיבִי עֲקֶרֶת הַבַּיִת, אֵם הַבָּנִים שְׂמֵחָה, הַלְלוּיָהּ.[1]

בְּצֵאת יִשְׂרָאֵל מִמִּצְרָיִם, בֵּית יַעֲקֹב מֵעַם לֹעֵז. הָיְתָה יְהוּדָה לְקָדְשׁוֹ, יִשְׂרָאֵל מַמְשְׁלוֹתָיו. הַיָּם רָאָה וַיָּנֹס, הַיַּרְדֵּן יִסֹּב לְאָחוֹר. הֶהָרִים רָקְדוּ כְאֵילִים, גְּבָעוֹת כִּבְנֵי צֹאן. מַה לְּךָ הַיָּם כִּי תָנוּס, הַיַּרְדֵּן תִּסֹּב לְאָחוֹר. הֶהָרִים תִּרְקְדוּ כְאֵילִים, גְּבָעוֹת כִּבְנֵי צֹאן. מִלִּפְנֵי אָדוֹן חוּלִי אָרֶץ, מִלִּפְנֵי אֱלוֹהַ יַעֲקֹב. הַהֹפְכִי הַצּוּר אֲגַם מָיִם, חַלָּמִישׁ לְמַעְיְנוֹ מָיִם.[2]

---

giving for our having been freed from the yoke of paganism, for being granted the Torah, and for being chosen by God to serve Him and His purposes in the human world. *Hallel* begins, therefore, by identifying ourselves as the servants of the Lord . The true servants of the Lord have no foreign or human masters, even if they are physically under the rule of others. The true test of a Jew is whether he or she is prepared to fulfill the will of the Master. Jews always say to God that we are willing to serve You and in fact ask Divine aid in helping and allowing us to so serve. The ability to serve God exists in myriad ways every day of our lives. It goes without saying that observance of Torah and its rituals and commandments is the direct method of such service of God. However, improving one's character traits, being a better parent, spouse, teacher, employer, and employee also qualifies as serving God and His purposes. Thus, we all are the servants of God, and by appreciating this, come to the praise of the Lord.

One of the cardinal principles of Judaism is that God is interested in the details, the small things in our lives, and in the physical universe generally. Paganism preached that the gods were uninterested in human affairs and that humans had to seek their attention through various means of behavior, bribery, and intercession. Conversely, Judaism teaches that God, so to speak, "lowers" Himself to be concerned with the minutest details of human behavior. The wondrous complexity of God's universe is reflected not only in the vastness of seemingly endless space but in the exquisite formation of the tiniest of creatures. It is in this realization of God's "lowering" that man catches a fleeting glimpse of the Creator's workings. The Lord therefore makes the barren woman — Sarah, Rachel, Chanah, the woman of Shunam, in fact, the Jewish people as a whole — the eventual mother of civilization and progress in humanity by working the small details. In the science of medicine, we know that the difference between fertility and barrenness is very small and minute. In modern times, ecological studies have shown us how vast changes can be caused in the ecological balance of nature by small changes somewhere in the chain of creatures and vegetation. God, Who above all else, deals

Who is enthroned on high, yet lowers Himself to look upon the heaven and the earth. He raises the destitute from the dust; from the trash heaps He lifts the needy — to seat them with nobles, with nobles of His people. He transforms the barren wife into a glad mother of children. Halleluyah![1]

When Israel went forth from Egypt, Jacob's household from a people of alien tongue, Judah became His sanctuary, Israel His dominion. The sea saw and fled; the Jordan turned backward. The mountains skipped like rams, and the hills like young lambs. What ails you, O sea, that you flee? O Jordan, that you turn backward? O mountains, that you skip like rams? O hills, like young lambs? Before HASHEM's presence — tremble, O earth, before the presence of the God of Jacob, Who turns the rock into a pond of water, the flint into a flowing fountain.[2]

(1) *Psalms* 113. (2) *Psalms* 114.

---

with small to create great, is therefore the source and object of our praise for our miraculous continuity and blessed generations.

§ בְּצֵאת יִשְׂרָאֵל — *When Israel went forth*

The word "לֹעֵז" means *something foreign or alien*. It is used widely in rabbinic literature to indicate a language other than Hebrew. It is also somehow related to the Hebrew word "לַעַז," meaning *a malicious rumor* or *tale meant to discredit others*. Since such tales and rumors are foreign to Jewish moral standards and halachah, the connection between the words is not farfetched at all. The basic unity of Israel throughout the years of its dispersion was the knowledge of Hebrew. One can certainly not claim to be a learned Jew without a knowledge of Hebrew.

The rabbis teach that the Jews in Egypt did not forsake their mother tongue, Hebrew, and this was one of the causes that enabled them to be redeemed from Egypt. So, too, throughout the exiles of Israel, even when Jews created their own alternate languages such as Ladino and Yiddish, they still never forgot Hebrew. In our time, Torah works written in English, French, or other languages are meant to be educational aids in attaining Torah knowledge. They are not meant to indicate in any fashion that English, or French, or any other language can substitute for Hebrew in prayer, study or Jewish knowledge.

The revitalization of Hebrew as a living and spoken language in this past century has been one of the many wonders of Jewish rebirth generally and of the Jewish national state in the Land of Israel particularly. The Roman Catholic Church in the last century has been forced to give up on Latin, and classical Greek speech disappeared long ago. Just as the Jews are the only ancient people of the Classical Era to survive in the Western world till our time, only Hebrew, of all of the ancient classical languages, is in use today as a living, language spoken by millions of

According to all customs the cup is lifted
and the matzos covered during the recitation of this blessing.

בָּרוּךְ אַתָּה יהוה אֱלֹהֵינוּ מֶלֶךְ הָעוֹלָם, אֲשֶׁר גְּאָלָנוּ וְגָאַל אֶת אֲבוֹתֵינוּ מִמִּצְרַיִם, וְהִגִּיעָנוּ הַלַּיְלָה הַזֶּה לֶאֱכָל בּוֹ מַצָּה וּמָרוֹר. כֵּן יהוה אֱלֹהֵינוּ וֵאלֹהֵי אֲבוֹתֵינוּ, יַגִּיעֵנוּ לְמוֹעֲדִים וְלִרְגָלִים אֲחֵרִים הַבָּאִים לִקְרָאתֵנוּ לְשָׁלוֹם, שְׂמֵחִים בְּבִנְיַן עִירֶךָ וְשָׂשִׂים בַּעֲבוֹדָתֶךָ, וְנֹאכַל שָׁם

(On *Motzaei Shabbos* the phrase in brackets substitutes for the preceding phrase.)

מִן הַזְּבָחִים וּמִן הַפְּסָחִים [מִן הַפְּסָחִים וּמִן הַזְּבָחִים] אֲשֶׁר יַגִּיעַ דָּמָם עַל קִיר מִזְבַּחֲךָ לְרָצוֹן. וְנוֹדֶה לְךָ שִׁיר חָדָשׁ עַל גְּאֻלָּתֵנוּ וְעַל פְּדוּת נַפְשֵׁנוּ. בָּרוּךְ אַתָּה יהוה, גָּאַל יִשְׂרָאֵל.

בָּרוּךְ אַתָּה יהוה אֱלֹהֵינוּ מֶלֶךְ הָעוֹלָם, בּוֹרֵא פְּרִי הַגָּפֶן.

The second cup is drunk while leaning on the left side —
preferably the entire cup, but at least most of it.

---

people. That is certainly no small achievement. It would behoove all Jewish educational institutions to intensify the study of Hebrew language in their curriculums. It is after all the key to true Torah knowledge and, in a great sense, to Jewish unity. It would undoubtedly serve as a strengthening bond between Jews the world over and especially between the Jews of the Diaspora and the Jews now living in the Land of Israel.

I have a story that I tell in some of my lectures about an incident concerning the Hebrew language that occurred a number of decades ago. I was scheduled to speak in Atlanta one evening and I had a flight on *TWA airlines (remember them?) from J.F.K. That day TWA announced that it was seeking Chapter 11 bankruptcy protection. When I arrived at the TWA terminal at J.F.K. two hours before departure, I was distressed to see that there was a very long line waiting to be processed by a lone harried clerk. I took my place in line and after waiting for more than one-and-a-half hours I was really certain that I would miss my flight.

When I finally approached the ticket counter, the clerk told me that the fearsome computer had somehow wiped out all of the previous reservations and that there was now no room for me on the flight. I explained how necessary it was for me to be on that flight — after all, the entire city of Atlanta was eagerly awaiting my arrival — and in an act of unparalleled kindness the clerk gave me a seat in first class!

I was the last person on the plane and when I entered the cabin, the flight attendant breathlessly whispered to me that I would be sitting next to a vice president of TWA. The vice president was already busily at work trying to save his airline, with his spreadsheets occupying both seats in the row when I arrived. He was visibly annoyed that he had to make room for me, but, being a pulpit rabbi of many years experience, I no longer took umbrage at people being

According to all customs the cup is lifted and the matzos covered during the recitation of this blessing.

Blessed are You, HASHEM, our God, King of the universe, Who redeemed us and redeemed our ancestors from Egypt and enabled us to reach this night that we may eat on it matzah and *maror*. So, HASHEM, our God and God of our fathers, bring us also to future holidays and festivals in peace, gladdened in the building of Your city and joyful at Your service. There we shall eat

(On *Motzaei Shabbos* the phrase in brackets substitutes for the preceding phrase.)

of the offerings and *pesach* sacrifices [of the *pesach* sacrifices and offerings] whose blood will reach the wall of Your Altar for gracious acceptance. We shall then sing a new song of praise to You for our redemption and for the liberation of our souls. Blessed are You, HASHEM, Who has redeemed Israel.

Blessed are You, HASHEM, our God, King of the universe, Who creates the fruit of the vine.

The second cup is drunk while leaning on the left side — preferably the entire cup, but at least most of it.

---

annoyed by my presence or words. As the plane took off, I took out a Hebrew Bible to peruse.

After a short while, the vice president leaned over and asked me what was that language that I was reading. When I told him it was Hebrew, he snorted that he could not believe that there were still people in this modern world who read and spoke Hebrew. I gently reminded him that his airline was at that time flying regularly to a country where millions of people spoke and read Hebrew. Now completely annoyed with me, he said: "Well, it is obvious that you and I have nothing in common." I softly told him that we had a great deal in common. He acidly said: "What do we have in common?" I answered so sweetly: "Neither of us paid for our first class seats on this plane." Well, *TWA is now grounded and gone forever, but there are still millions of us who are reading and speaking and studying in Hebrew.

בָּרוּךְ . . . אֲשֶׁר גְּאָלָנוּ —
Blessed . . . Who redeemed us

This blessing marks the conclusion of the first section of the Haggadah and of the Seder service itself. The portion of *Hallel* that is recited before this blessing is known as *Hallel Hamitzri,* the *Hallel* stated in praise of our deliverance from Egypt. The second part of the *Hallel* refers to the coming future redemption of Israel and is thus placed in the Haggadah after the appearance of the prophet Elijah (the eternal symbol of Jewish redemption and hope) at our Seder service and after all of the rituals regarding the remembrance of the Pesach service — the past redemption — have been observed and completed. The blessing itself contains both elements of

רָחְצָה

The hands are washed for matzah and the following blessing is recited.
It is preferable to bring water and a basin to the head of the household at the Seder table.

בָּרוּךְ אַתָּה יהוה אֱלֹהֵינוּ מֶלֶךְ הָעוֹלָם, אֲשֶׁר קִדְּשָׁנוּ בְּמִצְוֹתָיו, וְצִוָּנוּ עַל נְטִילַת יָדָיִם.

מוֹצִיא / מַצָּה

The following two blessings are recited over matzah; the first is recited over matzah as food, and the second for the special mitzvah of eating matzah on the night of Pesach. [The latter blessing is to be made with the intention that it also apply to the "sandwich" and the *afikoman*.] The head of the household raises all the matzos on the Seder plate and recites the following blessing:

בָּרוּךְ אַתָּה יהוה אֱלֹהֵינוּ מֶלֶךְ הָעוֹלָם, הַמּוֹצִיא לֶחֶם מִן הָאָרֶץ.

redemption — the past redemption from Egyptian slavery and the future redemption from all of the woes of exile and the Diaspora. We will yet again celebrate Pesach in Jerusalem in the Temple and with the service of the *pesach* sacrifice. The Lord Who redeemed us from Egypt will redeem us once more and we therefore now bless His Name for the past redemption and for the forthcoming one as well.

◆§ רָחְצָה / Rachtzah

Before eating bread — in this case, matzah — we wash our hands. This is not primarily a matter of cleanliness, though Judaism is very big on cleanliness, but a matter of spiritual purity. As I have already mentioned, eating in Judaism is seen as an act of holiness and dedication and not as matter of necessity, pure enjoyment, or gluttony. Washing one's hands in preparation of eating signifies that the meal to be eaten is to be sanctified, and not merely consumed. It conditions us to look at food and eating with an attitude of devotion and service to God, Who is the Provider for all living things.

This washing for the matzah requires a blessing, whereas the previous washing for *karpas* did not. Though there are clear halachic reasons for this difference, I think that a value is being taught here as well. At the beginning of the Seder service, when the *karpas* section of the Haggadah is being observed, the story of our deliverance from Egypt has not yet been told. Without the story of the Exodus being known and appreciated, it is harder to understand the holiness and spiritual heights of Judaism's ritual. Therefore, the washing of the hands is just that alone — the washing of the hands. But now, when we have all heard the wondrous story and recounted all of the miracles that accompanied that Exodus and we are aware of our debt to our Creator for what He did for us, then every act of ours, even washing our hands before eating, is an act of service to God — and that requires a blessing.

◆§ מוֹצִיא מַצָּה / Motzi — Matzah

The eating part of the Seder service commences after the drinking of the second cup of

RACHTZAH

The hands are washed for matzah and the following blessing is recited. It is preferable to bring water and a basin to the head of the household at the Seder table.

Blessed are You, HASHEM, our God, King of the universe, Who has sanctified us with His commandments, and has commanded us concerning the washing of the hands.

MOTZI / MATZAH

The following two blessings are recited over matzah; the first is recited over matzah as food, and the second for the special mitzvah of eating matzah on the night of Pesach. [The latter blessing is to be made with the intention that it also apply to the "sandwich" and the *afikoman*.] The head of the household raises all the matzos on the Seder plate and recites the following blessing:

Blessed are You, HASHEM, our God, King of the universe, Who brings forth bread from the earth.

wine and the washing of our hands. Before the matzah is eaten, two blessings are recited. One is the customary *hamotzi* blessing before bread, about drawing forth bread from the earth. Rabbi Zadok HaKohen states that this blessing signifies our ability not only to extract grain from the earth and convert it into bread but it symbolically symbolizes a human's ability to sanctify material things and to raise them, so to speak, from their inherent "earthiness" into a state of holiness and spirit. The Jewish means to do this is through all of the rituals connected with eating — washing hands before eating, making bless-ings before eating, consuming food carefully and respectfully, reciting grace after eating, and expressing thanks to man and God for the food given to us. Judaism is inherently anti-fast food and anti-junk food. The rituals regarding eating preclude treating food frivolously or taking it for granted.

The experience of Israel in eating manna from Heaven for forty years in the desert of Sinai conditioned the Jewish people to look at food as something more than mundane and ordinary. The blessings and rituals regarding the eating of food remind us that we are, so to speak, still eating manna from Heaven and that food should be treated accordingly with respect, care, and appreciation.

Once we have that appreciation of food that the *hamotzi* blessing represents, we can then proceed to the blessing over the mitzvah of matzah itself. I have already written much about matzah and *maror* previously and I will not repeat myself here. However, I do wish to make a comment about the amount of matzah and *maror* that is to be consumed in order to fulfill the mitzvah appropriately.

In the 18th century, Rabbi Yechezkel Landau, the rabbi of Prague, claimed that the size of an egg — one of the basic halachic measures of size and volume regarding food — differed markedly in his times from its size in Mishnaic times. Because of this, he proposed practically doubling the size or volume necessary to fulfill the halachic requirements of food in regard to the obligations of mitzvos, such as matzah and *maror*. Although his opinion was not universally adopted at first, it has gained adherents over the centuries. In the past century, Rabbi Abraham

The bottom matzah is put down and the following blessing is recited while the top (whole) matzah and the middle (broken) piece are still raised.

בָּרוּךְ אַתָּה יהוה אֱלֹהֵינוּ מֶלֶךְ הָעוֹלָם, אֲשֶׁר קִדְּשָׁנוּ בְּמִצְוֹתָיו, וְצִוָּנוּ עַל אֲכִילַת מַצָּה.

Each participant is required to eat an amount of matzah equal in volume to an egg. Since it is usually impossible to provide a sufficient amount of matzah from the two matzos for all members of the household, the other matzos should be available at the head of the table from which to complete the required amounts. However, each participant should receive a piece from each of the top two matzos. The matzos are to be eaten while reclining on the left side and without delay; they need not be dipped in salt.

מָרוֹר

The head of the household takes a half-egg-volume of *maror,* dips it into *charoses,* and gives each participant a like amount. The following blessing is recited with the intention that it also apply to the *maror* of the "sandwich." The *maror* is eaten without reclining, and without delay.

בָּרוּךְ אַתָּה יהוה אֱלֹהֵינוּ מֶלֶךְ הָעוֹלָם, אֲשֶׁר קִדְּשָׁנוּ בְּמִצְוֹתָיו, וְצִוָּנוּ עַל אֲכִילַת מָרוֹר.

Yeshayu Karelitz (the *Chazon Ish,* who passed away in the early 1950's) formalized Rabbi Landau's opinion as being correct, and because of this it has become the mainstream ruling in much of current halachic literature. Every family should follow its custom regarding these measures of size and volume. Suffice it to say that Jews were and are very exacting regarding the matzah and *maror* that is eaten at the Seder — both as to its preparation and source and as to the size and measure required for fulfilling the mitzvah properly.

In the 19th century, the matzah-producing machine was invented. It immediately caused a furor in the rabbinic world as to whether it may be used to produce Pesach matzos. There were many rabbinic decisors who opposed the newfangled machine, and for many different reasons. There were those who opposed it because of economic reasons — the machine would displace the workers who produced matzos previously by hand. In Eastern Europe, many of these workers were widows whose annual livelihood depended on this pre-Pesach employment. Other rabbinic authorities opposed the use of the machine for baking matzos on the grounds that the necessary element of *lishmah* — having express intent to bake the dough for the purpose of fulfilling the mitzvah of matzah — was inherently lacking with a machine. Still others were convinced that the machine could not control the problem of bits of the dough lingering in the machine long enough to rise and become *chametz,* and then mix with the matzah. Yet, there were many great rabbis who approved of the machine and pointed out its economic and even halachic benefits.

The original matzah machine of 1854 Austro-Hungary has been perfected over the last one hundred-fifty years so that no real question of *chametz* remains. Blowers, scrapers, Teflon-coated belts, etc. have all been integrated into

The bottom matzah is put down and the following blessing is recited while the top (whole) matzah and the middle (broken) piece are still raised.

Blessed are You, HASHEM, our God, King of the universe, Who has sanctified us with His commandments, and has commanded us concerning the eating of the matzah.

Each participant is required to eat an amount of matzah equal in volume to an egg. Since it is usually impossible to provide a sufficient amount of matzah from the two matzos for all members of the household, the other matzos should be available at the head of the table from which to complete the required amounts. However, each participant should receive a piece from each of the top two matzos. The matzos are to be eaten while reclining on the left side and without delay; they need not be dipped in salt.

MAROR

The head of the household takes a half-egg-volume of *maror,* dips it into *charoses,* and gives each participant a like amount. The following blessing is recited with the intention that it also apply to the *maror* of the "sandwich." The *maror* is eaten without reclining, and without delay.

Blessed are You, HASHEM, our God, King of the universe, Who has sanctified us with His commandments, and has commanded us concerning the eating of *maror.*

---

the machine, removing the possibility of bits of dough finding their way back into the production process. We have become accustomed and reconciled to the fact that machines must perforce replace manual labor and that temporary dislocation of employees is always present whenever any type of new technology is introduced. (Whatever happened to the carbon paper, mimeograph and ditto machines, seat covers for automobiles, typewriters, etc. of my youth?) And many rabbinic authorities today maintain that the *lishmah* requirement is fulfilled by the *mashgiach*/worker (rabbinic supervisor) who, before he turns on the machine, proclaims that the entire machine-driven matzah-production process is intended to produce matzos solely for the fulfillment of the *mitzvah.* It is also true that the machine-made matzos are more uniform, better baked, have less chance of being puffed up by air or bent and folded over, and that the machine does not get tired at the end of the day and work sloppily, as can certainly happen with us humans, no matter how well intentioned we may be. Thus, machine matzos are now almost the norm in much of the Jewish world, though many people still adhere rigorously to the exclusive use of hand-produced matzos for Pesach. The custom in my family is to use hand-produced matzah for the Seder (for after all, our ancestors when they left Egypt undoubtedly did not eat machine-made matzos!) while machine-made matzah as well is used for the other meals of the holiday.

◆§ מָרוֹר / Maror

Eastern European Jews traditionally used horseradish for *maror.* However, over the last century, although horseradish still appears symbolically on the Seder *ka'arah* plate, romaine lettuce, which is much easier to digest, is used for *maror.* Yemenite Jews use dandelion roots

כּוֹרֵךְ

The bottom (thus far unbroken) matzah is now taken. From it, with the addition of other matzos, each participant receives a half-egg-volume of matzah with an equal-volume portion of *maror* (dipped into *charoses,* which is shaken off). The following paragraph is recited and the "sandwich" is eaten while reclining.

זֵכֶר לְמִקְדָּשׁ כְּהִלֵּל. כֵּן עָשָׂה הִלֵּל בִּזְמַן שֶׁבֵּית הַמִּקְדָּשׁ הָיָה קַיָּם. הָיָה כּוֹרֵךְ [פֶּסַח] מַצָּה וּמָרוֹר וְאוֹכֵל בְּיַחַד. לְקַיֵּם מַה שֶּׁנֶּאֱמַר, עַל מַצּוֹת וּמְרֹרִים יֹאכְלֻהוּ.[1]

---

for *maror*, and other types of bitter herbs as well are used for *maror* by various communities the world over. The *maror* is dipped into the *charoses*, which removes some of the sting of its bitterness and makes the *maror* more palatable. I notice that at our family Seder the young usually eat *charoses* with some *maror*, instead of *maror* with some *charoses.*

Whatever the proper food may be, our historical experiences of the 20th century contribute mightily to our memory of the bitter suffering of the Egyptian exile. *Maror* is not only a vegetable; it is a memory as well. The ability of the Jews to eat *maror*, so to speak, and even recite a blessing over its consumption — all as part of our continuing national experience — and nevertheless to continue to build and create and prosper is one of the miracles of our national character.

כּוֹרֵךְ / Koreich

The matzah-maror-*charoses* sandwich attributed to the great Hillel (first-century B.C.E.) in Second Temple times also included meat from the *pesach* sacrifice. Since the *pesach* sacrifice cannot be brought because the Temple has not yet been rebuilt, our sandwich is much more bland than the ones of our ancestors in Jerusalem long ago. I think that the sandwich of Hillel sums up the basic difficulties of human living. Matzah is representative of the pressures of time and circumstance that all of us face daily. We seem to never have enough time to allow 'the bread to rise" properly in our lives. Especially in our modern world, the pressures of financial and social accomplishment, of the workplace and of the society generally, are immense.

We want more time for study, contemplation, even for relaxation and especially for our children and grandchildren. But the day is always too short. Life is really the skill of time management. Matzah teaches us that truth.

No human life passes without sadness, disappointment, loss, and tragedy. *Maror* is an unavoidable part of living. It too must be digested with our time-management skills. And sacrifice is inherent in any sense of accomplishment, in the achievement of anything worthwhile and lasting in our lives. "According to the effort and pain and sacrifice is the reward," is the dictum of the rabbis in *Pirkei Avos*. Children, marriage, study, career, nobility of behavior, all require constant sacrifice of personal wants and desires. Hillel, who in his own personal life reflected all of these human experiences, rolled them all into one with his famous sandwich. The taste of the meat of freedom and accomplishment,

KOREICH

The bottom (thus far unbroken) matzah is now taken. From it, with the addition of other matzos, each participant receives a half-egg-volume of matzah with an equal-volume portion of *maror* (dipped into *charoses*, which is shaken off). The following paragraph is recited and the "sandwich" is eaten while reclining.

In remembrance of the Temple we do as Hillel did in Temple times: He would combine (the *pesach* offering,) matzah and *maror* in a sandwich and eat them together, to fulfill what it says: They shall eat it with matzos and bitter herbs.[1]

(1) *Numbers* 9:11.

which is the meat of the *pesach* sacrifice — עַל מַצּוֹת וּמְרוֹרִים יֹאכְלֻהוּ — has to be eaten together with the pressures of time and circumstances in life, with the bitterness of loss and sadness and frustration and with the sacrifices that are inherent in any human achievement. This sandwich of Hillel is the philosophy of realistic and healthy living.

The sandwich is also זֵכֶר לְמִקְדָּשׁ — a remembrance of the Temple and its service. Over the millennia, the Jewish people never forgot Jerusalem or its Temple. In every prayer, the Temple was remembered and revered. Sometimes the remembrances were in imitation of the Temple service, such as Hillel's sandwich, and sometimes the remembrances were in purposely not imitating the Temple such as not erecting a seven-branched metal candelabra in a synagogue. But there were always remembrances of the Temple baked into the Jewish ritual, customs, and psyche. The longing to return to *Eretz Yisrael* was based on this omnipresent attitude of reverence toward the Temple, Jerusalem, and the Land. The genius of Judaism in transmitting ideas, values, and historical remembrance is represented in our observance of Hillel's sandwich at the Seder service.

Without ritual and observance, the values, ideas, and spirit of Judaism eventually fade and are never transmitted to later generations, no matter how good the intentions and lofty the ideals of those who wish to preserve a Judaism without Torah and mitzvos. This has proven to be an unfailing rule of Jewish history.

Justice Louis D. Brandeis, the first Jew to serve on the United States Supreme Court, had an uncle, Louis Dembitz, in Louisville, Kentucky, whom he loved greatly. Dembitz, an observant and knowledgeable Jew, had no children, and Brandeis changed his middle name from David to Dembitz in honor of his uncle. Brandeis wrote a letter to one of his friends regarding a Shabbos that he spent at the home of his Sabbath-observing uncle. He described the candles, the table set in gleaming white cloth, the delicious food, the serious but pleasant conversations at the table and the rest of the day, the serenity and peace that reigned in the home, and the blessed detachment from all worldly affairs. He ended the letter by saying: "How I long for such a serene Sabbath day, but without the restrictions."

The stark truth, however, is that without the restrictions, the serene Sabbath day can never be achieved. Without loyalty to Torah and an attitude of observance of mitzvot, there can be no true guarantee of Jewish survival whether in an individual family or regarding the Jewish people as a whole.

שֻׁלְחָן עוֹרֵךְ

The meal should be eaten in a combination of joy and solemnity, for the meal, too, is a part of the Seder service. While it is desirable that *zemiros* and discussion of the laws and events of Pesach be part of the meal, extraneous conversation should be avoided. It should be remembered that the *afikoman* must be eaten while there is still some appetite for it. In fact, if one is so sated that he must literally force himself to eat it, he is not credited with the performance of the mitzvah of *afikoman*. Therefore, it is unwise to eat more than a moderate amount during the meal.

◆§ שֻׁלְחָן עוֹרֵךְ / Shulchan Oreich

The Seder meal is always the deluxe repast of the Jewish year, topping even those of Purim and the other holidays. Even though, as the halachah requires, we leave room for the *afikoman* at the conclusion of the meal, no meal in our family is eaten with more gusto, appetite, and relish than the Seder meal. Two strong customs have proven to be both protective of Pesach, but somewhat divisive as between Jews. Beginning in the Geonic and early Middle Ages periods, Ashkenazic Jews took upon themselves the prohibition not to use rice and legumes, known as *kitniyos*, on Pesach. This was based upon the fact that in those times bread was manufactured from those sources and people would confuse that non-*chametz* bread with forbidden bread produced from grain. Another reason was that many times bits of these five grains that can become *chametz* were found to be mixed in sacks of rice and legumes.

This custom of not eating *kitniyos* was not accepted as binding in the Sephardic world, though some Sephardic communities refrain from eating rice on Pesach while nevertheless eating legumes. Only in serious years of famine did Ashkenazic rabbis consider allowing the consumption of *kitniyos* on Pesach. Over the past century, the ban on *kitniyos* has been extended to include even secondary products of *kitniyos* such as corn syrup, though there is much rabbinic opinion that the secondary products of *kitniyos* were never included in the original custom or ban.

The other custom deals with what was called in Yiddish *gebrokts* — foods made with matzah meal or matzos that are fried, baked, or dipped in any type of liquid. Here the fear is that if the matzah is not thoroughly baked through inside, when a bit of "raw" matzah comes into contact with liquid it will rise and perhaps become *chametz*. This custom of not eating *gebrokts* is widespread among chassidic groups and Jews of Polish, Ukrainian, and Hungarian descent. Jews who descend from Lithuanian, Russian, German, and Sephardic families did not adopt this custom. We Lithuanian Jews thus enjoy *kneidlach* (matzah balls in the chicken soup — heaven on earth) to our stomach's content. We also dip matzah in the soup, eat matzah *brei* (matzah fried with eggs or onions), put *kneidlach* in our Pesach Shabbos *cholent*, consume *gefilte* fish made with matzah meal, as well as eat cakes and pastries made with matzah meal. On the eighth day of Pesach in the Diaspora, even the non-*gebrokts* Jews allow themselves the luxury of eating *gebrokts*, thereby illustrating that it is only a matter of custom and not halachah.

SHULCHAN OREICH

The meal should be eaten in a combination of joy and solemnity, for the meal, too, is a part of the Seder service. While it is desirable that *zemiros* and discussion of the laws and events of Pesach be part of the meal, extraneous conversation should be avoided. It should be remembered that the *afikoman* must be eaten while there is still some appetite for it. In fact, if one is so sated that he must literally force himself to eat it, he is not credited with the performance of the mitzvah of *afikoman*. Therefore, it is unwise to eat more than a moderate amount during the meal.

צָפוּן

From the *afikoman* matzah (and from additional matzos to make up the required amount) a half-egg-volume portion — according to some, a full-egg-volume portion — is given to each participant. It should be eaten before midnight, while reclining, without delay, and uninterruptedly. Nothing may be eaten or drunk after the *afikoman* (with the exception of water and the like) except for the last two Seder cups of wine.

בָּרֵךְ

The third cup is poured and *Bircas Hamazon* (Grace After Meals) is recited. According to some customs, the Cup of Elijah is poured at this point.

שִׁיר הַמַּעֲלוֹת, בְּשׁוּב יהוה אֶת שִׁיבַת צִיּוֹן, הָיִינוּ כְּחֹלְמִים. אָז יִמָּלֵא שְׂחוֹק פִּינוּ וּלְשׁוֹנֵנוּ רִנָּה, אָז יֹאמְרוּ בַגּוֹיִם, הִגְדִּיל יהוה לַעֲשׂוֹת עִם אֵלֶּה. הִגְדִּיל יהוה

צָפוּן / Tzafun

The *afikoman* now makes its reappearance at the Seder table, many times having to be ransomed from gleeful little hands. I have already discussed the idea of the *afikoman,* but I now wish to add the following thought: The *afikoman* in Temple times was the meat of the *pesach* sacrifice itself, while in our times it is the piece that was broken from the whole matzah during the ceremony of *yachatz,* and hidden away till now. The Rabbis declared that this should be eaten last, at the conclusion of the Seder meal itself, so that its "taste" would remain with us. We are bidden to eat this *afikoman* while we are still satiated with the food of the Seder meal that has already filled us. Thus, we do not eat it out of hunger, but rather out of holy duty and memory. The *afikoman* fulfills a spiritual need for our soul and not a physical need for our stomachs. No matter how much food we consume at any given meal, we will most assuredly be hungry again hours later. However, spiritual food, Godly service, and traditional and family memory linger on throughout our entire lifetime. The *afikoman* food, like all spiritual qualities, knows no limits of time and place. Its "taste" remains with us always. Its memories allow us to survive the dark nights that are unavoidable in life.

I had a friend who was a Holocaust survivor. Before World War II, he was a wealthy man with a wife and family. In 1936 he traveled to the Land of Israel for a visit. While there, on impulse, he bought an apartment in Jerusalem. Since he did not really intend to actually live there in the foreseeable future, the Jerusalem apartment was far below the living standards of his more luxurious and comfortable home in Hungary. When the Germans took over Hungary in 1944, he and his family were deported to Auschwitz. His wife and children were murdered there, but he managed to wangle his way into a work battalion and miraculously survived ten horrible months until the

TZAFUN

From the *afikoman* matzah (and from additional matzos to make up the required amount) a half-egg§volume portion — according to some, a full-egg-volume portion — is given to each participant. It should be eaten before midnight, while reclining, without delay, and uninterruptedly. Nothing may be eaten or drunk after the *afikoman* (with the exception of water and the like) except for the last two Seder cups of wine.

BARECH

The third cup is poured and *Bircas Hamazon* (Grace After Meals) is recited. According to some customs, the Cup of EliJah is poured at this point.

A song of Ascents. When HASHEM brings back the exiles to Zion, we will have been like dreamers. Then our mouth will be filled with laughter, and our tongue with glad song. Then will it be said among the nations: HASHEM has done great things for these, HASHEM has

---

end of the war. He told me that he was able to survive because every night as he lay on his wooden plank, often with a newly expired corpse next to him, in his mind he furnished and rearranged his Jerusalem apartment. The memory of that Jerusalem apartment was his *afikoman,* whose "taste" would not desert him even in his darkest hour. Perhaps this is another reason for the custom of allowing the "stealing" of the *afikoman* and then ransoming it; it impresses upon us the importance that each of us must have an *afikoman* in our lives to hold on to, no matter the cost and bother of such an enterprise. So even though we are filled with the delicious food of the Seder meal, we should eat our *afikoman* with relish and enthusiasm. Its "taste" is meant to last us our entire lifetime.

בָּרֵךְ / Barech

The blessings after the meal are preceded by the recitation or (usually) the singing of Psalm 126 — *Shir Hama'alos*. This psalm states that at the moment of our ultimate deliverance from exile and diaspora we will be likened to dreamers. A dreamer is always an optimist who does not allow the difficulties of practicality to interfere with the hoped-for realization of his dream. Yet the Rabbis have taught us that no dream is ever fully fulfilled. "Just as there cannot be pure grain without some chaff mixed therein, so, too, there is no dream that does not contain unrealistic details." Jacob and Joseph, the prime dreamers in Jewish life, saw their dreams realized, but the exact details of reality differed from the hoped-for dream. So, too, when we deal with the eventual redemption of Zion and the advent of the messianic era, the goals of our dreams of freedom, redemption, greatness, and spiritual serenity will certainly be realized, but we cannot be certain as to the details of the process itself. What is certain is that the tears of sadness will finally be behind us and that now the songs of joy will fill our throats and lips.

לַעֲשׂוֹת עִמָּנוּ, הָיִינוּ שְׂמֵחִים. שׁוּבָה יהוה אֶת שְׁבִיתֵנוּ,
כַּאֲפִיקִים בַּנֶּגֶב. הַזֹּרְעִים בְּדִמְעָה בְּרִנָּה יִקְצֹרוּ. הָלוֹךְ
יֵלֵךְ וּבָכֹה נֹשֵׂא מֶשֶׁךְ הַזָּרַע, בֹּא יָבֹא בְרִנָּה, נֹשֵׂא
אֲלֻמֹּתָיו.[1]

תְּהִלַּת יהוה יְדַבֶּר פִּי וִיבָרֵךְ כָּל בָּשָׂר שֵׁם קָדְשׁוֹ לְעוֹלָם
וָעֶד.[2] וַאֲנַחְנוּ נְבָרֵךְ יָהּ מֵעַתָּה וְעַד עוֹלָם
הַלְלוּיָהּ.[3] הוֹדוּ לַיהוה כִּי טוֹב כִּי לְעוֹלָם חַסְדּוֹ.[4] מִי
יְמַלֵּל גְּבוּרוֹת יהוה יַשְׁמִיעַ כָּל תְּהִלָּתוֹ.[5]

If three or more males, aged thirteen or older, participated in the meal, the leader is required to formally invite the others to join him in the recitation of Grace After Meals. Following is the *zimun*, or formal invitation.

The leader begins:

רַבּוֹתַי נְבָרֵךְ.

The group responds:

יְהִי שֵׁם יהוה מְבֹרָךְ מֵעַתָּה וְעַד עוֹלָם.[6]

The leader continues:

יְהִי שֵׁם יהוה מְבֹרָךְ מֵעַתָּה וְעַד עוֹלָם.[6]

If ten men join in the *zimun*, the words [in brackets] are included.

בִּרְשׁוּת מָרָנָן וְרַבָּנָן וְרַבּוֹתַי,
נְבָרֵךְ [אֱלֹהֵינוּ] שֶׁאָכַלְנוּ מִשֶּׁלּוֹ.

The group responds:

בָּרוּךְ [אֱלֹהֵינוּ] שֶׁאָכַלְנוּ מִשֶּׁלּוֹ וּבְטוּבוֹ חָיִינוּ.

The leader continues:

בָּרוּךְ [אֱלֹהֵינוּ] שֶׁאָכַלְנוּ מִשֶּׁלּוֹ וּבְטוּבוֹ חָיִינוּ.

The psalm also teaches that at the time of the redemption we will all be "happy." In Jewish tradition the definition of "happy" is that one is satisfied with what one has and is not consumed with jealousy and envy of others. One of the famous descriptions of happiness in the Torah is that each person will dwell in peace "under *his* vine and under *his* fig tree." Appreciating what one has and not chasing the mechanical rabbit of what one *could* have or what *others*

done great things for us, and we rejoiced. Restore our captives, HASHEM, like streams in the dry land. Those who sow in tears shall reap in joy. Though the farmer bears the measure of seed to the field in tears, he shall come home with joy, bearing his sheaves.[1]

May my mouth declare the praise of HASHEM and may all flesh bless His Holy Name forever.[2] We will bless HASHEM from this time and forever. Halleluyah![3] Give thanks to God for He is good, His kindness endures forever.[4] Who can express the mighty acts of HASHEM? Who can declare all His praise?[5]

If three or more males, aged thirteen or older, participated in the meal, the leader is required to formally invite the others to join him in the recitation of Grace After Meals. Following is the *zimun*, or formal invitation.

The leader begins:

Gentlemen, let us bless.

The group responds:

Blessed is the Name of HASHEM
from this moment and forever![6]

The leader continues:

Blessed is the Name of HASHEM
from this moment and forever![6]

If ten men join in the *zimun*, the words [in brackets] are included.

With the permission of the distinguished people present, let us bless [our God] for we have eaten from what is His.

The group responds:

Blessed is He [our God] of Whose we have eaten
and through Whose goodness we live.

The leader continues:

Blessed is He [our God] of Whose we have eaten
and through Whose goodness we live.

(1) *Psalms* 126. (2) *Psalms* 145:21. (3) *Psalms* 115:18.
(4) *Psalms* 118:1 (5) *Psalms* 106:2. (6) *Psalms* 113:2.

The following line is recited if ten men join in the *zimun*.

בָּרוּךְ הוּא וּבָרוּךְ שְׁמוֹ.

בָּרוּךְ אַתָּה יהוה אֱלֹהֵינוּ מֶלֶךְ הָעוֹלָם, הַזָּן אֶת הָעוֹלָם כֻּלּוֹ, בְּטוּבוֹ, בְּחֵן בְּחֶסֶד וּבְרַחֲמִים, הוּא נֹתֵן לֶחֶם לְכָל בָּשָׂר, כִּי לְעוֹלָם חַסְדּוֹ.[1] וּבְטוּבוֹ הַגָּדוֹל, תָּמִיד לֹא חָסַר לָנוּ, וְאַל יֶחְסַר לָנוּ מָזוֹן לְעוֹלָם וָעֶד. בַּעֲבוּר שְׁמוֹ הַגָּדוֹל, כִּי הוּא אֵל זָן וּמְפַרְנֵס לַכֹּל, וּמֵטִיב לַכֹּל, וּמֵכִין מָזוֹן לְכָל בְּרִיּוֹתָיו אֲשֶׁר בָּרָא. בָּרוּךְ אַתָּה יהוה, הַזָּן אֶת הַכֹּל.

נוֹדֶה לְּךָ יהוה אֱלֹהֵינוּ, עַל שֶׁהִנְחַלְתָּ לַאֲבוֹתֵינוּ אֶרֶץ חֶמְדָּה טוֹבָה וּרְחָבָה. וְעַל שֶׁהוֹצֵאתָנוּ יהוה אֱלֹהֵינוּ מֵאֶרֶץ מִצְרַיִם, וּפְדִיתָנוּ מִבֵּית עֲבָדִים, וְעַל בְּרִיתְךָ שֶׁחָתַמְתָּ בִּבְשָׂרֵנוּ, וְעַל תּוֹרָתְךָ שֶׁלִּמַּדְתָּנוּ, וְעַל חֻקֶּיךָ שֶׁהוֹדַעְתָּנוּ, וְעַל חַיִּים חֵן וָחֶסֶד שֶׁחוֹנַנְתָּנוּ, וְעַל אֲכִילַת מָזוֹן שָׁאַתָּה זָן וּמְפַרְנֵס אוֹתָנוּ תָּמִיד, בְּכָל יוֹם וּבְכָל עֵת וּבְכָל שָׁעָה.

---

may have is the fundamental key to personal happiness and spiritual serenity. The forthcoming redemption of Zion can bring us no greater sense of happiness than this warm satisfaction in what one already has — family, wealth, and life itself.

This idea is also expressed at the conclusion of the blessings after the meal when we recite, "While lions may go hungry, those who seek God do not feel deprived of anything good." This naturally refers to an attitude rather than to actual wealth, for many a God-seeker has lived an economically minimal existence. One who seeks God in one's life never feels deprived of worldly possessions, while the "lions" among us roar on forever, always searching for more prey and never being satisfied with their lot.

The necessity for expressing thanks to God and man is central to Judaism. The lowest of all character traits is being *kafui tovah, ungrateful*. The ritual of blessing God after eating was introduced by our father Abraham who taught this essential lesson of sensitivity and good common sense to his guests. In our recitation of gratitude to God we not only thank Him for the meal just consumed, but also for the Land of Israel, for the Torah and its com-

The following line is recited if ten men join in the *zimun.*

Blessed is He and Blessed is His Name.

Blessed are You, HASHEM, our God, King of the universe, Who nourishes the entire world, in His goodness — with grace, with kindness, and with mercy. He gives nourishment to all flesh, for His kindness is eternal.[1] And through His great goodness, we have never lacked, and may we never lack, nourishment, for all eternity. For the sake of His Great Name, because He is God Who nourishes and sustains all, and benefits all, and He prepares food for all of His creatures which He has created. Blessed are You, HASHEM, Who nourishes all.

We thank You, HASHEM, our God, because You have given to our forefathers as a heritage a desirable, good, and spacious land; because You removed us, HASHEM, our God, from the land of Egypt and You redeemed us from the house of bondage; for Your covenant which You sealed in our flesh; for Your Torah which You taught us and for Your statutes which You made known to us; for life, grace, and kindness which You granted us; and for the provision of food with which You nourish and sustain us constantly, in every day, in every season, and in every hour.

(1) *Psalms* 136:25.

---

mandments, for the opportunity to serve Him, for the Temple and the Davidic royal dynasty, and for the inevitable restoration of Jewish sovereignty in all of the Land of Israel and the rebuilding of Jerusalem and the Temple once again. Included also is an expression of thanks for the hosts of the meal and blessings for all of those who have participated therein. One cannot proceed to the concluding portion of the Haggadah without expressing thanks for what has gone before. The same is true in life: one cannot really go forward in life without assessing the past and giving thanks for the good that has already been showered upon us. The blessings after eating are a symbol of reflection and contemplation, a backdrop and perspective to allow us to judge our daily life. This is true all year round, every day of our lives. It is doubly true on this special night of remembrance and reflection regarding our history and destiny.

וְעַל הַכֹּל יהוה אֱלֹהֵינוּ אֲנַחְנוּ מוֹדִים לָךְ, וּמְבָרְכִים אוֹתָךְ, יִתְבָּרַךְ שִׁמְךָ בְּפִי כָּל חַי תָּמִיד לְעוֹלָם וָעֶד. כַּכָּתוּב, וְאָכַלְתָּ וְשָׂבָעְתָּ, וּבֵרַכְתָּ אֶת יהוה אֱלֹהֶיךָ, עַל הָאָרֶץ הַטֹּבָה אֲשֶׁר נָתַן לָךְ.[1] בָּרוּךְ אַתָּה יהוה, עַל הָאָרֶץ וְעַל הַמָּזוֹן.

רַחֵם יהוה אֱלֹהֵינוּ עַל יִשְׂרָאֵל עַמֶּךָ, וְעַל יְרוּשָׁלַיִם עִירֶךָ, וְעַל צִיּוֹן מִשְׁכַּן כְּבוֹדֶךָ, וְעַל מַלְכוּת בֵּית דָּוִד מְשִׁיחֶךָ, וְעַל הַבַּיִת הַגָּדוֹל וְהַקָּדוֹשׁ שֶׁנִּקְרָא שִׁמְךָ עָלָיו. אֱלֹהֵינוּ אָבִינוּ רְעֵנוּ זוּנֵנוּ פַּרְנְסֵנוּ וְכַלְכְּלֵנוּ וְהַרְוִיחֵנוּ, וְהַרְוַח לָנוּ יהוה אֱלֹהֵינוּ מְהֵרָה מִכָּל צָרוֹתֵינוּ. וְנָא אַל תַּצְרִיכֵנוּ יהוה אֱלֹהֵינוּ, לֹא לִידֵי מַתְּנַת בָּשָׂר וָדָם, וְלֹא לִידֵי הַלְוָאָתָם, כִּי אִם לְיָדְךָ הַמְּלֵאָה הַפְּתוּחָה הַקְּדוֹשָׁה וְהָרְחָבָה, שֶׁלֹּא נֵבוֹשׁ וְלֹא נִכָּלֵם לְעוֹלָם וָעֶד.

On Shabbos add the following paragraph.

רְצֵה וְהַחֲלִיצֵנוּ יהוה אֱלֹהֵינוּ בְּמִצְוֹתֶיךָ, וּבְמִצְוַת יוֹם הַשְּׁבִיעִי הַשַּׁבָּת הַגָּדוֹל וְהַקָּדוֹשׁ הַזֶּה, כִּי יוֹם זֶה גָּדוֹל וְקָדוֹשׁ הוּא לְפָנֶיךָ, לִשְׁבָּת בּוֹ וְלָנוּחַ בּוֹ בְּאַהֲבָה כְּמִצְוַת רְצוֹנֶךָ, וּבִרְצוֹנְךָ הָנִיחַ לָנוּ יהוה אֱלֹהֵינוּ, שֶׁלֹּא תְהֵא צָרָה וְיָגוֹן וַאֲנָחָה בְּיוֹם מְנוּחָתֵנוּ, וְהַרְאֵנוּ יהוה אֱלֹהֵינוּ בְּנֶחָמַת צִיּוֹן עִירֶךָ, וּבְבִנְיַן יְרוּשָׁלַיִם עִיר קָדְשֶׁךָ, כִּי אַתָּה הוּא בַּעַל הַיְשׁוּעוֹת וּבַעַל הַנֶּחָמוֹת.

אֱלֹהֵינוּ וֵאלֹהֵי אֲבוֹתֵינוּ, יַעֲלֶה, וְיָבֹא, וְיַגִּיעַ, וְיֵרָאֶה, וְיֵרָצֶה, וְיִשָּׁמַע, וְיִפָּקֵד, וְיִזָּכֵר זִכְרוֹנֵנוּ וּפִקְדּוֹנֵנוּ, וְזִכְרוֹן אֲבוֹתֵינוּ, וְזִכְרוֹן מָשִׁיחַ בֶּן דָּוִד עַבְדֶּךָ, וְזִכְרוֹן יְרוּשָׁלַיִם עִיר קָדְשֶׁךָ, וְזִכְרוֹן כָּל עַמְּךָ בֵּית יִשְׂרָאֵל לְפָנֶיךָ, לִפְלֵיטָה לְטוֹבָה לְחֵן וּלְחֶסֶד וּלְרַחֲמִים, לְחַיִּים

For everything, HASHEM, our God, we thank You and bless You. May Your Name be blessed by the mouth of all the living, continuously for all eternity. As it is written: "And you shall eat and you shall be satisfied, and you shall bless HASHEM, your God, for the good land which He gave you."[1] Blessed are You, HASHEM, for the land and for the nourishment.

Have mercy HASHEM, our God, on Israel Your people; on Jerusalem, Your city, on Zion, the resting place of Your Glory; on the monarchy of the house of David, Your anointed; and on the great and holy House upon which Your Name is called. Our God, our Father — tend us, nourish us, sustain us, support us, relieve us; HASHEM, our God, grant us speedy relief from all our troubles. Please, make us not needful — HASHEM, our God — of the gifts of human hands nor of their loans, but only of Your Hand that is full, open, holy, and generous, that we not feel inner shame nor be humiliated for all eternity.

On Shabbos add the following paragraph.

May it please You to strengthen us, HASHEM, our God, in Your commandments, and in the commandment of the seventh day , this great and holy Shabbos. For this day is great and holy before You to rest on it and be content on it in love, as ordained by Your will. May it be Your will, HASHEM, our God, that there be no distress, grief, or lament on this day of our contentment. And show us, HASHEM, our God, the consolation of Zion, Your city, and the rebuilding of Jerusalem, city of Your holiness, for You are the Master of salvations and Master of consolations.

Our God and God of our forefathers, may there rise, come, reach, be noted, be favored, be heard, be considered, and be remembered — the remembrance and consideration of ourselves; the remembrance of our forefathers; the remembrance of Mashiach, son of David, Your servant; the remembrance of Jerusalem, the City of Your Holiness; the remembrance of all the House of Israel — before You for deliverance, for goodness, for grace, for kindness and for compassion, for life and for

(1) *Deuteronomy* 8:10.

וּלְשָׁלוֹם בְּיוֹם חַג הַמַּצּוֹת הַזֶּה. זָכְרֵנוּ יהוה אֱלֹהֵינוּ בּוֹ לְטוֹבָה, וּפָקְדֵנוּ בוֹ לִבְרָכָה, וְהוֹשִׁיעֵנוּ בוֹ לְחַיִּים. וּבִדְבַר יְשׁוּעָה וְרַחֲמִים, חוּס וְחָנֵּנוּ וְרַחֵם עָלֵינוּ וְהוֹשִׁיעֵנוּ, כִּי אֵלֶיךָ עֵינֵינוּ, כִּי אֵל חַנּוּן וְרַחוּם אָתָּה.[1]

וּבְנֵה יְרוּשָׁלַיִם עִיר הַקֹּדֶשׁ בִּמְהֵרָה בְיָמֵינוּ. בָּרוּךְ אַתָּה יהוה, בּוֹנֵה [בְרַחֲמָיו] יְרוּשָׁלָיִם. אָמֵן.

בָּרוּךְ אַתָּה יהוה אֱלֹהֵינוּ מֶלֶךְ הָעוֹלָם, הָאֵל אָבִינוּ מַלְכֵּנוּ אַדִּירֵנוּ בּוֹרְאֵנוּ גּוֹאֲלֵנוּ יוֹצְרֵנוּ קְדוֹשֵׁנוּ קְדוֹשׁ יַעֲקֹב, רוֹעֵנוּ רוֹעֵה יִשְׂרָאֵל, הַמֶּלֶךְ הַטּוֹב וְהַמֵּטִיב לַכֹּל, שֶׁבְּכָל יוֹם וָיוֹם הוּא הֵטִיב, הוּא מֵטִיב, הוּא יֵיטִיב לָנוּ. הוּא גְמָלָנוּ הוּא גוֹמְלֵנוּ הוּא יִגְמְלֵנוּ לָעַד, לְחֵן וּלְחֶסֶד וּלְרַחֲמִים וּלְרֶוַח הַצָּלָה וְהַצְלָחָה, בְּרָכָה וִישׁוּעָה נֶחָמָה פַּרְנָסָה וְכַלְכָּלָה וְרַחֲמִים וְחַיִּים וְשָׁלוֹם וְכָל טוֹב, וּמִכָּל טוּב לְעוֹלָם אַל יְחַסְּרֵנוּ.

הָרַחֲמָן הוּא יִמְלוֹךְ עָלֵינוּ לְעוֹלָם וָעֶד. הָרַחֲמָן הוּא יִתְבָּרַךְ בַּשָּׁמַיִם וּבָאָרֶץ. הָרַחֲמָן הוּא יִשְׁתַּבַּח לְדוֹר דּוֹרִים, וְיִתְפָּאַר בָּנוּ לָעַד וּלְנֵצַח נְצָחִים, וְיִתְהַדַּר בָּנוּ לָעַד וּלְעוֹלְמֵי עוֹלָמִים. הָרַחֲמָן הוּא יְפַרְנְסֵנוּ בְּכָבוֹד. הָרַחֲמָן הוּא יִשְׁבּוֹר עֻלֵּנוּ מֵעַל צַוָּארֵנוּ, וְהוּא יוֹלִיכֵנוּ קוֹמְמִיּוּת לְאַרְצֵנוּ. הָרַחֲמָן הוּא יִשְׁלַח לָנוּ בְּרָכָה מְרֻבָּה בַּבַּיִת הַזֶּה, וְעַל שֻׁלְחָן זֶה שֶׁאָכַלְנוּ עָלָיו. הָרַחֲמָן הוּא יִשְׁלַח לָנוּ אֶת אֵלִיָּהוּ הַנָּבִיא זָכוּר לַטּוֹב, וִיבַשֶּׂר לָנוּ בְּשׂוֹרוֹת טוֹבוֹת יְשׁוּעוֹת וְנֶחָמוֹת.

peace on this day of the Festival of Matzos. Remember us on it, HASHEM, our God, for goodness; consider us on it for blessing; and help us on it for life. In the matter of salvation and compassion, pity, be gracious and compassionate with us and help us, for our eyes are turned to You, because You are God, the gracious, and compassionate.[1]

Rebuild Jerusalem, the Holy City, soon in our days. Blessed are You, HASHEM, Who rebuilds Jerusalem [in His mercy]. Amen.

Blessed are You, HASHEM, our God, King of the universe, the Almighty, our Father, our King, our Sovereign, our Creator, our Redeemer, our Maker, our Holy One, Holy One of Jacob, our Shepherd, the Shepherd of Israel, the King Who is good and Who does good for all. For every single day He did good, He does good, and He will do good to us. He was bountiful with us, He is bountiful with us, and He will forever be bountiful with us — with grace and with kindness and with mercy, with relief, salvation, success, blessing, help, consolation, sustenance, support, mercy, life, peace, and all good; and of all good things may He never deprive us.

The compassionate One! May He reign over us forever. The compassionate One! May He be blessed in heaven and on earth. The compassionate One! May He be praised throughout all generations, may He be glorified through us forever to the ultimate ends, and be honored through us forever and for all eternity. The compassionate One! May He sustain us in honor. The compassionate One! May He break the yoke of oppression from our necks and guide us erect to our Land. The compassionate One! May He send us abundant blessing to this house and upon this table at which we have eaten. The compassionate One! May He send us Elijah the Prophet — he is remembered for good — to proclaim to us good tidings, salvations, and consolations.

---

(1) *Cf. Nehemiah* 9:31.

The following text — for a guest to recite at his host's table — appears in *Shulchan Aruch Orach Chaim* 201.

יְהִי רָצוֹן שֶׁלֹּא יֵבוֹשׁ וְלֹא יִכָּלֵם בַּעַל הַבַּיִת הַזֶּה, לֹא בָעוֹלָם הַזֶּה וְלֹא בָעוֹלָם הַבָּא, וְיַצְלִיחַ בְּכָל נְכָסָיו, וְיִהְיוּ נְכָסָיו מוּצְלָחִים וּקְרוֹבִים לָעִיר, וְאַל יִשְׁלוֹט שָׂטָן בְּמַעֲשֵׂה יָדָיו, וְאַל יִזְדַּקֵּק לְפָנָיו שׁוּם דְּבַר חֵטְא וְהִרְהוּר עָוֹן, מֵעַתָּה וְעַד עוֹלָם.

הָרַחֲמָן הוּא יְבָרֵךְ

Guests recite the following.
Children at their parents' table add the words in parentheses.

אֶת (אָבִי מוֹרִי) בַּעַל הַבַּיִת הַזֶּה,

וְאֶת (אִמִּי מוֹרָתִי) בַּעֲלַת הַבַּיִת הַזֶּה,

Those eating at their own table recite the following, adding the appropriate parenthesized phrases:

אוֹתִי (וְאֶת אִשְׁתִּי / בַּעְלִי. וְאֶת זַרְעִי)

וְאֶת כָּל אֲשֶׁר לִי.

All guests recite the following:

אוֹתָם וְאֶת בֵּיתָם וְאֶת זַרְעָם וְאֶת כָּל אֲשֶׁר לָהֶם.

All continue here:

אוֹתָנוּ וְאֶת כָּל אֲשֶׁר לָנוּ, כְּמוֹ שֶׁנִּתְבָּרְכוּ אֲבוֹתֵינוּ אַבְרָהָם יִצְחָק וְיַעֲקֹב בַּכֹּל מִכֹּל כֹּל,[1] כֵּן יְבָרֵךְ אוֹתָנוּ כֻּלָּנוּ יַחַד בִּבְרָכָה שְׁלֵמָה, וְנֹאמַר, אָמֵן.

בַּמָּרוֹם יְלַמְּדוּ עֲלֵיהֶם וְעָלֵינוּ זְכוּת, שֶׁתְּהֵא לְמִשְׁמֶרֶת שָׁלוֹם. וְנִשָּׂא בְרָכָה מֵאֵת יהוה, וּצְדָקָה מֵאֱלֹהֵי יִשְׁעֵנוּ, וְנִמְצָא חֵן וְשֵׂכֶל טוֹב בְּעֵינֵי אֱלֹהִים וְאָדָם.[2]

On Shabbos add the following sentence:

הָרַחֲמָן הוּא יַנְחִילֵנוּ יוֹם שֶׁכֻּלּוֹ שַׁבָּת וּמְנוּחָה לְחַיֵּי הָעוֹלָמִים.

The following text — for a guest to recite at his host's table — appears in *Shulchan Aruch Orach Chaim* 201.

May it be God's will that this host not be shamed nor humiliated in this world or in the World to Come. May he be successful in all his dealings. May his dealings be successful and conveniently close at hand. May no evil impediment reign over his handiwork, and may no semblance of sin or iniquitous thought attach itself to him from this time and forever.

The compassionate One! May He bless

Guests recite the following.
Children at their parents' table add the words in parentheses.

(my father, my teacher) the master of this house,

and (my mother, my teacher) lady of this house,

Those eating at their own table recite the following, adding the appropriate parenthesized phrases:

me (my wife/husband and family)

and all that is mine,

All guests recite the following:

them, their house, their family, and all that is theirs,

All continue here:

ours and all that is ours — just as our forefathers Abraham, Isaac, and Jacob were blessed with everything, from everything, with everything.[1] So may He bless all of us together, with a perfect blessing. And let us say: Amen!

On high, may merit be pleaded upon them and upon us, for a safeguard of peace. May we receive a blessing from HASHEM and just kindness from the God of our salvation, and find favor and good understanding in the eyes of God and man.[2]

On Shabbos add the following sentence:

The compassionate One! May He cause us to inherit the day which will be completely a Shabbos and rest day for eternal life.

(1) Cf. *Genesis* 24:1; 27:33; 33:11. (2) Cf. *Proverbs* 3:4.

The words in parentheses are added on the two Seder nights in some communities.

הָרַחֲמָן הוּא יַנְחִילֵנוּ יוֹם שֶׁכֻּלּוֹ טוֹב. [יוֹם שֶׁכֻּלּוֹ אָרוּךְ. יוֹם שֶׁצַּדִּיקִים יוֹשְׁבִים וְעַטְרוֹתֵיהֶם בְּרָאשֵׁיהֶם וְנֶהֱנִים מִזִּיו הַשְּׁכִינָה וִיהִי חֶלְקֵנוּ עִמָּהֶם.]

הָרַחֲמָן הוּא יְזַכֵּנוּ לִימוֹת הַמָּשִׁיחַ וּלְחַיֵּי הָעוֹלָם הַבָּא. מִגְדּוֹל יְשׁוּעוֹת מַלְכּוֹ וְעֹשֶׂה חֶסֶד לִמְשִׁיחוֹ לְדָוִד וּלְזַרְעוֹ עַד עוֹלָם.[1] עֹשֶׂה שָׁלוֹם בִּמְרוֹמָיו, הוּא יַעֲשֶׂה שָׁלוֹם עָלֵינוּ וְעַל כָּל יִשְׂרָאֵל. וְאִמְרוּ, אָמֵן.

יְראוּ אֶת יהוה קְדֹשָׁיו, כִּי אֵין מַחְסוֹר לִירֵאָיו. כְּפִירִים רָשׁוּ וְרָעֵבוּ, וְדֹרְשֵׁי יהוה לֹא יַחְסְרוּ כָל טוֹב.[2] הוֹדוּ לַיהוה כִּי טוֹב, כִּי לְעוֹלָם חַסְדּוֹ.[3] פּוֹתֵחַ אֶת יָדֶךָ, וּמַשְׂבִּיעַ לְכָל חַי רָצוֹן.[4] בָּרוּךְ הַגֶּבֶר אֲשֶׁר יִבְטַח בַּיהוה, וְהָיָה יהוה מִבְטַחוֹ.[5] נַעַר הָיִיתִי גַּם זָקַנְתִּי, וְלֹא רָאִיתִי צַדִּיק נֶעֱזָב, וְזַרְעוֹ מְבַקֶּשׁ לָחֶם.[6] יהוה עֹז לְעַמּוֹ יִתֵּן, יהוה יְבָרֵךְ אֶת עַמּוֹ בַשָּׁלוֹם.[7]

Upon completion of *Bircas Hamazon* the blessing over wine is recited and the third cup is drunk while reclining on the left side. It is preferable to drink the entire cup, but at the very least, most of the cup should be drained.

בָּרוּךְ אַתָּה יהוה אֱלֹהֵינוּ מֶלֶךְ הָעוֹלָם, בּוֹרֵא פְּרִי הַגָּפֶן.

The fourth cup is poured. According to most customs, the Cup of Elijah is poured at this point, after which the door is opened in accordance with the verse, "It is a guarded night." Then the following paragraph is recited.

שְׁפֹךְ חֲמָתְךָ אֶל הַגּוֹיִם אֲשֶׁר לֹא יְדָעוּךָ וְעַל מַמְלָכוֹת אֲשֶׁר בְּשִׁמְךָ לֹא קָרָאוּ. כִּי אָכַל אֶת יַעֲקֹב וְאֶת

שְׁפֹךְ חֲמָתְךָ — *Pour Your wrath*

This section of the Haggadah is apparently not part of the original Seder service. It does not figure in the introductory "table of contents," "Kadesh, U'rechatz," that precedes the actual recital of the Haggadah. However, it has been part of the Haggadah service since at least early Geonic times (seventh-century C.E.) and is commented upon by all of the scholars and commentators of medieval times. The words in this section are harsh and direct. It reflects our belief in the eventual retribution that the Lord

The words in parentheses are added on the two Seder nights in some communities.

The compassionate One! May He cause us to inherit that day which is altogether good (that everlasting day, the day when the just will sit with crowns on their heads, enjoying the reflection of God's majesty — and may our portion be with them!).

The compassionate One! May He make us worthy of the days of Mashiach and the life of the World to Come. He Who is a tower of salvations to His king and does kindness for His anointed, to David and to his descendants forever.[1] He Who makes peace in His heights, may He make peace upon us, and upon all Israel. Now respond: Amen!

Fear HASHEM, you, His holy ones, for there is no deprivation for His reverent ones. While young lions may go hungry, those who seek God do not feel deprived of anything good.[2] Give thanks to God for He is good; His kindness endures forever.[3] You open up Your hand and satisfy every living thing with contentment.[4] Blessed is the man who trusts in HASHEM, then HASHEM will be his security.[5] I was a youth and also have aged, and I have not seen a righteous man forsaken, with his children begging for bread.[6] HASHEM will give might to His people; HASHEM will bless His people with peace.[7]

Upon completion of *Bircas Hamazon* the blessing over wine is recited and the third cup is drunk while reclining on the left side. It is preferable to drink the entire cup, but at the very least, most of the cup should be drained.

Blessed are You, HASHEM, our God, King of the universe, Who creates the fruit of the vine.

The fourth cup is poured. According to most customs, the Cup of Elijah is poured at this point, after which the door is opened in accordance with the verse, "It is a guarded night." Then the following paragraph is recited.

Pour Your wrath upon the nations that do not recognize You and upon the kingdoms that do not invoke Your Name. For

(1) *Psalms* 18:51. (2) *Psalms* 34:10-11 (3) *Psalms* 136:1 et al. (4) *Psalms* 145:16. (5) *Jeremiah* 17:7 (6) *Psalms* 37:25. (7) *Psalms* 29:11

נָוֵהוּ הֵשַׁמּוּ.[1] שְׁפָךְ עֲלֵיהֶם זַעְמֶךָ וַחֲרוֹן אַפְּךָ יַשִּׂיגֵם.[2] תִּרְדֹּף בְּאַף וְתַשְׁמִידֵם מִתַּחַת שְׁמֵי יהוה.[3]

הַלֵּל

The door is closed and the recitation of the Haggadah is continued.

---

brings upon all evildoers, even on empires and mighty nations. The unwarranted hatred and persecution of the Jewish people is in itself an act of rebellion and spite toward God. We have suffered so much over the centuries in Christian Europe and in Moslem Levant that it is beyond human powers to wreak compensation for the cruelties done to us. We have no choice therefore but to leave the matter up to God. The treatment of the Jews by the nonJewish world is a shameful record of inhumanity and cruelty. It leaves a stain on the fabric of human civilization that is deep and abiding. Only in the messianic era, in the final redemption of Israel and through it of all humankind, as well, will that stain be removed.

The rabbis foresaw this time in the prophecy of Ezekiel regarding Gog and Magog — the terribly difficult events that precede the messianic era. Because of the fierceness of that struggle and the pain that it will yet engender, this section of the Haggadah serves as the proper and necessary introduction to the next part of *Hallel* that we will recite immediately after שְׁפֹךְ חֲמָתְךָ. It begins with the words לֹא לָנוּ — let us, the people of Israel, not be forced to suffer the pains and punishments of retribution that will mark that period of time.

☙ The Cup of Elijah

Prior to the recitation of שְׁפֹךְ חֲמָתְךָ, a cup of wine is filled. There is a dispute in the Mishnah as to whether the Seder service requires four or five cups of wine. Even though we drink only four cups, a fifth cup is nevertheless filled and placed on the table, in order to accommodate, so to speak, both opinions in the Mishnah. Those who require a fifth do so to commemorate God's promise of "I shall bring you to the land," just as the four cups symbolize the four facets of God's promise to bring about the Exodus (see above, The Four Cups).

This fifth cup of wine, which is named in honor of the prophet Elijah, represents the future complete restoration of the Jewish people to the Land of Israel. Elijah, who in rabbinic literature is seen as appearing at the beginning of the messianic era and answering all of the unsolved disputes in halachah that have gathered over the ages, will then decide what we are to do with this fifth cup as well.

Elijah, who never experienced the Angel of Death, is the symbol of the eternity of Israel. During his lifetime, he experienced moments of doubt regarding the future of the Jewish people. Living in a time of evil Jewish rulers, rampant paganism, and a wave of immorality, Elijah complained regarding the behavior and future of Israel. He despaired of his life, his mission, his people, and their future. The Lord therefore chose him to be His representative, so to speak, to visit the Jewish people regularly wherever they may reside, and bear witness to their fealty to Torah and Him.

Elijah is the "angel of the covenant" at every circumcision in a Jewish family. And he is a welcome "guest" at every Pesach Seder. In the words of the prophet Malachi, Elijah is the one who binds all of the Jewish generations

they have devoured Jacob and destroyed His habitation.[1] Pour Your fury upon them and let Your fierce anger overtake them.[2] Pursue them with wrath and annihilate them from beneath the heavens of HASHEM.[3]

HALLEL

The door is closed and the recitation of the Haggadah is continued.

(1) *Psalms* 79:6-7. (2) *Psalms* 69:25. (3) *Lamentations* 3:66.

לֹא לָנוּ יהוה לֹא לָנוּ, כִּי לְשִׁמְךָ תֵּן כָּבוֹד, עַל חַסְדְּךָ עַל אֲמִתֶּךָ. לָמָּה יֹאמְרוּ הַגּוֹיִם, אַיֵּה נָא אֱלֹהֵיהֶם. וֵאלֹהֵינוּ בַשָּׁמָיִם, כֹּל אֲשֶׁר חָפֵץ עָשָׂה. עֲצַבֵּיהֶם כֶּסֶף וְזָהָב, מַעֲשֵׂה יְדֵי אָדָם. פֶּה לָהֶם וְלֹא יְדַבֵּרוּ, עֵינַיִם לָהֶם וְלֹא יִרְאוּ. אָזְנַיִם לָהֶם וְלֹא יִשְׁמָעוּ, אַף לָהֶם וְלֹא יְרִיחוּן. יְדֵיהֶם וְלֹא יְמִישׁוּן, רַגְלֵיהֶם וְלֹא יְהַלֵּכוּ, לֹא יֶהְגּוּ בִּגְרוֹנָם. כְּמוֹהֶם יִהְיוּ עֹשֵׂיהֶם, כֹּל אֲשֶׁר בֹּטֵחַ בָּהֶם. יִשְׂרָאֵל בְּטַח בַּיהוה, עֶזְרָם וּמָגִנָּם הוּא. בֵּית אַהֲרֹן בִּטְחוּ בַיהוה, עֶזְרָם וּמָגִנָּם הוּא. יִרְאֵי יהוה בִּטְחוּ בַיהוה, עֶזְרָם וּמָגִנָּם הוּא.

---

together, who unites us and provides us with a sense of immortality and eternity. His presence keeps memory alive in the Jewish world and guarantees good hope for our future. Elijah is also the fierce avenger for God's people and is an instrument of the realization of the שְׁפֹךְ חֲמָתְךָ service itself.

To allow Elijah to enter our home we open the outside door, stand out of respect, and state: "*Baruch Haba*" — welcome. Aside from the Elijah theme to our opening the door, there are many other explanations given for this custom: it is an open demonstration that the night of Pesach is *leil shimurim* — a night wherein we are guarded from evil by Heaven; it exhibits to all the falseness of blood libel accusations; it expresses our hopes for the imminent coming of the messianic era; it declares our willingness to share the morality of Torah with the whole world, now that we have become free and redeemed and are no longer doomed to spiteful isolation. This list is not exhaustive and many other explanations are possible, as well.

Our children, when they were young, asked me, and lately, our current crop of young grandchildren ask me, why the Cup of Elijah remains full even after his visit to our home. Didn't Elijah stop to drink from it? I once told them that since Elijah has so many Jewish homes to visit on the Seder night, if he drank from every cup in every Jewish home he visited he would become drunk and be unable to fulfill his mission. Therefore, I triumphantly said, he does not drink from our cup or from anyone else's cup either. I thought that this was pretty clever of me. Nevertheless, one of our small grandchildren, reflecting on this piece of wisdom on my part, said that he thinks that Elijah does drink from the cup of wine in the last house he visits, since then he is no longer in danger of not fulfilling his task for the night. The child then asked me to arrange that next year Elijah should visit our house last and drink from our cup.

Well, I have long ago arranged for that, for I "see" Elijah drinking from our family cup every Seder night. I see it in the eyes of the future generations sitting around our table, in the warmth of the hospitality of being able to host guests to the Seder, and in the beauty of the Haggadah service itself. When the child grows older, I pray that he will also see, as I have learned to do, that Elijah does in truth drink from our family's cup

Not to us, HASHEM, not to us, but to Your Name give glory, for the sake of Your kindness and Your truth! Why should the nations say, "Where is their God now?" Our God is in the heavens; whatever He pleases, He does! Their idols are silver and gold, the handiwork of man. They have a mouth, but cannot speak; they have eyes, but cannot see; they have ears, but cannot hear; they have a nose, but cannot smell; their hands — they cannot feel; their feet — they cannot walk; nor can they utter a sound with their throat. Those who make them should become like them, whoever trusts in them! O Israel! Trust in HASHEM; He is their help and their shield! House of Aaron! Trust in HASHEM! He is their help and their shield! You who fear HASHEM — trust in HASHEM, He is their help and their shield!

---

and that this ability to so see him in mind and soul is the greatest guarantee of our family continuity and that of all of Israel as well.

הַלֵּל / Hallel

לֹא לָנוּ — *Not to us*

The "לֹא לָנוּ," "*not to us,*" part of *Hallel* refers to the period of pain and suffering that precedes the advent of the messianic era. As mentioned earlier, the view of the Rabbis toward the generations preceding the messianic era was somewhat apocalyptic. God is therefore beseeched to spare Israel the worst of that vision. The argument used to make this point is that the nations of the world will misinterpret the troubles that befall Israel and will come to mock God Himself. Again, as I mentioned earlier, this argument, which may appear specious on the surface, is employed throughout the Torah as a most valid point of debate. The Jewish people are therefore bidden to maintain their trust in God till the end, no matter what trials they must pass through.

The praise of God that is contained in this section of *Hallel* concerns itself with the denigration of pagan idols. It is certainly illogical and strange in the extreme that people should worship idols of stone, wood, and metal that they themselves created and fashioned. Yet, even in today's modern, sophisticated world, there are many hundreds of millions of humans who do so. We are thankful to God and praise Him for raising us from the pits of idolatry to the levels of trust and belief in the Creator of us all.

The words "לֹא לָנוּ," "*not to us*" can also be seen as a comment regarding our fervent hope that we remain "different" and apart from the idolaters and evildoers of the world. The very concept of being "different" has assured Jewish survival throughout the ages. Pride in oneself and people allows one to overcome the attendant difficulties of being "different." In fact, the fact of being "different" may often be the basic element in inducing pride in people, both old and young.

יהוה זְכָרָנוּ יְבָרֵךְ, יְבָרֵךְ אֶת בֵּית יִשְׂרָאֵל, יְבָרֵךְ אֶת בֵּית אַהֲרֹן. יְבָרֵךְ יִרְאֵי יהוה, הַקְּטַנִּים עִם הַגְּדֹלִים. יֹסֵף יהוה עֲלֵיכֶם, עֲלֵיכֶם וְעַל בְּנֵיכֶם. בְּרוּכִים אַתֶּם לַיהוה, עֹשֵׂה שָׁמַיִם וָאָרֶץ. הַשָּׁמַיִם שָׁמַיִם לַיהוה, וְהָאָרֶץ נָתַן לִבְנֵי אָדָם. לֹא הַמֵּתִים יְהַלְלוּ יָהּ, וְלֹא כָּל יֹרְדֵי דוּמָה. וַאֲנַחְנוּ נְבָרֵךְ יָהּ, מֵעַתָּה וְעַד עוֹלָם, הַלְלוּיָהּ.[1]

אָהַבְתִּי, כִּי יִשְׁמַע יהוה אֶת קוֹלִי, תַּחֲנוּנָי. כִּי הִטָּה אָזְנוֹ לִי, וּבְיָמַי אֶקְרָא. אֲפָפוּנִי חֶבְלֵי מָוֶת, וּמְצָרֵי שְׁאוֹל מְצָאוּנִי, צָרָה וְיָגוֹן אֶמְצָא. וּבְשֵׁם יהוה אֶקְרָא, אָנָּה יהוה מַלְּטָה נַפְשִׁי. חַנּוּן יהוה וְצַדִּיק, וֵאלֹהֵינוּ מְרַחֵם. שֹׁמֵר פְּתָאִים יהוה, דַּלּוֹתִי וְלִי יְהוֹשִׁיעַ. שׁוּבִי נַפְשִׁי לִמְנוּחָיְכִי, כִּי

ה׳ זְכָרָנוּ יְבָרֵךְ — *HASHEM Who has remembered us will bless*

The statement in *Hallel* that the dead no longer can praise God underscores the clear Jewish attitude toward life and living. The Psalmist sees life as an opportunity to serve God and humankind. Life, therefore, is precious above all else and not to be wasted or frittered away. It always presents many difficulties and there are circumstances of pain, suffering, and depression that force some to abandon life and wish for death. Much has been said in modern society about an indefinable measure of living called "quality of life." Judaism makes almost no allowance for such standards. Suicide or even hastening death is forbidden under Halachah.

As long as one is yet alive in this world, great and good things may yet still be achieved. It is reported that the great Vilna Gaon held his *tzi-tzis* in his hand as he felt himself leaving this world and wept, saying, "Where else can one fulfill such a glorious mitzvah for the cost of only a few kopeks?" The World to Come is the place of reward and serenity of soul. This world is the place of opportunity, growth, and achievement. As long as we are in this world we are bidden to serve God with words, attitudes, and deeds.

אָהַבְתִּי — *I love [Him]*

God guards the naive and the foolish. Many times in life, we make awful mistakes. Yet, the Lord saves us from the disastrous consequences of those mistakes. Naivete and innocence are sometimes very positive qualities in life. King David proclaims in *Hallel* that God protects פְּתָאִים, the simple. In the Talmud, Rabbi Akiva translates the word "פְּתָאִים" — usually meaning *naive* or *foolish* — as meaning children, especially the children of parents who were not very observent in their behavior or outlook. The children of such parents also are brought to immortality and the World to Come by God. Our generation is witness to the truth of Rabbi Akiva's statement. Jewish outreach groups and individuals have restored thousands of Jewish

HASHEM Who has remembered us will bless — He will bless the House of Israel; He will bless the House of Aaron; He will bless those who fear HASHEM, the small as well as the great. May HASHEM increase upon you, upon you and upon your children! You are blessed of HASHEM, Maker of heaven and earth. As for the heavens — the heavens are HASHEM's, but the earth He has given to mankind. The dead cannot praise God, nor can any who descend into silence; but we will bless God from this time and forever. Halleluyah![1]

I love [Him], for HASHEM hears my voice, my supplications. For He has inclined His ear to me, so in my days shall I call. The ropes of death encircled me; the confines of the grave have found me; trouble and grief have I found. Then I called upon the Name of HASHEM: "Please, HASHEM, save my soul." Gracious is HASHEM and righteous, our God is merciful. HASHEM protects the simple; I was brought low, but He saved me. Return, my soul, to

(1) *Psalms* 115.

---

children to their heritage in our generations.

It is easy to say that every person is false, that the situation is hopeless. Cynicism and pessimism are always present. The naysayers to every new idea and project always seem to outnumber the proponents of those ideas and projects. Yet, it is a mistake to be negative, to judge everyone harshly, to succumb to the cynicism engendered by the apparent falseness of human society and people individually. Such negative judgments are always made hastily, without thinking about the background and sweep of the Jewish story.

Positive thinking eventually creates positive results. The Ponivezher Rav, Rabbi Joseph Kahaneman, once told me in reference to a stone-throwing incident that stones were meant for building, not for throwing. Thus the realization that God guards the naive and foolish, that He provides opportunity for all Jewish children to become immortal, should be enough to dispel any hint of cynicism or negativity in our attitudes and behavior. There is always a new world waiting for us to build and we all have the ability to help build it.

Three times in *Hallel* does the phrase בְּשֵׁם ה' אֶקְרָא, *I will call out in God's Name,* occur:

(1) When one is in deep trouble צָרָה וְיָגוֹן אֶמְצָא. וּבְשֵׁם ה' אֶקְרָא (Trouble and grief have I found...) Nevertheless, one is then bidden to call out in the Name of God. Perhaps at times of such trouble and grief it is much more natural to call out to God, since there are no other man-made solutions.

(2) כּוֹס יְשׁוּעוֹת אֶשָּׂא, וּבְשֵׁם ה' אֶקְרָא (I will raise the cup of salvations...). In the moment of triumph and victory, when one is tempted to give credit only to oneself, to human ingenuity

יהוה גָּמַל עָלָיְכִי. כִּי חִלַּצְתָּ נַפְשִׁי מִמָּוֶת, אֶת עֵינִי מִן דִּמְעָה, אֶת רַגְלִי מִדֶּחִי. אֶתְהַלֵּךְ לִפְנֵי יהוה, בְּאַרְצוֹת הַחַיִּים. הֶאֱמַנְתִּי כִּי אֲדַבֵּר, אֲנִי עָנִיתִי מְאֹד. אֲנִי אָמַרְתִּי בְחָפְזִי, כָּל הָאָדָם כֹּזֵב.

מָה אָשִׁיב לַיהוה, כָּל תַּגְמוּלוֹהִי עָלָי. כּוֹס יְשׁוּעוֹת אֶשָּׂא, וּבְשֵׁם יהוה אֶקְרָא. נְדָרַי לַיהוה אֲשַׁלֵּם, נֶגְדָה נָּא לְכָל עַמּוֹ. יָקָר בְּעֵינֵי יהוה, הַמָּוְתָה לַחֲסִידָיו. אָנָּה יהוה כִּי אֲנִי עַבְדֶּךָ, אֲנִי עַבְדְּךָ, בֶּן אֲמָתֶךָ, פִּתַּחְתָּ לְמוֹסֵרָי. לְךָ אֶזְבַּח זֶבַח תּוֹדָה, וּבְשֵׁם יהוה אֶקְרָא. נְדָרַי לַיהוה אֲשַׁלֵּם, נֶגְדָה נָּא לְכָל עַמּוֹ. בְּחַצְרוֹת בֵּית יהוה, בְּתוֹכֵכִי יְרוּשָׁלָיִם הַלְלוּיָהּ.[1]

הַלְלוּ אֶת יהוה, כָּל גּוֹיִם, שַׁבְּחוּהוּ כָּל הָאֻמִּים. כִּי גָבַר עָלֵינוּ חַסְדּוֹ, וֶאֱמֶת יהוה לְעוֹלָם, הַלְלוּיָהּ.[2]

הוֹדוּ לַיהוה כִּי טוֹב, כִּי לְעוֹלָם חַסְדּוֹ.
יֹאמַר נָא יִשְׂרָאֵל, כִּי לְעוֹלָם חַסְדּוֹ.
יֹאמְרוּ נָא בֵית אַהֲרֹן, כִּי לְעוֹלָם חַסְדּוֹ.
יֹאמְרוּ נָא יִרְאֵי יהוה, כִּי לְעוֹלָם חַסְדּוֹ.

---

and wisdom and courage, I will nevertheless remember to call out in God's Name in recognition of the Divine aid that accompanies every human victory and accomplishment.

(3) The psalm teaches us that לְךָ אֶזְבַּח זֶבַח תּוֹדָה וּבְשֵׁם ה׳ אֶקְרָא (to You will I bring an offering of thanks...). At the moment of gratitude and understanding of the good we enjoy, then we offer God our appreciation and thanks and call out in His Name in gratitude.

In every situation in life, trouble, victory, thanksgiving, the Jewish response is always the same — to call out in the Name of God. The Exodus from Egypt contained all three situations. The Jews called out to God while in Egyptian bondage; they sang *Hallel* on the night of their deliverance from that bondage; and they completed the triumphal process of vanquishing Egyptian might by singing the great song of thanksgiving of Moses and Israel at the sea. We will yet again all call out in God's Name when we are privileged to be united again in harmony and peace in Jerusalem.

הוֹדוּ — *Give thanks*

The paragraphs of *Hallel* that deal almost exclusively with the praise of God — הוֹדוּ, מִן הַמֵּצַר, אָנָּא ה׳, בָּרוּךְ הַבָּא — are noteworthy

your rest; for HASHEM has been kind to you. You delivered my soul from death, my eyes from tears, my feet from stumbling. I shall walk before HASHEM in the lands of the living. I kept faith although I say: "I suffer exceedingly." I said in my haste: "All mankind is deceitful."

How can I repay (or respond to) HASHEM? All His benevolence is upon me! I will raise the cup of salvations and I will invoke the Name of HASHEM. My vows to HASHEM I will pay, in the presence, now, of His entire people. Precious in the eyes of HASHEM is the death of His devout ones. Please, HASHEM — for I am Your servant, I am Your servant, son of Your handmaid — You have released my bonds. To You will I bring an offering of thanks, and the Name of HASHEM I will invoke. My vows to HASHEM I will pay in the presence, now, of His entire people. In the courtyards of the House of HASHEM, in your midst, O Jerusalem, Halleluyah![1]

Praise HASHEM, all nations; extol Him, all the states! For His kindness has overwhelmed us, and the truth of HASHEM is eternal, Halleluyah![2]

Give thanks to HASHEM for He is good;
His kindness endures forever!

Let Israel say: His kindness endures forever!

Let the House of Aaron say:
His kindness endures forever!

Let those who fear HASHEM say:
His kindness endures forever!

(1) *Psalms* 116. (2) *Psalms* 117.

---

because of the repetitive nature of the verses involved. Why are the verses repeated, if not always verbatim, at least in terms of content? The simple answer is that the repetitions make our expressions of thanks to God even more emphatic and sincere. Yet, I have mentioned at our Seder table more than once that I feel that the repetition of the verses reveals another insight into life and events.

When the Lord extends a favor or a gift of sal-

מִן הַמֵּצַר קָרָאתִי יָּהּ, עָנָנִי בַמֶּרְחָב יָהּ. יהוה לִי לֹא אִירָא, מַה יַּעֲשֶׂה לִי אָדָם. יהוה לִי בְּעֹזְרָי, וַאֲנִי אֶרְאֶה בְשֹׂנְאָי. טוֹב לַחֲסוֹת בַּיהוה, מִבְּטֹחַ בָּאָדָם. טוֹב לַחֲסוֹת בַּיהוה, מִבְּטֹחַ בִּנְדִיבִים. כָּל גּוֹיִם סְבָבוּנִי, בְּשֵׁם יהוה כִּי אֲמִילַם. סַבּוּנִי גַם סְבָבוּנִי, בְּשֵׁם יהוה כִּי אֲמִילַם. סַבּוּנִי כִדְבֹרִים דֹּעֲכוּ כְּאֵשׁ קוֹצִים, בְּשֵׁם יהוה כִּי אֲמִילַם. דָּחֹה דְחִיתַנִי לִנְפֹּל, וַיהוה עֲזָרָנִי. עָזִּי וְזִמְרָת יָהּ, וַיְהִי לִי לִישׁוּעָה. קוֹל רִנָּה וִישׁוּעָה, בְּאָהֳלֵי צַדִּיקִים, יְמִין יהוה עֹשָׂה חָיִל. יְמִין יהוה רוֹמֵמָה, יְמִין יהוה עֹשָׂה חָיִל. לֹא אָמוּת כִּי אֶחְיֶה, וַאֲסַפֵּר מַעֲשֵׂי יָהּ. יַסֹּר יִסְּרַנִּי יָּהּ, וְלַמָּוֶת לֹא נְתָנָנִי. פִּתְחוּ לִי שַׁעֲרֵי צֶדֶק, אָבֹא בָם אוֹדֶה יָהּ. זֶה הַשַּׁעַר לַיהוה, צַדִּיקִים יָבֹאוּ בוֹ. אוֹדְךָ כִּי עֲנִיתָנִי, וַתְּהִי לִי לִישׁוּעָה. אוֹדְךָ כִּי עֲנִיתָנִי, וַתְּהִי לִי לִישׁוּעָה. אֶבֶן מָאֲסוּ הַבּוֹנִים, הָיְתָה לְרֹאשׁ פִּנָּה. אֶבֶן מָאֲסוּ הַבּוֹנִים, הָיְתָה לְרֹאשׁ פִּנָּה. מֵאֵת יהוה הָיְתָה זֹּאת, הִיא נִפְלָאת בְּעֵינֵינוּ. מֵאֵת יהוה הָיְתָה זֹּאת, הִיא נִפְלָאת בְּעֵינֵינוּ. זֶה הַיּוֹם עָשָׂה יהוה, נָגִילָה וְנִשְׂמְחָה בוֹ. זֶה הַיּוֹם עָשָׂה יהוה, נָגִילָה וְנִשְׂמְחָה בוֹ.

---

vation and succor to a human being, that person is certainly grateful for the immediate good that was done to him. However, as time passes the person realizes that aside from the immediate effects, there are other long-term benefits that continue to accrue, which were unknown and even unpredictable when the original favor was granted. In order to begin a business, a person borrows money from his friend. The immediate favor is that now that person can open his business. The business then prospers mightily and the person becomes wealthy, influential, a leader in his community. That person is able to do great things for his community, helping hundreds and thousands of others in bettering their lives. The person now realizes that the original favor done to him by his friend in lending him money to begin his business has had greater ramifications for him and for the community than he originally could have imagined. The person now has a new perspective on the original favor and therefore offers a new expression of thanks.

When we are blessed by God with life, good-

From the straits did I call to God; God answered me with expansiveness. HASHEM is for me; I have no fear; what can man possibly do to me? HASHEM is for me through my helpers; therefore I can face my foes. It is better to take refuge in HASHEM than to rely on man. It is better to take refuge in HASHEM than to rely on princes. All the nations surround me; but in the Name of HASHEM I cut them down! They encircle me; they surround me; but in the Name of HASHEM I cut them down! They encircle me like bees, but they are extinguished as a fire does thorns; in the Name of HASHEM I cut them down! You pushed me hard that I might fall, but HASHEM assisted me. My strength and song is God. He became my salvation. The sound of rejoicing and salvation is in the tents of the righteous: "The right hand of HASHEM does valiantly! The right hand of HASHEM is raised triumphantly! The right hand of HASHEM does valiantly!" I shall not die, but I shall live and relate the deeds of God. God afflicted me exceedingly but He did not let me die. Open for me the gates of righteousness, I will enter them and thank God. This is the gate of HASHEM; the righteous shall enter through it. I thank You for You answered me and became my salvation! I thank You for You answered me and became my salvation! The stone which the builders despised has become the cornerstone! The stone which the builders despised has become the cornerstone! This emanated from HASHEM; it is wondrous in our eyes! This emanated from HASHEM; it is wondrous in our eyes! This is the day HASHEM has made; we will rejoice and be glad in Him! This is the day HASHEM has made; we will rejoice and be glad in Him!

---

ness, family, wealth, and everything else that He showers upon us, we offer our thanks. However, only later in life do we reassess the true value of God's gifts to us and how they influenced our lives and fortunes. Then we repeat our thanks to God with greater understanding and fervor, for then we have a much truer evaluation of the worth of those gifts.

אָנָּא יהוה הוֹשִׁיעָה נָּא.
אָנָּא יהוה הוֹשִׁיעָה נָּא.
אָנָּא יהוה הַצְלִיחָה נָא.
אָנָּא יהוה הַצְלִיחָה נָא.

בָּרוּךְ הַבָּא בְּשֵׁם יהוה, בֵּרַכְנוּכֶם מִבֵּית יהוה. בָּרוּךְ הַבָּא בְּשֵׁם יהוה, בֵּרַכְנוּכֶם מִבֵּית יהוה. אֵל יהוה וַיָּאֶר לָנוּ, אִסְרוּ חַג בַּעֲבֹתִים, עַד קַרְנוֹת הַמִּזְבֵּחַ. אֵל יהוה וַיָּאֶר לָנוּ, אִסְרוּ חַג בַּעֲבֹתִים, עַד קַרְנוֹת הַמִּזְבֵּחַ. אֵלִי אַתָּה וְאוֹדֶךָּ, אֱלֹהַי אֲרוֹמְמֶךָּ. אֵלִי אַתָּה וְאוֹדֶךָּ, אֱלֹהַי אֲרוֹמְמֶךָּ. הוֹדוּ לַיהוה כִּי טוֹב, כִּי לְעוֹלָם חַסְדּוֹ. הוֹדוּ לַיהוה כִּי טוֹב, כִּי לְעוֹלָם חַסְדּוֹ.[1]

יְהַלְלוּךָ יהוה אֱלֹהֵינוּ כָּל מַעֲשֶׂיךָ, וַחֲסִידֶיךָ צַדִּיקִים עוֹשֵׂי רְצוֹנֶךָ, וְכָל עַמְּךָ בֵּית יִשְׂרָאֵל בְּרִנָּה יוֹדוּ וִיבָרְכוּ וִישַׁבְּחוּ וִיפָאֲרוּ וִירוֹמְמוּ וְיַעֲרִיצוּ וְיַקְדִּישׁוּ וְיַמְלִיכוּ אֶת שִׁמְךָ מַלְכֵּנוּ, כִּי לְךָ טוֹב לְהוֹדוֹת וּלְשִׁמְךָ נָאֶה לְזַמֵּר, כִּי מֵעוֹלָם וְעַד עוֹלָם אַתָּה אֵל.

הוֹדוּ לַיהוה כִּי טוֹב — כִּי לְעוֹלָם חַסְדּוֹ.
הוֹדוּ לֵאלֹהֵי הָאֱלֹהִים — כִּי לְעוֹלָם חַסְדּוֹ.
הוֹדוּ לַאֲדֹנֵי הָאֲדֹנִים — כִּי לְעוֹלָם חַסְדּוֹ.
לְעֹשֵׂה נִפְלָאוֹת גְּדֹלוֹת לְבַדּוֹ — כִּי לְעוֹלָם חַסְדּוֹ.

I compare it to gifts — usually scholarly books — received by a bar mitzvah boy or a bas mitzvah girl. At the time the gift is given there is a general sense of gratitude by the youngster for having received a gift and the required thank-you note is dutifully written and sent. However, ten years later, after having acquired a more intensive education, the young person now truly appreciates the gift and has a new sense of thanks regarding it. All of our expressions of thanks and praise to God for His beneficence to us are worthy of repetition many times over.

הַלֵּל הַגָּדוֹל / Hallel Hagadol

The twenty-six verses (corresponding to the

O, HASHEM, please save us!
O, HASHEM, please save us!
O, HASHEM, please make us prosper!

O, HASHEM, please make us prosper!

Blessed is he who comes in the Name of HASHEM; we bless you from the House of HASHEM. Blessed is he who comes in the Name of HASHEM; we bless you from the House of HASHEM. HASHEM is God and He illuminated for us; bind the festival offering with cords to the corners of the Altar. HASHEM is God and He illuminated for us; bind the festival offering with cords to the corners of the Altar. You are my God, and I shall thank You; my God, and I shall exalt You. You are my God, and I shall thank You; my God, and I shall exalt You. Give thanks to HASHEM, for He is good; His kindness endures forever. Give thanks to HASHEM, for He is good; His kindness endures forever![1]

They shall praise You, HASHEM our God, for all Your works, along with Your pious followers, the righteous, who do Your will, and Your entire people, the House of Israel, with joy will thank, bless, praise, glorify, exalt, revere, sanctify and coronate Your Name, our King! For to You it is fitting to give thanks, and unto Your Name it is proper to sing praises, for from eternity to eternity You are God.

Give thanks to HASHEM, for He is good;
His kindness endures forever!
Give thanks to the God of gods;
His kindness endures forever!
Give thanks to the Master of masters;
His kindness endures forever!
To Him Who alone does great wonders;
His kindness endures forever!

(1) *Psalms* 118.

לְעֹשֵׂה הַשָּׁמַיִם בִּתְבוּנָה כִּי לְעוֹלָם חַסְדּוֹ.
לְרֹקַע הָאָרֶץ עַל הַמָּיִם כִּי לְעוֹלָם חַסְדּוֹ.
לְעֹשֵׂה אוֹרִים גְּדֹלִים כִּי לְעוֹלָם חַסְדּוֹ.
אֶת הַשֶּׁמֶשׁ לְמֶמְשֶׁלֶת בַּיּוֹם כִּי לְעוֹלָם חַסְדּוֹ.
אֶת הַיָּרֵחַ וְכוֹכָבִים לְמֶמְשְׁלוֹת בַּלָּיְלָה כִּי לְעוֹלָם חַסְדּוֹ.
לְמַכֵּה מִצְרַיִם בִּבְכוֹרֵיהֶם כִּי לְעוֹלָם חַסְדּוֹ.
וַיּוֹצֵא יִשְׂרָאֵל מִתּוֹכָם כִּי לְעוֹלָם חַסְדּוֹ.
בְּיָד חֲזָקָה וּבִזְרוֹעַ נְטוּיָה כִּי לְעוֹלָם חַסְדּוֹ.
לְגֹזֵר יַם סוּף לִגְזָרִים כִּי לְעוֹלָם חַסְדּוֹ.
וְהֶעֱבִיר יִשְׂרָאֵל בְּתוֹכוֹ כִּי לְעוֹלָם חַסְדּוֹ.
וְנִעֵר פַּרְעֹה וְחֵילוֹ בְיַם סוּף כִּי לְעוֹלָם חַסְדּוֹ.
לְמוֹלִיךְ עַמּוֹ בַּמִּדְבָּר כִּי לְעוֹלָם חַסְדּוֹ.
לְמַכֵּה מְלָכִים גְּדֹלִים כִּי לְעוֹלָם חַסְדּוֹ.
וַיַּהֲרֹג מְלָכִים אַדִּירִים כִּי לְעוֹלָם חַסְדּוֹ.
לְסִיחוֹן מֶלֶךְ הָאֱמֹרִי כִּי לְעוֹלָם חַסְדּוֹ.
וּלְעוֹג מֶלֶךְ הַבָּשָׁן כִּי לְעוֹלָם חַסְדּוֹ.

---

numerical value of God's Ineffable Name) that comprise this song of praise to God are called in the Talmud *Hallel Hagadol* — The Great *Hallel* of praise of God. One of the reasons given for this title is that this hymn acknowledges God's unrivaled greatness in creating this vast universe and at the same time His ability to provide sustenance for every living creature. This concept that God's greatness lies in being able to sustain all life on our planet Earth, which is but a speck in His gigantic universe, is repeated by the rabbis of the Talmud in connection with the prayer of *Ashrei* (essentially Psalm 145) that Jews recite three times daily. The rabbis stated that the special importance of *Ashrei* lies in the verse that "[You, God,] open Your hand and sustain all living creatures graciously." All else in God's world pales before the wonder of the exquisite ecology of the food chain that sustains all living creatures in our world. This support of life, which we humans take for granted, is truly the miracle of all miracles, the apex of Godly wonders in our world.

Hallel Hagadol gives praise as well for selected miracles wrought by God for the benefit of the Jewish people in defeating our enemies and granting us the Land of Israel. The refrain כִּי לְעוֹלָם חַסְדּוֹ, *His kindness endures forever,* teaches us that God's wonders have an eternal and lasting effect, and even though they

To Him Who makes the heaven with understanding;
His kindness endures forever!
To Him Who stretched out the earth over the waters;
His kindness endures forever!
To Him Who makes great luminaries;
His kindness endures forever!
The sun for the reign of the day;
His kindness endures forever!
The moon and the stars for the reign of the night;
His kindness endures forever!
To Him Who smote Egypt through their firstborn;
His kindness endures forever!
And took Israel out from their midst;
His kindness endures forever!
With strong hand and outstretched arm;
His kindness endures forever!
To Him Who divided the Sea of Reeds into parts;
His kindness endures forever!
And caused Israel to pass through it;
His kindness endures forever!
And threw Pharaoh and his army into the Sea of Reeds;
His kindness endures forever!
To Him Who led His people through the Wilderness;
His kindness endures forever!
To Him Who smote great kings;
His kindness endures forever!
And slew mighty kings;
His kindness endures forever!
Sichon, king of the Emorites;
His kindness endures forever!
And Og, king of Bashan;
His kindness endures forever!

וְנָתַן אַרְצָם לְנַחֲלָה   כִּי לְעוֹלָם חַסְדּוֹ.
נַחֲלָה לְיִשְׂרָאֵל עַבְדּוֹ   כִּי לְעוֹלָם חַסְדּוֹ.
שֶׁבְּשִׁפְלֵנוּ זָכַר לָנוּ   כִּי לְעוֹלָם חַסְדּוֹ.
וַיִּפְרְקֵנוּ מִצָּרֵינוּ   כִּי לְעוֹלָם חַסְדּוֹ.
נֹתֵן לֶחֶם לְכָל בָּשָׂר   כִּי לְעוֹלָם חַסְדּוֹ.
הוֹדוּ לְאֵל הַשָּׁמָיִם   כִּי לְעוֹלָם חַסְדּוֹ.[1]

נִשְׁמַת כָּל חַי תְּבָרֵךְ אֶת שִׁמְךָ יהוה אֱלֹהֵינוּ וְרוּחַ כָּל בָּשָׂר תְּפָאֵר וּתְרוֹמֵם זִכְרְךָ מַלְכֵּנוּ תָּמִיד. מִן הָעוֹלָם וְעַד הָעוֹלָם אַתָּה אֵל וּמִבַּלְעָדֶיךָ אֵין לָנוּ מֶלֶךְ גּוֹאֵל וּמוֹשִׁיעַ פּוֹדֶה וּמַצִּיל וּמְפַרְנֵס וּמְרַחֵם בְּכָל עֵת צָרָה וְצוּקָה. אֵין לָנוּ מֶלֶךְ אֶלָּא אָתָּה. אֱלֹהֵי הָרִאשׁוֹנִים וְהָאַחֲרוֹנִים אֱלוֹהַּ כָּל בְּרִיּוֹת אֲדוֹן כָּל תּוֹלָדוֹת הַמְהֻלָּל בְּרֹב הַתִּשְׁבָּחוֹת הַמְנַהֵג עוֹלָמוֹ בְּחֶסֶד וּבְרִיּוֹתָיו בְּרַחֲמִים

---

occur in a specific time frame, they are of eternal value and influence.

We are also taught in *Hallel Hagadol* that matters seemingly unconnected to the Jewish people may in the end have profound meaning. The references in *Hallel Hagadol* to Sichon and Og, the Emorite kings of Transjordan at the time of Moses, are an example of this. The Jewish people were forbidden to take the lands of Amon and Moab due to the descent of Amon and Moab from Lot, the nephew of our father Abraham. Sichon and Og conquered and captured these lands prior to the arrival of the Jewish people in the area. The lands therefore were now subject to conquest by Israel, since they were now considered to be Emorite territory. I am certain that this is not what Sichon and Og had in mind when they embarked upon their wars of territorial expansion. But, as in most cases in life, the human intent may be one thing, but the Lord's plans may certainly be different, and it is His will that always prevails.

A more modern example of heavenly serendipity may be found in the visit of Pope Paul to Israel in 1963. The pope was planning to cross into Israel from the northern West Bank that was then under Jordanian control. The road from that crossing point to Jerusalem, on which the pope would travel, was old and poorly paved, with many narrow curves and rutted inclines. The Jordanians felt that it would not be proper for the pope to travel through their territory on such a road, and they therefore built a new, wider, straighter road for his journey to Jerusalem. The American government helped fund the project and the new road was completed on record time (for the Middle East) and of good quality (again, for the Middle East). The pope arrived, traveled on the road, visited Jerusalem, and returned to Rome. In the Six-Day

And gave their land as an inheritance;
His kindness endures forever!
An inheritance to Israel His servant;
His kindness endures forever!
Who remembered us in our lowliness;
His kindness endures forever!
And released us from our foes;
His kindness endures forever!
He gives food to all living creatures;
His kindness endures forever!
Give thanks to God of heaven;
His kindness endures forever![1]

The soul of every living being shall bless Your Name, HASHEM our God; the spirit of all flesh shall always glorify and exalt Your remembrance, our King. From eternity to eternity You are God, and other than You we have no king, redeemer, or savior. Liberator, Rescuer, Sustainer, and Merciful One in every time of trouble and anguish, we have no king but You — God of the first and of the last, God of all human beings, Master of all generations, Who is extolled through a multitude of praises, Who guides His world with kindness and His creatures with

(1) *Psalms* 136.

War that took place four years later in 1967, it was this new wider tank-supporting road that allowed Israeli armored columns to outflank the Jordanian army and force the Jordanians to retreat eastward across the Jordan River. In the absence of this road, the Six-Day War may have taken far longer to end.

So for whom was this road really built? In life, oftentimes much more is hidden than apparent. Therefore, the prayer of *Hallel Hagadol* is always timely and relevant.

בִּרְכַּת הַשִּׁיר / נִשְׁמַת

נִשְׁמַת כָּל חַי is an ancient prayer of praise of God, dating back to the beginning of the Common Era. Its author is unknown to us; nevertheless, because of its immense popularity and the magnificence of its language and content, legends swirl about concerning its origins. Some even saw it as a hymn of repentance from a *Jew who had strayed badly and now found his way back to his roots.* Whoever the author and whatever the reason for its composition, *Nish-*

וַיהוה לֹא יָנוּם וְלֹא יִישָׁן הַמְעוֹרֵר יְשֵׁנִים וְהַמֵּקִיץ נִרְדָּמִים וְהַמֵּשִׂיחַ אִלְּמִים וְהַמַּתִּיר אֲסוּרִים וְהַסּוֹמֵךְ נוֹפְלִים וְהַזּוֹקֵף כְּפוּפִים לְךָ לְבַדְּךָ אֲנַחְנוּ מוֹדִים. אִלּוּ פִינוּ מָלֵא שִׁירָה כַּיָּם וּלְשׁוֹנֵנוּ רִנָּה כַּהֲמוֹן גַּלָּיו וְשִׂפְתוֹתֵינוּ שֶׁבַח כְּמֶרְחֲבֵי רָקִיעַ וְעֵינֵינוּ מְאִירוֹת כַּשֶּׁמֶשׁ וְכַיָּרֵחַ וְיָדֵינוּ פְרוּשׂוֹת כְּנִשְׁרֵי שָׁמָיִם וְרַגְלֵינוּ קַלּוֹת כָּאַיָּלוֹת אֵין אֲנַחְנוּ מַסְפִּיקִים לְהוֹדוֹת לְךָ יהוה אֱלֹהֵינוּ וֵאלֹהֵי אֲבוֹתֵינוּ וּלְבָרֵךְ אֶת שְׁמֶךָ עַל אַחַת מֵאָלֶף אֶלֶף אַלְפֵי אֲלָפִים וְרִבֵּי רְבָבוֹת פְּעָמִים הַטּוֹבוֹת [נִסִּים וְנִפְלָאוֹת] שֶׁעָשִׂיתָ עִם אֲבוֹתֵינוּ וְעִמָּנוּ. מִמִּצְרַיִם גְּאַלְתָּנוּ יהוה אֱלֹהֵינוּ וּמִבֵּית עֲבָדִים פְּדִיתָנוּ בְּרָעָב זַנְתָּנוּ וּבְשָׂבָע כִּלְכַּלְתָּנוּ מֵחֶרֶב הִצַּלְתָּנוּ וּמִדֶּבֶר מִלַּטְתָּנוּ וּמֵחֳלָיִם רָעִים וְנֶאֱמָנִים דִּלִּיתָנוּ. עַד הֵנָּה עֲזָרוּנוּ רַחֲמֶיךָ וְלֹא עֲזָבוּנוּ חֲסָדֶיךָ וְאַל תִּטְּשֵׁנוּ יהוה אֱלֹהֵינוּ לָנֶצַח. עַל כֵּן אֵבָרִים שֶׁפִּלַּגְתָּ בָּנוּ וְרוּחַ וּנְשָׁמָה שֶׁנָּפַחְתָּ בְּאַפֵּינוּ וְלָשׁוֹן אֲשֶׁר שַׂמְתָּ בְּפִינוּ הֵן הֵם יוֹדוּ וִיבָרְכוּ וִישַׁבְּחוּ וִיפָאֲרוּ וִירוֹמְמוּ וְיַעֲרִיצוּ וְיַקְדִּישׁוּ וְיַמְלִיכוּ אֶת שִׁמְךָ מַלְכֵּנוּ. כִּי כָל פֶּה לְךָ יוֹדֶה וְכָל לָשׁוֹן לְךָ תִשָּׁבַע וְכָל בֶּרֶךְ לְךָ תִכְרַע וְכָל קוֹמָה לְפָנֶיךָ תִשְׁתַּחֲוֶה וְכָל לְבָבוֹת יִירָאוּךָ וְכָל קֶרֶב וּכְלָיוֹת יְזַמְּרוּ לִשְׁמֶךָ. כַּדָּבָר שֶׁכָּתוּב כָּל עַצְמֹתַי תֹּאמַרְנָה יהוה מִי

---

mas has a special place in the soul of Jewish prayer. Its holiness is such that its recitation is reserved for *Shabbos* and holidays, when there is time for its contemplation and appreciation.

It is recited here in the Haggadah on the night of Pesach since this night is also a night of remembrance, contemplation, historical perspective and appreciation, and of thanks to God for His ongoing miracles and kindnesses in sustaining all living creatures and especially for His relationship to the Jewish people. It also emphasizes the vision of universality of service of God evinced and enunciated by Judaism. All living creatures sing His praises, but we humans realize the inadequacy of our words of praise. Even if we possessed all the attributes of the animal kingdom's beauty and strength and were able to give our mouths the never-ending roar of the sea, we would still find ourselves praising and thanking God. In the famous poem of *Akdamus* that is

mercy. HASHEM neither slumbers nor sleeps; He rouses the sleepers and awakens the slumberers; He makes the mute speak and releases the bound; He supports the fallen and straightens the bent. To You alone we give thanks. Were our mouth as full of song as the sea, and our tongue as full of jubilation as its multitude of waves, and our lips as full of praise as the breadth of the heavens, and our eyes as brilliant as the sun and the moon, and our hands as outspread as eagles of the sky and our feet as swift as hinds — we still could not sufficiently thank You, HASHEM our God and God of our forefathers, and to bless Your Name for even one of the thousands upon thousands, and myriads upon myriads of the favors (miracles and wonders) that You performed for our ancestors and for us. You redeemed us from Egypt, HASHEM our God, and liberated us from the house of bondage. In famine You nourished us and in plenty You sustained us. From sword You saved us; from plague You let us escape; and You spared us from severe and enduring diseases. Until now Your mercy has helped us and Your kindness has not forsaken us; do not abandon us, HASHEM our God, forever. Therefore, the limbs which You have set within us, and the spirit and soul which You have breathed into our nostrils, and the tongue which You have placed in our mouth — they shall thank, bless, praise, glorify, exalt, revere, sanctify, and do homage to Your Name, our King. For every mouth shall offer thanks to You; every tongue shall vow allegiance to You; every knee shall bend to You; all who stand erect shall bow before You; all hearts shall fear You, and all men's innermost feelings and thoughts shall sing praises to Your Name, as it is written: "All my bones declare: 'HASHEM, who

---

recited on the holiday of *Shavuos*, the author borrows from the ideas of *Nishmas* when he states there that even if all of the seas were ink and all of nature were parchment, it would not suffice to write upon it all of the praises due God for the magnificence of His universe and His sus-

כָּמוֹךָ מַצִּיל עָנִי מֵחָזָק מִמֶּנּוּ וְעָנִי וְאֶבְיוֹן מִגֹּזְלוֹ. מִי יִדְמֶה לָּךְ וּמִי יִשְׁוֶה לָּךְ וּמִי יַעֲרָךְ לָךְ הָאֵל הַגָּדוֹל הַגִּבּוֹר וְהַנּוֹרָא אֵל עֶלְיוֹן קֹנֵה שָׁמַיִם וָאָרֶץ. נְהַלֶּלְךָ וּנְשַׁבֵּחֲךָ וּנְפָאֶרְךָ וּנְבָרֵךְ אֶת שֵׁם קָדְשֶׁךָ כָּאָמוּר לְדָוִד בָּרְכִי נַפְשִׁי אֶת יהוה וְכָל קְרָבַי אֶת שֵׁם קָדְשׁוֹ:

הָאֵל בְּתַעֲצֻמוֹת עֻזֶּךָ הַגָּדוֹל בִּכְבוֹד שְׁמֶךָ הַגִּבּוֹר לָנֶצַח וְהַנּוֹרָא בְּנוֹרְאוֹתֶיךָ הַמֶּלֶךְ הַיּוֹשֵׁב עַל כִּסֵּא רָם וְנִשָּׂא:

שׁוֹכֵן עַד מָרוֹם וְקָדוֹשׁ שְׁמוֹ. וְכָתוּב רַנְּנוּ צַדִּיקִים בַּיהוה לַיְשָׁרִים נָאוָה תְהִלָּה: בְּפִי יְשָׁרִים תִּתְהַלָּל וּבְדִבְרֵי צַדִּיקִים תִּתְבָּרַךְ וּבִלְשׁוֹן חֲסִידִים תִּתְרוֹמָם וּבְקֶרֶב קְדוֹשִׁים תִּתְקַדָּשׁ:

וּבְמַקְהֲלוֹת רִבְבוֹת עַמְּךָ בֵּית יִשְׂרָאֵל בְּרִנָּה יִתְפָּאַר שִׁמְךָ מַלְכֵּנוּ בְּכָל דּוֹר וָדוֹר שֶׁכֵּן חוֹבַת כָּל הַיְצוּרִים לְפָנֶיךָ יהוה אֱלֹהֵינוּ וֵאלֹהֵי אֲבוֹתֵינוּ לְהוֹדוֹת לְהַלֵּל לְשַׁבֵּחַ לְפָאֵר לְרוֹמֵם לְהַדֵּר לְבָרֵךְ לְעַלֵּה וּלְקַלֵּס עַל כָּל דִּבְרֵי שִׁירוֹת וְתִשְׁבְּחוֹת דָּוִד בֶּן יִשַׁי עַבְדְּךָ מְשִׁיחֶךָ.

יִשְׁתַּבַּח שִׁמְךָ לָעַד מַלְכֵּנוּ הָאֵל הַמֶּלֶךְ הַגָּדוֹל וְהַקָּדוֹשׁ בַּשָּׁמַיִם וּבָאָרֶץ כִּי לְךָ נָאֶה יהוה אֱלֹהֵינוּ וֵאלֹהֵי

---

tenance of Israel in its perilous tale of survival. Special attention is paid in *Nishmas* to the story of the Exodus from Egypt, and these particular stanzas in the prayer are alone sufficient to warrant the prayer's inclusion in the Haggadah service. In short, *Nishmas* is the supreme prayer of gratitude and thanks for the miraculous deliverance of Israel from Egyptian bondage.

יִשְׁתַּבַּח שִׁמְךָ —
May Your Name be praised

The concluding prayers of the *Hallel* section are those that are recited on *Shabbos* and holidays after נִשְׁמַת. The final prayer sums up all the types of praise and gratitude that we have recited before it to God. Again, these concluding prayers of the *Hallel* section are all prayers of thanksgiving to God and a reiteration of our obligation to recite His praise daily and regularly. Obviously God does not need our praise, but we need this constant reminder of our obliis like You?' You save the poor man from one stronger than he, the poor and destitute from one who would rob him." Who is like unto You? Who is equal to You? Who can be compared to You? O great, mighty, and awesome God, supreme God, Maker of heaven and earth. We shall praise, acclaim, and glorify You and bless Your holy Name, as it is said: "Of David: Bless HASHEM, O my soul, and let all my innermost being bless His holy Name!"

O God, in the omnipotence of Your strength, great in the honor of Your Name, powerful forever and awesome through Your awesome deeds, O King enthroned upon a high and lofty throne!

He Who abides forever, exalted and holy is His Name. And it is written: "Rejoice in HASHEM, you righteous; for the upright, praise is fitting." By the mouth of the upright You shall be lauded; by the words of the righteous You shall be praised; by the tongue of the pious You shall be exalted; and amid the holy You shall be sanctified.

And in the assemblies of the myriads of Your people, the House of Israel, with jubilation shall Your Name, our King, be glorified, in every generation. For such is the duty of all creatures — before You, HASHEM, our God, and God of our forefathers, to thank, praise, laud, glorify, exalt, adore, bless, raise high, and sing praises — even beyond all expressions of the songs and praises of David the son of Jesse, Your servant, Your anointed.

May Your Name be praised forever, our King, the God, and King Who is great and holy in heaven and on earth; for to You, HASHEM, our God, and the God of our

---

gations of appreciation and thanks.

After a while, the obligation to deliver expressions of gratitude begins to grate. Children wail: "I said thank-you once already!" But

אֲבוֹתֵינוּ שִׁיר וּשְׁבָחָה הַלֵּל וְזִמְרָה עֹז וּמֶמְשָׁלָה נֶצַח גְּדֻלָּה וּגְבוּרָה תְּהִלָּה וְתִפְאֶרֶת קְדֻשָּׁה וּמַלְכוּת בְּרָכוֹת וְהוֹדָאוֹת מֵעַתָּה וְעַד עוֹלָם: בָּרוּךְ אַתָּה יהוה אֵל מֶלֶךְ גָּדוֹל בַּתִּשְׁבָּחוֹת אֵל הַהוֹדָאוֹת אֲדוֹן הַנִּפְלָאוֹת הַבּוֹחֵר בְּשִׁירֵי זִמְרָה מֶלֶךְ אֵל חֵי הָעוֹלָמִים.

The blessing over wine is recited and the fourth cup is drunk while reclining to the left side. It is preferable that the entire cup be drunk.

בָּרוּךְ אַתָּה יהוה אֱלֹהֵנוּ מֶלֶךְ הָעוֹלָם בּוֹרֵא פְּרִי הַגָּפֶן:

After drinking the fourth cup, the concluding blessing is recited. On Shabbos include the passage in brackets.

בָּרוּךְ אַתָּה יהוה אֱלֹהֵינוּ מֶלֶךְ הָעוֹלָם עַל הַגֶּפֶן וְעַל פְּרִי הַגֶּפֶן וְעַל תְּנוּבַת הַשָּׂדֶה וְעַל אֶרֶץ חֶמְדָּה טוֹבָה וּרְחָבָה שֶׁרָצִיתָ וְהִנְחַלְתָּ לַאֲבוֹתֵינוּ לֶאֱכוֹל מִפִּרְיָהּ וְלִשְׂבּוֹעַ מִטּוּבָהּ. רַחֵם נָא יהוה אֱלֹהֵינוּ עַל יִשְׂרָאֵל עַמֶּךָ וְעַל יְרוּשָׁלַיִם עִירֶךָ וְעַל צִיּוֹן מִשְׁכַּן כְּבוֹדֶךָ וְעַל מִזְבְּחֶךָ וְעַל הֵיכָלֶךָ. וּבְנֵה יְרוּשָׁלַיִם עִיר הַקֹּדֶשׁ בִּמְהֵרָה בְיָמֵינוּ וְהַעֲלֵנוּ לְתוֹכָהּ וְשַׂמְּחֵנוּ בְּבִנְיָנָהּ, וְנֹאכַל מִפִּרְיָהּ וְנִשְׂבַּע מִטּוּבָהּ וּנְבָרֶכְךָ עָלֶיהָ בִּקְדֻשָּׁה וּבְטָהֳרָה. [וּרְצֵה וְהַחֲלִיצֵנוּ בְּיוֹם הַשַּׁבָּת הַזֶּה] וְשַׂמְּחֵנוּ בְּיוֹם חַג הַמַּצּוֹת הַזֶּה. כִּי אַתָּה יהוה טוֹב וּמֵטִיב לַכֹּל וְנוֹדֶה לְּךָ עַל הָאָרֶץ וְעַל פְּרִי הַגָּפֶן: בָּרוּךְ אַתָּה יהוה עַל הָאָרֶץ וְעַל פְּרִי הַגָּפֶן:

---

the truth is that true gratitude knows no limits. All of family life is built upon the realization that gratitude should be constant and unending. Rabbi Yose the Galilean in the Talmud told those who complained to him about his wife's difficult behavior toward him: "Is it not sufficient that she raises our children and saves me from sin?" Gratitude is difficult to maintain. The Torah therefore bids us to stay in practice, so to speak, by having us constantly express our gratitude to God. Somehow, it is psychologically easier to say thank-you to an eternal but unseen God than to a mortal but physically present human being. Nevertheless, the constant repetition of thanks to God does allow our psyche to absorb the message of the importance

forefathers, it is fitting to render song and praise, lauding and hymns, power and dominion, triumph, greatness and strength, praise and splendor, holiness and sovereignty, blessings and thanksgivings from now and forever. Blessed are You, HASHEM, God, King, great in praises, God of thanksgivings, Master of wonders, Who favors songs of praise — King, God, Lifegiver of the world.

The blessing over wine is recited and the fourth cup is drunk while reclining to the left side. It is preferable that the entire cup be drunk.

Blessed are You, HASHEM, our God, King of the universe, Who creates the fruit of the vine.

After drinking the fourth cup, the concluding blessing is recited. On Shabbos include the passage in brackets.

Blessed are You, HASHEM, our God, King of the universe, for the vine and the fruit of the vine, and for the produce of the field. For the desirable, good, and spacious land that You were pleased to give our forefathers as a heritage, to eat of its fruit and to be satisfied with its goodness. Have mercy, we beg You, HASHEM, our God, on Israel Your people; on Jerusalem, Your city; on Zion, resting place of Your glory; Your Altar, and Your Temple. Rebuild Jerusalem the city of holiness, speedily in our days. Bring us up into it and gladden us in its rebuilding, and let us eat from its fruit and be satisfied with its goodness and bless You upon it in holiness and purity. [Favor us and strengthen us on this Shabbos day] and grant us happiness on this Festival of Matzos; for You, HASHEM, are good and do good to all, and we thank You for the land and for the fruit of the vine. Blessed are You, HASHEM, for the land and for the fruit of the vine.

---

of expressing gratitude, willingly and constantly. There is no smoother path to human harmony than the ability to express such gratitude appropriately and voluntarily.

נִרְצָה

חֲסַל סִדּוּר פֶּסַח כְּהִלְכָתוֹ. כְּכָל מִשְׁפָּטוֹ וְחֻקָּתוֹ. כַּאֲשֶׁר זָכִינוּ לְסַדֵּר אוֹתוֹ. כֵּן נִזְכֶּה לַעֲשׂוֹתוֹ: זָךְ שׁוֹכֵן מְעוֹנָה. קוֹמֵם קְהַל עֲדַת מִי מָנָה. בְּקָרוֹב נַהֵל נִטְעֵי כַנָּה. פְּדוּיִם לְצִיּוֹן בְּרִנָּה:

לְשָׁנָה הַבָּאָה בִּירוּשָׁלָיִם:

☙ נִרְצָה / Nirtzah

The concluding part of the Haggadah — נִרְצָה — makes the obvious but nevertheless sometimes-overlooked point that an offering, gift, or service must ultimately be acceptable and meaningful, both to the giver and the receiver, in order to fulfil its real purpose. We have completed the Seder service for the night of Pesach, and we pray that the Lord has found our service acceptable. But we also hope and pray that the Seder service has made a lasting impression upon all those seated at our Seder table, as well. The rabbis of Mussar and Chassidus stated that if one finds meaning and inspiration in one's service to God, then that is an indicator that God also finds, so to speak, pleasure in that service. This idea is derived from the words in *Avos* that "everything (literally, everyone) in which humans find pleasure in, i.e., people and actions that find favor in human eyes, God also finds, so to speak, pleasure therein." This idea is expressed three times a day when we ask God to find our prayers favorable and acceptable in His eyes. Similarly we cannot leave the Seder table without asking that all that we did not be in vain.

Remembrances of the family Seder are many times the strongest bonds that attach a family to one another and to Judaism itself. When we say חֲסַל סִדּוּר פֶּסַח — the Pesach Seder is now concluded — we are really saying that we have now solidified our faith and strengthened our belief in our destiny. This goal gives Pesach and the Seder special significance in Jewish life. Therefore, even though we say חֲסַל סִדּוּר פֶּסַח — the Pesach Seder is now concluded — it really is not. For like the taste of the *afikoman,* the Pesach Seder and its message is meant to last us for our entire lifetimes.

☙ לְשָׁנָה הַבָּאָה בִּירוּשָׁלָיִם — *Next year in Jerusalem!*

Twice a year, at moments of supreme joy — the end of Yom Kippur and the end of the Pesach Seder — Jews state their determination to live once more in the Holy City of Jerusalem. In our time, this statement has turned into reality for hundreds of thousands of Jews, this author included. The Rabbis of the Talmud taught us that every Jew is a citizen of Jerusalem, even while living outside of Israel. We are all "born" in Jerusalem, for Jerusalem alone sums up the whole Jewish story, past, present, and future. It is of little wonder then that the name *Jerusalem* appears so many hundreds of times in the Bible.

(Parenthetically, it appears not even once in Islam's Koran. In Christianity, the connection to Jerusalem is only through the Jewish roots of that faith and the belief that the history of early Christianity took place in Jerusalem. Christiani-

NIRTZAH

The Seder is now concluded in accordance with its laws, with all its ordinances and statutes. Just as we were privileged to arrange it, so may we merit to perform it. O Pure One, Who dwells on high, raise up the countless congregation, soon guide the offshoots of Your plants, redeemed to Zion with glad song.

NEXT YEAR IN JERUSALEM!

ty's main cities were Byzantium (Constantinople/Istanbul) and Rome; Jerusalem was mainly peripheral to either religion — the Crusades were an exception — until, of course, our times when the Jews returned there to claim it as their own.)

For the Jew, Jerusalem continually and uninterruptedly occupied a central place in our faith. Without Jerusalem, Jewish history is incomplete and the Jewish future almost meaningless. It was not only that forgetting Jerusalem would cause our "right hand to lose its cunning"; forgetting Jerusalem means divorcing oneself from much of traditional Jewish life and attitudes. Throughout the ages Jews longed to return to Jerusalem and Jerusalem waited, in humility and silence, but also in great expectation, for their return. Our generation has been blessed to see this circle closed and Jewish Jerusalem exists and prospers against all of the odds and predictions of the wise men of the world. Our exclamation at this climactic moment of the Seder expresses the longing for the spiritual ecstasy of the future Jerusalem, the Jerusalem of the Third Temple, and the perfection of the Messianic era.

Jerusalem, the most beautiful of all cities according to the Rabbis of the Talmud, reveals itself very slowly and with great reluctance and modesty to its visitors and even to its inhabitants. On the surface, a visitor will find that the city is crowded, in some places not too clean, subject to traffic jams that rival London, Los Angeles, and New York, and composed of a polyglot population that often get on one another's nerves. But that it is only the surface Jerusalem. It does not reveal the true Jerusalem that lies hidden, modestly but royally, under its modern, bustling urban surface. The true Jerusalem is experienced in the silence of Friday afternoon in the city. *Shabbos* in Jerusalem is special, but *erev Shabbos* — Sabbath eve — is unique. Jerusalem is golden in the late-afternoon sunlight that shines upon its stone buildings. It is a city of moods and atmosphere, of the ghosts of prophets and kings. One feels prophecy and destiny within its precincts. It is a place where Jews feel intimately at home and comfortable, as though they have always lived there. Personally, I experience Jerusalem always with a sense of *d'ej'a, vu* even though I have only lived here for seven years, as of this writing. I constantly have the eerie feeling that I have been here before and therefore no turn around any corner of Jerusalem's streets surprises me. I understand better than ever before the comment of the Rabbis in the Talmud that I quoted earlier that "all of us were born in Jerusalem." Somehow I am back in my old neighborhood, in the milieu of my essence.

The true secret of Jerusalem, and in fact of all of the Land of Israel, lies in a letter written by Rabbi Abraham Hakohen of Kalisk, who arrived in the land in 1793. Four years later, he wrote to his friends back in Eastern Europe as follows:

> Before Coming to *Eretz Yisrael*
> "This do I write from the depths of my heart to answer those of you who ask my opinion regarding settling here in the Holy Land. This is therefore a public declaration of the problem confronting all of those who come here and the nature of the land itself. Everyone who comes to this land is, in the words of the Rabbis, 'born' here. Therefore, settling in the land requires a period of pregnancy and labor, of nursing and growing to maturity until one truly sees the land for what it is, and then one's soul becomes united with the soul of the land itself. Here there come Torah scholars, bearing their vast knowledge with them, and being accustomed to their usual honors and character traits [developed in the Exile]. They are unable originally

to adjust themselves to the circumstances of life here. Their minds literally go berserk at the lack of security and serenity that they feel. Their ambivalence and state of mind is like a ship that is trapped in the midst of a raging sea of giant waves. They rise to heaven and sink to the depths and they disturb others to help them with their activities and social adjustment. They moan, 'Is this Torah and its reward?' But what was [in the Exile] will no longer be again [here]. Until finally the Lord God shines His countenance upon this person and then one will find rest and suddenly be at ease with oneself.

This process has no definite time limit and no one can know how long the process of adjustment will take and what form it will yet take. It all depends on the individual, one's merits and good deeds, and the true source and depth of one's soul. Therefore, one who wishes to come here and come near to the inner sanctum of the holiness of the Land of Israel has to prepare oneself for all of the trials that I have outlined above. One has to determine beforehand if one will be able to withstand the rigors of these tests and 'not allow one's ears to be cut off' [a Talmudic saying about a mythical camel that desired to have horns and in the process of attempting to have the horns grafted to its head lost its ears. In rabbinic literature, this phrase was always used to warn people against attempting to overreach one's abilities and potential in spiritual matters].

One should therefore assess that one's faith and character traits are in order and under one's control [before attempting to settle here]. Then one can walk confidently in this holy place in harmony with the advice and counsel of the great men of one's time and anyone who heeds this message will then dwell here in security and serenity."

The Land of Israel and Jerusalem must be viewed with a special spiritual lens in order to be truly seen and appreciated. The words of Rabbi Abraham Hakohen of Kalisk are as true today as they were when they were first penned over two centuries ago. Jerusalem today, as always, can break your heart or uplift it and strengthen it. Jerusalem is not only the goal of every Jew;" it is just as much the test of every Jew as well. Jerusalem has to be won personally by each and every Jew and is not easily acquired. That is what makes it the most exciting and challenging place in the world for Jews.

◆§ Jerusalem

In the Lithuanian Ashkenazic rite of the *Selichos* (special penitential prayers) for the third day (after *Rosh Hashanah*) of the Ten Days of Repentance, there is a long poem regarding the centrality of Jerusalem in Jewish life and the terrible damage done to the Jewish people due to the loss of it. It would appear that this poem would be much more fitting to be recited on *Tishah B'Av* (the ninth day of Av, the fast day commemorating the destruction of the Temples and of Jerusalem) as part of the *Kinnos* (dirges and lamentations) of that day, rather than as a *selichah* — a prayer of penitence attached to the High Holy Days. I nevertheless believe that it is included as a penitential prayer because, just as it is within our power to repent, so we can restore Jerusalem to its central place in our hearts and thoughts. Like all of the penitential prayers, the poet presupposes that we can and should do something about our previous shortcomings and improve our attitude and attachment to Jerusalem. Jerusalem is not only a geographical place for the Jewish people; it is a state of mind. As such, our efforts to rebuild it and remain loyal to it can always find room for

On the first night recite the following.
On the second night continue on page 180.

וּבְכֵן וַיְהִי בַּחֲצִי הַלַּיְלָה:

improvement. As the poet himself states in that magnificent *selichah:*

> "Jerusalem! May those who love you be serene; and may your ruins be rebuilt; for near [cities] and far once made you the paradigm of all praise; to uphold in you the vision of Godly salvations. Elderly men and women will once again sit in the streets of Jerusalem [and watch children at play]. Jerusalem!"

In the darkest cellars hiding from the Inquisition, in the labor camps of the Gulag, even in the concentration and killing camps of the Nazis, Jews still dreamt of Jerusalem. Jerusalem has sustained Jewish hope and survival throughout the Exile and the Jewish people reciprocally have never abandoned Jerusalem, not physically, mentally or emotionally.

Now, at the beginning of the 21st century, the city of Jerusalem is building a light rail system to ease its strangling automobile traffic-congestion problem. As the infrastructure for this massive project is dug, the past of Jerusalem is uncovered. Ancient buildings, burial sites, remnants of walls and fortifications are being unearthed and see the light of day for the first time in many, many centuries.

How, I wonder, does this ancient Jerusalem, now rising from its slumber, view the modern Jerusalem that the Jews have built on its ruins? I think that our ancestors are mightily proud of much that their progeny have accomplished. Jerusalem today is a city of holiness and piety, of thousands of full-time Torah students and scholars, and hundreds of *yeshivos* and *kollelim*. It is a city of great charity and compassion, both private and public, of caring and voluntarism. It is a city of national and municipal governments with their attendant majestic buildings, of gardens and parks and innovative architecture, of markets and of *souks* that would be recognizable to our ancestors and also of sparkling new gigantic shopping malls.

It is also a city of neighborhoods, some strictly "segregated" and others with a very mixed population base. My neighborhood of Rechaviah resonates with the many languages spoken on its streets — Hebrew, English, French, Spanish, Russian, Arabic (many of the city employees who service our neighborhood are Jerusalemite Arabs), and German (the elderly remnant of the German immigration that arrived here just before World War II). I think that the neighborhood clearly is representative of both the diversity and unity of the Jewish people and of the population of the Land of Israel all at one and the same time. Jerusalem is the most "mixed" of all of the cities in Israel, both Jewishly and generally speaking. It is truly what the Psalmist called it: "the city that binds all [the tribes of Israel] together."

There is a special quality about being able to say, "I am from Jerusalem." Even in our most difficult world of secular values, latent and often obvious anti-Semitism, and pacifist political correctness, there still is a magical quality in the name of Jerusalem. Some time ago, I was in San Diego, California. On a spare morning I visited Tijuana, Mexico. Walking back from Mexico across the border and showing my U.S.A. passport to the American immigration officer, I was asked: "Where do you reside?" I answered: "Jerusalem." The officer's eyes literally lit up and he said to me: "You must feel so blessed." I never thought about it quite that way before, but I realized how correct his assessment was.

On the first night recite the following.
On the second night continue on page 181.

And therefore it came to pass at midnight.

Anyone who has the privilege of living in Jerusalem is undoubtedly truly blessed. As an Arab taxi driver in Atlanta, Georgia told me upon learning that I live in Jerusalem, "At least that is better than Tel Aviv!" I cannot judge better or worse, but I do feel that being able to live in Jerusalem is a spiritual gift as much as it is a physical fact of life. Jerusalem is just the most special place on earth. The whole world, Jewish and non-Jewish, appreciates this fact. This gives our declaration of loyalty to Jerusalem at the conclusion of our Seder service even greater meaning and importance. Special is special.

☙ Jerusalem — Above and Below

There is a "Jerusalem of Above" just as there is a Jerusalem here on earth. The Talmud represents these two Jerusalems as facing each other across the seemingly never-ending space of God's creation. The Talmud records God saying, so to speak, that the Jerusalem of Above will not house Him until the Jerusalem of this earth is permanently established and inhabited by His children, the people of Israel. It is not an easy task to build and populate the Jerusalem on this earth in such a way that it can honestly be called the Holy City. Many are the obstacles, the naysayers, the pettiness, the disputes, the enemies of Jerusalem and Israel, the difficulties of urban life in our modern world. Yet, when we declare at the end of the Haggadah service, "Next year in the rebuilt Jerusalem!" we re-affirm our commitment to the task of building the great Jerusalem here on earth. The Lord stated that He would not rest or be at ease until Jerusalem — the Godly Jerusalem — is firmly established and is the light unto all of mankind. Peace all over the world, peace for all of war-weary mankind, is thus wholly dependent on the peace of Jerusalem. We tell God when we say, "Next year in rebuilt Jerusalem!" that we want to aid Him, so to speak, to complete and enter the "Jerusalem of Above." We become partners with God in the great project of Jerusalem, which is the center of our national life and existence. Only building the Jerusalem on earth will allow the "Jerusalem of Above" to be fulfilled.

By declaring our faith, both to the "Jerusalem of Above" and the earthly Jerusalem, we say to God that we are ready for the tasks and burdens that freedom imposes upon us. "Next year in rebuilt Jerusalem" is our version of the Biblical answer of *hineni* — I am here to do God's work on earth. What an exalted way to conclude our Seder service and the celebration of our freedom from Egyptian bondage! Just as we elevate Jerusalem to a higher plane over and above all of the moments of our personal joy and happiness, so too we cannot leave the Seder table, the occasion and symbol of our national joy and happiness, without again "raising Jerusalem over the head of personal joy."

☙ The Poems that Conclude the Seder

In the Ashkenazic rite of the Haggadah, six poems are added to the Seder service after *Nirtzah* Just as we rabbis often "take the liberty of saying a few words" before we actually deliver our speech, so too the Haggadah still has something to say to us after the official conclusion of *Nirtzah*. The first five poems are clearly related to the Pesach theme and praise of God. The sixth poem, *Chad Gadya*, is much more problematic, for its connection to Pesach is quite obscure, as are the general idea and details of the poem. But let us proceed in the order of the poems.

☙ וּבְכֵן וַיְהִי בַּחֲצִי הַלַּיְלָה —

And therefore it came to pass at midnight.

This poem deals with the history of the night

אָז רוֹב נִסִּים הִפְלֵאתָ בַּלַּֽיְלָה.
בְּרֹאשׁ אַשְׁמוֹרֶת זֶה הַלַּֽיְלָה.
גֵּר צֶדֶק נִצַּחְתּוֹ כְּנֶחֱלַק לוֹ לַֽיְלָה.
וַיְהִי בַּחֲצִי הַלַּֽיְלָה.

דַּֽנְתָּ מֶֽלֶךְ גְּרָר בַּחֲלוֹם הַלַּֽיְלָה.
הִפְחַֽדְתָּ אֲרַמִּי בְּאֶמֶשׁ לַֽיְלָה.
וַיָּֽשַׂר יִשְׂרָאֵל לְמַלְאָךְ וַיּֽוּכַל לוֹ לַֽיְלָה.
וַיְהִי בַּחֲצִי הַלַּֽיְלָה.

זֶֽרַע בְּכוֹרֵי פַתְרוֹס מָחַֽצְתָּ בַּחֲצִי הַלַּֽיְלָה.
חֵילָם לֹא מָצְאוּ בְּקוּמָם בַּלַּֽיְלָה.
טִיסַת נְגִיד חֲרוֹשֶׁת סִלִּֽיתָ בְּכוֹכְבֵי לַֽיְלָה.
וַיְהִי בַּחֲצִי הַלַּֽיְלָה.

יָעַץ מְחָרֵף לְנוֹפֵף אִוּוּי הוֹבַֽשְׁתָּ פְגָרָיו בַּלַּֽיְלָה.
כָּֽרַע בֵּל וּמַצָּבוֹ בְּאִישׁוֹן לַֽיְלָה.
לְאִישׁ חֲמוּדוֹת נִגְלָה רָז חֲזוֹת לַֽיְלָה.
וַיְהִי בַּחֲצִי הַלַּֽיְלָה.

---

of Pesach in Jewish history. Many miraculous events over the millennia took place on this night, and its historic importance is not limited only to the Exodus from Egypt, though that event is certainly the main centerpiece of this night's history. The word וּבְכֵן has the inference of "therefore," of being connected with what preceded it in the Haggadah. Since we have discussed the miracles of this night as far as the Exodus from Egypt is concerned, "therefore" it is in place for us to recall other of God's miracles that took place on Pesach night or on other nights throughout Jewish history. The use of the word וּבְכֵן here is in line with its use in the High Holy Days' prayers where we also say וּבְכֵן תֵּן פַּחְדְּךָ, etc. There also it implies that after reciting the opening prayers of praise of God, let us therefore continue to add further words of praise.

This poem makes reference to the following miracles and special events that occurred on this night of the fifteenth of Nissan and that are not part of the Exodus narrative, or to other events that took place at night, night-time being the common denominator of the events mentioned in the poem. Included in this list of special night-time occurrences are the defeat of the kings by our father Abraham; God's warnings to Abimelech, the Philistine king, not to harm Abraham and Sarah, and to

You have, of old, performed many wonders by night.
At the head of the watches of this night.
To the righteous convert (Abraham),
You gave triumph by dividing for him the night.
And therefore it came to pass at midnight.
You judged the king of Gerar (Abimelech),
in a dream by night.
You frightened the Aramean (Laban),
in the dark of night.
Israel (Jacob) fought with an angel
and overcame him by night.
And therefore it came to pass at midnight.
Egypt's firstborn You crushed at midnight.
Their host they found not upon arising at night.
The army of the prince of Charoshes (Sisera)
You swept away with stars of the night.
And therefore it came to pass at midnight.
The blasphemer (Sennacherib) planned to raise
his hand against Jerusalem —
but You withered his corpses by night.
Bel was overturned with its pedestal,
in the darkness of night.
To the man of Your delights (Daniel)
was revealed the mystery of the visions of night.
And therefore it came to pass at midnight.

Laban regarding the safety of Jacob and his family; Jacob's triumph in wrestling with Esau's angel; the plague of the firstborn in Egypt and the loss of the Egyptians' wealth; the defeat of Sisera and his iron chariots by Barak, Deborah, and Jael, with the aid of the stars of the night; the defeat of Sennacherib's Assyrian army outside the walls of Jerusalem; the destruction of Nebuchadnezzar's idol; the interpretation of Nebuchadnezzar's nightmare by Daniel; the killing of Belshazzar, Nebuchadnezzar's grandson, after he had profaned the holy vessels of the First Temple that were brought into Babylonian captivity by his grandfather; Daniel's miraculous escape from the lions' den; Haman's writing of the decree against the Jews at night, and the foiling of his genocidal plan through Ahasuerus' inabil-

מִשְׁתַּכֵּר בִּכְלֵי קֹדֶשׁ נֶהֱרַג בּוֹ בַּלַּֽיְלָה.
נוֹשַׁע מִבּוֹר אֲרָיוֹת פּוֹתֵר בִּעֲתוּתֵי לַֽיְלָה.
שִׂנְאָה נָטַר אֲגָגִי וְכָתַב סְפָרִים בַּלַּֽיְלָה.
וַיְהִי בַּחֲצִי הַלַּֽיְלָה.

עוֹרַרְתָּ נִצְחֲךָ עָלָיו בְּנֶדֶד שְׁנַת לַֽיְלָה.
פּוּרָה תִדְרוֹךְ לְשׁוֹמֵר מַה מִלַּֽיְלָה.
צָרַח כַּשּׁוֹמֵר וְשָׂח אָתָא בֹקֶר וְגַם לַֽיְלָה.
וַיְהִי בַּחֲצִי הַלַּֽיְלָה.

קָרֵב יוֹם אֲשֶׁר הוּא לֹא יוֹם וְלֹא לַֽיְלָה.
רָם הוֹדַע כִּי לְךָ הַיּוֹם אַף לְךָ הַלַּֽיְלָה.
שׁוֹמְרִים הַפְקֵד לְעִירְךָ כָּל הַיּוֹם וְכָל הַלַּֽיְלָה.
תָּאִיר כְּאוֹר יוֹם חֶשְׁכַת לַֽיְלָה.
וַיְהִי בַּחֲצִי הַלַּֽיְלָה.

---

ity to sleep at night. The poem concludes by referring to the forthcoming time of redemption and salvation — a time that will be neither day nor night — when the darkness of the Exile will be ended in the blinding light of the messianic era.

All the events listed in this poem were pivotal to the creation and survival of the Jewish people. Sometimes, Jewry seems but a hairsbreadth away from extinction and the events leading to its survival are sometimes almost unnoticeable except in retrospect and hindsight. This is also part of the message of "nighttime" in the poem. We don't see very well at night and often God's miracles pass us by unnoticed and unappreciated. But on the night of Pesach — *leil shimurim,* the watchful night — we do see things clearly and therefore praise God for having sustained us throughout history so that we may serve Him and advance the cause of all humankind.

In the centuries since the composition of this poem many events have occurred to the Jewish people that would allow us to add even more stanzas to this poem, but these latter events are dressed in natural clothing: The defeat of Byzantine Christendom by Islam just before the Byzantines were to embark on the genocide of the Jews in the Middle East; the defeat of the Crusaders before they, too, would have destroyed the Jews; the ability to migrate into Eastern Europe as a place of Jewish refuge from Western European anti-Semitism; the rise of the United States of America and its place in the survival of world Jewry; the resettlement of the Land of Israel by millions of Jews and the existence of a Jewish state there after nearly two thousand years of absence; the Six-Day War and the Yom Kippur War; the collapse of the Soviet

He (Belshazzar) who caroused from the holy vessels
was killed that very night.
From the lions' den was rescued he (Daniel)
who interpreted the "terrors" of the night.
The Agagite (Haman) nursed hatred
and wrote decrees at night.
And therefore it came to pass at midnight.
You began Your triumph over him when You
disturbed (Ahasuerus') sleep at night.
Trample the winepress to help those who ask the
watchman, "What of the long night?"
He will shout, like a watchman, and say:
"Morning shall come after night."
And therefore it came to pass at midnight.
Hasten the day (of Mashiach),
that is neither day nor night.
Most High — make known that Yours
are day and night.
Appoint guards for Your city,
all the day and all the night.
Brighten like the light of day
the darkness of night.
And therefore it came to pass at midnight.

Union and the freeing of Soviet Jewry — all these events and many more are each worthy of a stanza in a poem of thanksgiving to God.

Earlier in the Haggadah we pledged ourselves to sing a new song at the end of days to God in appreciation of what has been wrought for the Jewish people. That new song will undoubtedly contain many more stanzas than does the poem that we currently recite at the conclusion of our Seder service. The survival of the Jewish people over the millennia contains so many twists and turns, so many "what ifs," so many vitally pivotal moments and choices, that the supernatural becomes the only natural explanation of the story. The almost-imperceptible miracles performed on our behalf during the dark night of our Exile will be added to the list of all of the other night-time miracles that the Lord performed on our behalf in Biblical times.

On the second night recite the following. On the first night continue on page 182.

וּבְכֵן וַאֲמַרְתֶּם זֶבַח פֶּסַח:

אֹמֶץ גְּבוּרוֹתֶיךָ הִפְלֵאתָ בַּפֶּסַח.
בְּרֹאשׁ כָּל מוֹעֲדוֹת נִשֵּׂאתָ פֶּסַח.
גִּלִּיתָ לְאֶזְרָחִי חֲצוֹת לֵיל פֶּסַח.
וַאֲמַרְתֶּם זֶבַח פֶּסַח.

דְּלָתָיו דָּפַקְתָּ כְּחֹם הַיּוֹם בַּפֶּסַח.
הִסְעִיד נוֹצְצִים עֻגוֹת מַצּוֹת בַּפֶּסַח.
וְאֶל הַבָּקָר רָץ זֵכֶר לְשׁוֹר עֵרֶךְ פֶּסַח.
וַאֲמַרְתֶּם זֶבַח פֶּסַח.

זוֹעֲמוּ סְדוֹמִים וְלוֹהֲטוּ בָּאֵשׁ בַּפֶּסַח.
חֻלַּץ לוֹט מֵהֶם וּמַצּוֹת אָפָה בְּקֵץ פֶּסַח.
טִאטֵאתָ אַדְמַת מוֹף וְנוֹף בְּעָבְרְךָ בַּפֶּסַח.
וַאֲמַרְתֶּם זֶבַח פֶּסַח.

יָהּ רֹאשׁ כָּל אוֹן מָחַצְתָּ בְּלֵיל שִׁמּוּר פֶּסַח.
כַּבִּיר עַל בֵּן בְּכוֹר פָּסַחְתָּ בְּדַם פֶּסַח.
לְבִלְתִּי תֵּת מַשְׁחִית לָבֹא בִּפְתָחַי בַּפֶּסַח.
וַאֲמַרְתֶּם זֶבַח פֶּסַח.

וּבְכֵן וַאֲמַרְתֶּם זֶבַח פֶּסַח — *And Therefore You Shall Say: This Is the Feast of Pesach.*

The second in this series of poems that conclude the Seder service refers directly to events that occurred on the days that would be Pesach itself. Again, the poem is introduced with the word וּבְכֵן, indicating that it comes as additional praise to God on top of what has been recited already. In the Land of Israel where there is only one Seder night, the poems וַיְהִי בַּחֲצִי הַלַּיְלָה and וַאֲמַרְתֶּם זֶבַח פֶּסַח are both recited at the single Seder. However, outside of the Land of Israel, where there are two Seder nights, the recitation of this second poem, וַאֲמַרְתֶּם זֶבַח פֶּסַח, is reserved for the second Seder night while וַיְהִי בַּחֲצִי הַלַּיְלָה is recited at the first Seder.

Having celebrated two Seder nights and services for most of my life, I must admit that now, having settled permanently in Jerusalem, having only one Seder requires some adjustment of mind and attitude. In spite of all of the expectation and longing that always preceded the first Seder in our home, I always found the second Seder to be more relaxed, friendlier, and in

On the second night recite the following. On the first night continue on page 183.

And therefore you shall say: This is the feast of Pesach.

You displayed wondrously Your
mighty powers on Pesach.
Above all festivals You elevated Pesach.
To the Oriental (Abraham) You revealed
the future midnight of Pesach.
And therefore you shall say: This is the feast of Pesach.
At his door You knocked in the
heat of the day on Pesach;
He satiated the angels with matzah-
cakes on Pesach.
And he ran to the herd — symbolic of
the sacrificial beast of Pesach.
And therefore you shall say: This is the feast of Pesach.
The Sodomites provoked (God) and were devoured
by fire on Pesach;
Lot was withdrawn from them — he had baked
matzos at the time of Pesach.
You swept clean the soil of Mof and Nof (in Egypt)
when You passed through on Pesach.
And therefore you shall say: This is the feast of Pesach.
God, You crushed every firstborn of On (in Egypt)
on the watchful night of Pesach.
But Master — Your own firstborn, You skipped
by merit of the blood of Pesach,
Not to allow the Destroyer to enter
my doors on Pesach.
And therefore you shall say: This is the feast of Pesach.

---

many ways more spiritually and educationally successful than the first. The kinks have been ironed out, the quarrels and competitiveness between the children and, in later life, the grandchildren became muted, and the holiday atmosphere was already absorbed into our

מְסֻגֶּרֶת סֻגָּרָה בְּעִתּוֹתֵי פֶּסַח.
נִשְׁמְדָה מִדְיָן בִּצְלִיל שְׂעוֹרֵי עֹמֶר פֶּסַח.
שׂוֹרְפוּ מִשְׁמַנֵּי פּוּל וְלוּד בִּיקַד יְקוֹד פֶּסַח.
וַאֲמַרְתֶּם זֶבַח פֶּסַח.
עוֹד הַיּוֹם בְּנֹב לַעֲמוֹד עַד גָּעָה עוֹנַת פֶּסַח.
פַּס יַד כָּתְבָה לְקַעֲקֵעַ צוּל בַּפֶּסַח.
צָפֹה הַצָּפִית עָרוֹךְ הַשֻּׁלְחָן בַּפֶּסַח.
וַאֲמַרְתֶּם זֶבַח פֶּסַח.
קָהָל כִּנְּסָה הֲדַסָּה צוֹם לְשַׁלֵּשׁ בַּפֶּסַח.
רֹאשׁ מִבֵּית רָשָׁע מָחַצְתָּ בְּעֵץ חֲמִשִּׁים בַּפֶּסַח.
שְׁתֵּי אֵלֶּה רֶגַע תָּבִיא לְעוּצִית בַּפֶּסַח.
תָּעֹז יָדְךָ וְתָרוּם יְמִינְךָ כְּלֵיל הִתְקַדֵּשׁ חַג פֶּסַח.
וַאֲמַרְתֶּם זֶבַח פֶּסַח.

On both nights continue here:

כִּי לוֹ נָאֶה, כִּי לוֹ יָאֶה:

אַדִּיר בִּמְלוּכָה, בָּחוּר כַּהֲלָכָה, גְּדוּדָיו יֹאמְרוּ לוֹ, לְךָ

---

weary bones. The second Seder was conducted by a well-rested, holiday-happy, group of people. It was a wonderful experience. Thus one of the tests of living in the Land of Israel to me is having only one Seder and somehow making it suffice for two. Like many other things here in the Holy Land, this is still a work in progress.

This second poem deals with the revelation of God to Abraham regarding the forthcoming miraculous birth of Isaac; the destruction of Sodom and the story of Lot and his angelic guests; the war of Gideon against the Midianites; the fall of Jericho to Joshua and the army of Israel; the Divine decimation of Sennacherib and his army outside the walls of Jerusalem; the handwriting on the wall of the Babylonian emperor; the fast days of Esther and Mordechai at the time of Haman's threat of genocide; and the hoped-for final redemption of Israel and humankind.

The poem is in the form of an alphabetical acrostic, as was the first poem, and emphasizes many of the same ideas that we saw and learned in reciting the first poem. The binding theme of this poem is not so much the miracles of the night that highlighted the previous poem, but rather the occurrence of all these events on the days of the calendar that now mark Pesach. These first two poems are usually recited in a singsong sort of recitative instead of being put to melody and song — at least that is what hap-

The beleaguered (Jericho) was besieged on Pesach.
Midian was destroyed with a barley cake,
from the Omer of Pesach.
The mighty nobles of Pul and Lud (Assyria) were
consumed in a great conflagration on Pesach.
And therefore you shall say: This is the feast of Pesach.
He (Sennacherib) would have stood that day at Nob,
but for the advent of Pesach.
A hand inscribed the destruction of Zul
(Babylon) on Pesach.
As the watch was set, and the royal
table decked on Pesach.
And therefore you shall say: This is the feast of Pesach.
Hadassah (Esther) gathered a congregation
for a three-day fast on Pesach.
You caused the head of the evil clan (Haman) to be
hanged on a fifty-cubit gallows on Pesach.
Doubly, will You bring in an instant
upon Utzis (Edom) on Pesach.
Let Your hand be strong, and Your right arm exalted,
as on that night when You hallowed
the festival of Pesach.
And therefore you shall say: This is the feast of Pesach.

On both nights continue here:

To Him praise is due! To Him praise is fitting!

Mighty in kingship, perfectly distinguished, His companies of angels say to Him: Yours and only Yours;

---

pens in our home. However, the next four songs are always sung to definite tunes and with much gusto — at least by those then still awake to do so.

אַדִּיר בִּמְלוּכָה — *Mighty in Kingship*

The third poem/song אַדִּיר בִּמְלוּכָה, is again an alphabetical acrostic. Jewish poetry, especially liturgical poetry from the time of David onward and stretching through medieval times, used acrostics, and especially alphabetical acrostics, often and regularly. In fact, there is even a Hebrew liturgical poem that contains

וּלְךָ, לְךָ כִּי לְךָ, לְךָ אַף לְךָ, לְךָ יהוה הַמַּמְלָכָה, כִּי לוֹ נָאֶה, כִּי לוֹ יָאֶה.

דָּגוּל בִּמְלוּכָה, הָדוּר כַּהֲלָכָה, וָתִיקָיו יֹאמְרוּ לוֹ, לְךָ וּלְךָ, לְךָ כִּי לְךָ, לְךָ אַף לְךָ, לְךָ יהוה הַמַּמְלָכָה, כִּי לוֹ נָאֶה, כִּי לוֹ יָאֶה.

זַכַּאי בִּמְלוּכָה, חָסִין כַּהֲלָכָה, טַפְסְרָיו יֹאמְרוּ לוֹ, לְךָ וּלְךָ, לְךָ כִּי לְךָ, לְךָ אַף לְךָ, לְךָ יהוה הַמַּמְלָכָה, כִּי לוֹ נָאֶה, כִּי לוֹ יָאֶה.

יָחִיד בִּמְלוּכָה, כַּבִּיר כַּהֲלָכָה, לִמּוּדָיו יֹאמְרוּ לוֹ, לְךָ וּלְךָ, לְךָ כִּי לְךָ, לְךָ אַף לְךָ, לְךָ יהוה הַמַּמְלָכָה, כִּי לוֹ נָאֶה, כִּי לוֹ יָאֶה.

מוֹשֵׁל בִּמְלוּכָה, נוֹרָא כַּהֲלָכָה, סְבִיבָיו יֹאמְרוּ לוֹ, לְךָ וּלְךָ, לְךָ כִּי לְךָ, לְךָ אַף לְךָ, לְךָ יהוה הַמַּמְלָכָה, כִּי לוֹ נָאֶה, כִּי לוֹ יָאֶה.

עָנָיו בִּמְלוּכָה, פּוֹדֶה כַּהֲלָכָה, צַדִּיקָיו יֹאמְרוּ לוֹ, לְךָ וּלְךָ, לְךָ כִּי לְךָ, לְךָ אַף לְךָ, לְךָ יהוה הַמַּמְלָכָה, כִּי לוֹ נָאֶה, כִּי לוֹ יָאֶה.

---

one thousand words, each word beginning with the same letter, א! The refrain of this poem is כִּי לוֹ נָאֶה. כִּי לוֹ יָאֶה — basically meaning that these praises of God are fitting and worthy of Him. The second line of each stanza contains abridged verses from *Psalms* that testify to God's omnipotence and omniscience. Each of those verses contains the word לְךָ — *to You* — twice, and therefore the second line of the stanza (composed of the shortened version of the verses from *Psalms*) sums up the praises of God that the first line of the stanza described. In the poem itself, the first phrase in the first line describes an aspect of God's sovereignty, the second phrase refers to God's greatness and correctness, and the third and final phrase of the line refers to the adoring angels and humans who constantly sing God's praises.

There are poems whose natural construction of words and phrases lend themselves to melodious interpretation. (The poem welcoming the *Shabbos*, *Lechah Dodi,* is to my mind the prime example of such a poem, regarding which hundreds of melodies have been developed over the years.) This poem is one of those types, and our family has sung many tunes for it over the

Yours, yes Yours; Yours, surely Yours; Yours, HASHEM, is the sovereignty. To Him praise is due! To Him praise is fitting!

Supreme in kingship, perfectly glorious, His faithful say to Him: Yours and only Yours; Yours, yes Yours; Yours, surely Yours; Yours, HASHEM, is the sovereignty. To Him praise is due! To Him praise is fitting!

Pure in kingship, perfectly mighty, His angels say to Him: Yours and only Yours; Yours, yes Yours; Yours, surely Yours; Yours, HASHEM, is the sovereignty. To Him praise is due! To Him praise is fitting!

Alone in kingship, perfectly omnipotent, His scholars say to Him: Yours and only Yours; Yours, yes Yours; Yours, surely Yours; Yours, HASHEM, is the sovereignty. To Him praise is due! To Him praise is fitting!

Commanding in kingship, perfectly wondrous, His surrounding (angels) say to Him: Yours and only Yours; Yours, yes Yours; Yours, surely Yours; Yours, HASHEM, is the sovereignty. To Him praise is due! To Him praise is fitting!

Modest in kingship, perfectly the Redeemer, His righteous say to Him: Yours and only Yours; Yours, yes Yours; Yours, surely Yours; Yours, HASHEM, is the sovereignty. To Him praise is due! To Him praise is fitting!

---

years. I am tone deaf and cannot carry a tune in a paper bag. However, none of my children or their spouses has acquired that exquisite trait from me, and most of my grandchildren have excellent musical voices and sing very well. One of my grandsons however is not much of a singer — though nowhere as tone deaf as his grandfather — and for a time he felt bad about his lack of musical talent. I assured him that it was a sure sign of genius and that he should not fret over the matter. Be that as it may, from this part of the Seder till its conclusion, my services as the leader of the Seder are dispensed with and the singers in the family take over. Depending therefore on who my substitute will be in leading us to the very end of the Seder service, a number of possible (and sometimes impossible) tunes have been employed at our table over the years for the singing of this joyous poem of praise and fealty to God.

I have often wondered why these particular songs and poems were chosen to be included in the Haggadah. After all, literally hundreds of other poems regarding God's greatness and even regarding the connection of that greatness to Pesach and the Seder could have been

קָדוֹשׁ בִּמְלוּכָה, רַחוּם כַּהֲלָכָה, שִׁנְאַנָּיו יֹאמְרוּ לוֹ, לְךָ וּלְךָ, לְךָ כִּי לְךָ, לְךָ אַף לְךָ, לְךָ יהוה הַמַּמְלָכָה, כִּי לוֹ נָאֶה, כִּי לוֹ יָאֶה.

תַּקִּיף בִּמְלוּכָה, תּוֹמֵךְ כַּהֲלָכָה, תְּמִימָיו יֹאמְרוּ לוֹ, לְךָ וּלְךָ, לְךָ כִּי לְךָ, לְךָ אַף לְךָ, לְךָ יהוה הַמַּמְלָכָה, כִּי לוֹ נָאֶה, כִּי לוֹ יָאֶה.

אַדִּיר הוּא יִבְנֶה בֵיתוֹ בְּקָרוֹב, בִּמְהֵרָה, בִּמְהֵרָה, בְּיָמֵינוּ בְּקָרוֹב. אֵל בְּנֵה, אֵל בְּנֵה, בְּנֵה בֵיתְךָ בְּקָרוֹב.

בָּחוּר הוּא. גָּדוֹל הוּא. דָּגוּל הוּא. יִבְנֶה בֵיתוֹ בְּקָרוֹב, בִּמְהֵרָה, בִּמְהֵרָה, בְּיָמֵינוּ בְּקָרוֹב. אֵל בְּנֵה, אֵל בְּנֵה, בְּנֵה בֵיתְךָ בְּקָרוֹב.

הָדוּר הוּא. וָתִיק הוּא. זַכַּאי הוּא. חָסִיד הוּא. יִבְנֶה בֵיתוֹ בְּקָרוֹב, בִּמְהֵרָה, בִּמְהֵרָה, בְּיָמֵינוּ בְּקָרוֹב. אֵל בְּנֵה, אֵל בְּנֵה, בְּנֵה בֵיתְךָ בְּקָרוֹב.

---

included in the Haggadah. These six poems that are part of the Haggadah are all of anonymous authorship. So, why these and not the others? The Rabbis of the *Midrash* have taught us that "everything depends on *mazal,* even as regards the Torah scroll in the Ark." Well, there certainly is an element of *mazal* present here. But perhaps on a more sublime level, the thread running through these poems is their upbeat nature. The Seder should be concluded on a joyous note with a feeling of triumph and satisfaction. These poems assure us that eventually right will prevail and that there will be better times for Israel and all humankind. The message of serene confidence and unmitigated hope that dominates these poetic words gain them permanent entrance into the immortal Pesach Haggadah.

Pesach is all about hope for the future and not merely remembrance of the past. All progress in personal life and human civilization is based upon hope for the future. Only those who hope eventually achieve and accomplish. So, now, at the conclusion of the Seder service, we express our confidence and hope for the future with these songs and poems that speak to our souls and comfort our emotions. This hymm meant not only as a praise of God, but also as a description of our relationship to Pesach, where a spirit of optimism and hope should pervade our holiday celebration.

אַדִּיר הוּא — *He Is Most Mighty.*

This poem is an alphabetical acrostic of praise to God. Its refrain — יִבְנֶה בֵיתוֹ בְּקָרוֹב — is an appeal to God that He should establish the Third and final Temple speedily in our time. It

Holy in kingship, perfectly merciful, His troops of angels say to Him: Yours and only Yours; Yours, yes Yours; Yours, surely Yours; Yours, HASHEM, is the sovereignty. To Him praise is due! To Him praise is fitting.

Almighty in kingship, perfectly sustaining, His perfect ones say to Him: Yours and only Yours; Yours, yes Yours; Yours, surely Yours; Yours, HASHEM, is the sovereignty. To Him praise is due! To Him praise is fitting!

He is most mighty. May He soon rebuild His House, speedily, yes speedily, in our days, soon. God, rebuild, God, rebuild, rebuild Your House soon!

He is distinguished, He is great, He is exalted. May He soon rebuild His House, speedily, yes speedily, in our days, soon. God, rebuild, God, rebuild, rebuild Your House soon!

He is all glorious, He is faithful, He is faultless, He is kind. May He soon rebuild His House, speedily, yes speedily, in our days, soon. God, rebuild, God, rebuild, rebuild Your House soon!

---

is, however, not only a plea to God but also a statement of our faith and assurance that He will do so. This is in line with the entire thrust of the Haggadah, that even though its main focus is on the past — the Exodus from Egypt — it is also the book that deals with our future and our final redemption. Jewish history is a continuum. The Exodus from Egypt is its starting point but it stretches for thousands of years till our day and will continue till the days of the final redemption of Israel and humankind and even thereafter. As such, the songs about the future such as אַדִּיר הוּא are an integral part of the Seder service.

It is our firm faith in the hopes for our better future that allows us to celebrate our past glories. If it were not for our future, our past would have little meaning for us. It is not for naught that most historians are pessimistic about humankind and the future. Because by dealing only with the past and seeing the road of human existence so strewn with folly and evil, it is more than natural to have a jaundiced view of the human race. Yet, by projecting a better future and a hope that humankind can progress morally and socially as well as technologically and economically, a more optimistic view of life and of our future can emerge.

Pesach embodies optimism. It teaches us that even the most vile circumstances — slavery, immorality, paganism, etc. — all can be overcome by human faith and effort and with the help of the Almighty. And that is really the theme of this poem of אַדִּיר הוּא.

טָהוֹר הוּא. יָחִיד הוּא. כַּבִּיר הוּא. לָמוּד הוּא. מֶלֶךְ הוּא. נוֹרָא הוּא. סַגִּיב הוּא. עִזּוּז הוּא. פּוֹדֶה הוּא. צַדִּיק הוּא. יִבְנֶה בֵיתוֹ בְּקָרוֹב, בִּמְהֵרָה, בִּמְהֵרָה, בְּיָמֵינוּ בְּקָרוֹב. אֵל בְּנֵה, אֵל בְּנֵה, בְּנֵה בֵיתְךָ בְּקָרוֹב.

קָדוֹשׁ הוּא. רַחוּם הוּא. שַׁדַּי הוּא. תַּקִּיף הוּא. יִבְנֶה בֵיתוֹ בְּקָרוֹב, בִּמְהֵרָה, בִּמְהֵרָה, בְּיָמֵינוּ בְּקָרוֹב. אֵל בְּנֵה, אֵל בְּנֵה, בְּנֵה בֵיתְךָ בְּקָרוֹב.

אֶחָד מִי יוֹדֵעַ? אֶחָד אֲנִי יוֹדֵעַ. אֶחָד אֱלֹהֵינוּ שֶׁבַּשָּׁמַיִם וּבָאָרֶץ.

שְׁנַיִם מִי יוֹדֵעַ? שְׁנַיִם אֲנִי יוֹדֵעַ. שְׁנֵי לֻחוֹת הַבְּרִית, אֶחָד אֱלֹהֵינוּ שֶׁבַּשָּׁמַיִם וּבָאָרֶץ.

שְׁלֹשָׁה מִי יוֹדֵעַ? שְׁלֹשָׁה אֲנִי יוֹדֵעַ. שְׁלֹשָׁה אָבוֹת, שְׁנֵי לֻחוֹת הַבְּרִית, אֶחָד אֱלֹהֵינוּ שֶׁבַּשָּׁמַיִם וּבָאָרֶץ.

There is discussion in the Talmud and among the *Rishonim* (the rabbinic scholars of the early Middle Ages) regarding the building of the Third Temple. How will it be built? There is one opinion (*Rashi*, among others) — probably the majority opinion — that the Third Temple will be built in heaven and miraculously descend to earth, whole and fully finished. The other opinion (Rabbi Menachem HaMeiri, among others) is that the Third Temple will be built by human talent, labor, and planning, as were the first two Temples. Jewish tradition certainly leans toward the first opinion and the intimation of the words of the poem here are in line with the idea of a heavenly Temple being established on earth. However, since the poem does not necessarily exclude a Temple constructed by human hands, the question remains open. Whatever and however, we pray that the Lord facilitate the building of that Temple and that it be done speedily (hence the use of the double מְהֵרָה — *speedily, speedily* — in the refrain of the poem) and in our days.

אֶחָד מִי יוֹדֵעַ — *Who Knows One?*

This is one of the most famous and beloved of the Pesach poem songs. The numbers one through thirteen are used to represent the great beliefs and personalities of Judaism, as well as parts of the life cycle of a Jewish home. The song is sung with the refrain, covering all of the previous stanzas and thus continually growing longer, repeated at the end of each number stanza. The number one naturally represents God's unique Oneness, which has no equal, and therefore the number implies One alone and apart from all else. As such, this number one differs from all of the other twelve numbers that are used in the poem, for those numbers are

He is pure, He is unique, He is powerful, He is all-wise, He is King, He is awesome, He is sublime, He is all-powerful, He is the Redeemer, He is the all-righteous. May He soon rebuild His House, speedily, yes speedily, in our days, soon. God, rebuild, God, rebuild, rebuild Your House soon!

He is holy, He is compassionate, He is Almighty, He is omnipotent. May He soon rebuild His House, speedily, yes speedily, in our days, soon. God, rebuild, God, rebuild, rebuild Your House soon!

Who knows one? I know one: One is our God, in heaven and on earth.

Who knows two? I know two: two are the Tablets of the Covenant; One is our God, in heaven and on earth.

Who knows three? I know three: three are the Patriarchs; two are the Tablets of the Covenant; One is our God, in heaven and on earth.

---

intended to be seen as part of a numerical sequence. The poem is phrased in a question-and-answer format: Who knows one, or two, or three, etc? I know one, or two, or three, etc. This format alone has made this poem a longstanding favorite among Jewish children over the ages.

I remember that at one of our family Sedarim, one of the younger members of the group, badly in need of sleep by then (and the adults were by then badly in need of the child being put to sleep by his mother), insisted that he was not going to sleep until אֶחָד מִי יוֹדֵעַ was sung. Sensing the emergency nature of the situation — the child was on the verge of a temper tantrum — I wisely ruled that even though we were yet in the middle of *Maggid,* the poem could be sung then and there. Mollified by his triumph, the little angel then finally marched off to sleep, and we at the table continued our own march toward liberation and freedom, albeit without his endearing presence. Since that incident I have never again underestimated the importance of אֶחָד מִי יוֹדֵעַ in achieving a serene and meaningful Seder service.

The numbers two, five, six, ten, and thirteen all deal with the Torah and its written and oral laws. The two tablets of stone upon which the Ten Commandments were inscribed represent the Written Torah as acquired from Sinai by our teacher, Moses. The Five Books of Moses — the *Chumash* — are themselves the full written law as dictated to Moses by God. The six sections of the *Mishnah* are the repository of the Oral Law, derived from Sinai as well, and edited and codified by Rabbi Yehudah HaNassi (second-century C.E. Land of Israel). These six main sections — *Zeraim* (laws of agriculture, food, and blessings), *Moed* (laws of Sabbath and holy days), *Nashim* (laws regarding marriage, divorce, and domestic relations), *Nezikim* (torts and commercial law),

אַרְבַּע מִי יוֹדֵעַ? אַרְבַּע אֲנִי יוֹדֵעַ. אַרְבַּע אִמָּהוֹת, שְׁלֹשָׁה אָבוֹת, שְׁנֵי לֻחוֹת הַבְּרִית, אֶחָד אֱלֹהֵינוּ שֶׁבַּשָּׁמַיִם וּבָאָרֶץ.

חֲמִשָּׁה מִי יוֹדֵעַ? חֲמִשָּׁה אֲנִי יוֹדֵעַ. חֲמִשָּׁה חֻמְשֵׁי תוֹרָה, אַרְבַּע אִמָּהוֹת, שְׁלֹשָׁה אָבוֹת, שְׁנֵי לֻחוֹת הַבְּרִית, אֶחָד אֱלֹהֵינוּ שֶׁבַּשָּׁמַיִם וּבָאָרֶץ.

שִׁשָּׁה מִי יוֹדֵעַ? שִׁשָּׁה אֲנִי יוֹדֵעַ. שִׁשָּׁה סִדְרֵי מִשְׁנָה, חֲמִשָּׁה חֻמְשֵׁי תוֹרָה, אַרְבַּע אִמָּהוֹת, שְׁלֹשָׁה אָבוֹת, שְׁנֵי לֻחוֹת הַבְּרִית, אֶחָד אֱלֹהֵינוּ שֶׁבַּשָּׁמַיִם וּבָאָרֶץ.

שִׁבְעָה מִי יוֹדֵעַ? שִׁבְעָה אֲנִי יוֹדֵעַ. שִׁבְעָה יְמֵי שַׁבַּתָּא, שִׁשָּׁה סִדְרֵי מִשְׁנָה, חֲמִשָּׁה חֻמְשֵׁי תוֹרָה, אַרְבַּע אִמָּהוֹת, שְׁלֹשָׁה אָבוֹת, שְׁנֵי לֻחוֹת הַבְּרִית, אֶחָד אֱלֹהֵינוּ שֶׁבַּשָּׁמַיִם וּבָאָרֶץ.

שְׁמוֹנָה מִי יוֹדֵעַ? שְׁמוֹנָה אֲנִי יוֹדֵעַ. שְׁמוֹנָה יְמֵי מִילָה, שִׁבְעָה יְמֵי שַׁבַּתָּא, שִׁשָּׁה סִדְרֵי מִשְׁנָה, חֲמִשָּׁה חֻמְשֵׁי תוֹרָה, אַרְבַּע אִמָּהוֹת, שְׁלֹשָׁה אָבוֹת, שְׁנֵי לֻחוֹת הַבְּרִית, אֶחָד אֱלֹהֵינוּ שֶׁבַּשָּׁמַיִם וּבָאָרֶץ.

Kodashim (laws regarding the Temple service, sacrifices, and *kashrus*,) and *Taharos* (laws regarding purity and impurity) — are further subdivided into sixty-three tractates, and serve as the basis for the Talmud.

The use of the number ten as representing the Ten Commandments is obvious. Ten is always an important number in Jewish life since it also signifies the basic unit for Jewish prayer and public life — a *minyan*. Much has been written, naturally, about the Ten Commandments but, my friends, the hour is late and this may not be the right time to delve into the matter as deeply as it certainly deserves.

One thing to be noted, however, is that the beginning of the Ten Commandments is the word *Anochi* — one of the Hebrew words for *I*. This is the form of "I" that God used in telling our father Jacob that He would yet raise the people of Israel from Egypt and return them to the Land of Israel; hence the connection that God Himself, so to speak, makes in the first sentence of the Ten Commandments between His "I" and the Exodus from Egypt, eschewing there any reference to Himself as the Creator of the universe.

Who knows four? I know four: four are the Matriarchs; three are the Patriarchs; two are the Tablets of the Covenant; One is our God, in heaven and on earth.

Who knows five? I know five: five are the Books of the Torah; four are the Matriarchs; three are the Patriarchs; two are the Tablets of the Covenant; One is our God, in heaven and on earth.

Who knows six? I know six: six are the Orders of the Mishnah; five are the Books of the Torah; four are the Matriarchs; three are the Patriarchs; two are the Tablets of the Covenant; One is our God, in heaven and on earth.

Who knows seven? I know seven: seven are the days of the week; six are the Orders of the Mishnah; five are the Books of the Torah; four are the Matriarchs; three are the Patriarchs; two are the Tablets of the Covenant; One is our God, in heaven and on earth.

Who knows eight? I know eight: eight are the days of circumcision; seven are the days of the week; six are the Orders of the Mishnah; five are the Books of the Torah; four are the Matriarchs; three are the Patriarchs; two are the Tablets of the Covenant; One is our God, in heaven and on earth.

The numbers three, four, eleven, and twelve all deal with Biblical narrative and the foundation blocks of our nationhood — the three Patriarchs, the four Matriarchs, the eleven tribes represented by the stars in Joseph's second dream as related to his father and brothers, and, finally, the twelve tribes of Israel that together form the Jewish nation. All of these represent the basic personalities that molded and shaped and formed the Jewish people and prepared them to survive the ordeal of Egyptian slavery and then to commit themselves to the acceptance of the Torah and its Godly way of life and its values system.

The numbers seven, eight, and nine represent the cycle of life in a Jewish home — the Sabbath, children, the Covenant of Abraham. As much as the Jewish people are a nation, they are also a family, and family life is therefore the cornerstone of Jewish existence. One of the main safeguards of Jewish family life is the Sabbath, which binds the individual members of the family together as a unit for at least one day a week. The Seder service strengthens family continuity and generational bonding. It marks our transition from bondage to bonding, and that is

תִּשְׁעָה מִי יוֹדֵעַ? תִּשְׁעָה אֲנִי יוֹדֵעַ. תִּשְׁעָה יַרְחֵי לֵדָה, שְׁמוֹנָה יְמֵי מִילָה, שִׁבְעָה יְמֵי שַׁבַּתָּא, שִׁשָּׁה סִדְרֵי מִשְׁנָה, חֲמִשָּׁה חֻמְשֵׁי תוֹרָה, אַרְבַּע אִמָּהוֹת, שְׁלֹשָׁה אָבוֹת, שְׁנֵי לֻחוֹת הַבְּרִית, אֶחָד אֱלֹהֵינוּ שֶׁבַּשָּׁמַיִם וּבָאָרֶץ.

עֲשָׂרָה מִי יוֹדֵעַ? עֲשָׂרָה אֲנִי יוֹדֵעַ. עֲשָׂרָה דִבְּרַיָּא, תִּשְׁעָה יַרְחֵי לֵדָה, שְׁמוֹנָה יְמֵי מִילָה, שִׁבְעָה יְמֵי שַׁבַּתָּא, שִׁשָּׁה סִדְרֵי מִשְׁנָה, חֲמִשָּׁה חֻמְשֵׁי תוֹרָה, אַרְבַּע אִמָּהוֹת, שְׁלֹשָׁה אָבוֹת, שְׁנֵי לֻחוֹת הַבְּרִית, אֶחָד אֱלֹהֵינוּ שֶׁבַּשָּׁמַיִם וּבָאָרֶץ.

אַחַד עָשָׂר מִי יוֹדֵעַ? אַחַד עָשָׂר אֲנִי יוֹדֵעַ. אַחַד עָשָׂר כּוֹכְבַיָּא, עֲשָׂרָה דִבְּרַיָּא, תִּשְׁעָה יַרְחֵי לֵדָה, שְׁמוֹנָה יְמֵי מִילָה, שִׁבְעָה יְמֵי שַׁבַּתָּא, שִׁשָּׁה סִדְרֵי מִשְׁנָה, חֲמִשָּׁה חֻמְשֵׁי תוֹרָה, אַרְבַּע אִמָּהוֹת, שְׁלֹשָׁה אָבוֹת, שְׁנֵי לֻחוֹת הַבְּרִית, אֶחָד אֱלֹהֵינוּ שֶׁבַּשָּׁמַיִם וּבָאָרֶץ.

שְׁנֵים עָשָׂר מִי יוֹדֵעַ? שְׁנֵים עָשָׂר אֲנִי יוֹדֵעַ. שְׁנֵים עָשָׂר שִׁבְטַיָּא, אַחַד עָשָׂר כּוֹכְבַיָּא, עֲשָׂרָה דִבְּרַיָּא, תִּשְׁעָה יַרְחֵי לֵדָה, שְׁמוֹנָה יְמֵי מִילָה, שִׁבְעָה יְמֵי שַׁבַּתָּא, שִׁשָּׁה סִדְרֵי מִשְׁנָה, חֲמִשָּׁה חֻמְשֵׁי תוֹרָה, אַרְבַּע אִמָּהוֹת, שְׁלֹשָׁה אָבוֹת, שְׁנֵי לֻחוֹת הַבְּרִית, אֶחָד אֱלֹהֵינוּ שֶׁבַּשָּׁמַיִם וּבָאָרֶץ.

---

an essential part of our understanding of freedom and its holy and eternal purpose. At the conclusion of the thirteenth stanza of אֶחָד מִי יוֹדֵעַ, we repeat in the final refrain all the lessons that the thirteen numbers have taught us, and end with the triumphant declaration of God's Oneness, uniqueness, and mastery over everything "in heaven and on earth." Thus, אֶחָד מִי יוֹדֵעַ is a song of belief and understanding of the fundamental ideas of Jewish life.

As an additional note, this poem alone, out of the six that traditionally are part of the con-

Who knows nine? I know nine: nine are the months of pregnancy; eight are the days of circumcision; seven are the days of the week; six are the Orders of the Mishnah; five are the Books of the Torah; four are the Matriarchs; three are the Patriarchs; two are the Tablets of the Covenant; One is our God, in heaven and on earth.

Who knows ten? I know ten: ten are the Ten Commandments; nine are the months of pregnancy; eight are the days of circumcision; seven are the days of the week; six are the Orders of the Mishnah; five are the Books of the Torah; four are the Matriarchs; three are the Patriarchs; two are the Tablets of the Covenant; One is our God, in heaven and on earth.

Who knows eleven? I know eleven: eleven are the stars (in Joseph's dream); ten are the Ten Commandments; nine are the months of pregnancy; eight are the days of circumcision; seven are the days of the week; six are the Orders of the Mishnah; five are the Books of the Torah; four are the Matriarchs; three are the Patriarchs; two are the Tablets of the Covenant; One is our God, in heaven and on earth.

Who knows twelve? I know twelve: twelve are the tribes; eleven are the stars (in Joseph's dream); ten are the Ten Commandments; nine are the months of pregnancy; eight are the days of circumcision; seven are the days of the week; six are the Orders of the Mishnah; five are the Books of the Torah; four are the Matriarchs; three are the Patriarchs; two are the Tablets of the Covenant; One is our God, in heaven and on earth.

---

clusion of the Haggadah, was recited at the Seder table of the Gaon of Vilna. According to the disciples of the Gaon, he considered it a restatement of all Jewish beliefs, and therefore was most appropriate to be used for the conclusion of the exalted Seder service of the night.

שְׁלֹשָׁה עָשָׂר מִי יוֹדֵעַ? שְׁלֹשָׁה עָשָׂר אֲנִי יוֹדֵעַ. שְׁלֹשָׁה עָשָׂר מִדַּיָּא, שְׁנֵים עָשָׂר שִׁבְטַיָּא, אַחַד עָשָׂר כּוֹכְבַיָּא, עֲשָׂרָה דִבְּרַיָּא, תִּשְׁעָה יַרְחֵי לֵדָה, שְׁמוֹנָה יְמֵי מִילָה, שִׁבְעָה יְמֵי שַׁבַּתָּא, שִׁשָּׁה סִדְרֵי מִשְׁנָה, חֲמִשָּׁה חֻמְשֵׁי תוֹרָה, אַרְבַּע אִמָּהוֹת, שְׁלֹשָׁה אָבוֹת, שְׁנֵי לֻחוֹת הַבְּרִית, אֶחָד אֱלֹהֵינוּ שֶׁבַּשָּׁמַיִם וּבָאָרֶץ.

חַד גַּדְיָא, חַד גַּדְיָא, דְּזַבִּין אַבָּא בִּתְרֵי זוּזֵי, חַד גַּדְיָא חַד גַּדְיָא.

חַד גַּדְיָא, חַד גַּדְיָא — *One kid, one kid.*

This is the most beloved song poem of the six that mark the conclusion of the Seder service. The poem is of ancient authorship, written in the Aramaic spoken in Babylonia in Talmudic times, albeit the author is unknown. The meaning of this poem is also shrouded in mystery and over the centuries many interpretations and commentaries have been offered as to its hidden meanings. Its apparent connection to Pesach is also not too easily discernible.

Because on the surface it appears as a simple children's song, there have been those in the past who have doubted its holiness and even ridiculed its inclusion in the Haggadah. Chida (Rabbi Chaim Joseph David Azulai, 18th-century Jerusalem) describes a Jewish community that banned a member because he ridiculed the חַד גַּדְיָא poem. Chida approved of the community's action, stating that the poem had hidden holiness to it and, since it had already been sung for so many centuries at the Seder service, it had rightfully acquired its permanent place in the Haggadah.

The Gaon of Vilna interpreted the characters in the song — the goat, the cat, the dog, the stick, the fire, the water, the ox, the *shochet* (ritual slaughterer), the Angel of Death — and the final intervention of God as a description of the process of Jewish history from the time of our father Jacob to the final days of the messianic era and the fulfillment of the prophetic promise that death will be swallowed up forever by the Lord Himself. Many other commentators, some preceding the Gaon and some coming after him, foreshadowed or followed him in these ideas, however with different identities to the characters mentioned in the poem than those chosen by the Gaon.

The complicated message of *Chad Gadya,* with all of its various characters and events, gave birth to the famous Yiddish idiom always used in describing a complicated, long drawn out narrative or difficult problem or complex situation. In Yiddish, things of such nature were called a *gantzer chad gadya* — an entire *chad gadya* — a complete, complicated matter. The phrase has even been preserved in modern Israeli Hebrew to describe the same sort of situation — a *chad gadya gamur.*

What is clear is that *Chad Gadya* is basically a song of encouragement and hope and that eventually God will do justice in the world and

Who knows thirteen? I know thirteen: thirteen are the attributes of God; twelve are the tribes; eleven are the stars (in Joseph's dream); ten are the Ten Commandments; nine are the months of pregnancy; eight are the days of circumcision; seven are the days of the week; six are the Orders of the Mishnah; five are the Books of the Torah; four are the Matriarchs; three are the Patriarchs; two are the Tablets of the Covenant; One is our God, in heaven and on earth.

One kid, one kid; that father bought for two zuzim, one kid, one kid.

וְאָתָא שׁוּנְרָא וְאָכְלָה לְגַדְיָא, דְּזַבִּין אַבָּא בִּתְרֵי זוּזֵי, חַד גַּדְיָא חַד גַּדְיָא.

וְאָתָא כַלְבָּא וְנָשַׁךְ לְשׁוּנְרָא, דְּאָכְלָה לְגַדְיָא, דְּזַבִּין אַבָּא בִּתְרֵי זוּזֵי, חַד גַּדְיָא חַד גַּדְיָא.

וְאָתָא חוּטְרָא וְהִכָּה לְכַלְבָּא, דְּנָשַׁךְ לְשׁוּנְרָא, דְּאָכְלָה לְגַדְיָא, דְּזַבִּין אַבָּא בִּתְרֵי זוּזֵי, חַד גַּדְיָא חַד גַּדְיָא.

וְאָתָא נוּרָא וְשָׂרַף לְחוּטְרָא, דְּהִכָּה לְכַלְבָּא, דְּנָשַׁךְ לְשׁוּנְרָא, דְּאָכְלָה לְגַדְיָא, דְּזַבִּין אַבָּא בִּתְרֵי זוּזֵי, חַד גַּדְיָא חַד גַּדְיָא.

וְאָתָא מַיָּא וְכָבָה לְנוּרָא, דְּשָׂרַף לְחוּטְרָא, דְּהִכָּה לְכַלְבָּא, דְּנָשַׁךְ לְשׁוּנְרָא, דְּאָכְלָה לְגַדְיָא, דְּזַבִּין אַבָּא בִּתְרֵי זוּזֵי, חַד גַּדְיָא חַד גַּדְיָא.

וְאָתָא תוֹרָא וְשָׁתָה לְמַיָּא, דְּכָבָה לְנוּרָא, דְּשָׂרַף לְחוּטְרָא, דְּהִכָּה לְכַלְבָּא, דְּנָשַׁךְ לְשׁוּנְרָא, דְּאָכְלָה לְגַדְיָא, דְּזַבִּין אַבָּא בִּתְרֵי זוּזֵי, חַד גַּדְיָא חַד גַּדְיָא.

וְאָתָא הַשּׁוֹחֵט וְשָׁחַט לְתוֹרָא, דְּשָׁתָה לְמַיָּא, דְּכָבָה לְנוּרָא, דְּשָׂרַף לְחוּטְרָא, דְּהִכָּה לְכַלְבָּא, דְּנָשַׁךְ לְשׁוּנְרָא, דְּאָכְלָה לְגַדְיָא, דְּזַבִּין אַבָּא בִּתְרֵי זוּזֵי, חַד גַּדְיָא חַד גַּדְיָא.

וְאָתָא מַלְאַךְ הַמָּוֶת וְשָׁחַט לְשׁוֹחֵט, דְּשָׁחַט לְתוֹרָא, דְּשָׁתָה לְמַיָּא, דְּכָבָה לְנוּרָא, דְּשָׂרַף לְחוּטְרָא, דְּהִכָּה לְכַלְבָּא, דְּנָשַׁךְ לְשׁוּנְרָא, דְּאָכְלָה לְגַדְיָא, דְּזַבִּין אַבָּא בִּתְרֵי זוּזֵי, חַד גַּדְיָא חַד גַּדְיָא.

---

all evil — and even death itself — will be confounded and defeated. Thus we all leave the Seder table on a note of great optimism and confidence, in the conviction that all will yet come right. And that certainly is the essential message of the entire night — *leil shimurim* —

A cat then came and devoured the kid that father bought for two zuzim, one kid, one kid.

A dog then came and bit the cat, that devoured the kid that father bought for two zuzim, one kid, one kid.

A stick then came and beat the dog, that bit the cat, that devoured the kid that father bought for two zuzim, one kid, one kid.

A fire then came and burnt the stick, that beat the dog, that bit the cat, that devoured the kid that father bought for two zuzim, one kid, one kid.

Water then came and quenched the fire, that burnt the stick, that beat the dog, that bit the cat, that devoured the kid that father bought for two zuzim, one kid, one kid.

An ox then came and drank the water, that quenched the fire, that burnt the stick, that beat the dog, that bit the cat, that devoured the kid that father bought for two zuzim, one kid, one kid.

A slaughterer then came and slaughtered the ox, that drank the water, that quenched the fire, that burnt the stick, that beat the dog, that bit the cat, that devoured the kid that father bought for two zuzim, one kid, one kid.

The angel of death then came and killed the slaughterer, who slaughtered the ox, that drank the water, that quenched the fire, that burnt the stick, that beat the dog, that bit the cat, that devoured the kid that father bought for two zuzim, one kid, one kid.

---

come right. And that certainly is the essential message of the entire night — *leil shimurim* — a night of protection and hope, a night when we express our confident hopes for the future and our gratitude for the past. There is no greater joy than being able to join the past and the future in confidence and optimism, all at one's family table.

וְאָתָא הַקָּדוֹשׁ בָּרוּךְ הוּא וְשָׁחַט לְמַלְאַךְ הַמָּוֶת, דְּשָׁחַט לְשׁוֹחֵט, דְּשָׁחַט לְתוֹרָא, דְּשָׁתָה לְמַיָּא, דְּכָבָה לְנוּרָא, דְּשָׂרַף לְחוּטְרָא, דְּהִכָּה לְכַלְבָּא, דְּנָשַׁךְ לְשׁוּנְרָא, דְּאָכְלָה לְגַדְיָא, דְּזַבִּין אַבָּא בִּתְרֵי זוּזֵי, חַד גַּדְיָא חַד גַּדְיָא.

Although the Haggadah formally ends at this point,
one should continue to occupy himself with the story of the Exodus,
and the laws of Pesach, until sleep overtakes him.

☙ After The Seder

There is a custom to recite *Shir Hashirim*, Solomon's lofty poem describing the intimacy of the relationship between God and Israel, after the conclusion of the Seder service. The custom of many congregations is to read this book on the Sabbath of Pesach. Pesach, the season of spring and renewal, of freedom and optimism, is the ideal time for reciting and studying this song of longing and inseparability between the God of Israel and His people. I must admit that there have been times that I dozed off before finishing *Shir Hashirim* after the Seder. But I at least have tried to fulfill this beautiful custom. Jewish tradition teaches us that heavenly credit is given for effort as well as for accomplishment. That tradition always gives me comfort, not only on the night of the Seder service, but all year round as well.

In our home, the post-Seder cleanup chores

The Holy One, Blessed is He, then came and slew the angel of death, who killed the slaughterer, who slaughtered the ox, that drank the water, that quenched the fire, that burnt the stick, that beat the dog, that bit the cat, that devoured the kid that father bought for two zuzim, one kid, one kid.

Although the Haggadah formally ends at this point, one should continue to occupy himself with the story of the Exodus, and the laws of Pesach, until sleep overtakes him.

---

are divided between the adults (those who are still awake) and the younger generation, mainly the teenagers and young adults. I have always assumed the role of supervisor of these activities (that is, when I was still awake enough to do so). Some of the most meaningful conversations between my younger generations and me have taken place during this post-Seder cleanup process. I think that it is the lingering atmosphere of the Seder itself that lends itself to having such warm, intimate, and treasured discussions. Though the conversations are usually about serious topics — the Haggadah, study, careers, finding a spouse, etc. — they are always punctuated with gleeful laughter and good spirits. Finally retiring to sleep at 2 o'clock in the morning or thereabouts, I do so with a heavy stomach and a light heart. The night of the Seder is truly a *leil shimurim* — a night to be savored and stored into memory and guarded fiercely in one's heart and soul.

שיר השירים

SHIR HASHIRIM/SONG OF SONGS

א

א-ב שִׁיר הַשִּׁירִים אֲשֶׁר לִשְׁלֹמֹה: יִשָּׁקֵנִי מִנְּשִׁיקוֹת פִּיהוּ כִּי־טוֹבִים דֹּדֶיךָ מִיָּיִן:
ג-ד לְרֵיחַ שְׁמָנֶיךָ טוֹבִים שֶׁמֶן תּוּרַק שְׁמֶךָ עַל־כֵּן עֲלָמוֹת אֲהֵבוּךָ: מָשְׁכֵנִי אַחֲרֶיךָ
נָּרוּצָה הֱבִיאַנִי הַמֶּלֶךְ חֲדָרָיו נָגִילָה וְנִשְׂמְחָה בָּךְ נַזְכִּירָה דֹדֶיךָ מִיַּיִן מֵישָׁרִים
ה אֲהֵבוּךָ: שְׁחוֹרָה אֲנִי וְנָאוָה בְּנוֹת יְרוּשָׁלִָם כְּאָהֳלֵי קֵדָר כִּירִיעוֹת
ו שְׁלֹמֹה: אַל־תִּרְאוּנִי שֶׁאֲנִי שְׁחַרְחֹרֶת שֶׁשְּׁזָפַתְנִי הַשָּׁמֶשׁ בְּנֵי אִמִּי נִחֲרוּ־בִי
ז שָׂמֻנִי נֹטֵרָה אֶת־הַכְּרָמִים כַּרְמִי שֶׁלִּי לֹא נָטָרְתִּי: הַגִּידָה לִּי שֶׁאָהֲבָה נַפְשִׁי
אֵיכָה תִרְעֶה אֵיכָה תַּרְבִּיץ בַּצָּהֳרָיִם שַׁלָּמָה אֶהְיֶה כְּעֹטְיָה עַל עֶדְרֵי חֲבֵרֶיךָ:
ח אִם־לֹא תֵדְעִי לָךְ הַיָּפָה בַּנָּשִׁים צְאִי־לָךְ בְּעִקְבֵי הַצֹּאן וּרְעִי אֶת־גְּדִיֹּתַיִךְ עַל
ט-י מִשְׁכְּנוֹת הָרֹעִים: לְסֻסָתִי בְּרִכְבֵי פַרְעֹה דִּמִּיתִיךְ רַעְיָתִי: נָאווּ
יא לְחָיַיִךְ בַּתֹּרִים צַוָּארֵךְ בַּחֲרוּזִים: תּוֹרֵי זָהָב נַעֲשֶׂה־לָּךְ עִם נְקֻדּוֹת הַכָּסֶף:

NOTES INCLUDING PHRASE-BY-PHRASE LITERAL TRANSLATION

1:1. שִׁיר הַשִּׁירִים — *The song that excels all songs* [lit., *The song of songs*]. The greatest song uttered to God by Israel.

אֲשֶׁר לִשְׁלֹמֹה — *dedicated to God, Him to Whom peace belongs* [lit., *which is Solomon's*]. In *Proverbs* and *Ecclesiastes,* Solomon is identified as the "son of David." The omission of David's name here implies that there is a second שְׁלֹמֹה, namely מֶלֶךְ שֶׁהַשָּׁלוֹם שֶׁלּוֹ, "the King to Whom peace belongs," i.e., God, the Source of peace.

1:2. יִשָּׁקֵנִי מִנְּשִׁיקוֹת פִּיהוּ — *Communicate Your innermost wisdom to me again in loving closeness* [lit., *May He kiss me with the kisses of His mouth*]. Exiled Israel longs for God to teach the Torah, "mouth to mouth," as at Sinai.

כִּי טוֹבִים דֹּדֶיךָ מִיָּיִן — *for Your love is dearer to me than all earthly delights* [lit., *for Your love is better than wine*]. The love You showed when You redeemed us from Egypt and gave us the Torah is dearer to us than wine or any other earthly pleasure.

1:3. לְרֵיחַ שְׁמָנֶיךָ טוֹבִים — *Like the scent of goodly oils is the spreading fame of Your great deeds* [lit., *For fragrance Your oils are good*]. The "fragrance" of God's miracles in Egypt was felt everywhere.

שֶׁמֶן תּוּרַק שְׁמֶךָ — *Your very name is "Flowing Oil"* [lit., *Your name is oil poured forth*]. Your reputation is like fine oil; the more it is poured, the more its fragrance spreads.

עַל כֵּן עֲלָמוֹת אֲהֵבוּךָ — *therefore have nations loved You* [lit., *therefore do young maidens love You*]. "Maidens" refers to the nations of the world.

1:4. מָשְׁכֵנִי אַחֲרֶיךָ נָּרוּצָה — *Upon perceiving a mere hint that You wished to draw me [near], we rushed with perfect faith after You into the wilderness* [lit., *Draw me, we will run after You!*]. We followed God faithfully, without food or drink (see *Jeremiah* 2:2,6).

הֱבִיאַנִי הַמֶּלֶךְ חֲדָרָיו — *The King brought me into His cloud-pillared chamber* [lit., *the King has brought me into His chambers*]. God protected us with His clouds of glory (see *Exodus* 13:21-22).

נָגִילָה וְנִשְׂמְחָה בָּךְ — *whatever our travail, we shall always be glad and rejoice in Your Torah* [lit., *we will rejoice and be glad in You*]. We take delight in Your Torah.

נַזְכִּירָה דֹדֶיךָ מִיַּיִן — *We recall Your love more than earthly delights* [lit., *we will commemorate Your love (better) than wine*]. We recall Your former love as the finest of all pleasures.

מֵישָׁרִים אֲהֵבוּךָ — *unrestrainedly do they love You* [lit., *sincerely do they love You*].

1:5. שְׁחוֹרָה אֲנִי וְנָאוָה — *Though I am black with sin, I am comely with virtue* [lit., *I am black, yet comely*]. Though my Husband left me because my sins blackened me, I am comely by virtue of my forefathers' deeds.

בְּנוֹת יְרוּשָׁלָיִם — *O nations destined to ascend to Jerusalem* [lit., *O daughters of Jerusalem*]. Ultimately, all peoples will stream to honor Jerusalem, and you nations, earlier called "maidens" (v. 3), will become "her daughters."

כְּאָהֳלֵי קֵדָר כִּירִיעוֹת שְׁלֹמֹה — *though sullied as the tents of Kedar, I will be immaculate as the draperies of Him to whom peace belongs* [lit., *as the tents of Kedar, as the curtains of Solomon*].

1:6. אַל תִּרְאוּנִי שֶׁאֲנִי שְׁחַרְחֹרֶת — *Do not view me with contempt despite my swarthiness* [lit., *Do not look upon me that I am swarthy*].

שֶׁשְּׁזָפַתְנִי הַשָּׁמֶשׁ — *for it is but the sun which has glared upon me* [lit., *because the sun has gazed upon me*]. My darkness, i.e., sinfulness, is not genetic; it will go away when I avoid the sun.

בְּנֵי אִמִּי נִחֲרוּ בִי — *The alien children of my mother incited me* [lit., *my mother's sons kindled in me*]. The mixed multitude of Egyptians and other aliens who accompanied us at the Exodus incited us to worship idols.

שָׂמֻנִי נֹטֵרָה אֶת הַכְּרָמִים — *and made me a keeper of the vineyards of idols* [lit., *they made me keeper of the vineyards*]. . .

כַּרְמִי שֶׁלִּי לֹא נָטָרְתִּי — *but the vineyard of my own true God I did not keep* [lit., *my own vineyard I did not guard*]. I served strange gods, but not the God of my fathers.

1:7. Israel addresses God as a woman addressing her beloved Husband, and compares herself to sheep, as she contends that the exile is too difficult for her and unbecoming to Him.

הַגִּידָה לִּי שֶׁאָהֲבָה נַפְשִׁי — *Tell me, O You Whom my soul loves* . . .

ALLEGORICAL RENDERING FOLLOWING RASHI

1 *Prologue* 1 *The song that excels all songs dedicated to God, Him to Whom peace belongs:*
Israel in exile to God 2 *Communicate Your innermost wisdom to me again in loving closeness, for*
Your love is dearer to me than all earthly delights. 3 *Like the scent of goodly oils is*
the spreading fame of Your great deeds; Your very name is "Flowing Oil," therefore
have nations loved You. 4 *Upon perceiving a mere hint that You wished to draw me*
[near], we rushed with perfect faith after You into the wilderness. The King brought
me into His cloud-pillared chamber; whatever our travail, we shall always be glad
and rejoice in Your Torah. We recall Your love more than earthly delights,
unrestrainedly do they love You.

Israel to the nations 5 *Though I am black with sin, I am comely with virtue, O nations destined to*
ascend to Jerusalem; though sullied as the tents of Kedar, I will be immaculate as
the draperies of Him to Whom peace belongs. 6 *Do not view me with contempt*
despite my swarthiness, for it is but the sun which has glared upon me. The alien
children of my mother incited me and made me a keeper of the vineyards of idols,
but the vineyard of my own true God I did not keep.

Israel to God 7 *Tell me, O You Whom my soul loves: Where will You graze Your flock? Where*
will You rest them under the fiercest sun of harshest exile? Why shall I be like one
veiled in mourning among the flocks of Your fellow shepherds?

God responds to Israel 8 *If you know not where to graze, O fairest of nations, follow the footsteps of the*
sheep, your forefathers, who traced a straight, unswerving path after My Torah.
Then you can graze your tender kids even among the dwellings of foreign
shepherds. 9 *With My mighty steeds who battled Pharaoh's riders I revealed that*
you are My beloved. 10 *Your cheeks are lovely with rows of gems, your neck with*
necklaces, My gifts to you from the splitting sea, 11 *by inducing Pharaoh to engage*
in pursuit, to add circlets of gold to your spangles of silver.

NOTES INCLUDING PHRASE-BY-PHRASE LITERAL TRANSLATION

אֵיכָה תִרְעֶה אֵיכָה תַּרְבִּיץ בַּצָּהֳרָיִם — *Where will You graze your flock? Where will You rest them under the fiercest sun of harshest exile?* [lit., *Where will You graze (Your flock), where will You rest (them) at noon*?]. Where will You graze us, Your flock, among the seventy wolflike nations? Where will You give us rest in the fierce lands of our exile?

שַׁלָּמָה אֶהְיֶה כְּעֹטְיָה — *Why shall I be like one veiled in mourning* [lit., *for what reason should I be as one veiled*]. It is unbecoming to You that I display grief.

עַל עֶדְרֵי חֲבֵרֶיךָ — *among the flocks of Your fellow shepherds* [lit., *by the flocks of Your colleagues*]? The other nations, who are "shepherded" by their rulers.

1:8. אִם לֹא תֵדְעִי לָךְ הַיָּפָה בַּנָּשִׁים — *If you know not where to graze, O fairest of nations* [lit., *If you do not know, O fairest of women*]. . .

צְאִי לָךְ בְּעִקְבֵי הַצֹּאן — *follow the footsteps of the sheep, your forefathers, who traced a straight, unswerving path after My Torah* [lit., *go out in the tracks of the sheep*]. If you do not know how to safeguard your children from alien cultures, follow the example of your ancestors who observed My commandments.

וּרְעִי אֶת גְּדִיֹּתַיִךְ עַל מִשְׁכְּנוֹת הָרֹעִים — *Then you can graze your tender kids even among the dwellings of foreign shepherds* [lit., *and graze your kids by the shepherds' tents*]. Then you will be able to raise your children among the nations.

1:9. לְסֻסָתִי בְּרִכְבֵי פַרְעֹה — *With My mighty steeds who battled Pharaoh's riders* [lit., *To a steed in Pharaoh's chariot*]. God saved the Jews from Pharaoh's army at the Sea of Reeds (*Exodus* Chs. 14-15).

דִּמִּיתִיךְ רַעְיָתִי — *I revealed that you are My beloved* [lit., *I have compared you, My beloved*].

1:10. נָאווּ לְחָיַיִךְ בַּתֹּרִים צַוָּארֵךְ בַּחֲרוּזִים — *Your cheeks are lovely with rows of gems, your neck with necklaces, My gifts to you from the splitting sea* [lit., *your cheeks are comely with circlets, your neck with strings of jewels*]. . .

1:11. תּוֹרֵי זָהָב נַעֲשֶׂה לָּךְ עִם נְקֻדּוֹת הַכָּסֶף — *by inducing Pharaoh to engage in pursuit, to add circlets of gold to your spangles of silver* [lit., *circlets of gold will We make for you and points of silver*]. God influenced the pursuing Egyptians to wear their treasures, so that, upon their defeat, Israel could claim the booty.

יב־יד עַד־שֶׁהַמֶּלֶךְ בִּמְסִבּוֹ נִרְדִּי נָתַן רֵיחוֹ׃ צְרוֹר הַמֹּר ׀ דּוֹדִי לִי בֵּין שָׁדַי יָלִין׃ אֶשְׁכֹּל
טו הַכֹּפֶר ׀ דּוֹדִי לִי בְּכַרְמֵי עֵין גֶּדִי׃ הִנָּךְ יָפָה רַעְיָתִי הִנָּךְ יָפָה עֵינַיִךְ
טז־יז יוֹנִים׃ הִנְּךָ יָפֶה דוֹדִי אַף נָעִים אַף־עַרְשֵׂנוּ רַעֲנָנָה׃ קֹרוֹת בָּתֵּינוּ אֲרָזִים °רחיטנו
ב א־ב [°רָהִיטֵנוּ ק׳] בְּרוֹתִים׃ אֲנִי חֲבַצֶּלֶת הַשָּׁרוֹן שׁוֹשַׁנַּת הָעֲמָקִים׃ כְּשׁוֹשַׁנָּה בֵּין
ג הַחוֹחִים כֵּן רַעְיָתִי בֵּין הַבָּנוֹת׃ כְּתַפּוּחַ בַּעֲצֵי הַיַּעַר כֵּן דּוֹדִי בֵּין הַבָּנִים בְּצִלּוֹ
ד חִמַּדְתִּי וְיָשַׁבְתִּי וּפִרְיוֹ מָתוֹק לְחִכִּי׃ הֱבִיאַנִי אֶל־בֵּית הַיָּיִן וְדִגְלוֹ עָלַי אַהֲבָה׃
ה־ו סַמְּכוּנִי בָּאֲשִׁישׁוֹת רַפְּדוּנִי בַּתַּפּוּחִים כִּי־חוֹלַת אַהֲבָה אָנִי׃ שְׂמֹאלוֹ תַּחַת
ז לְרֹאשִׁי וִימִינוֹ תְּחַבְּקֵנִי׃ הִשְׁבַּעְתִּי אֶתְכֶם בְּנוֹת יְרוּשָׁלַםִ בִּצְבָאוֹת אוֹ בְּאַיְלוֹת
ח הַשָּׂדֶה אִם־תָּעִירוּ ׀ וְאִם־תְּעוֹרְרוּ אֶת־הָאַהֲבָה עַד שֶׁתֶּחְפָּץ׃ קוֹל דּוֹדִי
ט הִנֵּה־זֶה בָּא מְדַלֵּג עַל־הֶהָרִים מְקַפֵּץ עַל־הַגְּבָעוֹת׃ דּוֹמֶה דוֹדִי לִצְבִי אוֹ לְעֹפֶר
הָאַיָּלִים הִנֵּה־זֶה עוֹמֵד אַחַר כָּתְלֵנוּ מַשְׁגִּיחַ מִן־הַחַלֹּנוֹת מֵצִיץ מִן־הַחֲרַכִּים׃

NOTES INCLUDING PHRASE-BY-PHRASE LITERAL TRANSLATION

1:12. עַד שֶׁהַמֶּלֶךְ בִּמְסִבּוֹ נִרְדִּי נָתַן רֵיחוֹ — *While the King was yet at Sinai my malodorous deed gave forth its scent as my Golden Calf defiled the covenant* [lit., *While the King was* (still) *at His table, my nard gave forth its fragrance*]. Nard is a fragrant herb, but is used here as a euphemism for the bad odor of idolatry.

1:13. צְרוֹר הַמֹּר דּוֹדִי לִי — *But my Beloved responded with a bundle of myrrh, the fragrant atonement of erecting a Tabernacle* [lit., *A bag of myrrh is my Beloved to me*]. After the disaster of the Golden Calf, God offered me a new fragrance. "Contribute toward the construction of the Tabernacle to atone for the gold you gave to make the Calf."

בֵּין שָׁדַי יָלִין — *where His Presence would dwell between the Holy Ark's staves* [lit., *lodged between my breasts*], i.e., the *Shechinah* (God's immanent Presence) dwelled between the two staves of the Ark. The long staves of the Ark pressed against the curtain that separated between it and the other appurtenances of the Tabernacle, causing breastlike protrusions on the other side of the curtain (*Yoma* 54a; *Menachos* 98a).

1:14. אֶשְׁכֹּל הַכֹּפֶר דּוֹדִי לִי בְּכַרְמֵי עֵין גֶּדִי — *Like a cluster of henna in En-gedi vineyards has my Beloved multiplied His forgiveness to me* [lit., *A cluster of henna is my Beloved to me, in the vineyards of En-gedi*]. The word כֹּפֶר, "henna," is linguistically related to כַּפָּרָה, "atonement."

1:15. הִנָּךְ יָפָה רַעְיָתִי הִנָּךְ יָפָה עֵינַיִךְ יוֹנִים — *He said, "I forgive you, My friend, for you are lovely in deed and lovely in resolve. The righteous among you are loyal as a dove"* [lit., *Behold, you are beautiful, My beloved; behold, you are beautiful, your eyes are doves*]. Your righteous leaders — the "eyes" of the generation — have cleaved to Me like doves, who are faithful to their mates.

1:16. הִנְּךָ יָפֶה דוֹדִי אַף נָעִים — *It is You Who are lovely, my Beloved, so pleasant that You pardoned my sin* [lit., *You are handsome, my Beloved, indeed pleasant*]. The beauty is Yours, for having forgiven us.

אַף עַרְשֵׂנוּ רַעֲנָנָה — *enabling our Temple to make me ever fresh* [lit., *even our couch is full of vigor*]. "Couch" refers to the Tabernacle, whose existence led to flourishing growth of the Jewish population.

1:17. קֹרוֹת בָּתֵּינוּ אֲרָזִים רָהִיטֵנוּ בְּרוֹתִים — *The beams of our houses are cedar, our panels are cypress.*

2:1. אֲנִי חֲבַצֶּלֶת הַשָּׁרוֹן שׁוֹשַׁנַּת הָעֲמָקִים — *I am but a rose of Sharon, even an ever-fresh rose of the valleys* [lit., *I am a rose of the Sharon, a rose of the valleys*].

2:2. כְּשׁוֹשַׁנָּה בֵּין הַחוֹחִים כֵּן רַעְיָתִי בֵּין הַבָּנוֹת — *Like the rose maintaining its beauty among the thorns, so is My faithful beloved among the nations* [lit., *As a rose among thorns, so is My beloved among the daughters*]. Just as the rose retains its beauty though surrounded by thorns, so My beloved people maintains her faith despite the torments of her neighbors.

2:3. כְּתַפּוּחַ בַּעֲצֵי הַיַּעַר כֵּן דּוֹדִי בֵּין הַבָּנִים — *Like the fruitful, fragrant apple among the barren trees of the forest, so is my Beloved among the gods* [lit., *Like an apple tree among the trees of the forest, so is my Beloved among the sons*]. God is superior to all the fruitless idols of the nations.

בְּצִלּוֹ חִמַּדְתִּי וְיָשַׁבְתִּי — *In His shade I delighted and [there] I sat . . .* וּפִרְיוֹ מָתוֹק לְחִכִּי — *and the fruit of His Torah was sweet to my palate* [lit., *and His fruit is sweet to my palate*]. We spent twelve months at Mount Sinai enjoying the sweetness of His Torah.

2:4. הֱבִיאַנִי אֶל בֵּית הַיָּיִן — *He brought me to the chamber of Torah delights* [lit., *He has brought me to the house of wine*]; an allusion to the Tent of the Meeting, where Moses expounded the Torah's commandments.

וְדִגְלוֹ עָלַי אַהֲבָה — *and clustered my encampments about Him in love* [lit., *and His banner upon me is love*]. He gathered the tribes about His Tabernacle.

2:5. סַמְּכוּנִי בָּאֲשִׁישׁוֹת רַפְּדוּנִי בַּתַּפּוּחִים — *I say to Him, "Sustain me in exile with dainty cakes, spread fragrant apples about me to comfort my dispersion* [lit., *Sustain me with dainties, spread out apples around me*]. . .

כִּי חוֹלַת אַהֲבָה אָנִי — *for, bereft of Your Presence, I am sick with love"* [lit., *for I am sick with love*]. In exile, I am sick for want of

Israel about God 12 *While the King was yet at Sinai my malodorous deed gave forth its scent as my*
Golden Calf defiled the covenant. 13 *But my Beloved responded with a bundle of myrrh,*
the fragrant atonement of erecting a Tabernacle where His Presence would dwell
between the Holy Ark's staves. 14 *Like a cluster of henna in En-gedi vineyards has my*
Beloved multiplied His forgiveness to me. 15 *He said, "I forgive you, My friend, for you*
are lovely in deed and lovely in resolve. The righteous among you are loyal as a dove."

Israel to God 16 *It is You Who are lovely, my Beloved, so pleasant that You pardoned my sin*
enabling our Temple to make me ever fresh. 17 *The beams of our houses are cedar, our*
2 *panels are cypress.* 1 *I am but a rose of Sharon, even an ever-fresh rose of the valleys.*

God to Israel 2 *Like the rose maintaining its beauty among the thorns, so is My faithful beloved*
among the nations.

Israel reminisces . . . 3 *Like the fruitful, fragrant apple among the barren trees of the forest, so is my Beloved*
among the gods. In His shade I delighted and [there] I sat, and the fruit of His Torah
was sweet to my palate. 4 *He brought me to the chamber of Torah delights and*
clustered my encampments about Him in love. 5 *I say to Him, "Sustain me in exile with*
dainty cakes, spread fragrant apples about me to comfort my dispersion, for, bereft of
Your Presence, I am sick with love." 6 *With memories of His loving support in the desert,*
of His left hand under my head, of His right hand enveloping me.

. . . turns to the nations . . . 7 *I adjure you, O nations destined to ascend to Jerusalem, for if you violate your oath,*
you will become as defenseless as gazelles or hinds of the field, if you dare provoke God
to hate me or disturb His love for me while He still desires it.

. . . then reminisces further 8 *The voice of my Beloved! Behold, it came suddenly to redeem me, as if leaping over*
mountains, skipping over hills. 9 *In His swiftness to redeem me, my Beloved is like a*
gazelle or a young hart. I thought I would be forever alone, but behold! He was standing
behind our wall, observing through the windows, peering through the lattices.

NOTES INCLUDING PHRASE-BY-PHRASE LITERAL TRANSLATION

His love; I thirst for Him here in exile.

2:6. שְׂמֹאלוֹ תַּחַת לְרֹאשִׁי וִימִינוֹ תְּחַבְּקֵנִי — *With memories of His loving support in the desert, of His left hand under my head, of His right hand enveloping me* [lit., *His left hand is under my head and His right arm embraces me*]. Ecstatically, I recall how I was accompanied by God's Ark, enveloped in His cloud, eating His manna.

2:7. הִשְׁבַּעְתִּי אֶתְכֶם בְּנוֹת יְרוּשָׁלַםִ — *I adjure you, O nations destined to ascend to Jerusalem* [lit., *I have adjured you, O daughters of Jerusalem*]. See 1:5.

בִּצְבָאוֹת אוֹ בְּאַיְלוֹת הַשָּׂדֶה — *for if you violate your oath, you will become as defenseless as gazelles or hinds of the field* [lit., *by gazelles or by hinds of the field*] . . .

אִם תָּעִירוּ וְאִם תְּעוֹרְרוּ אֶת הָאַהֲבָה עַד שֶׁתֶּחְפָּץ — *if you dare provoke God to hate me or disturb His love for me while He still desires it* [lit., *should you wake or rouse the love until it pleases*].

2:8. With this verse, Israel begins a recapitulation of God's remembrance of His people in Egypt.

קוֹל דּוֹדִי הִנֵּה זֶה בָּא — *The voice of my Beloved! Behold it came suddenly to redeem me* [lit., *The voice of my Beloved! Behold He comes*]. . .

מְדַלֵּג עַל הֶהָרִים מְקַפֵּץ עַל הַגְּבָעוֹת — *as if leaping over mountains, skipping over hills* [lit., *leaping upon the mountains skipping upon the hills*]. God leaped and skipped, so to speak, redeeming the Jews one hundred and ninety years before the completion of the prophecy of four hundred years of bondage.

2:9. דּוֹמֶה דוֹדִי לִצְבִי אוֹ לְעֹפֶר הָאַיָּלִים — *In His swiftness to redeem me, my Beloved is like a gazelle or a young hart* [lit., *My Beloved is like a gazelle or a young hart*].

הִנֵּה זֶה עוֹמֵד אַחַר כָּתְלֵנוּ מַשְׁגִּיחַ מִן הַחַלֹּנוֹת מֵצִיץ מִן הַחֲרַכִּים — *I thought I would be forever alone, but behold! He was standing behind our wall, observing through the windows, peering through the lattices* [lit., *behold He stands behind our wall looking through the windows, peering through the lattices*]. I was like a woman resigned to being an *agunah* (bereft of husband, yet legally bound to him), for a still undetermined period of time. Then, suddenly, He came to tell me that He is peering through the windows of the heavens taking notice of my plight (see *Exodus* 3:7), reassuring me that whatever my travail, He will never fail to keep the closest watch over me.

י־יא עָנָ֥ה דוֹדִ֖י וְאָ֣מַר לִ֑י ק֥וּמִי לָ֛ךְ רַעְיָתִ֥י יָפָתִ֖י וּלְכִי־לָֽךְ׃ כִּֽי־הִנֵּ֥ה הַסְּתָ֖ו עָבָ֑ר
יב הַגֶּ֕שֶׁם חָלַ֖ף הָלַ֥ךְ לֽוֹ׃ הַנִּצָּנִים֙ נִרְא֣וּ בָאָ֔רֶץ עֵ֥ת הַזָּמִ֖יר הִגִּ֑יעַ וְק֥וֹל הַתּ֖וֹר
יג נִשְׁמַ֥ע בְּאַרְצֵֽנוּ׃ הַתְּאֵנָה֙ חָֽנְטָ֣ה פַגֶּ֔יהָ וְהַגְּפָנִ֥ים ׀ סְמָדַ֖ר נָ֣תְנוּ רֵ֑יחַ ק֥וּמִי °לכי
יד [°לָ֛ךְ ק׳] רַעְיָתִ֥י יָפָתִ֖י וּלְכִי־לָֽךְ׃ יוֹנָתִ֞י בְּחַגְוֵ֣י הַסֶּ֗לַע בְּסֵ֙תֶר֙
הַמַּדְרֵגָ֔ה הַרְאִ֙ינִי֙ אֶת־מַרְאַ֔יִךְ הַשְׁמִיעִ֖ינִי אֶת־ קוֹלֵ֑ךְ כִּי־קוֹלֵ֥ךְ עָרֵ֖ב וּמַרְאֵ֥יךְ
טו נָאוֶֽה׃ אֶֽחֱזוּ־לָ֙נוּ֙ שֽׁוּעָלִ֔ים שֽׁוּעָלִ֖ים קְטַנִּ֑ים מְחַבְּלִ֣ים כְּרָמִ֔ים וּכְרָמֵ֖ינוּ
טז־יז סְמָדַֽר׃ דּוֹדִ֥י לִי֙ וַאֲנִ֣י ל֔וֹ הָרֹעֶ֖ה בַּשּׁוֹשַׁנִּֽים׃ עַ֤ד שֶׁיָּפ֙וּחַ֙ הַיּ֔וֹם וְנָ֖סוּ הַצְּלָלִ֑ים
ג א סֹב֩ דְּמֵה־לְךָ֨ דוֹדִ֜י לִצְבִ֗י א֛וֹ לְעֹ֥פֶר הָאַיָּלִ֖ים עַל־הָ֥רֵי בָֽתֶר׃ עַל־
מִשְׁכָּבִי֙ בַּלֵּיל֔וֹת בִּקַּ֕שְׁתִּי אֵ֥ת שֶׁאָהֲבָ֖ה נַפְשִׁ֑י בִּקַּשְׁתִּ֖יו וְלֹ֥א מְצָאתִֽיו׃
ב אָק֩וּמָה נָּ֨א וַאֲסוֹבְבָ֜ה בָעִ֗יר בַּשְּׁוָקִים֙ וּבָ֣רְחֹב֔וֹת אֲבַקְשָׁ֕ה אֵ֥ת שֶׁאָהֲבָ֖ה
ג נַפְשִׁ֑י בִּקַּשְׁתִּ֖יו וְלֹ֥א מְצָאתִֽיו׃ מְצָא֙וּנִי֙ הַשֹּׁ֣מְרִ֔ים הַסֹּבְבִ֖ים בָּעִ֑יר אֵ֛ת שֶׁאָהֲבָ֥ה
ד נַפְשִׁ֖י רְאִיתֶֽם׃ כִּמְעַט֙ שֶׁעָבַ֣רְתִּי מֵהֶ֔ם עַ֣ד שֶׁמָּצָ֔אתִי אֵ֥ת שֶׁאָהֲבָ֖ה נַפְשִׁ֑י

NOTES INCLUDING PHRASE-BY-PHRASE LITERAL TRANSLATION

2:10. עָנָה דוֹדִי וְאָמַר לִי — *When He redeemed me from Egypt, my Beloved called out and said to me,* [lit., *My Beloved lifted His voice and said to me,*]. . .

קוּמִי לָךְ רַעְיָתִי יָפָתִי וּלְכִי לָךְ — *"Arise My love, My fair one, and go forth* [lit., *Arise My love, My fair one, and go forth for yourself*]. "Carry out My precepts, and I will bring you up out of the affliction of Egypt" (*Exodus* 3:17).

2:11-13. A poetic picture describing the season of Redemption. Metaphorically, the verses conjure up an image of the worst being over, of redemption being at hand.

2:11. כִּי הִנֵּה הַסְּתָו עָבָר — *For the winter of bondage has passed* [lit., *For, behold, the winter is past*]. The years of bondage are over. It is time to travel forth.

הַגֶּשֶׁם חָלַף הָלַךְ לוֹ — *the deluge of suffering is over and gone* [lit., *the rain is over and gone*].

2:12. הַנִּצָּנִים נִרְאוּ בָאָרֶץ — *The righteous blossoms are seen in the land* [lit., *The blossoms have appeared in the land*]. The "blossoms" are Moses and Aaron who blossomed in response to Israel's needs.

עֵת הַזָּמִיר הִגִּיעַ — *The time of your song has arrived* [lit., *the time of singing has come*], to praise God, by singing the Song of the Sea (*Exodus* Ch. 15).

וְקוֹל הַתּוֹר נִשְׁמַע בְּאַרְצֵנוּ — *and the voice of your guide is heard in the land* [lit., *and the voice of the turtledove is heard in the land*]. The word תּוֹר, "turtledove," is linguistically related to תַּיָּר, "guide," an allusion to Moses.

2:13. הַתְּאֵנָה חָנְטָה פַגֶּיהָ וְהַגְּפָנִים סְמָדַר נָתְנוּ רֵיחַ — *The fig tree has formed its first small figs, ready for ascent to the Temple; the vines are in blossom, their fragrance declaring they are ready for libation* [lit., *The fig tree has formed its first figs, and the vines in blossom give forth fragrance*]. The time is drawing near for you to bring the first fruits and the wine libations in the Temple.

קוּמִי לָךְ רַעְיָתִי יָפָתִי וּלְכִי לָךְ — *Arise, My beloved, My fair one, and go forth"* [lit., *Arise, My beloved, My fair one, and go forth for yourself*].

2:14. יוֹנָתִי בְּחַגְוֵי הַסֶּלַע בְּסֵתֶר הַמַּדְרֵגָה — *At the sea, He said to me, "O My dove, trapped at the sea as if in the clefts of the rock, the concealment of the terrace* [lit., *O My dove, in the crannies of the rock, in the covert of the step*]. When the Jews were trapped between the sea and the Egyptian army, they were like a dove fleeing a hawk. It flew into the cleft of a rock, and found a serpent lurking there. It could neither enter, because of the snake, nor turn back, because of the hawk.

הַרְאִינִי אֶת מַרְאַיִךְ — *"Show Me your prayerful gaze* [lit., *show Me your countenance*]. Show Me to whom you turn when you are in trouble.

הַשְׁמִיעִנִי אֶת קוֹלֵךְ — *let Me hear your supplicating voice* [lit., *let Me hear your voice*]. . .

כִּי קוֹלֵךְ עָרֵב וּמַרְאֵיךְ נָאוֶה — *for your voice is sweet and your countenance comely."*

2:15. אֶחֱזוּ לָנוּ שֻׁעָלִים שֻׁעָלִים קְטַנִּים מְחַבְּלִים כְּרָמִים וּכְרָמֵינוּ סְמָדַר — *Then He told the sea, "Seize for us the Egyptian foxes, even the small foxes who spoiled Israel's vineyards while our vineyards had just begun to blossom"* [lit., *The foxes have seized us, the little foxes that ruin the vineyard, and our vineyards were in blossom*].

2:16. דּוֹדִי לִי וַאֲנִי לוֹ — *My Beloved is mine, He fills all my needs and I seek from Him and none other* [lit., *My Beloved is mine, and I am His*]. He makes demands upon us and we rely on none other but Him.

הָרֹעֶה בַּשּׁוֹשַׁנִּים — *He grazes me in roselike bounty* [lit., *Who grazes (others) among the roses*]. God grazes us, His flock, in pastures of tranquil beauty.

2:17. עַד שֶׁיָּפוּחַ הַיּוֹם וְנָסוּ הַצְּלָלִים — *Until my sin blows His friendship away and sears me like the midday sun and His protection departs* [lit., *until the day blows and the shadows flee*]. The condition of "My Beloved is mine, and I am His" was dispelled when the sins of the Golden Calf (*Exodus* Ch. 32) and the Spies (*Numbers* Chs. 13-14) blackened us with the ferocity of the noontime sun.

סֹב — *My sin caused Him to turn away* [lit., *turn*].

[10] When He redeemed me from Egypt, my Beloved called out and said to me,
"Arise My love, My fair one, and go forth. [11] For the winter of bondage has passed,
the deluge of suffering is over and gone. [12] The righteous blossoms are seen in the
land, the time of your song has arrived, and the voice of your guide is heard in the
land. [13] The fig tree has formed its first small figs, ready for ascent to the Temple; the
vines are in blossom, their fragrance declaring they are ready for libation. Arise, My
beloved, My fair one, and go forth!"

[14] At the sea, He said to me, "O My dove, trapped at the sea as if in the clefts of
the rock, the concealment of the terrace. Show Me your prayerful gaze, let Me hear
your supplicating voice, for your voice is sweet and your countenance comely."
[15] Then He told the sea, "Seize for us the Egyptian foxes, even the small foxes who
spoiled Israel's vineyards while our vineyards had just begun to blossom."

[16] My Beloved is mine, He fills all my needs and I seek from Him and none other.
He grazes me in roselike bounty. [17] Until my sin blows His friendship away and sears
me like the midday sun and His protection departs. My sin caused Him to turn away.

I say to him, "My Beloved, You became like a gazelle or like a young hart on the
distant mountains."

3 *Israel to the nations*

[1] As I lay on my bed in the night of my desert travail, I sought Him Whom my soul
loves. I sought Him but I found Him not, for He maintained His aloofness. [2] I
resolved to arise then, and roam through the city, in the streets and squares;
that through Moses I would seek Him Whom my soul loved. I sought Him, but I found
Him not. [3] They, Moses and Aaron, the watchmen patrolling the city, found me. "You
have seen Him Whom my soul loves; what has He said?" [4] Scarcely had I departed
from them, when, in the days of Joshua, I found Him Whom my soul loves.

NOTES INCLUDING PHRASE-BY-PHRASE LITERAL TRANSLATION

דְּמֵה לְךָ דוֹדִי לִצְבִי אוֹ לְעֹפֶר הָאַיָּלִים — *I say to him, "My Beloved, You became like a gazelle or like a young hart* [lit., *My Beloved, and be like a gazelle or a young hart*]. Through my sins I caused Him to depart from me, as swiftly as a gazelle. . .

עַל הָרֵי בָתֶר — *on the distant mountains"* [lit., *upon the mountains of separation*], out of reach.

3:1. עַל מִשְׁכָּבִי בַּלֵּילוֹת בִּקַּשְׁתִּי אֵת שֶׁאָהֲבָה נַפְשִׁי — *As I lay on my bed in the night of my desert travail, I sought Him Whom my soul loves* [lit., *Upon my bed during the nights I sought the One my soul loves*]. After the sin of the Spies, God did not speak directly to Moses for thirty-eight years (see *Deuteronomy* 2:14-17), a period depicted as "during the nights." This chapter depicts the anguish of Israel, bereft of its former uninhibited relationship with God, longing for a resumption of His love.

בִּקַּשְׁתִּיו וְלֹא מְצָאתִיו — *I sought Him, but I found Him not, for He maintained His aloofness* [lit., *I sought Him, but I found Him not*]. As He warned, "For I will not go up in your midst" (*Exodus* 33:3); "For I am not among you" (*Deuteronomy* 1:42).

3:2. אָקוּמָה נָּא וַאֲסוֹבְבָה בָעִיר בַּשְּׁוָקִים וּבָרְחֹבוֹת — *I resolved to arise then, and roam through the city, in the streets and squares* [lit., *I will rise now and roam about the city, through the streets and through the squares*]. We were determined to seek God by every possible avenue.

אֲבַקְשָׁה אֵת שֶׁאָהֲבָה נַפְשִׁי — *that through Moses I would seek Him Whom my soul loved* [lit., *I will seek the One I love*]. As Moses said, "I will go up to HASHEM; perhaps I can win atonement for your sins" (*Exodus* 32:30).

בִּקַּשְׁתִּיו וְלֹא מְצָאתִיו — *I sought Him, but I found Him not.*

3:3. מְצָאוּנִי הַשֹּׁמְרִים הַסֹּבְבִים בָּעִיר — *They, Moses and Aaron, the watchmen patrolling the city, found me* [lit., *The watchmen who circle the city found me*]. Moses and Aaron went among us to instill us with the love of God. They guided us, and inspired us to be patient, for Redemption was at hand.

אֵת שֶׁאָהֲבָה נַפְשִׁי רְאִיתֶם — *"You have seen Him Whom my soul loves; what has He said?"* [lit., *Have you seen Him Whom my soul loves?*].

3:4. כִּמְעַט שֶׁעָבַרְתִּי מֵהֶם עַד שֶׁמָּצָאתִי אֵת שֶׁאָהֲבָה נַפְשִׁי – *Scarcely had I departed from them, when, in the days of Joshua, I found Him Whom my soul loves* [lit., *Scarcely had I passed them, when I found Him Whom my soul loves*]. When Moses and Aaron died, God remained with Joshua, helping him to conquer the thirty-one kings of Canaan.

ה אֲחַזְתִּיו וְלֹא אַרְפֶּנּוּ עַד־שֶׁהֲבֵיאתִיו אֶל־בֵּית אִמִּי וְאֶל־חֶדֶר הוֹרָתִי: הִשְׁבַּעְתִּי
אֶתְכֶם בְּנוֹת יְרוּשָׁלִַם בִּצְבָאוֹת אוֹ בְּאַיְלוֹת הַשָּׂדֶה אִם־תָּעִירוּ | וְאִם־תְּעוֹרְרוּ
ו אֶת־הָאַהֲבָה עַד שֶׁתֶּחְפָּץ: מִי זֹאת עֹלָה מִן־הַמִּדְבָּר כְּתִימְרוֹת
ז עָשָׁן מְקֻטֶּרֶת מֹר וּלְבוֹנָה מִכֹּל אַבְקַת רוֹכֵל: הִנֵּה מִטָּתוֹ שֶׁלִּשְׁלֹמֹה שִׁשִּׁים
ח גִּבֹּרִים סָבִיב לָהּ מִגִּבֹּרֵי יִשְׂרָאֵל: כֻּלָּם אֲחֻזֵי חֶרֶב מְלֻמְּדֵי מִלְחָמָה אִישׁ חַרְבּוֹ
ט עַל־יְרֵכוֹ מִפַּחַד בַּלֵּילוֹת: אַפִּרְיוֹן עָשָׂה לוֹ הַמֶּלֶךְ שְׁלֹמֹה מֵעֲצֵי
י הַלְּבָנוֹן: עַמּוּדָיו עָשָׂה כֶסֶף רְפִידָתוֹ זָהָב מֶרְכָּבוֹ אַרְגָּמָן תּוֹכוֹ רָצוּף אַהֲבָה
יא מִבְּנוֹת יְרוּשָׁלִָם: צְאֶינָה | וּרְאֶינָה בְּנוֹת צִיּוֹן בַּמֶּלֶךְ שְׁלֹמֹה בָּעֲטָרָה
ד א שֶׁעִטְּרָה־לּוֹ אִמּוֹ בְּיוֹם חֲתֻנָּתוֹ וּבְיוֹם שִׂמְחַת לִבּוֹ: הִנָּךְ יָפָה רַעְיָתִי
הִנָּךְ יָפָה עֵינַיִךְ יוֹנִים מִבַּעַד לְצַמָּתֵךְ שַׂעְרֵךְ כְּעֵדֶר הָעִזִּים שֶׁגָּלְשׁוּ מֵהַר גִּלְעָד:
ב שִׁנַּיִךְ כְּעֵדֶר הַקְּצוּבוֹת שֶׁעָלוּ מִן־הָרַחְצָה שֶׁכֻּלָּם מַתְאִימוֹת וְשַׁכֻּלָה אֵין בָּהֶם:

NOTES INCLUDING PHRASE-BY-PHRASE LITERAL TRANSLATION

אֲחַזְתִּיו וְלֹא אַרְפֶּנּוּ — *I grasped Him, determined that my deeds would never again cause me to lose hold of Him* [lit., *I have grasped Him and I would not let Him go*] . . .

עַד שֶׁהֲבֵיאתִיו אֶל בֵּית אִמִּי וְאֶל חֶדֶר הוֹרָתִי — *until I brought His Presence to the Tabernacle of my mother and to the chamber of the one who conceived me* [lit., *until I brought Him to my mother's house, and to the chamber of the one who conceived me*]. I built the Tabernacle at Shiloh, in return for all that He wrought for me.

3:5. הִשְׁבַּעְתִּי אֶתְכֶם בְּנוֹת יְרוּשָׁלִַם — *I adjure you, O nations destined to ascend to Jerusalem* [lit., *I have adjured you, O daughters of Jerusalem*]. See 1:5.

בִּצְבָאוֹת אוֹ בְּאַיְלוֹת הַשָּׂדֶה — *for if you violate your oath, you will become as defenseless as gazelles or hinds of the field* [lit., *by gazelles or by hinds of the field*] . . .

אִם תָּעִירוּ וְאִם תְּעוֹרְרוּ אֶת הָאַהֲבָה עַד שֶׁתֶּחְפָּץ — *if you dare provoke God to hate me or disturb His love for me while He still desires it* [lit., *if you will wake or rouse the love until it pleases*].

3:6. מִי זֹאת עֹלָה מִן הַמִּדְבָּר — *You nations have asked, "Who is this ascending from the wilderness* [lit., *Who is it that rises up from the wilderness*]. In the wilderness, Israel was led by the pillar of fire and the pillar of cloud (*Exodus* 13:21 ff), which killed snakes and scorpions, and burned thorns and thistles to clear the way. The nations exclaimed: "Who is this [i.e., How great is this spectacle] that comes up from the wilderness?"

כְּתִימְרוֹת עָשָׁן — *its way secured and smoothed by palmlike pillars of smoke* [lit., *like columns of smoke*]. The word תִּימְרָה, "column," is linguistically related to תָּמָר, "date-palm." The pillar of clouds that accompanied Israel through the wilderness was tall and erect as a palm tree . . .

מְקֻטֶּרֶת מֹר וּלְבוֹנָה מִכֹּל אַבְקַת רוֹכֵל — *burning fragrant myrrh and frankincense, of all the perfumer's powders?"* [lit., *perfumed with myrrh and frankincense, with every powder of the merchant*] . . . like the "cloud of the incense" (*Leviticus* 16:13) that ascended from the Altar in the Tabernacle.

3:7. הִנֵּה מִטָּתוֹ שֶׁלִּשְׁלֹמֹה — *Behold the resting place of Him to Whom peace belongs* [lit., *Behold, it is the couch of Solomon*], i.e., the Tent of Meeting and the Ark . . .

שִׁשִּׁים גִּבֹּרִים סָבִיב לָהּ מִגִּבֹּרֵי יִשְׂרָאֵל — *with sixty myriads of Israel's mighty encircling it* [lit., *sixty mighty men round about it, of the mighty men of Israel*]. Sixty times ten thousand men were eligible to fight in the Israelite army (see *Numbers* 1:45-46).

3:8. כֻּלָּם אֲחֻזֵי חֶרֶב מְלֻמְּדֵי מִלְחָמָה — *All of them gripping the sword of tradition, skilled in the battle of Torah* [lit., *They all handle the sword, learned in warfare*].

אִישׁ חַרְבּוֹ עַל יְרֵכוֹ מִפַּחַד בַּלֵּילוֹת — *each with his sword ready at his side, lest he succumb in the nights of exile* [lit., *each with his sword on his thigh, because of terror in the nights*]. "Sword" refers to the means by which to transmit the Torah intact from one generation to the next.

3:9. אַפִּרְיוֹן עָשָׂה לוֹ הַמֶּלֶךְ שְׁלֹמֹה מֵעֲצֵי הַלְּבָנוֹן — *A Tabernacle for His Presence has the King to Whom peace belongs made of the wood of Lebanon* [lit., *A sedan chair has King Solomon made unto Him, of the wood of Lebanon*], a metaphor for a private chamber for His glory.

3:10. עַמּוּדָיו עָשָׂה כֶסֶף — *Its pillars He made of silver.* A reference to the silver hooks of the Tabernacle's courtyard pillars (see *Exodus* 27:10).

רְפִידָתוֹ זָהָב — *His resting place was gold* [lit., *its covering was gold*]. God's Presence rested upon the golden Cover of the Ark, from which He spoke to Moses (see *Exodus* 27:17,22).

מֶרְכָּבוֹ אַרְגָּמָן — *Its suspended curtain was purple wool* [lit., *its seat was purple wool*]. The dominant color of the *Paroches* (Curtain) between the Holy and the Holy of Holies was purple (see *Exodus* 26:31-33).

תּוֹכוֹ רָצוּף אַהֲבָה — *Its midst was decked with implements bespeaking love* [lit., *its inner side was decked with love*]. The Ark, its Cover, its Cherubim and Tablets were all symbolic of the love between God and Israel.

מִבְּנוֹת יְרוּשָׁלִָם — *by the daughters of Jerusalem.* Throughout the rest of the Book (see, e.g., 1:5) "daughters of Jerusalem" refers

I grasped Him, determined that my deeds would never again cause me to lose hold of Him,
until I brought His Presence to the Tabernacle of my mother and to the chamber of the one
who conceived me. 5 *I adjure you, O nations destined to ascend to Jerusalem, for if you*
violate your oath, you will become as defenseless as gazelles or hinds of the field, if you
dare provoke God to hate me or disturb His love for me while He still desires it.

Quoting the nations

6 *You nations have asked, "Who is this ascending from the wilderness, its way secured*
and smoothed by palmlike pillars of smoke, burning fragrant myrrh and frankincense, of
all the perfumer's powders?" 7 *Behold the resting place of Him to Whom peace belongs,*
with sixty myriads of Israel's mighty encircling it. 8 *All of them gripping the sword of*
tradition, skilled in the battle of Torah, each with his sword ready at his side, lest he
succumb in the nights of exile.

9 *A Tabernacle for His presence has the King to Whom peace belongs made of the wood*
of Lebanon: 10 *Its pillars He made of silver; His resting place was gold; its suspended*
curtain was purple wool, its midst was decked with implements bespeaking love by the
daughters of Jerusalem. 11 *Go forth and gaze, O daughters distinguished by loyalty to*
God, upon the King to Whom peace belongs adorned with the crown His nation made for
Him, on the day His Law was given and He became one with Israel, and on the day His
heart was gladdened by His Tabernacle's consecration.

4

God to Israel

1 *Behold, you are lovely, My beloved, behold you are lovely, your very appearance*
radiates dovelike constancy. The most common sons within your encampments are
as dearly beloved as the children of Jacob in the goatlike procession descending the slopes
of Mount Gilead. 2 *Accountable in deed are your mighty leaders like a well-*
numbered flock come up from the washing, all of them unblemished with no miscarriage
of action in them.

NOTES INCLUDING PHRASE-BY-PHRASE LITERAL TRANSLATION

to the heathen nations who will flock to Jerusalem in the future; here it refers to the Jews.

3:11. צְאֶינָה וּרְאֶינָה בְּנוֹת צִיּוֹן בַּמֶּלֶךְ שְׁלֹמֹה — *Go forth and gaze, O daughters distinguished by loyalty to God, upon the King to Whom peace belongs* [lit., *Go forth and gaze, O daughters of Zion, upon King Solomon*]. צִיּוֹן, "Zion," is linguistically related to צִיּוּן, "distinguishing mark." The daughters of Zion, Israel, are distinguished in their loyalty to God and to His commandments.

בָּעֲטָרָה שֶׁעִטְּרָה לוֹ אִמּוֹ — *adorned with the crown His nation made for Him* [lit., *with the crown with which his mother crowned him*]. The Tabernacle was "crowned" with coverings of colored skins; of blue, purple and scarlet wool, and fine linen; and of goat's hair (*Exodus* 26:1,7,14).

בְּיוֹם חֲתֻנָּתוֹ — *on the day His Law was given and He became one with Israel* [lit., *on His wedding day*]; the day the Torah was given.

וּבְיוֹם שִׂמְחַת לִבּוֹ — *and on the day His heart was gladdened by His Tabernacle's consecration* [lit., *and on the day of His heart's bliss*]. The dedication day of the Tabernacle in the wilderness.

4:1. הִנָּךְ יָפָה רַעְיָתִי הִנָּךְ יָפָה עֵינַיִךְ יוֹנִים — *Behold, you are lovely, My beloved, behold you are lovely, your very appearance radiates dovelike constancy* [lit., *Behold, you are beautiful, My beloved; behold, you are beautiful, your eyes are doves*]. You are like the dove which is loyal to its mate.

מִבַּעַד לְצַמָּתֵךְ שַׂעְרֵךְ כְּעֵדֶר הָעִזִּים שֶׁגָּלְשׁוּ מֵהַר גִּלְעָד — *The most common sons within your encampments are as dearly beloved as the children of Jacob in the goatlike procession descending the slopes of Mount Gilead* [lit., *Within your kerchief, your hair is like a flock of goats streaming down from Mount Gilead*]. Even your common people, whose merits are hidden by veils, are as dear to Me as Jacob and his sons who streamed down Mount Gilead when Laban pursued them (see *Genesis* 31:23ff).

4:2. שִׁנַּיִךְ כְּעֵדֶר הַקְּצוּבוֹת שֶׁעָלוּ מִן הָרַחְצָה — *Accountable in deed are your mighty leaders like a well-numbered flock come up from the washing* [lit., *Your teeth are like a flock well counted, which have come up from the washing*]. Israel's warriors who "tear apart and consume" their enemies are allegorized as teeth. By refraining from plunder and lewdness, the warriors remain untainted by sin, as if they "came up from the washing."

שֶׁכֻּלָּם מַתְאִימוֹת וְשַׁכֻּלָה אֵין בָּהֶם — *all of them unblemished with no miscarriage of action in them* [lit., *all of them are perfect and there is none blemished among them*].

ג כְּחוּט הַשָּׁנִי֙ שִׂפְתוֹתַ֔יִךְ וּמִדְבָּרֵ֖ךְ נָאוֶ֑ה כְּפֶ֤לַח הָֽרִמּוֹן֙ רַקָּתֵ֔ךְ מִבַּ֖עַד לְצַמָּתֵֽךְ:
ד כְּמִגְדַּ֤ל דָּוִיד֙ צַוָּארֵ֔ךְ בָּנ֖וּי לְתַלְפִּיּ֑וֹת אֶ֤לֶף הַמָּגֵן֙ תָּל֣וּי עָלָ֔יו כֹּ֖ל שִׁלְטֵ֥י הַגִּבֹּרִֽים:
ה-ו שְׁנֵ֥י שָׁדַ֛יִךְ כִּשְׁנֵ֥י עֳפָרִ֖ים תְּאוֹמֵ֣י צְבִיָּ֑ה הָרוֹעִ֖ים בַּשּׁוֹשַׁנִּֽים: עַ֤ד שֶׁיָּפ֙וּחַ֙ הַיּ֔וֹם
ז וְנָ֖סוּ הַצְּלָלִ֑ים אֵ֤לֶךְ לִי֙ אֶל־הַ֣ר הַמּ֔וֹר וְאֶל־גִּבְעַ֖ת הַלְּבוֹנָֽה: כֻּלָּ֤ךְ יָפָה֙ רַעְיָתִ֔י
ח וּמ֖וּם אֵ֥ין בָּֽךְ: אִתִּ֤י מִלְּבָנוֹן֙ כַּלָּ֔ה אִתִּ֖י מִלְּבָנ֣וֹן תָּב֑וֹאִי תָּשׁ֣וּרִי ׀
ט מֵרֹ֣אשׁ אֲמָנָ֗ה מֵרֹ֤אשׁ שְׂנִיר֙ וְחֶרְמ֔וֹן מִמְּעֹנ֣וֹת אֲרָי֔וֹת מֵהַרְרֵ֖י נְמֵרִֽים: לִבַּבְתִּ֖נִי
אֲחֹתִ֣י כַלָּ֑ה לִבַּבְתִּ֙נִי֙ °באחד [°בְּאַחַ֣ת ק׳] מֵעֵינַ֔יִךְ בְּאַחַ֥ד עֲנָ֖ק מִצַּוְּרֹנָֽיִךְ:
י מַה־יָּפ֥וּ דֹדַ֖יִךְ אֲחֹתִ֣י כַלָּ֑ה מַה־טֹּ֤בוּ דֹדַ֙יִךְ֙ מִיַּ֔יִן וְרֵ֥יחַ שְׁמָנַ֖יִךְ מִכָּל־בְּשָׂמִֽים:
יא נֹ֛פֶת תִּטֹּ֥פְנָה שִׂפְתוֹתַ֖יִךְ כַּלָּ֑ה דְּבַ֤שׁ וְחָלָב֙ תַּ֣חַת לְשׁוֹנֵ֔ךְ וְרֵ֥יחַ שַׂלְמֹתַ֖יִךְ
יב כְּרֵ֥יחַ לְבָנֽוֹן: גַּ֥ן ׀ נָע֖וּל אֲחֹתִ֣י כַלָּ֑ה גַּ֥ל נָע֖וּל מַעְיָ֥ן חָתֽוּם:
יג-יד שְׁלָחַ֙יִךְ֙ פַּרְדֵּ֣ס רִמּוֹנִ֔ים עִ֖ם פְּרִ֣י מְגָדִ֑ים כְּפָרִ֖ים עִם־נְרָדִֽים: נֵ֣רְדְּ ׀ וְכַרְכֹּ֗ם
קָנֶה֙ וְקִנָּמ֔וֹן עִ֖ם כָּל־עֲצֵ֣י לְבוֹנָ֑ה מֹ֚ר וַאֲהָל֔וֹת עִ֖ם כָּל־רָאשֵׁ֥י בְשָׂמִֽים:

NOTES INCLUDING PHRASE-BY-PHRASE LITERAL TRANSLATION

4:3. כְּחוּט הַשָּׁנִי שִׂפְתוֹתַיִךְ — *Like the scarlet thread, guarantor of Rahab's safety, is the sincerity of your lips* [lit., *Your lips are like a thread of scarlet*]. This refers to the sincere pledge that Joshua's spies made to Rahab in Jericho. They guaranteed her safety if she would display a scarlet thread as a signal to the conquering Jews (see *Joshua* Ch. 2).

וּמִדְבָּרֵךְ נָאוֶה — *and your word is unfeigned* [lit., *and your speech is comely*].

כְּפֶלַח הָרִמּוֹן רַקָּתֵךְ מִבַּעַד לְצַמָּתֵךְ — *As many as a pomegranate's seeds are the merits of your unworthiest within your modest veil* [lit., *Your cheeks are like a slice of pomegranate, from behind your veil*]. The word רַקָּה, "cheeks," is linguistically related to רֵק, "empty," and is a metaphor for those who are relatively empty of mitzvos; rosy cheeks also resemble a pomegranate. Even the comparatively few merits of the lowest among you are as numerous as a pomegranate's seeds.

4:4. כְּמִגְדַּל דָּוִיד צַוָּארֵךְ בָּנוּי לְתַלְפִּיּוֹת — *As stately as the Tower of David is the site of your Sanhedrin built as a model to emulate* [lit., *Your neck is the Tower of David, built as an ornament*]. The verse alludes to the Stronghold of Zion, a beautiful, stately fortification, and to the chamber of the Sanhedrin, the spiritual stronghold of Israel.

אֶלֶף הַמָּגֵן תָּלוּי עָלָיו כֹּל שִׁלְטֵי הַגִּבֹּרִים — *with a thousand shields of Torah armor hung upon it, all the disciple-filled quivers of the mighty* [lit., *a thousand shields are hung upon it; all the quivers of the mighty men*]. Students are likened to arrows (see *Psalms* 127:4-5).

4:5. שְׁנֵי שָׁדַיִךְ כִּשְׁנֵי עֳפָרִים תְּאוֹמֵי צְבִיָּה — *Moses and Aaron, your two sustainers, are like two fawns, twins of the gazelle* [lit., *Your breasts are like two fawns, twins of a gazelle*]. Moses and Aaron are like the breasts that nurtured Israel. They are called "twins" because they were of equal stature.

הָרוֹעִים בַּשּׁוֹשַׁנִּים — *who graze their sheep in roselike bounty* [lit., *who feed among the roses*]. Like shepherds, Moses and Aaron guided their nation along tranquil paths.

4:6. עַד שֶׁיָּפוּחַ הַיּוֹם וְנָסוּ הַצְּלָלִים — *Until My sunny benevolence was withdrawn from Shiloh and the protective shadows were dispersed by your sin* [lit., *Until the day breathes and the shadows flee*]. God had been Israel's protective shade, until they sinned.

אֵלֶךְ לִי אֶל הַר הַמּוֹר וְאֶל גִּבְעַת הַלְּבוֹנָה — *I will go to Mount Moriah and the hill of frankincense* [lit., *I will get me to the mountain of myrrh, and to the hill of frankincense*]. After His anger abated, He chose Mount Moriah as the site of the Temple, where incense would be offered.

4:7. כֻּלָּךְ יָפָה רַעְיָתִי וּמוּם אֵין בָּךְ — *where [on Mount Moriah] you will be completely fair, My beloved, and no blemish will be in you* [lit., *You are entirely fair, My beloved, and there is no blemish in you*].

4:8. אִתִּי מִלְּבָנוֹן כַּלָּה אִתִּי מִלְּבָנוֹן תָּבוֹאִי — *With Me will you be exiled from the Temple, O bride, with Me from the Temple until you return* [lit., *With Me from Lebanon, O bride! With Me from Lebanon shall you come*]. The Temple is called Lebanon (לְבָנוֹן, lit., "whitener") because it whitens the sins of Israel (Talmud, *Yoma* 39b). You will be exiled "with Me," says God, "for in all your afflictions, I, too, am afflicted" (see *Isaiah* 63:9).

תָּשׁוּרִי מֵרֹאשׁ אֲמָנָה — *then to contemplate the fruits of your faith from its earliest beginnings* [lit., *Look from the peak of Amanah*]. The word ראש means both "head (or, peak)" and "beginning"; אֲמָנָה means "covenant of faith" and is the name of a mountain on the northern border of the Land of Israel.

מֵרֹאשׁ שְׂנִיר וְחֶרְמוֹן מִמְּעֹנוֹת אֲרָיוֹת מֵהַרְרֵי נְמֵרִים — *from your first arrival at the summits of Senir and Hermon, the lands of mighty Sihon and Og, as impregnable as dens of lions, and as mountains of leopards* [lit., *from the peak of Senir and Hermon, from the dens of lions, from the mountains of leopards*].

4:9. לִבַּבְתִּנִי אֲחֹתִי כַלָּה — *You have captured My heart, My sister, O bride*.

לִבַּבְתִּנִי בְּאַחַת מֵעֵינַיִךְ בְּאַחַד עֲנָק מִצַּוְּרֹנָיִךְ — *you have captured My heart with but one of your virtues, with but one of the precepts that adorn you like beads of a necklace resplendent* [lit., *You have*

*[3] Like the scarlet thread, guarantor of Rahab's safety, is the sincerity of your lips,
and your word is unfeigned. As many as a pomegranate's seeds are the merits of
your unworthiest within your modest veil. [4] As stately as the Tower of David is the
site of your Sanhedrin built as a model to emulate, with a thousand shields of Torah
armor hung upon it, all the disciple-filled quivers of the mighty. [5] Moses and Aaron,
your two sustainers, are like two fawns, twins of the gazelle, who graze their sheep
in roselike bounty.*

*[6] Until My sunny benevolence was withdrawn from Shiloh and the protective
shadows were dispersed by your sin. I will go to Mount Moriah and the hill of
frankincense — [7] where you will be completely fair, My beloved, and no blemish
will be in you.*

*[8] With Me will you be exiled from the Temple, O bride, with Me from the Temple
until you return; then to contemplate the fruits of your faith from its earliest
beginnings, from your first arrival at the summits of Senir and Hermon, the lands of
mighty Sihon and Og, as impregnable as dens of lions, and as mountains of
leopards.*

*[9] You have captured My heart, My sister, O bride; you have captured My heart
with but one of your virtues, with but one of the precepts that adorn you like beads
of a necklace resplendent. [10] How fair was your love in so many settings, My sister,
O bride; so superior is your love to wine and your spreading fame to all perfumes.*

*[11] The sweetness of Torah drips from your lips, like honey and milk it lies
under your tongue; your very garments are scented with precepts like the
scent of Lebanon. [12] As chaste as a garden locked, My sister, O bride; a
spring locked up, a fountain sealed. [13] Your least gifted ones are a pomegranate
orchard with luscious fruit; henna with nard; [14] nard and saffron, calamus and
cinnamon, with all trees of frankincense, myrrh and aloes with all the chief spices;*

NOTES INCLUDING PHRASE-BY-PHRASE LITERAL TRANSLATION

captured my heart with one of your eyes, with one bead of your necklace]. I would have loved you even had you possessed only one of your endearing qualities; how much more so since you possess so many!

4:10. מַה יָּפוּ דֹדַיִךְ אֲחֹתִי כַלָּה — *How fair was your love in so many settings, My sister, O bride* [lit., *How fair was your love, My sister O bride!*]. Your love is pleasing everywhere, whether in the Tabernacle or in the Temple.

מַה טֹּבוּ דֹדַיִךְ מִיַּיִן וְרֵיחַ שְׁמָנַיִךְ מִכָּל בְּשָׂמִים — *so superior is your love to wine and your spreading fame to all perfumes* [lit., *how much better your love than wine, and the fragrance of your oils than all spices!*].

4:11. נֹפֶת תִּטֹּפְנָה שִׂפְתוֹתַיִךְ כַּלָּה דְּבַשׁ וְחָלָב תַּחַת לְשׁוֹנֵךְ — *The sweetness of Torah drips from your lips, like honey and milk it lies under your tongue* [lit., *Honey drops from your lips, O bride, honey and milk are under your tongue*].

וְרֵיחַ שַׂלְמֹתַיִךְ כְּרֵיחַ לְבָנוֹן — *your very garments are scented with precepts like the scent of Lebanon* [lit., *and the scent of your garments is like the scent of Lebanon*]. This refers to the precepts associated with clothing, such as the commandment of wearing *tzitzis* and the prohibition against wearing *shaatnez* (see *Deuteronomy* 22:11).

4:12. גַּן נָעוּל אֲחֹתִי כַלָּה גַּל נָעוּל מַעְיָן חָתוּם — *As chaste as a garden locked, My sister, O bride; a spring locked up, a fountain sealed* [lit., *A garden locked up is my sister, the bride, a spring locked up, a fountain sealed*]. The beauty and charm of the daughters of Israel are guided by modesty and purity.

4:13. שְׁלָחַיִךְ פַּרְדֵּס רִמּוֹנִים עִם פְּרִי מְגָדִים — *Your least gifted ones are a pomegranate orchard with luscious fruit* [lit., *Your arid areas are an orchard of pomegranates with precious fruits*]. Like a field in need of irrigation, your youngsters strive to be "moistened" with Torah and good deeds.

כְּפָרִים עִם נְרָדִים — *henna with nard.* Types of spices (see 1:14).

4:14. נֵרְדְּ וְכַרְכֹּם קָנֶה וְקִנָּמוֹן עִם כָּל עֲצֵי לְבוֹנָה מֹר וַאֲהָלוֹת עִם כָּל רָאשֵׁי בְשָׂמִים — *Nard and saffron, calamus and cinnamon, with all trees of frankincense, myrrh, and aloes, with all the chief spices.*

טו־טז מַעְיַן גַּנִּים בְּאֵר מַיִם חַיִּים וְנֹזְלִים מִן־לְבָנוֹן: עוּרִי צָפוֹן וּבוֹאִי תֵימָן הָפִיחִי גַנִּי
ה א יִזְּלוּ בְשָׂמָיו יָבֹא דוֹדִי לְגַנּוֹ וְיֹאכַל פְּרִי מְגָדָיו: בָּאתִי לְגַנִּי אֲחֹתִי כַלָּה אָרִיתִי
מוֹרִי עִם־בְּשָׂמִי אָכַלְתִּי יַעְרִי עִם־דִּבְשִׁי שָׁתִיתִי יֵינִי עִם־חֲלָבִי אִכְלוּ רֵעִים
ב שְׁתוּ וְשִׁכְרוּ דּוֹדִים: אֲנִי יְשֵׁנָה וְלִבִּי עֵר קוֹל ׀ דּוֹדִי דוֹפֵק פִּתְחִי־לִי
ג אֲחֹתִי רַעְיָתִי יוֹנָתִי תַמָּתִי שֶׁרֹּאשִׁי נִמְלָא־טָל קְוֻצּוֹתַי רְסִיסֵי לָיְלָה: פָּשַׁטְתִּי
ד אֶת־כֻּתָּנְתִּי אֵיכָכָה אֶלְבָּשֶׁנָּה רָחַצְתִּי אֶת־רַגְלַי אֵיכָכָה אֲטַנְּפֵם: דּוֹדִי שָׁלַח
ה יָדוֹ מִן־הַחֹר וּמֵעַי הָמוּ עָלָיו: קַמְתִּי אֲנִי לִפְתֹּחַ לְדוֹדִי וְיָדַי נָטְפוּ־מוֹר
ו וְאֶצְבְּעֹתַי מוֹר עֹבֵר עַל כַּפּוֹת הַמַּנְעוּל: פָּתַחְתִּי אֲנִי לְדוֹדִי וְדוֹדִי חָמַק עָבָר
ז נַפְשִׁי יָצְאָה בְדַבְּרוֹ בִּקַּשְׁתִּיהוּ וְלֹא מְצָאתִיהוּ קְרָאתִיו וְלֹא עָנָנִי: מְצָאֻנִי
הַשֹּׁמְרִים הַסֹּבְבִים בָּעִיר הִכּוּנִי פְצָעוּנִי נָשְׂאוּ אֶת־רְדִידִי מֵעָלַי שֹׁמְרֵי הַחֹמוֹת:

NOTES INCLUDING PHRASE-BY-PHRASE LITERAL TRANSLATION

4:15. מַעְיַן גַּנִּים בְּאֵר מַיִם חַיִּים וְנֹזְלִים מִן לְבָנוֹן — *purified in a garden spring, a well of waters alive and flowing clean from Lebanon* [lit., *(You are) a garden spring; a well of living waters streams from Lebanon*]. God praises the women of Israel whose ritual immersion is like a spring enabling the fields to be fruitful.

4:16. עוּרִי צָפוֹן וּבוֹאִי תֵימָן הָפִיחִי גַנִּי יִזְּלוּ בְשָׂמָיו — *Awake from the north and come from the south! Like the winds let My exiles return to My garden, let their fragrant goodness flow in Jerusalem* [lit., *Awake, O north (wind), and come, O south! Blow (upon) my garden, let its spices flow out*]. Having found delight in you, command the winds to waft your fragrance afar. Allegorically, Israel's host nations will be so overwhelmed by the miracles preceding the Redemption that they will bring the Jews to Eretz Yisrael (see *Isaiah* 66:20). In the Temple, the Jews will say to God . . .

יָבֹא דוֹדִי לְגַנּוֹ וְיֹאכַל פְּרִי מְגָדָיו — *Let but my Beloved come to His garden and enjoy His precious people* [lit., *Let my Beloved come to His garden and eat its precious fruit*]. If You are there, all is there.

5:1. בָּאתִי לְגַנִּי אֲחֹתִי כַלָּה — *To your Tabernacle Dedication, My sister, O bride, I came as if to My garden* [lit., *I have come into My garden, My sister, O bride*]. When the Tabernacle was set up, God's glory filled it (*Exodus* 40:33,34).

אָרִיתִי מוֹרִי עִם בְּשָׂמִי — *I gathered My myrrh with My spice from your princely incense* [lit., *I have gathered My myrrh with My spice*]. The princes of the tribes offered incense at the Dedication of the Tabernacle (*Numbers* Ch. 7).

אָכַלְתִּי יַעְרִי עִם דִּבְשִׁי — *I accepted your unbidden as well as your bidden offerings to Me* [lit., *I have eaten My honeycomb with My honey*]. After its sweetness has been sucked, the comb is discarded. However, God's love of Israel was such that, during the inauguration of the Tabernacle, He accepted even offerings that would have otherwise been inappropriate. The tribal princes brought not only incense, but also sin-offerings, even though sin-offerings are not appropriate to be brought voluntarily.

שָׁתִיתִי יֵינִי עִם חֲלָבִי — *I drank your libations pure as milk* [lit., *I have drunk My wine with My milk*].

אִכְלוּ רֵעִים שְׁתוּ וְשִׁכְרוּ דוֹדִים — *Eat, My beloved priests! Drink and become God-intoxicated, O friends* [lit., *Eat, friends; drink and become intoxicated, O beloved ones*], you who partook of the flesh of the peace-offerings.

5:2. [The following verses allegorize the period of the First Temple and its destruction, Israel's sins, God's pleas for repentance, and Israel's recalcitrance — until it was too late.]

אֲנִי יְשֵׁנָה וְלִבִּי עֵר — *I let my devotion slumber, but the God of my heart was awake* [lit., *I (was) asleep but my heart (was) awake*]. Secure in the peaceful period of feeling secure, Israel neglected the service of God, as if asleep, but, "my heart," i.e., God, was wakeful to guard me and grant me goodness.

קוֹל דּוֹדִי דוֹפֵק — *A sound! My Beloved knocks* [lit., *The sound of my Beloved knocking!*]. Throughout my slumber, He issued daily warnings through the prophets (see *Jeremiah* 7:25).

פִּתְחִי לִי אֲחֹתִי רַעְיָתִי יוֹנָתִי תַמָּתִי — *He said, "Open your heart to Me, My sister, My love, My dove, My perfection* [lit., *Open to Me* (i.e., Let Me in), *My sister, My love, My dove, My perfect one*]. Do not cause Me to depart from you.

שֶׁרֹּאשִׁי נִמְלָא טָל — *admit Me and My head is filled with dewlike memories of Abraham* [lit., *for My head is filled with dew*]. Through His prophets, He said to me, "Abraham's deeds were pleasing to Me as dew, and I will shower you with blessings if you will but return to Me."

קְוֻצּוֹתַי רְסִיסֵי לָיְלָה — *spurn Me and I bear collections of punishing rains in exile-nights* [lit., *My locks (with) the rains of the night*].

5:3. פָּשַׁטְתִּי אֶת כֻּתָּנְתִּי אֵיכָכָה אֶלְבָּשֶׁנָּה רָחַצְתִּי אֶת רַגְלַי אֵיכָכָה אֲטַנְּפֵם — *And I responded, "I have doffed my robe of devotion; how can I don it? I have washed my feet that trod Your path; how can I soil them?"* [lit., *I have taken off my robe, how shall I don it? I have washed my feet, how shall I soil them?*]. In reaction to God's knock on the door, we thought, "We have accustomed ourselves to serve other gods — how can we return to our God?"

5:4. דּוֹדִי שָׁלַח יָדוֹ מִן הַחֹר — *In anger at my recalcitrance, my Beloved sent forth His hand from the portal in wrath* [lit., *My*

[15] purified in a garden spring, a well of waters alive and flowing clean from Lebanon.
[16] Awake from the north and come from the south! Like the winds let My exiles
return to My garden, let their fragrant goodness flow in Jerusalem.
Israel responds Let but my Beloved come to His garden and enjoy His precious people.

5 God replies [1] To your Tabernacle Dedication, My sister, O bride, I came as if to My garden. I
gathered My myrrh with My spice from your princely incense; I accepted your
unbidden as well as your bidden offerings to Me; I drank your libations pure as milk.
Eat, My beloved priests! Drink and become God-intoxicated, O friends!
[2] I let my devotion slumber, but the God of my heart was awake! A sound! My
Israel reminisces regretfully Beloved knocks!
He said, "Open your heart to Me, My sister, My love, My dove, My perfection;
admit Me and My head is filled with dewlike memories of Abraham; spurn Me and
I bear collections of punishing rains in exile-nights."
[3] And I responded, "I have doffed my robe of devotion; how can I don it? I have
washed my feet that trod Your path; how can I soil them?"
[4] In anger at my recalcitrance, my Beloved sent forth His hand from the portal in
wrath, and my intestines churned with longing for Him. [5] I arose to open for my
Beloved and my hands dripped myrrh of repentant devotion to Torah and God, and
my fingers flowing with myrrh to remove the traces of my foolish rebuke from the
handles of the lock. [6] I opened for my Beloved; but, alas, my Beloved had turned His
back on my plea and was gone. My soul departed at His decree! I sought His
closeness, but could not find it; I beseeched Him, but He would not answer.
[7] They found me, the enemy watchmen patrolling the city; they struck me, they
bloodied me wreaking God's revenge on me. They stripped my mantle of holiness
from me, the angelic watchmen of the wall.

NOTES INCLUDING PHRASE-BY-PHRASE LITERAL TRANSLATION

Beloved sent forth His hand from the portal]. When we spurned Him, God brought Aram upon us and our king, Ahaz (see *II Chronicles* 28:5,6).

וּמֵעַי הָמוּ עָלָיו — *and my intestines churned with longing for Him* [lit., *and my intestines stirred for Him*]. We changed our ways, and became righteous in the service of God.

5:5. קַמְתִּי אֲנִי לִפְתֹּחַ לְדוֹדִי וְיָדַי נָטְפוּ מוֹר — *I arose to open for my Beloved and my hands dripped myrrh of repentant devotion to Torah and God* [lit., *I rose to open for my Beloved and my hands dripped with myrrh*]. Hezekiah, Ahaz's son, became a model of piety. His entire generation was perfect; and there never arose another generation like it (*Talmud, Sanhedrin* 94b).

וְאֶצְבְּעֹתַי מוֹר עֹבֵר עַל כַּפּוֹת הַמַּנְעוּל — *and my fingers flowing with myrrh to remove the traces of my foolish rebuke from the handles of the lock* [lit., *and my fingers flowing with myrrh upon the handles of the lock*].

5:6. But, His Decree was to be enforced.

פָּתַחְתִּי אֲנִי לְדוֹדִי וְדוֹדִי חָמַק עָבָר — *I opened for my Beloved; but, alas, my Beloved had turned His back on my plea and was gone* [lit., *I opened for my Beloved, but my Beloved had turned and gone*]. Belatedly, I responded to my Beloved, but, alas, He did not annul His decree.

נַפְשִׁי יָצְאָה בְדַבְּרוֹ — *My soul departed at His decree* [lit., *my soul departed* (i.e., I became faint) *as He spoke*]. In effect, He said, "I will not enter, since at first you had refused to let Me in."

בִּקַּשְׁתִּיהוּ וְלֹא מְצָאתִיהוּ — *I sought His closeness, but could not find it* [lit., *I sought Him, but did not find Him*].

קְרָאתִיו וְלֹא עָנָנִי — *I beseeched Him, but He would not answer* [lit., *I called Him, but He did not answer me*].

5:7. מְצָאֻנִי הַשֹּׁמְרִים הַסֹּבְבִים בָּעִיר — *They found me, the enemy watchmen patrolling the city* [lit., *The watchmen who circle the city found me*]. Nebuchadnezzar's forces lay siege to Jerusalem . . .

הִכּוּנִי פְצָעוּנִי — *they struck me, they bloodied me, wreaking God's revenge on me* [lit., *they struck me, they wounded me*]. The Destruction of the First Temple was beginning.

נָשְׂאוּ אֶת רְדִידִי מֵעָלַי שֹׁמְרֵי הַחֹמוֹת — *They stripped my mantle of holiness from me, the angelic watchmen of the wall* [lit., *the guards of the walls stripped my mantle from me*]. Even the angels that had formerly been assigned to protect the city now took part in the destruction (see *Lamentations* 1:13).

ח הִשְׁבַּעְתִּי אֶתְכֶם בְּנוֹת יְרוּשָׁלָם אִם־תִּמְצְאוּ אֶת־דּוֹדִי מַה־תַּגִּידוּ לוֹ שֶׁחוֹלַת
ט אַהֲבָה אָנִי׃ מַה־דּוֹדֵךְ מִדּוֹד הַיָּפָה בַּנָּשִׁים מַה־דּוֹדֵךְ מִדּוֹד שֶׁכָּכָה הִשְׁבַּעְתָּנוּ׃
י־יא דּוֹדִי צַח וְאָדוֹם דָּגוּל מֵרְבָבָה׃ רֹאשׁוֹ כֶּתֶם פָּז קְוֻצּוֹתָיו תַּלְתַּלִּים שְׁחֹרוֹת
יב־יג כָּעוֹרֵב׃ עֵינָיו כְּיוֹנִים עַל־אֲפִיקֵי מָיִם רֹחֲצוֹת בֶּחָלָב יֹשְׁבוֹת עַל־מִלֵּאת׃ לְחָיָו
יד כַּעֲרוּגַת הַבֹּשֶׂם מִגְדְּלוֹת מֶרְקָחִים שִׂפְתוֹתָיו שׁוֹשַׁנִּים נֹטְפוֹת מוֹר עֹבֵר׃ יָדָיו
טו גְּלִילֵי זָהָב מְמֻלָּאִים בַּתַּרְשִׁישׁ מֵעָיו עֶשֶׁת שֵׁן מְעֻלֶּפֶת סַפִּירִים׃ שׁוֹקָיו עַמּוּדֵי
טז שֵׁשׁ מְיֻסָּדִים עַל־אַדְנֵי־פָז מַרְאֵהוּ כַּלְּבָנוֹן בָּחוּר כָּאֲרָזִים׃ חִכּוֹ מַמְתַקִּים וְכֻלּוֹ
ו א מַחֲמַדִּים זֶה דוֹדִי וְזֶה רֵעִי בְּנוֹת יְרוּשָׁלָם׃ אָנָה הָלַךְ דּוֹדֵךְ הַיָּפָה בַּנָּשִׁים אָנָה
ב פָּנָה דוֹדֵךְ וּנְבַקְשֶׁנּוּ עִמָּךְ׃ דּוֹדִי יָרַד לְגַנּוֹ לַעֲרֻגוֹת הַבֹּשֶׂם לִרְעוֹת בַּגַּנִּים
ג וְלִלְקֹט שׁוֹשַׁנִּים׃ אֲנִי לְדוֹדִי וְדוֹדִי לִי הָרֹעֶה בַּשּׁוֹשַׁנִּים׃

NOTES INCLUDING PHRASE-BY-PHRASE LITERAL TRANSLATION

5:8. הִשְׁבַּעְתִּי אֶתְכֶם בְּנוֹת יְרוּשָׁלָם — *I adjure you, O nations destined to ascend to Jerusalem* [lit., *I adjure you, O daughters of Jerusalem*]. You, our oppressors, should testify that we remained loyal to our God.

אִם תִּמְצְאוּ אֶת דּוֹדִי — *when you see my Beloved on the future Day of Judgment* [lit., *If you find my Beloved*], when the nations will be called upon to bear witness for Israel . . .

מַה תַּגִּידוּ לוֹ שֶׁחוֹלַת אַהֲבָה אָנִי — *will you not tell Him that I bore all travails for love of Him*? [lit., *What shall you tell him? That I am sick with love*]. Tell Him that only for love of Him were we afflicted with harsh suffering.

5:9. מַה דּוֹדֵךְ מִדּוֹד הַיָּפָה בַּנָּשִׁים — *With what does your beloved God excel all others that you suffer for His Name, O fairest of nations?* [lit., *What (makes) your Beloved (better) than (another) beloved, O fairest among women?*]. How is your God so superior to other gods that you are ready to be burned and tortured for Him? You are handsome, you are mighty; come intermingle with us!

מַה דּוֹדֵךְ מִדּוֹד שֶׁכָּכָה הִשְׁבַּעְתָּנוּ — *With what does your beloved God excel all others that you dare to adjure us?* [lit., *What (makes) your Beloved (better) than (another) beloved, that you so adjure us?*].

5:10. דּוֹדִי צַח וְאָדוֹם — *My Beloved is pure and purifies sin, and is ruddy with vengeance to punish betrayers* [lit., *My Beloved is white, yet ruddy*]. Even when He sits in judgment, He is anxious to purify my deeds. But when exacting retribution from His enemies, He is depicted as clad in blood-red vestments (see *Isaiah* 63:2).

דָּגוּל מֵרְבָבָה — *surrounded with myriad angels* [lit., *preeminent above ten thousand*].

5:11. רֹאשׁוֹ כֶּתֶם פָּז — *His opening words were finest gold* [lit., *His head is finest gold*]. When He gave us the Ten Commandments, His words were like fine gold.

קְוֻצּוֹתָיו תַּלְתַּלִּים — *His crowns hold mounds of statutes* [lit., *His locks are wavy*]. From every one of the scribal crowns that adorn the tops of many letters in the Torah script, mounds and mounds of laws can be derived (*Eruvin* 21b).

שְׁחֹרוֹת כָּעוֹרֵב — *written in raven-black flame* [lit., *black as the raven*]. In Heaven, the Torah is written in black fire upon white fire.

5:12. עֵינָיו כְּיוֹנִים עַל אֲפִיקֵי מָיִם — *Like the gaze of doves toward their cotes, His eyes are fixed on the waters of Torah* [lit., *His eyes are like doves besides brooks of water*].

רֹחֲצוֹת בֶּחָלָב — *bathing all things in clarity* [lit., *bathing in milk*]. God's "eyes" see clearly, rewarding the righteous, and condemning the wicked.

יֹשְׁבוֹת עַל מִלֵּאת — *established upon Creation's fullness* [lit., *sitting upon the fullness*]. His judgment is upon the fullness of the earth.

5:13. לְחָיָו כַּעֲרוּגַת הַבֹּשֶׂם מִגְדְּלוֹת מֶרְקָחִים — *Like a bed of spices are His words at Sinai, like towers of perfume* [lit., *His cheeks are like a bed of spices, towers of perfume*]. God's utterances at Mount Sinai during which He displayed a friendly, smiling demeanor were like beds of spices and mounds of sweet herbs to be processed into perfumes.

שִׂפְתוֹתָיו שׁוֹשַׁנִּים נֹטְפוֹת מוֹר עֹבֵר — *His comforting words from the Tabernacle are roses dripping flowing myrrh* [lit., *His lips are like roses; they drip flowing myrrh*]. In the Tabernacle, God taught us about the offerings that atone for sin.

5:14. יָדָיו גְּלִילֵי זָהָב — *The Tablets, His handiwork, are desirable above even rolls of gold* [lit., *His arms are rods of gold*]. The Tablets of the Ten Commandments, written by the "finger" of God (*Exodus* 31:18), "are more desirable than gold, than even much fine gold" (*Psalms* 19:11).

מְמֻלָּאִים בַּתַּרְשִׁישׁ — *they are studded with commandments precious as gems* [lit., *studded with crystal*].

מֵעָיו עֶשֶׁת שֵׁן מְעֻלֶּפֶת סַפִּירִים — *the Torah's innards are sparkling as ivory intricately inlaid with precious stone* [lit., *his innards are as shiny as ivory inlaid with sapphires*].

5:15. שׁוֹקָיו עַמּוּדֵי שֵׁשׁ מְיֻסָּדִים עַל אַדְנֵי פָז — *The Torah's columns are marble set in contexts of finest gold* [lit., *His legs are pillars of marble set upon sockets of fine gold*] . . .

מַרְאֵהוּ כַּלְּבָנוֹן בָּחוּר כָּאֲרָזִים — *its contemplation flowers like Lebanon, it is sturdy as cedars* [lit., *his appearance is like (the forest of) Lebanon, choicest among cedars*]. Just as one sees beautiful

Israel to the nations

8 *I adjure you, O nations destined to ascend to Jerusalem, when you see my*
Beloved on the future Day of Judgment, will you not tell Him that I bore all travails
for love of Him?

The nations ask Israel

9 *With what does your beloved God excel all others that you suffer for His Name,*
O fairest of nations? With what does your beloved God excel all others that you dare
to adjure us?

Israel responds

10 *My Beloved is pure and purifies sin, and is ruddy with vengeance to punish*
betrayers, surrounded with myriad angels. 11 *His opening words were finest gold,*
His crowns hold mounds of statutes written in raven-black flame.
12 *Like the gaze of doves toward their cotes, His eyes are fixed on the waters of*
Torah, bathing all things in clarity, established upon Creation's fullness. 13 *Like a bed*
of spices are His words at Sinai, like towers of perfume. His comforting words from
the Tabernacle are roses dripping flowing myrrh. 14 *The Tablets, His handiwork, are*
desirable above even rolls of gold; they are studded with commandments precious
as gems, the Torah's innards are sparkling as ivory intricately inlaid with precious
stone. 15 *The Torah's columns are marble set in contexts of finest gold, its*
contemplation flowers like Lebanon, it is sturdy as cedars. 16 *The words of His*
palate are sweet and He is all delight.

This is my Beloved and this is my Friend, O nations destined to ascend to Jerusalem.

6 *The nations, derisively, to Israel*

1 *Where has your Beloved gone, O fairest among women? Where has your*
Beloved turned to rejoin you? Let us seek Him with you and build His Temple
with you.

Israel responds

2 *My Beloved has descended to His Temple garden, to His Incense Altar, yet still*
He grazes my brethren remaining in gardens of exile to gather the roseate fragrance
of their words of Torah. 3 *I alone am my Beloved's and my Beloved is mine, He Who*
grazes His sheep in roselike pastures.

NOTES INCLUDING PHRASE-BY-PHRASE LITERAL TRANSLATION

flowers and lofty trees in a forest, so one discovers limitless wisdom in the Torah.

5:16. חִכּוֹ מַמְתַקִּים וְכֻלּוֹ מַחֲמַדִּים — *The words of His palate are sweet and He is all delight* [lit., *His palate is most sweet; and all of him is a delight*].

זֶה דוֹדִי וְזֶה רֵעִי בְּנוֹת יְרוּשָׁלָםִ — *This is my Beloved and this is my Friend, O nations destined to ascend to Jerusalem* [lit., *this is my Beloved, and this is my Friend, O daughters of Jerusalem*].

6:1. The nations continue to taunt Israel:

אָנָה הָלַךְ דּוֹדֵךְ הַיָּפָה בַּנָּשִׁים — *Where has your Beloved gone, O fairest among women*? Why has He left you alone, widowed?

אָנָה פָּנָה דוֹדֵךְ וּנְבַקְשֶׁנּוּ עִמָּךְ — *Where has your Beloved turned to rejoin you? Let us seek Him with you and build His Temple with you* [lit., *Where has your Beloved turned, that we may seek Him with you*?]. When King Cyrus permitted the rebuilding of the Temple, the heathens tried to undermine the work by joining the builders and sabotaging the construction (see *Ezra* 4:1-2).

6:2. דּוֹדִי יָרַד לְגַנּוֹ לַעֲרֻגוֹת הַבֹּשֶׂם — *My Beloved has descended to His Temple garden, to His Incense Altar* [lit., *My Beloved has gone down to His garden, to the beds of spices*]. He commanded us to build His Temple, and He will surely be there with us.

לִרְעוֹת בַּגַּנִּים וְלִלְקֹט שׁוֹשַׁנִּים — *yet still He grazes my brethren remaining in gardens of exile to gather the roseate fragrance of their words of Torah* [lit., *to graze in the gardens and to pick roses*]. God did not neglect those of His children who chose not to return to the land. He manifested His Presence in their synagogues and study halls.

6:3. In reply to the nations' insincere offer to help Israel:

אֲנִי לְדוֹדִי — *I alone am my Beloved's* [lit., *I am My Beloved's*]. I, alone, am my Beloved's. You are not His, and you will not assist us in the construction (see *Ezra* 4:3).

וְדוֹדִי לִי — *and my Beloved is mine*.

הָרוֹעֶה בַּשּׁוֹשַׁנִּים — *He Who grazes His sheep in roselike pastures* [lit., *Who feeds (others) among the roses*].

יָפָה אַתְּ רַעְיָתִי כְּתִרְצָה נָאוָה כִּירוּשָׁלָםִ אֲיֻמָּה כַּנִּדְגָּלוֹת: הָסֵבִּי עֵינַיִךְ מִנֶּגְדִּי ד־ה
שֶׁהֵם הִרְהִיבֻנִי שַׂעְרֵךְ כְּעֵדֶר הָעִזִּים שֶׁגָּלְשׁוּ מִן־הַגִּלְעָד: שִׁנַּיִךְ כְּעֵדֶר הָרְחֵלִים ו
שֶׁעָלוּ מִן־הָרַחְצָה שֶׁכֻּלָּם מַתְאִימוֹת וְשַׁכֻּלָה אֵין בָּהֶם: כְּפֶלַח הָרִמּוֹן רַקָּתֵךְ ז
מִבַּעַד לְצַמָּתֵךְ: שִׁשִּׁים הֵמָּה מְלָכוֹת וּשְׁמֹנִים פִּילַגְשִׁים וַעֲלָמוֹת אֵין מִסְפָּר: ח
אַחַת הִיא יוֹנָתִי תַמָּתִי אַחַת הִיא לְאִמָּהּ בָּרָה הִיא לְיוֹלַדְתָּהּ רָאוּהָ ט
בָנוֹת וַיְאַשְּׁרוּהָ מְלָכוֹת וּפִילַגְשִׁים וַיְהַלְלוּהָ: מִי־זֹאת הַנִּשְׁקָפָה י
כְּמוֹ־שָׁחַר יָפָה כַלְּבָנָה בָּרָה כַּחַמָּה אֲיֻמָּה כַּנִּדְגָּלוֹת: אֶל־גִּנַּת אֱגוֹז יא
יָרַדְתִּי לִרְאוֹת בְּאִבֵּי הַנָּחַל לִרְאוֹת הֲפָרְחָה הַגֶּפֶן הֵנֵצוּ הָרִמֹּנִים: לֹא יָדַעְתִּי יב
נַפְשִׁי שָׂמַתְנִי מַרְכְּבוֹת עַמִּי נָדִיב: שׁוּבִי שׁוּבִי הַשּׁוּלַמִּית שׁוּבִי שׁוּבִי וְנֶחֱזֶה־ א ז
בָּךְ מַה־תֶּחֱזוּ בַּשּׁוּלַמִּית כִּמְחֹלַת הַמַּחֲנָיִם: מַה־יָּפוּ פְעָמַיִךְ בַּנְּעָלִים בַּת־ ב

NOTES INCLUDING PHRASE-BY-PHRASE LITERAL TRANSLATION

6:4. יָפָה אַתְּ רַעְיָתִי כְּתִרְצָה — *You are beautiful, My love, when your deeds are pleasing* [lit., *You are beautiful, My love, as Tirzah*]. Tirzah was a beautiful city that was the capital for a succession of kings of the Northern Kingdom of Israel (see *I Kings* 15:33; 16:8-9,15,23).

נָאוָה כִּירוּשָׁלָםִ — *as comely now as you once were in Jerusalem of old* [lit., *comely as Jerusalem*].

אֲיֻמָּה כַּנִּדְגָּלוֹת — *hosts of angels stand in awe of you* [lit., *awe inspiring as an army with banners*]. See *Ezra* Ch. 5.

6:5. הָסֵבִּי עֵינַיִךְ מִנֶּגְדִּי שֶׁהֵם הִרְהִיבֻנִי — *Turn your pleading eyes from Me lest I be tempted to bestow upon you holiness more than you can bear* [lit., *Turn your eyes away from Me, for they overwhelm Me*]. As the Second Temple was being built, God said figuratively, "You are as beautiful to Me now as you were before, but in this Temple I will not return the Ark, the Cherubim and the *Paroches*-Curtain that you had in the First Temple. They invoke special love in Me that you cannot have now that you have sinned. But in every other way you have maintained the former virtues that endeared you to Me."

שַׂעְרֵךְ כְּעֵדֶר הָעִזִּים שֶׁגָּלְשׁוּ מִן הַגִּלְעָד — *But with all your flaws, your most common sons are as dearly beloved as the children of Jacob in the goatlike procession descending the slopes of Mount Gilead* [lit., *your hair is like a flock of goats streaming down from Gilead*]. Even the young, tender and insignificant among you are praiseworthy.

6:6. שִׁנַּיִךְ כְּעֵדֶר הָרְחֵלִים שֶׁעָלוּ מִן הָרַחְצָה שֶׁכֻּלָּם מַתְאִימוֹת וְשַׁכֻּלָה אֵין בָּהֶם — *Your mighty leaders are perfect, as a flock of ewes come up from the washing, all of them unblemished with no miscarriage of action in them* [lit., *Your teeth are like a flock of ewes which have come up from the washing, all of them are perfect and there is none blemished among them*] (see 4:2).

6:7. כְּפֶלַח הָרִמּוֹן רַקָּתֵךְ מִבַּעַד לְצַמָּתֵךְ — *As many as a pomegranate's seeds are the merits of your unworthiest within your modest veil* [lit., *Your cheeks are like a slice of pomegranate, from behind your veil*] (see 4:3).

6:8. שִׁשִּׁים הֵמָּה מְלָכוֹת — *The queenly offspring of Abraham are sixty* [lit., *There are sixty queens*]. Abraham's male descendants through the children of Jacob (*Genesis* 25:1-4, 12-15; 35:23-36:19) numbered sixty (see Appendix B, charts 2 and 4).

וּשְׁמֹנִים פִּילַגְשִׁים וַעֲלָמוֹת אֵין מִסְפָּר — *compared to whom the eighty Noachides and all their countless nations are like mere concubines* [lit., *and eighty concubines and maidens without number*]. Noah's descendants, until Abraham (*Genesis* Chs. 10-11), numbered eighty (See Appendix B, chart 1). Each of them branched out into many families.

6:9. אַחַת הִיא יוֹנָתִי תַמָּתִי — *Unique is she, My constant dove, My perfect one* [lit., *One is My dove, My perfect one*]. Israel is My chosen nation, like a perfect dove, loyal to her mate.

אַחַת הִיא לְאִמָּהּ — *Unique is she, this nation striving for the truth* [lit., *one is she to her mother*]. To comprehend Torah in its fundamentals and its truth.

בָּרָה הִיא לְיוֹלַדְתָּהּ — *pure is she to Jacob who begot her* [lit., *she is pure to the one that begot her*]. All of Jacob's sons were righteous.

רָאוּהָ בָנוֹת וַיְאַשְּׁרוּהָ מְלָכוֹת וּפִילַגְשִׁים וַיְהַלְלוּהָ — Nations [lit., *maidens*] *saw her and they extolled her; queens and concubines, and they praised her* (see *Malachi* 3:12).

6:10. God now quotes to Israel how the nations will extol and praise her:

מִי זֹאת הַנִּשְׁקָפָה כְּמוֹ שָׁחַר — *"Who is this that gazes down from atop the Temple Mount, brightening like the dawn* [lit., *Who is that gazing down like dawn?*]. Like a steadily brightening dawn, Israel began the Second Temple era in subjugation, but later became independent under the Hasmonean dynasty.

יָפָה כַלְּבָנָה בָּרָה כַּחַמָּה — *beautiful as the moon, brilliant as the sun* [lit., *beautiful as the moon, pure as the sun*]. At first, Israel was like the moon, because it could only reflect the power permitted it by King Cyrus.

אֲיֻמָּה כַּנִּדְגָּלוֹת — *awesome as the bannered hosts of kings?"* [lit., *awe inspiring as an army with banners*].

6:11. אֶל גִּנַּת אֱגוֹז יָרַדְתִּי — *I descended upon the deceptively simple holiness of the Second Temple* [lit., *I went down to the garden of nuts*]. Israel is modest and unpretentious; her scholars are not

God to Israel

4 You are beautiful, My love, when your deeds are pleasing, as comely now as you
once were in Jerusalem of old, hosts of angels stand in awe of you. 5 Turn your
pleading eyes from Me lest I be tempted to bestow upon you holiness more than you
can bear. But with all your flaws, your most common sons are as dearly beloved as
the children of Jacob in the goatlike procession descending the slopes of Mount
Gilead. 6 Your mighty leaders are perfect, as a flock of ewes come up from the
washing, all of them unblemished with no miscarriage of action in them. 7 As many
as a pomegranate's seeds are the merits of your unworthiest within your modest veil.
8 The queenly offspring of Abraham are sixty, compared to whom the eighty
Noachides and all their countless nations are like mere concubines.
9 Unique is she, My constant dove, My perfect one. Unique is she, this nation
striving for the truth; pure is she to Jacob who begot her. Nations saw her and they
extolled her; queens and concubines, and they praised her: 10 "Who is this that gazes
down from atop the Temple Mount, brightening like the dawn, beautiful as the moon,
brilliant as the sun, awesome as the bannered hosts of kings?"
11 I descended upon the deceptively simple holiness of the Second Temple to see
your moisture-laden deeds in the river beds; to see whether your Torah scholars had
budded on the vine, whether your merit-laden righteous had flowered like the
pomegranates filled with seeds.

Israel responds sadly

12 Alas, I knew not how to guard myself from sin! My own devices harnessed me,
like chariots subject to a foreign nation's mercies.

7 *1 The nations have said to me, "Turn away, turn away from God, O nation whose*
faith in Him is perfect, turn away, turn away, and we shall choose nobility from you."
But I replied to them, "What can you bestow upon a nation of perfect faith
commensurate even with the desert camps encircling?"

The nations to Israel

2 But your footsteps were so lovely when shod in pilgrim's sandals, O daughter

NOTES INCLUDING PHRASE-BY-PHRASE LITERAL TRANSLATION

conspicuous, but they are full of wisdom.

לִרְאוֹת בְּאִבֵּי הַנָּחַל — *to see your moisture-laden deeds in the river beds* [lit., *to look at the green plants of the streams*], to examine the good deeds that I could find in you . . .

לִרְאוֹת הֲפָרְחָה הַגֶּפֶן — *to see whether your Torah scholars had budded on the vine* [lit., *to see whether the vine has budded*] . . .

הֵנֵצוּ הָרִמֹּנִים — *whether your merit-laden righteous had flowered like the pomegranates filled with seeds* [lit., *if the pomegranates were in flower*].

6:12. Hearing God's praise of her glorious past, Israel reflects on her current plight and responds sadly:

לֹא יָדַעְתִּי נַפְשִׁי שָׂמַתְנִי מַרְכְּבוֹת עַמִּי נָדִיב — *Alas, I knew not how to guard myself from sin! My own devices harnessed me, like chariots subject to a foreign nation's mercies* [lit., *I did not know; my soul set me (as) chariots of a noble nation*]. Instead of avoiding sin, I stumbled into the sin of hatred and controversy, which caused Jews to invite Rome into the land and take control. From that point, I became a chariot driven by foreign nations.

7:1. שׁוּבִי שׁוּבִי הַשּׁוּלַמִּית — *The nations have said to me, "Turn away, turn away from God, O nation whose faith in Him is perfect* [lit., *Turn, turn, O Shulammite*]. The word שׁוּלַמִּית, "Shulammite," is linguistically related to שָׁלֵם, "whole, perfect."

שׁוּבִי שׁוּבִי וְנֶחֱזֶה בָּךְ — *turn away, turn away, and we shall choose nobility from you"* [lit., *turn, turn, that we may see you*]. Join us and we will discern what greatness to bestow upon you.

מַה תֶּחֱזוּ בַּשּׁוּלַמִּית כִּמְחֹלַת הַמַּחֲנָיִם — *But I replied to them, "What can you bestow upon a nation of perfect faith commensurate even with the desert camps encircling?"* [lit., *What will you see in the Shulammite like a dance of the camps*?]. Your highest honors are not equal even to the greatness of the encircling encampments in the desert. See *Numbers* Ch. 2.

7:2. מַה יָּפוּ פְעָמַיִךְ בַּנְּעָלִים בַּת נָדִיב — *But your footsteps were so lovely when shod in pilgrim's sandals, O daughter of nobles* [lit., *How lovely are your steps in sandals, O daughter of nobility*!]. The word פְּעָמִים means both "footsteps," (hence, "pilgrimage") and "times, repeated occasions." The nations were impressed by Israel's pilgrimages to the Temple three times each year to celebrate the festivals.

ג נָדִיב חַמּוּקֵי יְרֵכַיִךְ כְּמוֹ חֲלָאִים מַעֲשֵׂה יְדֵי אָמָּן: שָׁרְרֵךְ אַגַּן הַסַּהַר
ד אַל־יֶחְסַר הַמָּזֶג בִּטְנֵךְ עֲרֵמַת חִטִּים סוּגָה בַּשּׁוֹשַׁנִּים: שְׁנֵי שָׁדַיִךְ כִּשְׁנֵי
ה עֳפָרִים תָּאֳמֵי צְבִיָּה: צַוָּארֵךְ כְּמִגְדַּל הַשֵּׁן עֵינַיִךְ בְּרֵכוֹת בְּחֶשְׁבּוֹן עַל־שַׁעַר
ו בַּת־רַבִּים אַפֵּךְ כְּמִגְדַּל הַלְּבָנוֹן צוֹפֶה פְּנֵי דַמָּשֶׂק: רֹאשֵׁךְ עָלַיִךְ כַּכַּרְמֶל וְדַלַּת
ז רֹאשֵׁךְ כָּאַרְגָּמָן מֶלֶךְ אָסוּר בָּרְהָטִים: מַה־יָּפִית וּמַה־נָּעַמְתְּ אַהֲבָה
ח־ט בַּתַּעֲנוּגִים: זֹאת קוֹמָתֵךְ דָּמְתָה לְתָמָר וְשָׁדַיִךְ לְאַשְׁכֹּלוֹת: אָמַרְתִּי אֶעֱלֶה
בְתָמָר אֹחֲזָה בְּסַנְסִנָּיו וְיִהְיוּ־נָא שָׁדַיִךְ כְּאֶשְׁכְּלוֹת הַגֶּפֶן וְרֵיחַ אַפֵּךְ כַּתַּפּוּחִים:
י־יא וְחִכֵּךְ כְּיֵין הַטּוֹב הוֹלֵךְ לְדוֹדִי לְמֵישָׁרִים דּוֹבֵב שִׂפְתֵי יְשֵׁנִים: אֲנִי לְדוֹדִי וְעָלַי
יב־יג תְּשׁוּקָתוֹ: לְכָה דוֹדִי נֵצֵא הַשָּׂדֶה נָלִינָה בַּכְּפָרִים: נַשְׁכִּימָה לַכְּרָמִים נִרְאֶה
אִם־פָּרְחָה הַגֶּפֶן פִּתַּח הַסְּמָדַר הֵנֵצוּ הָרִמּוֹנִים שָׁם אֶתֵּן אֶת־דֹּדַי לָךְ:

NOTES INCLUDING PHRASE-BY-PHRASE LITERAL TRANSLATION

חַמּוּקֵי יְרֵכַיִךְ כְּמוֹ חֲלָאִים מַעֲשֵׂה יְדֵי אָמָּן — *The rounded shafts for your libations' abysslike trenches, handiwork of the Master Craftsman* [lit., *The roundness of your flanks are like jewels, the work of a master's hand*]. The wine libations, poured onto the top of the Temple's Courtyard Altar, flowed through pipes into deep pits under the Altar. Those pits had been placed there by God Himself during the Six Days of Creation. They were rounded like a thigh and descended into the abyss.

7:3. שָׁרְרֵךְ אַגַּן הַסַּהַר — *At earth's very center your Sanhedrin site is a crescent basin* [lit., *Your umbilicus is like a moonshaped basin*]. The seat of the Sanhedrin (high court) was in the Temple complex, at the center of the world. Its members were seated in a semicircle, like the crescent moon, so they could see each other and speak face to face.

אַל יֶחְסַר הַמָּזֶג — *of ceaseless, flowing teaching* [lit., *wherein no mixed wine is lacking*]. The Sanhedrin was an endless source of wisdom.

בִּטְנֵךְ עֲרֵמַת חִטִּים — *your national center an indispensable heap of nourishing knowledge* [lit., *your stomach is like a heap of wheat*]. Wheat is an indispensable staple.

סוּגָה בַּשּׁוֹשַׁנִּים — *Hedged about with roses.* Just as a hedge of roses is hardly an imposing barrier, similarly, the sanctions of the Torah are gentle reminders to refrain from trespass against the handiwork of God.

7:4. שְׁנֵי שָׁדַיִךְ כִּשְׁנֵי עֳפָרִים תָּאֳמֵי צְבִיָּה — *Your twin sustainers, the Tablets of the Law, are like two fawns, twins of the gazelle* [lit., *Your two breasts are like two fawns, twins of a gazelle*]. This refers to the twin Tablets of the Covenant (see also 4:5).

7:5. צַוָּארֵךְ כְּמִגְדַּל הַשֵּׁן — *Your Altar and Temple, erect and stately as an ivory tower* [lit., *Your neck is like a tower of ivory*]. The Sanctuary and Altar, which stood erect and tall, provided spiritual strength and protection like an ivory tower.

עֵינַיִךְ בְּרֵכוֹת בְּחֶשְׁבּוֹן עַל שַׁעַר בַּת רַבִּים — *your wise men aflow with springs of complex wisdom at the gate of the many-peopled city* [lit., *your eyes are (like the) pools in Heshbon by the gate of Bath-rabbim*]. Your wise men (the "eyes" of the nation) sit at the gates of Jerusalem (Bath-rabbim, lit., "of great population") where they are involved in the complex calculations of the Hebrew calendar.

אַפֵּךְ כְּמִגְדַּל הַלְּבָנוֹן צוֹפֶה פְּנֵי דַמָּשֶׂק — *your face, like the tower of Lebanon, looks to your future boundary as far as Damascus* [lit., *your face is like the tower of Lebanon facing toward Damascus*]. An allusion to the prophetic vision (see *Zechariah* 9:1) that in the future the gates of Jerusalem will stretch forth until Damascus.

7:6. רֹאשֵׁךְ עָלַיִךְ כַּכַּרְמֶל — *The Godly name on your head is as mighty as Carmel* [lit., *Your head upon you is like (Mount) Carmel*]. This refers to the *tefillin* of the head, of which the verse says, "Then all the peoples of the earth will see that the Name of HASHEM is proclaimed over you, and they will revere you" (*Deuteronomy* 28:10). The *tefillin* are Israel's strength; they are as awe inspiring as the lofty cliffs of Mount Carmel.

וְדַלַּת רֹאשֵׁךְ כָּאַרְגָּמָן — *your crowning braid is royal purple* [lit., *and the locks of your head are like purple*]. The locks of your Nazirites are as comely as garments of royal purple.

מֶלֶךְ אָסוּר בָּרְהָטִים — *your King is bound in Naziritic tresses* [lit., *a king bound in tresses*]. The crown of the King (God) is associated with the Nazirite's hair (see *Numbers* 6:7).

7:7. מַה יָּפִית וּמַה נָּעַמְתְּ אַהֲבָה בַּתַּעֲנוּגִים — *How beautiful and pleasant are you, befitting the pleasures of spiritual love* [lit., *How beautiful you are, and how pleasant, love in delights*]. The nations now praise Israel's lofty spiritual ideals.

7:8. זֹאת קוֹמָתֵךְ דָּמְתָה לְתָמָר — *Such is your stature, likened to a towering palm tree* [lit., *This is your stature, like unto a palm tree*]. We witnessed your lovely stature in the days of Nebuchadnezzar, when all the nations bowed down to the statue (see *Daniel* Ch. 3).

וְשָׁדַיִךְ לְאַשְׁכֹּלוֹת — *from your teachers flow sustenance like wine-filled clusters* [lit., *and your breasts are like clusters*]. "Your breasts," your sources of spiritual nourishment, i.e., Daniel and his companions Hananiah, Mishael, and Azariah, nurtured everyone with the knowledge that there is no fear of God like yours.

7:9. אָמַרְתִּי אֶעֱלֶה בְתָמָר — *I boast on High that your deeds cause Me to ascend on your palm tree* [lit., *I said: I will ascend in the palm tree*]. I boast about you among the Celestial Hosts, that I am

of nobles. The rounded shafts for your libations' abysslike trenches, handiwork of the Master Craftsman. [3] *At earth's very center your Sanhedrin site is a crescent basin of ceaseless, flowing teaching; your national center an indispensable heap of nourishing knowledge hedged about with roses.* [4] *Your twin sustainers, the Tablets of the Law, are like two fawns, twins of the gazelle.* [5] *Your Altar and Temple, erect and stately as an ivory tower; your wise men aflow with springs of complex wisdom at the gate of the many-peopled city; your face, like the tower of Lebanon, looks to your future boundary as far as Damascus.*

[6] *The Godly name on your head is as mighty as Carmel; your crowning braid is royal purple, your King is bound in Naziritic tresses.* [7] *How beautiful and pleasant are you, befitting the pleasures of spiritual love.* [8] *Such is your stature, likened to a towering palm tree, from your teachers flow sustenance like wine-filled clusters.*

God to Israel

[9] *I boast on High that your deeds cause Me to ascend on your palm tree, I grasp onto your branches. I beg now your teachers that they may remain like clusters of grapes from which flow strength to your weakest ones, and the fragrance of your countenance like apples,* [10] *and may your utterance be like finest wine.*

Israel to God. . .

I shall heed Your plea to uphold my faith before my Beloved in love so upright and honest that my slumbering fathers will move their lips in approval.

. . . to the nations . . .

[11] *I am my Beloved's and He longs for my perfection.*

. . . to God

[12] *Come, my Beloved, let us go to the fields where Your children serve You in want, there let us lodge with Esau's children who are blessed with plenty yet still deny.*

[13] *Let us wake at dawn in vineyards of prayer and study. Let us see if students of Writ have budded, if students of Oral Law have blossomed, if ripened scholars have bloomed; there I will display my finest products to You.*

NOTES INCLUDING PHRASE-BY-PHRASE LITERAL TRANSLATION

elevated through your actions on earth.

אֹחֲזָה בְּסַנְסִנָּיו — *I grasp onto your branches* [lit., *I will take hold of its branches*]. I cleave to the branches, i.e., the children, of this palm tree, Israel.

וְיִהְיוּ נָא שָׁדַיִךְ כְּאֶשְׁכְּלוֹת הַגֶּפֶן וְרֵיחַ אַפֵּךְ כַּתַּפּוּחִים — *I beg now your teachers that they may remain like clusters of grapes from which flow strength to your weakest ones, and the fragrance of your countenance like apples* [lit., *and let your breasts be like clusters of the vine, and the fragrance of your countenance like apples*]. May the righteous and wise inspire the young to withstand the taunts of their heathen neighbors who wish to lead Israel astray.

7:10. וְחִכֵּךְ כְּיֵין הַטּוֹב — *and may your utterance be like finest wine* [lit., *your palate is like choice wine*]. May your response to the taunts of the heathens be as clear and potent as fine wine.

הוֹלֵךְ לְדוֹדִי לְמֵישָׁרִים — *I shall heed Your plea to uphold my faith before my Beloved in love so upright and honest* [lit., *it goes to my Beloved in righteousness*].

דּוֹבֵב שִׂפְתֵי יְשֵׁנִים — *that my slumbering fathers will move their lips in approval* [lit., *causing the lips of sleepers to speak*]. My love is so intense that even my departed ancestors will rejoice in me and be thankful for their lot.

7:11. אֲנִי לְדוֹדִי וְעָלַי תְּשׁוּקָתוֹ — *I am my Beloved's and He longs for my perfection* [lit., *I am my Beloved's and His longing is upon me*].

7:12. לְכָה דוֹדִי נֵצֵא הַשָּׂדֶה — *Come, my Beloved, let us go to the fields where Your children serve You in want* [lit., *Come, my Beloved, let us go forth into the field*]. Do not judge me by the affluent people who indulge in robbery and immorality; come, let me show You scholars who study the Torah in poverty.

נָלִינָה בַּכְּפָרִים — *there let us lodge with Esau's children who are blessed with plenty yet still deny* [lit., *let us lodge in the villages*]. I will show You the children of Esau, upon whom You have bestowed much bounty, yet they do not believe in You.

7:13. נַשְׁכִּימָה לַכְּרָמִים — *Let us wake at dawn in vineyards of prayer and study* [lit., *Let us rise early for the vineyards*].

נִרְאֶה אִם פָּרְחָה הַגֶּפֶן פִּתַּח הַסְּמָדַר הֵנֵצוּ הָרִמּוֹנִים — *Let us see if students of Writ have budded, if students of Oral Law have blossomed, if ripened scholars have bloomed* [lit., *Let us see if the vine has budded, if the blossom has opened, if the pomegranates are in bloom*]. The stages of the ripening grape — budding, flowering, fruiting — symbolize the progress of the developing Torah scholars, from Scripture to Mishnah to Talmud.

שָׁם אֶתֵּן אֶת דֹּדַי לָךְ — *there I will display my finest products to You* [lit., *there I will give my love to You*]. I will show You my glory and my greatness, my sons and my daughters.

יד הַדּוּדָאִים נָתְנוּ־רֵיחַ וְעַל־פְּתָחֵינוּ כָּל־מְגָדִים חֲדָשִׁים גַּם־יְשָׁנִים דּוֹדִי צָפַנְתִּי
ח א לָךְ: מִי יִתֶּנְךָ כְּאָח לִי יוֹנֵק שְׁדֵי אִמִּי אֶמְצָאֲךָ בַחוּץ אֶשָּׁקְךָ גַּם לֹא־יָבֻזוּ לִי:
ב אֶנְהָגְךָ אֲבִיאֲךָ אֶל־בֵּית אִמִּי תְּלַמְּדֵנִי אַשְׁקְךָ מִיַּיִן הָרֶקַח מֵעֲסִיס רִמֹּנִי:
ג־ד שְׂמֹאלוֹ תַּחַת רֹאשִׁי וִימִינוֹ תְּחַבְּקֵנִי: הִשְׁבַּעְתִּי אֶתְכֶם בְּנוֹת יְרוּשָׁלָם מַה־
ה תָּעִירוּ | וּמַה־תְּעֹרְרוּ אֶת־הָאַהֲבָה עַד שֶׁתֶּחְפָּץ: מִי זֹאת עֹלָה מִן־
הַמִּדְבָּר מִתְרַפֶּקֶת עַל־דּוֹדָהּ תַּחַת הַתַּפּוּחַ עוֹרַרְתִּיךָ שָׁמָּה חִבְּלַתְךָ אִמֶּךָ
ו שָׁמָּה חִבְּלָה יְלָדַתְךָ: שִׂימֵנִי כַחוֹתָם עַל־לִבֶּךָ כַּחוֹתָם עַל־זְרוֹעֶךָ כִּי־עַזָּה
ז כַמָּוֶת אַהֲבָה קָשָׁה כִשְׁאוֹל קִנְאָה רְשָׁפֶיהָ רִשְׁפֵּי אֵשׁ שַׁלְהֶבֶתְיָה: מַיִם רַבִּים
לֹא יוּכְלוּ לְכַבּוֹת אֶת־הָאַהֲבָה וּנְהָרוֹת לֹא יִשְׁטְפוּהָ אִם־יִתֵּן אִישׁ אֶת־כָּל־הוֹן
ח בֵּיתוֹ בָּאַהֲבָה בּוֹז יָבוּזוּ לוֹ: אָחוֹת לָנוּ קְטַנָּה וְשָׁדַיִם אֵין לָהּ מַה־
ט נַּעֲשֶׂה לַאֲחֹתֵנוּ בַּיּוֹם שֶׁיְּדֻבַּר־בָּהּ: אִם־חוֹמָה הִיא נִבְנֶה עָלֶיהָ טִירַת כָּסֶף

NOTES INCLUDING PHRASE-BY-PHRASE LITERAL TRANSLATION

7:14. הַדּוּדָאִים נָתְנוּ רֵיחַ — *All my baskets, good and bad, emit a fragrance* [lit., *The baskets yield fragrance*]. "Good figs" are an allusion to the righteous; "bad figs," to the wicked. In time, even the wicked will seek out God.

וְעַל פְּתָחֵינוּ כָּל מְגָדִים חֲדָשִׁים גַּם יְשָׁנִים — *all at our doors have the precious fruits of comely deeds, both the Scribes' new ordinances and the Torah's timeless wisdom* [lit., *and at our door are all precious fruits, both new and old*].

דּוֹדִי צָפַנְתִּי לָךְ — *for You, O Beloved, has my heart stored them* [lit., *I have hidden for You, my Beloved*]. Your commandments are in the depths of my heart.

8:1. מִי יִתֶּנְךָ כְּאָח לִי יוֹנֵק שְׁדֵי אִמִּי — *If only, despite my wrongs, You could comfort me as Joseph did, like a brother nurtured at my mother's breast* [lit., *If only You were as a brother to me, who had nursed at my mother's breast!*]. If only You would comfort me as Joseph comforted his brothers (see *Genesis* 50:21).

אֶמְצָאֲךָ בַחוּץ אֶשָּׁקְךָ גַּם לֹא יָבֻזוּ לִי — *if in the streets I found Your prophets I would kiss You and embrace You through them, nor could anyone despise me for it* [lit., *(when) I would find You in the street I would kiss You and no one would scorn me*]. I would find Your prophets speaking in Your Name and I would embrace and kiss them.

8:2. אֶנְהָגְךָ אֲבִיאֲךָ אֶל בֵּית אִמִּי תְּלַמְּדֵנִי — *I would lead You, I would bring You to my mother's Temple for You to teach me as You did in Moses' Tent* [lit., *I would lead You, I would bring You to my mother's house that You should instruct me*].

אַשְׁקְךָ מִיַּיִן הָרֶקַח מֵעֲסִיס רִמֹּנִי — *to drink I would give You spiced libations, wines like pomegranate nectar* [lit., *I would give You spiced wine to drink, of the juice of my pomegranate*].

8:3. שְׂמֹאלוֹ תַּחַת רֹאשִׁי וִימִינוֹ תְּחַבְּקֵנִי — *Despite my laments in exile, His left hand supports my head and His right hand embraces me in support* [lit., *His left hand is under my head and His right arm embraces me*].

8:4. הִשְׁבַּעְתִּי אֶתְכֶם בְּנוֹת יְרוּשָׁלָם מַה תָּעִירוּ וּמַה תְּעֹרְרוּ אֶת הָאַהֲבָה עַד שֶׁתֶּחְפָּץ — *I adjure you, O nations who are destined to ascend to Jerusalem, if you dare provoke God to hate me or disturb His love for me while He still desires it* [lit., *I have adjured you O daughters of Jerusalem: should you wake or rouse the love until it pleases*]. Your efforts will be of no avail! (see 2:6-7).

8:5. מִי זֹאת עֹלָה מִן הַמִּדְבָּר מִתְרַפֶּקֶת עַל דּוֹדָהּ — *How worthy she is ascending from the wilderness bearing Torah and His Presence, clinging to her Beloved!* [lit., *Who is she that rises up from the wilderness leaning upon her Beloved?*]. Israel ascended from the desert bearing wonderful gifts from God; there she rose spiritually by cleaving to the Divine Presence.

תַּחַת הַתַּפּוּחַ עוֹרַרְתִּיךָ — *Under Sinai suspended above me, there I roused Your love* [lit., *Under the apple tree I roused You*]. Remember, how, beneath Mount Sinai, which was suspended over my head like an apple ["and they stood beneath the mountain" (*Deuteronomy* 4:11)], I manifested my love for You.

שָׁמָּה חִבְּלַתְךָ אִמֶּךָ שָׁמָּה חִבְּלָה יְלָדַתְךָ — *there was Your people born; a mother to other nations, there she endured the travail of her birth* [lit., *there Your mother was in travail for You; she who bore You was in travail*].

8:6. שִׂימֵנִי כַחוֹתָם עַל לִבֶּךָ כַּחוֹתָם עַל זְרוֹעֶךָ — *For the sake of my love, place me like a seal on Your heart, like a seal to dedicate Your strength for me* [lit., *Set me as a seal upon Your heart, as a seal upon Your arm*]. And because of that love, seal me upon Your heart so that You do not forget me.

כִּי עַזָּה כַמָּוֶת אַהֲבָה — *for strong till the death is my love* [lit., *that love is strong as death*].

קָשָׁה כִשְׁאוֹל קִנְאָה — *though their zeal for vengeance is hard as the grave* [lit., *jealousy is hard as the grave*], i.e., the unjust complaints, rivalries and jealousies that the nations provoked against me because of You.

רְשָׁפֶיהָ רִשְׁפֵּי אֵשׁ שַׁלְהֶבֶתְיָה — *its flashes are flashes of fire, the flame of God.* Its flashes are of a fierce fire emanating from the flames of Gehinnom.

8:7. מַיִם רַבִּים לֹא יוּכְלוּ לְכַבּוֹת אֶת הָאַהֲבָה — *Many waters of heathen tribulation cannot extinguish the fire of this love* [lit., *Many waters*

*14 All my baskets, good and bad, emit a fragrance; all at our doors have the precious
fruits of comely deeds, both the Scribes' new ordinances and the Torah's timeless
wisdom; for You, Beloved, has my heart stored them.*

8

*1 If only, despite my wrongs, You could comfort me as Joseph did, like a brother
nurtured at my mother's breasts, if in the streets I found Your prophets I would kiss You
and embrace You through them, nor could anyone despise me for it. 2 I would lead You,
I would bring You to my mother's Temple for You to teach me as You did in Moses' Tent;
to drink I would give You spiced libations, wines like pomegranate nectar.*

Israel to the nations

*3 Despite my laments in exile, His left hand supports my head and His right hand
embraces me in support. 4 I adjure you, O nations who are destined to ascend to
Jerusalem, if you dare provoke God to hate me or disturb His love for me while He still
desires it.*

God and the Heavenly Tribunal

*5 How worthy she is ascending from the wilderness bearing Torah and His Presence,
clinging to her Beloved!*

Israel interjects

*Under Sinai suspended above me, there I roused Your love, there was Your people
born; a mother to other nations, there she endured the travail of her birth. 6 For the sake
of my love, place me like a seal on Your heart, like a seal to dedicate Your strength for
me, for strong till the death is my love; though their zeal for vengeance is hard as the
grave, its flashes are flashes of fire, the flame of God. 7 Many waters of heathen
tribulation cannot extinguish the fire of this love, nor rivers of royal seduction or torture
wash it away.*

God replies to Israel

*Were any man to offer all the treasure of his home to entice you away from your love,
they would scorn him to extreme.*

The Heavenly Tribunal reflects

*8 Israel desires to cleave to us, the small and humble one, but her time of spiritual
maturity has not come. What shall we do for our cleaving one on the day the nations
plot against her?
9 If her faith and belief are strong as a wall withstanding incursions from without, we
shall become her fortress and beauty, building her city and Holy Temple;*

NOTES INCLUDING PHRASE-BY-PHRASE LITERAL TRANSLATION

cannot extinguish the love]. "Many waters" refers to the heathen nations (see *Isaiah* 17:12,13).

וּנְהָרוֹת לֹא יִשְׁטְפוּהָ — *nor rivers of royal seduction or torture wash it away* [lit., *and rivers cannot drown it*]. Their leaders and kings cannot drown it, neither by force, nor by terror, nor by seductive enticement.

אִם יִתֵּן אִישׁ אֶת כָּל הוֹן בֵּיתוֹ בָּאַהֲבָה בּוֹז יָבוּזוּ לוֹ — *Were any man to offer all the treasure of his home to entice you away from your love, they would scorn him to extreme* [lit., *If a man would give all the substance of his house in exchange for love, he would be laughed to scorn*]. God and His Tribunal bear witness to Israel's love for her Beloved.

8:8. אָחוֹת לָנוּ קְטַנָּה — *Israel desires to cleave to us, the small and humble one* [lit., *We have a little sister*]. The words אָח, "brother," and אָחוֹת, "sister," are linguistically related to the verb אחה, "to join together." The Heavenly Tribunal said, "One small, humble nation longs to join with us."

וְשָׁדַיִם אֵין לָהּ — *but her time of spiritual maturity has not come* [lit., *but she has no breasts*]. She is not yet ripe for Redemption (see *Ezekiel* 16:7).

מַה נַּעֲשֶׂה לַאֲחוֹתֵנוּ בַּיּוֹם שֶׁיְּדֻבַּר בָּהּ — *What shall we do for our cleaving one on the day the nations plot against her?* [lit., *What shall we do for our sister on the day she is spoken for*?]. How will we treat her when she seeks our protection?

8:9. אִם חוֹמָה הִיא נִבְנֶה עָלֶיהָ טִירַת כָּסֶף — *If her faith and belief are strong as a wall withstanding incursions from without, we shall become her fortress and beauty, building her city and Holy Temple* [lit., *If she be a wall, we will build upon her a turret of silver*]. Our response depends upon how she conducts herself in exile: If Israel will gird herself with faith and act toward the nations as if fortified with impenetrable "walls of copper" (*Jeremiah* 1:18), i.e., if she will neither intermarry nor intermingle with them, then we will rebuild the Holy City and Temple.

י וְאִם־דֶּ֥לֶת הִ֖יא נָצ֣וּר עָלֶ֑יהָ ל֥וּחַ אָֽרֶז׃ אֲנִ֣י חוֹמָ֔ה וְשָׁדַ֖י כַּמִּגְדָּל֑וֹת אָ֛ז הָיִ֥יתִי
יא בְעֵינָ֖יו כְּמוֹצְאֵ֥ת שָׁלֽוֹם׃ כֶּ֣רֶם הָיָ֤ה לִשְׁלֹמֹה֙ בְּבַ֣עַל הָמ֔וֹן נָתַ֥ן אֶת הַכֶּ֖רֶם
יב לַנֹּטְרִ֑ים אִ֛ישׁ יָבִ֥א בְּפִרְי֖וֹ אֶ֥לֶף כָּֽסֶף׃ כַּרְמִ֥י שֶׁלִּ֖י לְפָנָ֑י הָאֶ֤לֶף לְךָ֙ שְׁלֹמֹ֔ה
יג וּמָאתַ֖יִם לְנֹטְרִ֥ים אֶת־פִּרְיֽוֹ׃ הַיּוֹשֶׁ֣בֶת בַּגַּנִּ֗ים חֲבֵרִ֛ים מַקְשִׁיבִ֥ים לְקוֹלֵ֖ךְ
יד הַשְׁמִיעִֽנִי׃ בְּרַ֣ח דּוֹדִ֗י וּֽדְמֵה־לְךָ֤ לִצְבִי֙ א֚וֹ לְעֹ֣פֶר הָֽאַיָּלִ֔ים עַ֖ל הָרֵ֥י בְשָׂמִֽים׃

NOTES INCLUDING PHRASE-BY-PHRASE LITERAL TRANSLATION

וְאִם דֶּלֶת הִיא נָצוּר עָלֶיהָ לוּחַ אָרֶז — *but if she wavers like a door, succumbing to every alien knock, with fragile cedar panels shall we then enclose her* [lit., *But if she be a door we will enclose her with cedar panel*]. If she is open to all blandishments, like a door that always swings open, then we will line her doors with wooden panels that will rot, thus exposing her to danger.

8:10. אֲנִי חוֹמָה וְשָׁדַי כַּמִּגְדָּלוֹת — *My faith is firm as a wall, and my nourishing synagogues and study halls are strong as towers!* [lit., *I am a wall, and my breasts are like towers!*]. I comport myself like a wall, strong in the love of my Beloved. My synagogues and study halls nurture Israel with words of Torah; they "are like towers."

אָז הָיִיתִי בְעֵינָיו כְּמוֹצְאֵת שָׁלוֹם — *Then, having said so, I become in His eyes like a bride found perfect* [lit., *Then I am in His eyes like one who found peace*].

8:11. כֶּרֶם הָיָה לִשְׁלֹמֹה בְּבַעַל הָמוֹן — *Israel was the vineyard of Him to Whom peace belongs in populous Jerusalem* [lit., *Solomon had a vineyard in Baal-hamon*]. "Solomon" refers to God (see 1:1); "vineyard" to Israel (see *Isaiah* 5:7); "Baal-hamon" [lit., "the owner of the multitude"] to Jerusalem, the greatly populated city.

נָתַן אֶת הַכֶּרֶם לַנֹּטְרִים — *He gave His vineyard to harsh, cruel guardians* [lit., *He gave over the vineyard to guardians*]. He handed over His people to harsh rulers: Babylon, Media, Greece and Rome.

אִישׁ יָבִא בְּפִרְיוֹ אֶלֶף כָּסֶף — *each one came to extort his fruit, even a thousand silver pieces* [lit., *everyone would bring for its fruit a thousand silver pieces*]. The "guardians" would impose exorbitant levies and taxes to feed their lusts.

8:12. כַּרְמִי שֶׁלִּי לְפָנָי — *The vineyard is Mine! Your iniquities are before Me!* [lit., *My vineyard, which is Mine, is before Me!*]

but if she wavers like a door, succumbing to every alien knock, with fragile cedar panels shall we then enclose her.

Israel replies proudly . . .

10 *My faith is firm as a wall, and my nourishing synagogues and study halls are strong as towers! Then, having said so, I become in His eyes like a bride found perfect.*

. . . and reminisces

11 *Israel was the vineyard of Him to Whom peace belongs in populous Jerusalem. He gave His vineyard to harsh, cruel guardians; each one came to extort his fruit, even a thousand silver pieces.*

God to the nations, on judgment day

12 *The vineyard is Mine! Your iniquities are before Me!*

The nations will reply

The thousand silver pieces are Yours, You to Whom peace belongs, and two hundred more to the Sages who guarded the fruit of Torah from our designs.

God to Israel

13 *O My beloved, dwelling in far-flung gardens, your fellows, the angels, hearken to your voice of Torah and prayer. Let Me hear it, that they may then sanctify Me.*

Israel to God

14 *Flee, my Beloved, from our common exile and be like a gazelle or a young hart in Your swiftness to redeem and rest Your Presence among us on the fragrant Mount Moriah, site of Your Temple.*

NOTES INCLUDING PHRASE-BY-PHRASE LITERAL TRANSLATION

Although I transferred My vineyard to you, I am still the sole owner. All your injustices against Israel are before Me; nothing eludes Me.

הָאֶלֶף לְךָ שְׁלֹמֹה — *The thousand silver pieces are Yours, You to Whom peace belongs* [lit., *You, Solomon, can have Your thousand*]. Whatever we stole from them will all be returned to You.

וּמָאתַיִם לְנֹטְרִים אֶת פִּרְיוֹ — *and two hundred more to the Sages who guarded the fruit of Torah from our designs* [lit., *and two hundred to the tenders of its fruit*]. We will recompense Israel's leaders and Sages (see *Isaiah* 60:17).

8:13. הַיּוֹשֶׁבֶת בַּגַּנִּים חֲבֵרִים מַקְשִׁיבִים לְקוֹלֵךְ — *O My beloved, dwelling in far-flung gardens, your fellows, the angels, hearken to your voice of Torah and prayer* [lit., *O you who dwell in the gardens, companions are attentive to your voice*]. The angels listen to the prayers of Israel in the Diaspora, tending the gardens of others, and who dwell in the synagogues and study halls.

הַשְׁמִיעִנִי — *Let Me hear it, that they may then sanctify Me* [lit., *let Me hear it*]. Let Me hear your voice, for after you are finished, the ministering angels will commence to sanctify Me.

8:14. בְּרַח דּוֹדִי — *Flee, my Beloved, from our common exile* [lit., *Flee, my Beloved*]. Flee away with us, O God Who has accompanied us throughout every exile! And let us leave this exile together.

וּדְמֵה לְךָ לִצְבִי אוֹ לְעֹפֶר הָאַיָּלִים — *and be like a gazelle or a young hart in Your swiftness to redeem and rest Your Presence among us* [lit., *and be like a gazelle or a young hart*]. Hasten the Redemption.

עַל הָרֵי בְשָׂמִים — *on the fragrant Mount Moriah, site of Your Temple* [lit., *upon the mountains of spices*], may it be rebuilt speedily in our days. Amen.